Bird Finding Guide to Western Massachusetts

Illustrations
Andrew Finch Magee

Editors
Jan Ortiz
David A. Spector
Pete Westover
Mary Alice Wilson

Regional Editors
Seth Kellogg, Hampden County
Mark C. Lynch, Western Worcester Region
Noreen Mole, Berkshire County
Jan Ortiz, Franklin and Hampshire Counties
Dave Small, Quabbin Region

Introduction and Bar Chart Data
Seth Kellogg

Maps
Bill and Mary Alice Wilson

2003

D1478044

Illustrations © 2003 Andrew Finch Magee, Northampton, MA 01060

Library of Congress Control Number: 2002112452

ISBN 1892893029 First Edition

Printed in the United States of America

Published by University of Massachusetts Extension http://www.umassextension.org
Sales information: (413)545-2717

Copy Editor
Elizabeth Carr Adams

Project Managers
Joe Shoenfeld
Susan W. Handlen

Graphic Design
Mary Zyskowski

Graphic Production
Plouffe, Inc.

Photography of Art
Stephen Petegorsky

Marketing Manager
Nathanael Schildbach

Printer
Gazette Printing Co., Inc.

BLUE JAY FEATHERS AND EGG

The book is dedicated to all those individuals and
organizations who have helped protect habitat for nesting, migrating,
and wintering birds in Western Massachusetts.

Please join us in actively supporting both public and private efforts
to promote environmental education and to protect and
enhance bird habitat at the local, state, national, and international level.
These groups need your expertise, your time, and your
financial support. A list of many of these organizations appears
near the end of the book.

When Birding in Western Massachusetts . . .

We have included the American Birding Association's Code of Ethics and assume that all readers will comply with it. We assume also that all birders will judiciously adhere to responsible behavior especially in regard to issues of public and private property and the welfare of birds and their environment.

While birding in Western Massachusetts is not especially hazardous, below are some precautions that might make life more pleasant for you, for other people, and for the birds.

- **Be sensible** about New England weather. As always when birding, check the local forecast. Be prepared with extra warm clothing throughout the year and protection from the sun in the summer. Carry water.

- **In spring and summer** expect an array of biting insects. Wear protective clothing and bring bug repellent. Ticks, both dog and deer, are common here. Dog ticks are merely irritating, but deer ticks may carry Lyme disease. Check yourself thoroughly after birding in any possible deer tick habitat. Consult a physician if you have any concerns about the possibility of exposure to Lyme disease.

- **Poison ivy** is abundant in many areas. Be on the lookout for this three-leaved irritant.

- **Always park** in a way that allows other vehicles to pass safely. Never park in front of gates or block boat launches.

- **Do not walk on railroad tracks** and be cautious when crossing them. Tracks that seem little used may be active.

- **Do not walk in agricultural fields** that have crops or that might be seeded.

- **Especially during mud season** (late winter and early spring), be careful before driving onto a dirt road or parking on the side of any road. In winter snow- and ice-covered roads can be treacherous; use caution.

- **Always lock your car** and make sure that valuables are out of sight. Be aware of personal safety in all locations; it may not be advisable to bird some sites alone.

- **Avoid certain areas** during hunting season. Shotgun deer hunting usually starts the Monday after Thanksgiving and lasts for two weeks. Many state Wildlife Management Areas are stocked with Ring-necked

Pheasants and are best avoided in pheasant season. Hunting seasons and regulations can be obtained at any town clerk's office or on the web (www.state.ma.us/dfwele/dfw/dfwrec.htm). Hunting is prohibited in Massachusetts on Sundays.

- **Please use common sense and courtesy.**

Bird Sightings

To learn what birds are currently being seen in Western Massachusetts, as well as in the three other regions in the state (Eastern, Cape Cod, and Nantucket), call the Massachusetts Audubon's Voice (Rare Bird Alert) at 1-888-224-6444 (toll free).

Please report your sightings to the above number. Should you encounter a rare bird that you assume local birders would like to know about immediately, please call 1-413-549-1768.

American Birding Association's Principles of Birding Ethics

Everyone who enjoys birds and birding must always respect wildlife, its environment, and the rights of others. In any conflict of interest between birds and birders, the welfare of the birds and their environment comes first.

Code of Birding Ethics
1. Promote the welfare of birds and their environment.

1(a) Support the protection of important bird habitat.

1(b) To avoid stressing birds or exposing them to danger, exercise restraint and caution during observation, photography, sound recording, or filming.

Limit the use of recordings and other methods of attracting birds, and never use such methods in heavily birded areas, or for attracting any species that is Threatened, Endangered, or of Special Concern, or is rare in your local area.

Keep well back from nests and nesting colonies, roosts, display areas, and important feeding sites. In such sensitive areas, if there is a need for extended observation, photography, filming, or recording, try to use a blind or hide, and take advantage of natural cover.

Use artificial light sparingly for filming or photography, especially for close-ups.

1(c) Before advertising the presence of a rare bird, evaluate the potential for disturbance to the bird, its surroundings, and other people in the area, and proceed only if access can be controlled, disturbance minimized, and permission has been obtained from private land owners. The sites of rare nesting birds should be divulged only to the proper conservation authorities.

1(d) Stay on roads, trails, and paths where they exist; otherwise, keep habitat disturbance to a minimum.

2. Respect the law, and the rights of others.

2(a) Do not enter private property without the owner's explicit permission.

2(b) Follow all laws, rules, and regulations governing use of roads and public areas, both at home and abroad.

2(c) Practice common courtesy in contacts with other people. Your exemplary behavior will generate good will with birders and non-birders alike.

3. Ensure that feeders, nest structures, and other artificial bird environments are safe.

3(a) Keep dispensers, water, and food clean, and free of decay or disease. It is important to feed birds continually during harsh weather.

3(b) Maintain and clean nest structures regularly.

3(c) If you are attracting birds to an area, ensure the birds are not exposed to predation from cats and other domestic animals, or dangers posed by artificial hazards.

4. Group birding, whether organized or impromptu, requires special care.

Each individual in the group, in addition to the obligations spelled out in Items #1 and #2, has responsibilities as a Group Member.

4(a) Respect the interests, rights, and skills of fellow birders, as well as people participating in other legitimate outdoor activities. Freely share your knowledge and experience, except where code 1(c) applies. Be especially helpful to beginning birders.

4(b) If you witness unethical birding behavior, assess the situation, and intervene if you think it prudent. When interceding, inform the person(s) of the inappropriate action, and attempt, within reason, to have it stopped. If the behavior continues, document it, and notify appropriate individuals or organizations.

Group Leader Responsibilities (amateur and professional trips, tours).

4(c) Be an exemplary ethical role model for the group. Teach through word and example.

4(d) Keep groups to a size that limits impact on the environment, and does not interfere with others using the same area.

4(e) Ensure everyone in the group knows of and practices this code.

4(f) Learn and inform the group of any special circumstances applicable to the areas being visited (e.g., no tape recorders allowed).

4(g) Acknowledge that professional tour companies bear a special responsibility to place the welfare of birds and the benefits of public knowledge ahead of the company's commercial interests. Ideally, leaders should keep track of tour sightings, document unusual occurrences, and submit records to appropriate organizations.

PLEASE FOLLOW THIS CODE AND DISTRIBUTE AND TEACH IT TO OTHERS.

We thank the American Birding Association for developing and promoting this code. See http://americanbirding.org for more information.

The Maps

You should know that:

The maps in this book include primarily those roads and features mentioned in the text. We suggest that you carry at least a state road map. You might also consider having a Western Massachusetts fold-out map, a spiral-bound book of town maps, and/or USGS topographic maps. Some places listed in the book also have trail maps available at a kiosk. Assume that all maps have occasional errors.

Most roads in Western Massachusetts change their names when they cross town lines. Sometimes more often than that. Those changes do not make map-making or map-following any easier.

Roads are going to change. There will be new roads and intersections; old roads will be closed by development, deterioration, or the work of beavers. We will try to update maps for new editions. We welcome your suggestions.

○	approximate center of town	▬	interstate highway
□	exit from limited-access road	▬	federal or major state road
P	parking	▬	paved or unpaved local road
↦	gate (may be closed)	- - - -	farm or woods road
· — —	buried gas line	- - - ⌐	path, trail
⤙—⤙	transmission line	⊢—⊢—⊢	railroad
▭	box on regional map = the approximate location of the account		

For those interested in the technical side of this project, we based our maps on the USGS maps in TOPO!® and did all the drawing and lettering in Adobe Illustrator 9®. We thank all the authors and regional editors who so patiently corrected and improved our drafts.

Mary Alice and Bill Wilson

Acknowledgements

Over the past five years many people have contributed in countless ways to the production of this book. We thank first of all the authors for their enthusiasm for the sites and birds they describe, and for the experience and wisdom they share. We regret not having enough space to include all the wonderful stories and descriptions in their original texts. We thank Seth Kellogg for his historical perspective on birding Western Massachusetts and for sharing the material that he has been accumulating toward an authoritative book on the birds of Western Massachusetts. We thank Bill Wilson for the endless hours spent creating and editing the maps and his highly evolved sense of direction. We thank Harvey Allen and Dave Ziomek for their energy in helping initiate the project and the members of the bar chart committee for their painstaking review of each revision. We thank Bill Buchanan, Sally Hills, Lola Reid, and Nancy Young for their patient checking of maps and text. We thank the people too numerous to list who have answered questions, commented on accounts, checked directions, and helped in many small but essential ways. We thank our families who are glad to see this book finished. We thank the Kestrel Trust for financing the initial stages of this project. We thank the wonderful people of the University of Massachusetts Extension for their commitment to public education and the production of a high quality book.

A very special thanks to Andrew Finch Magee for the exquisite illustrations that reflect his love and knowledge of the natural world.

Finally, as you visit these sites, enjoy the birds, and contribute to environmental education and conservation, we thank you.

Jan Ortiz, David A. Spector, Pete Westover, and Mary Alice Wilson

Editors Note: *To save space and to avoid repetition, many common resident species, such as Blue Jay and Black-capped Chickadee, and, to a lesser extent, common migrant species, such as Common Yellowthroat, are not mentioned or are mentioned infrequently in the site accounts. The bar chart at the back of this book, habitat descriptions in field guides, and time in the field should help you find these common species.*

Contents

Illustrations

All illustrations by Andrew Finch Magee

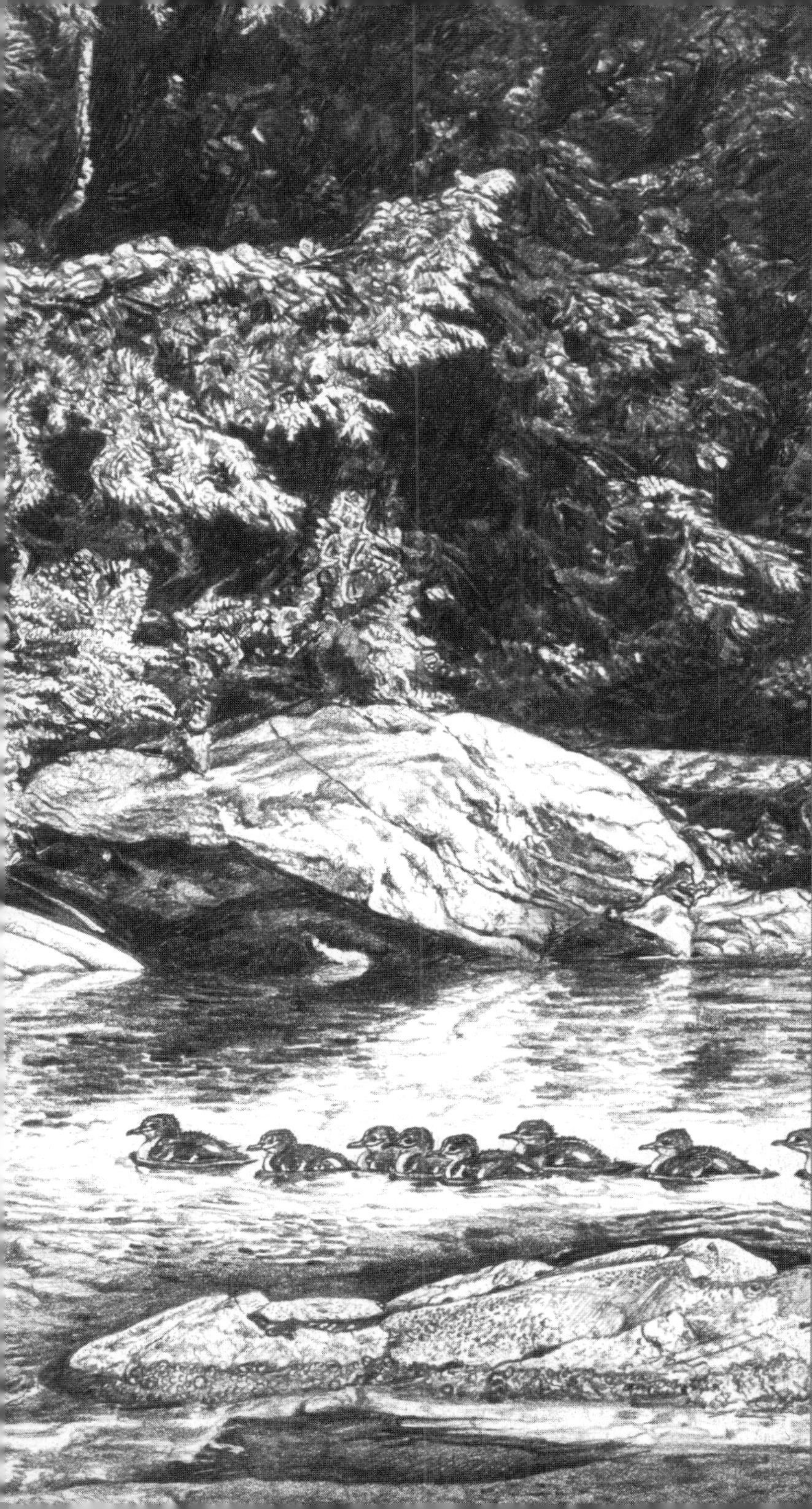

Introduction

GREAT HORNED OWL FEATHERS

Introduction

Introduction to Western Massachusetts Birding

See Western Massachusetts map (on the inside back cover)

Western Massachusetts has an extraordinary mixture of habitats with a great variety of bird life. The Connecticut River Valley is one of the most beautiful and diverse agricultural valleys in the country, with a long history of intense birding and bird record keeping. The Berkshire Hills and lakes and the valleys of the Housatonic and Hoosic Rivers are almost equally diverse. The Quabbin Reservoir, with its eagle and loon populations and great numbers of water birds and birds typical of the central New England forest, is also a tremendous wildlife resource. East of the Quabbin is the forested, hilly land of western Worcester County dotted by small lakes, ponds, and rivers. Together these make Western Massachusetts a beautiful and productive birding region.

This volume draws on the records and skills of dozens of the top birders of the region. It also draws on work that dates back to the early parts of the century, including *Birds of the Connecticut Valley in Massachusetts* by Aaron C. Bagg and Samuel A. Eliot, published in 1937; *The Birds of Berkshire County* by Bartlett Hendricks, first published in 1994 with a third edition in 1999; and *Birding Western Massachusetts: The Kestrel Trust Area,* published by the Kestrel Trust and the Hampshire Bird Club in 1996.

The Valleys and Hills of Western Massachusetts

The post-glacial period began in New England about 12,000 years ago. Much of the eastern part of the continent in this period was covered by open grassy country with scattered spruce trees. This was largely succeeded by forest by about 10,000 years ago. Even then mastodons and other large herbivores persisted and kept large areas in open grasslands for some time. Other animals that moved onto the newly available land included humans, for whom there is clear evidence of coastal settlement beginning about 9,000 years ago. Birds also moved into the area, and migration patterns of advance and retreat developed with the seasons. As the large grazers died out and the forest closed in further, human activities such as burning and agriculture kept some areas open. Beaver moved in to create periodic ponds and meadows. The variety of habitat produced the amazing diversity of bird life Europeans found when they arrived.

Preceeding Pages: **COMMON MERGANSER**

By the late 1600s, forest was the predominant vegetation. Much clearing for agriculture took place in the eighteenth and nineteenth centuries, but through the twentieth century much of the forest returned. We now have a mixture of northern forests to the west and north in higher elevations, advancing southern vegetation in the lowland valleys along our southern edge, and an intermediate mixture in between. Add to this the many lakes and ponds, marshlands, and our position as a migration path to and from the sea and between north and south, and you have a situation ideal for birds and bird study.

Geographic Areas

Western Massachusetts has four distinct geographic areas. Each stretches the entire north-south distance between Connecticut and New Hampshire/Vermont. For the convenience of the reader, the chapters in this book use somewhat different lines than the geographic areas. Most of the Western Highlands and Connecticut River Valley geographic areas are combined into the Connecticut River Region chapter; the Eastern Highlands is split into the Quabbin and Western Worcester Region chapters.

Berkshire County. Starting on the New York border are the Housatonic and Hoosic River Valleys, with steep, high ridges on their eastern and western edges. The Hoosic River in the north drains the Taconic and Hoosac Mountain ranges, which are "island" extensions of the Green Mountains and contain the largest proportion of spruce-fir and northern hardwood vegetation in Massachusetts. The highest such island is Mount Greylock, rising in the center of the valley to almost 3500 feet, but there are more extensive evergreen forests in the Hoosac Range east of Mount Greylock. Here the birder will find the summer nesting specialties of this forest habitat and the winter visitors that overflow from the far north.

The southern slopes drain south into the Housatonic River. The valley widens and cleared meadows surround the built-up areas of Pittsfield and Lee. Four large lakes are the first bodies of water available to migrant waterfowl that pass over the ridges after leaving the Hudson/Mohawk River Valley or the Lake Champlain Valley. The river continues south and meanders through fertile farmland flanked by slightly more modest hills. Extensive marshes also attract wetland species. They are good stopping points for species migrating between the St. Lawrence Valley and the Chesapeake Bay and veering a little eastward into our region.

Connecticut River Region. As you can see on the Western Massachusetts map at the back of the book, this chapter covers most of two geographic areas: the Western Highlands and the Connecticut River Valley.

Western Highlands. Once past the steep ridges on the east side of the Berkshire County valleys, the hills form a wide plateau of uplands. (This area is sometimes called the Berkshire Hills.) This plateau takes up almost half of Western Massachusetts and is now heavily forested with only small islands of farmland. Elevations rise as one goes north and the mix of spruce and fir increases. Some of the rivers in the Western Highlands flow westward to the Housatonic, but tributaries of the Connecticut River drain most of the plateau. The Deerfield River is the largest, forming the watershed of the entire northern third of the Western Highlands. The Westfield River watershed is nearly as large, draining most of the central and southeastern portions of the plateau. The Western Highlands are the stronghold of the mixed forest upland species that form the bulk of the breeding birds of Western Massachusetts. They include evergreen specialists, upland marsh and stream birds, and secretive species of craggy hillsides.

Connecticut River Valley. By the time the Connecticut River reaches Massachusetts, this major New England river has collected much of the water that falls on Vermont and New Hampshire. Here it enters the wider floodplains that characterize the lower part of the river's course. The first rich farmland is at Northfield; then the river hits the dam and rapids at Turners Falls. Below the rapids the river enters the flat fertile expanse that once was the bottom of ancient Lake Hitchcock. This is the most extensive agricultural area in western Massachusetts, where both summer and winter open country species are most likely to be found. It is also the migration route for many birds that are forced into islands of natural vegetation by intense farming or urban development. Along the entire length of the river there are summer sandbars and shallows that attract migrating shorebirds and dispersing waders. Major oxbows of the central part of the river in Hatfield and Northampton provide unique habitat for migrating waterfowl and wetland breeders.

The river then passes through the notch between the Mount Holyoke and Mount Tom ranges and shortly arrives at a dam and rapids at Holyoke. The valley widens further with a spine of hills separating it into two sections, and the remaining farmland is more broken and rolling. Westover Air Reserve Base forms the only large open area and is home to several state endangered and threatened species of grassland birds. Here the Chicopee and Westfield Rivers meet the Connecticut. This area is highly developed but valuable to birders for its migrant traps with a few pockets of breeding habitat. Just before the river enters Connecticut there is a large floodplain on the east side of the river in Longmeadow, where wise land preservation has protected a wetland for waders, waterfowl, and shorebirds.

Quabbin Region and Western Worcester Region. The fourth geographic area, the Eastern Highlands, has been split into two chapters. The Eastern Highlands is made up of a second series of hills, an extension of the southern New Hampshire mountain ranges. The Quabbin Reservation is a near-wilderness large enough to provide a home to some unique wildlife. Migrant water birds are specialties here along with forest breeding birds, eagles, and winter finches. South and east of Quabbin is the valley of the Ware and Quaboag Rivers, featuring many low hills, scattered farmland, a good number of ponds and lakes important to waterfowl, and some of the largest cattail marshes in western Massachusetts. To the south of the Quaboag lie the areas of the Quinnebaug River watershed with rural towns that feature hilly terrain, mixed forest, and numerous ponds and lakes. Northern Worcester County is also hilly and features large tracks of mixed upland forest and a breeding avifauna more closely related to the Berkshires. The northern tier remains one of the most consistent spots in the entire state, along with the northern Berkshires, for winter finches, including Pine Grosbeak, and Bohemian Waxwing.

Winter

There are two major water systems important in the cold weather season: the Connecticut River and its tributaries, and the Quabbin Reservoir. Some bird species are present on the Quabbin and a few other large bodies of water until they are forced out by ice. The Connecticut River rarely freezes over completely, and there are always sections near rapids where waterfowl are found. Open water can also be found in park ponds, landfills, and other urbanized sites. There are usually a few individuals of other species that have lingered with the winter waterfowl.

If the cone crop is heavy in our northern areas, groups of winter finches will visit the highest hills. If regions even farther north and west have a light cone crop at the same time, their numbers may be greater and some birds will overflow into the rest of our area. Some northern finches now nest with us, and there are always a few of them present all winter, mostly in the highlands, but also a stray handful in the valleys.

Spring and Early Summer Migration

First Arrival Stage. February to early March: Birds arrive in our region from the south in several stages. First, a warm front will sweep up into the northeast as early as mid-February. Usually around March 1 the earliest new arrivals alight on rivers and fields. All the new species in this early stage have a few individual that have lingered all winter.

The first habitat to thaw is the larger rivers and their floodplains. The Connecticut River is the largest, but its major tributaries and the

Housatonic and Hoosic also have areas where birds first find refuge. The floodplains have been altered by intensive agriculture to the detriment of those species. The habitat that remains is restricted to the Quaboag Valley, Longmeadow Flats, Northampton Meadows, Connecticut River in Hadley and Hatfield, Deerfield and Northfield Meadows, and the coves at Gill and Turners Falls. In the west, Sheffield, Lenox, and Pittsfield also have important floodplains. Arriving waterfowl will linger for several days or even weeks in a spot that provides food, and their numbers can be quite impressive.

The second habitat type to thaw includes various local sites on these rivers as well as the lakes and reservoirs. A few important lakes have become built up, but some birds still make short visits. Major bodies of water are Congamond Lakes, Ashley Reservoir, Ludlow Reservoir, the Brookfield Lakes, and the Quabbin. The forests are the last to see the snow disappear, so the birds that can find food there in the early spring are few and specialized.

Second Arrival Stage. Late March through early April: As the weather slowly warms, the pace of arrival quickens. The next stage still has many species that favor open wetlands and fields, but a few woodland birds creep into the mix. Many birds come to earth only when forced down by weather. The few migrating shorebirds that stray inland find food in small rainpools.

Though it is hard to tell when the secretive marsh species arrive, it is generally early, as soon as the frogs, snails, and worms emerge. Most of the early arriving birds are drawn to open country. More and more of these areas are being lost to development, so many of these species are decreasing. The first of the true woodland birds now find their way quietly to our forests.

Third Arrival Stage. Mid- to late April: On the first warming days with southwest winds, the snow disappears except for a few patches in the deep woods. Now insects emerge and the first tropical birds arrive to devour them. Most come from Central and South America or the West Indies. Some winter along the Gulf Coast of the United States. There are only a few wetland birds left to arrive, and they spread out to small ponds and marshes. With them are the swallows and swifts, which feed over wetlands where flying insects are thickest. With fewer farms and old chimneys, it is more difficult for these and other open country species to find homes.

Fourth Arrival Stage. May: Now the forest leaves burst from their buds and the larvae that feed on them emerge. Then the long distance

COMMON NIGHTHAWK

migrants arrive and restore the energy expended during the final stages of migration. Some species are on the way much farther north to boreal breeding grounds, but many are back to stay in the extensive woods and edges of our hills and valleys. Ridgetops as well as parks and sanctuaries in the valleys now harbor plenty of birds. Near rivers or lakes, insects and birds are even more abundant.

Spring and Early Summer Nesting

There are now at least 165 species nesting yearly in Western Massachusetts, and best represented are the forest species. Grassland birds and species of early successional growth are generally in decline because of habitat loss and forest growth. Modern agricultural methods have also made it harder for those species. Wetland birds are recovering in the hill country where the beaver has returned. Many of the marshes along the large rivers are gone, but some remain to harbor remnant ducks and rails.

Late Summer Dispersal and Early Fall Migration

When breeding is over, birds start to move around the landscape. As the first days of July pass, birders concentrate on the receding banks of rivers and pools to see the birds that leave the Arctic at the end of its short summer. Sandbars are important to sandpipers and plovers. Herons and egrets forage the shallows.

In years when the rivers are high, the shorebirds use soggy fields that were recently harvested and plowed. The corn and potatoes are gone but insects still abound. In those fields the rarest of shorebirds are most often found. Sometimes it is a hurricane that brings in surprises like South Atlantic terns, seabirds, and a few uncommon ducks. Wood Ducks have gathered, teal arrive in August, and wigeons and pintails come in September. Nighthawks, swifts, and swallows swarm through the evening skies. Then come migrating flycatchers, thrushes, fall warblers, and hawks. Broad-winged Hawks move in enormous kettles, kestrels beat their way through, and hummingbirds flash by.

Late Fall Migration

With the cold weather, ducks and geese fill the sky and raptors careen down the ridges. The bigger lakes attract a variety of ducks. This may be the only time you can find certain sea ducks in Western Massachusetts. In October and November, your chances are good of encountering all the ducks regularly seen in interior northeastern North America.

A few birds of brushy and open country arrive in October, especially sparrows and western strays. As the days get really cold and flurries begin, tundra and boreal forest sparrows arrive, and with the sparrows come a few other northern birds that like bare ground. Blackbirds reappear to feast on unharvested kernels. As December approaches, most of the birds that are left are the resident species.   *Seth Kellogg*

Birds and Landscape Change in Western Massachusetts

Most of Western Massachusetts has undergone the same pattern of forest clearing for agriculture and subsequent reforestation as the rest of southern New England. The Berkshire Hills were not cleared to the same extent as the rest of the state, but even there the face of the land has changed and is constantly changing. The familiar pattern in southern New England involved small clearings for subsistence agriculture until about 1750, when the rate of clearing began increasing steadily until 1820-1840. By that time 90 percent of the arable land had been cleared for crops and pasture.

The opening of the Erie Canal in 1825, the California gold rush, and the Civil War all contributed to the exodus of farmers from the stony farms of New England. Land abandonment gradually resulted in Western Massachusetts resuming an ever more forested character. Now, old cellar holes and miles of stone fences running through the woods are all that remain of that agrarian society. Although the pattern of clearing, settlement, abandonment, and reforestation stands as the most dramatic change in landscape in Massachusetts, other factors keep the landscape in a state of constant flux.

The composition of the region's vegetation has developed since the retreat of the last glacier and resultant climate change over the past 12,000 years. Pollen records show that both deciduous and coniferous trees moved northward independently of one another and that forests consisted of chance combinations of tree species that were rarely stable for more than a few thousand years. Because of the differences in seed dispersal rates between hardwoods and conifers, between light-seeded and heavy-seeded species, and between wind-dispersed and animal-dispersed species, forest composition has been very different through time since the melting of the last glacier.

Against the background of climate change, five major types of disturbance have altered the region's forests: windthrow, fire, logging, agriculture, and exotic pests and pathogens. In addition, ice storms, drought, and flood have caused minor, and occasionally major, disturbances. Windthrow from catastrophic disturbances in New England occurs at long intervals averaging approximately 800 years for fire and 1,100 years for wind. Localized disturbances, sometimes severe, occur at much shorter intervals. Major hurricanes and windstorms occurred several times during the last century; the last severe hurricane occurred in 1938, when several billion board feet of timber were blown down from Rhode Island to central New Hampshire. Storms of similar size occurred in 1635 and 1815 and occur on average about every 150 years.

Intense forest fires generally occur on dry sites, especially outwash sands and gravels and shallow soils over bedrock. Where it occurs, the impact of fire on forests is more severe than that of wind. Pitch pine barrens such as the Montague Plains occupy repeatedly burned areas that were originally in white pine or oak-pine. In addition to natural fire, Indians in southern New England burned the forest periodically, in spring or fall, to drive game for hunting, clear fields for planting, and open the forest for traveling. Many such fires burned until extinguished by rain. As a result of Indian fires, the earliest explorers in New England encountered a quite open landscape, especially in southern New England. Early declines of Indian populations from disease and persecution in the 1600s allowed the forest to develop to the point that later settlers penetrating into the interior encountered a more forested landscape than that which had existed for at least a thousand years previously. Fire prevention throughout much of the twentieth century has further reduced the occurrence of open habitats in much of southern New England, and especially in Western Massachusetts east of the Berkshires.

Few tracts of land in Western Massachusetts remain unlogged. Most logging, as opposed to land clearing for agriculture, occurred in the mid- to late 1800s when primarily pines and other softwoods were harvested. It is only fairly recently that hardwoods have been heavily cut. Around 1910 the clearing of vast pine stands that seeded into abandoned fields represented the last major land clearing in southern New England. Logging, like wind damage, did not affect subsequent forest development or soils except when intense fires fueled by slash burned the organic soil layer, resulting in the establishment of birch.

As noted, most of Western Massachusetts was cultivated or grazed and then reverted to forest. The effects of agriculture on the subsequent forest were dramatic: the loss of nutrients, changes in soil profiles, and major conversions from hardwoods to old-field white pine. Introduced pests

1997, and 1998 on 12 survey routes throughout the watersheds of the Farmington River (Connecticut), Deerfield River (Massachusetts), Ashuelot River (New Hampshire), and White River (Vermont). The routes were divided between habitat types: adjacent to the Connecticut River ("A" sites), adjacent to major tributaries ("B" sites), and upland sites unassociated with rivers ("C" sites).

During the three years of the study our observers counted over 100,000 birds within the four state study areas, 60,000 of which fell into the count circles. Of those 60,000 birds, 36 percent were found in Connecticut's Farmington River watershed and 26 percent in Massachusetts' Deerfield River watershed. As you move north into New Hampshire and Vermont, 19 percent of the birds were observed in each of those states. Migrants using the Eastern Flyway reach the mouth of the CRV in larger numbers, then disperse throughout the valley and beyond as they continue north.

A similar pattern was seen in the number of bird species observed migrating within the CRV ecosystem. The number of species varied from a high of 113 to a low of 84. The highest number of species in any given year always occurred farther south, in Connecticut, and the lowest in the most northern study area, the White River watershed of Vermont. Only 5 or 6 percent of the species turn over between years, and those that appear in one year and disappear in the next are typically the rarer species such as Merlin, Bicknell's Thrush, and Orange-crowned Warbler. Those are in contrast to the species that over the three years were typically the most abundant, including Red-eyed Vireo, Veery, Chestnut-sided Warbler, Black-throated Blue Warbler, Yellow-rumped Warbler, Black-and-white Warbler, American Redstart, and Ovenbird.

The most dramatic result our surveyors found was that 47 percent of all the birds observed used the "A" sites, those along the main stem of the Connecticut River. The south to north pattern continued in regard to habitat use. The highest percentage of "A" use was in Connecticut (56%), followed by Massachusetts (42%). Migrant use of riverside "A" sites in the two more northern areas was about equal (38%).

To this point, we have been lumping all species together, which could give the impression that all species behave the same way. In reality, there were dozens of behavioral and evolutionary strategies observed within CRV migration that help a bird advance its species to the next generation.

One strategy is to arrive very early on the breeding grounds, if the problem of a dependable food supply can be solved. Early April in the forested hills of Massachusetts, New Hampshire, and Vermont often means deep snow cover, freezing temperatures and resultant delays in insect hatches and tree flower blooming. Those are staples in the diets of many migrants. However, for the Yellow-bellied Sapsucker, which arrives before the first survey count, the early supply of tree sap provides a high-energy food supply at a time when the majority of migrants have yet to enter the CRV.

The survey's first, late-April count is lonely and quiet for the eager surveyor looking to record birds. The welcomed calls and partial songs of a flock of Yellow-rumped Warblers break the silence. Like the non-migratory chickadee, the Yellow-rumped is less dependent on warming temperatures, insect emergence and blooming flowers because it forages on persistent seeds and fruits. Yellow-rumps begin appearing early in Connecticut and, as their migration progresses up the valley, their numbers decrease in Connecticut while increasing in Massachusetts. Their numbers also diminish in the CRV as they disperse to higher elevations and northern coniferous forest breeding grounds.

The American Redstart is a mid-season migrant whose population in Connecticut is relatively small in early May but increases rapidly from mid- to late May when both insects and tree flowers are abundant. American Redstarts begin their CRV migration in Connecticut using predominantly main stem "A" sites, and as spring and migration progress they begin using "B" sites along tributaries. Late in migration, as winter lifts, their use of "B" sites becomes dominant in the higher elevations of tributaries as territories become suitable for breeding.

In contrast, the Red-eyed Vireo forgoes all the early or mid-season variability in weather and food supply and simply does not appear in the CRV until mid- to late May. It shows a bias toward the higher elevation upland forests where food is now abundant and breeding territories await. By migrating later in the season when winter is long gone, Red-eyed Vireos are not bound to the milder climate lower in the valley near the main river.

How does this information help a refuge manager develop a conservation policy that protects the future of migrant birds? First, we have a better understanding of the stopover habitat needs of each species, so our management recommendations can be more precise: preserve upland deciduous tree habitat for Yellow-bellied Sapsuckers; acquire conservation easements along tributary sites preferred by Yellow-rumped Warblers; conduct restoration projects on "A" sites used early in American Redstart migration. They all make sense. But, in the CRV, with its population of two million people and high rate of sprawl, there are even more urgent priorities. Due to historical and current land use patterns, the land along the Connecticut River's shores and floodplains ("A" sites) seems in most urgent need of reclamation and protection.

YELLOW-RUMPED WARBLER

Native Americans traditionally used the Connecticut River as a corridor for transportation and commerce. This pattern accelerated with European settlement. Cities like Hartford, Springfield, Brattleboro, and Hanover grew from small settlements into the centers of population and commerce we know today. Floodplain forests with their rich soils were cleared for agriculture. Today, with this historical momentum, Interstate 91 not only links those centers but also clearly defines the corridor as a place for expanded economic and residential activity. These otherwise important growth activities are nothing more than a haphazard plan for sprawl without a regional landscape plan that includes protection of water and air quality, historical features, and wildlife communities. With so many nationwide examples of sprawl's economic and environmental failures to draw upon, the Connecticut River Valley has the opportunity to serve as a national planning model. Migrant birds tell us so.

Thomas S. Litwin, Clark Science Center, Smith College
Trevor Lloyd-Evans, Manomet Center for Conservation Science
Katherine Halvorsen, Department of Mathematics, Smith College

Based on a collaborative effort involving the following individuals and organizations: Beth Goettel, S.O. Conte National Fish and Wildlife Refuge; State Coordinators: Mark Szantyr, Connecticut Nature Conservancy; Wayne Petersen, Massachusetts Audubon Society; Richard Cook, Audubon Society of New Hampshire; Chris Rimmer, Vermont Institute of Natural Science.

Further reading:

Able, K.P.(ed.). 1999. *Gathering of Angels: Migrating Birds and their Ecology.* Ithaca, NY: Cornell University Press.

Moore, F.R. (ed.). 2000. *Stopover Ecology of Nearctic-Neotropical Landbird Migrants: Habitat Relations and Conservation Implications. Studies in Avian Biology No. 20.* The Cooper Ornithological Society.

Roddis, H., and J. Steel. 1998. *Shaping the Future of Your Community: A Guide to Growth Management and Land Protection in Massachusetts.* Lincoln, MA: Massachusetts Audubon Society.

Steel, J. 1999. *Losing Ground: An Analysis of Patterns of Development and Their Effects on Open Space.* Lincoln, MA: Massachusetts Audubon Society.

Weidensaul, S. 1999. *Living on the Wind.* New York: North Point Press.

Bird Habitat Protection in Western Massachusetts

A map of open space and bird habitat in Western Massachusetts shows a mosaic of protected and unprotected land. Some of the best birding areas are fully protected from development: Fanny Stebbins Wildlife Refuge in Longmeadow (owned by the Allen Bird Club together with other conservation groups), Bartholomew's Cobble Reservation in Sheffield (The Trustees of Reservations), Mount Sugarloaf in Deerfield and Mount Greylock in northern Berkshire County (Department of Environmental Management), the Quabbin Reservation (Metropolitan District Commission), and Canoe Meadows Wildlife Sanctuary in Pittsfield and Elm Hill Farm in Brookfield (Massachusetts Audubon Society). Others are only partly protected: the Montague Plains (partly owned by the Division of Fisheries and Wildlife), Mount Toby in Sunderland and Leverett (University of Massachusetts and many private owners), the Holyoke Range in eastern Hampshire County, the marshes of the Quaboag River, and others. A third group, including many of the best lakes, ponds, riparian areas, open fields, and roadside birding areas in Western Massachusetts, are unprotected and vulnerable.

The good news is that many conservation groups are increasingly active in land preservation throughout Western Massachusetts. Regional land trusts like the three-county Valley Land Fund, which focuses on the Connecticut River Valley and adjacent hilltowns, and the Berkshire Natural Resources Council in Berkshire County typically pull together coalitions of state agencies and land trusts to complete complicated purchases. Local land trusts play an equally important role in identifying and protecting land in their own communities. Additional funding for land protection sometimes comes from groups like the Sweetwater Trust and the Norcross Wildlife Foundation.

In general, bird habitat in Western Massachusetts has been protected by a variety of mechanisms, including outright governmental purchase, acquisition by private conservation or educational groups, the establishment of Conservation Restrictions or Agricultural Preservation Restrictions, and the implementation of management partnerships involving private owners, conservation land trusts, state conservation agencies, the Silvio O. Conte National Fish and Wildlife Refuge, and others.

With this book we hope to inspire serious birders to relay bird records and local knowledge of special birding locations to the groups best able to act. For habitat on active farmland, for example, the state Department of Food and Agriculture's Agricultural Preservation Restriction (APR) program, headed by Rich Hubbard, has already protected some 50,000 acres statewide, often with help from towns and land trusts. There are still many vulnerable farms, however, particularly in the central Connecticut River Valley, the Brookfields, and the Hoosic and Housatonic Valleys.

Through the persistent work of Terry Blunt and many others, the Department of Environmental Management (DEM) controls many state parks described in this volume. Together with The Nature Conservancy, the Massachusetts Audubon Society, The Trustees of Reservations, and others, the DEM has recently protected exceptional land complexes with fine bird habitat near the French King Bridge in Gill, on the Holyoke Range and Mount Tom, and elsewhere. The Division of Fisheries and Wildlife cares for many state Wildlife Management Areas and has an interest in protecting both game and non-game habitat as well as land with rare species. The state Natural Heritage & Endangered Species Program's recent BioMap publications are valuable tools for anyone interested in conservation.

In some cases, as with Hadley Cove on the Connecticut River, recent Conservation Restrictions (which permanently prevent development) given to land trusts or to the DEM now protect special habitats even though they remain in private ownership. Many fine birding spots are municipally owned and managed as conservation land. Others, such as Hawley Bog in Franklin County, are owned by research or educational institutions like Five Colleges, Inc., or the community colleges, or by electric utilities or municipal water districts.

The big picture is one of nervous hope for the remaining unprotected areas of critical bird habitat. State funding for open space protection is not always adequate, but private grants and gifts to the land trusts have often allowed those trusts to come to the rescue by acting quickly in the face of development threats. We invite both resident and visiting birders to contribute to those land trusts and to help supply birding information to the trusts and the state and municipal conservation agencies that continue to do such an admirable land protection and habitat management job, watching over the best birding areas despite scarce resources. See the list of Conservation Resources near the end of this book for addresses and more information.

We also wish to thank those who have worked diligently to identify important tracts of habitat, support land protection, help with fundraising, and contribute skills and expertise by collecting data and helping with management decisions and land management. Western Massachusetts has a wealth of beautiful and important natural areas and birding sites. Through continuing collaborative efforts we hope to maintain those sites into the distant future.

Pete Westover, Conservation Department, Town of Amherst

The University of Massachusetts and Bird Conservation

As part of the Land Grant system in the United States, the University of Massachusetts fulfills its mission through a combination of teaching, basic and applied research, and outreach. Resources of the University support bird and habitat conservation in a variety of ways.

The University offers degree programs in biology, botany, zoology, organismic and evolutionary biology, wildlife and fisheries conservation, forestry, natural resource studies, building materials and wood technology, landscape architecture, regional planning, resource economics, civil and environmental engineering, geosciences, environmental science, and public health. Many University of Massachusetts graduates work for federal and state environmental agencies, conservation organizations, environmental consulting firms, and natural resource based businesses.

Faculty and graduate students conduct both basic and applied research that enhances our understanding of birds, their habitats, and the array of issues that affect bird populations: bird anatomy, physiology, behavior, and ecology, and applied research on population genetics, conservation biology, and habitat requirements. University faculty and students are involved in studies in New England and around the world, continuing to add to our body of knowledge about birds. Research in the fields of habitat management, invasive plants and animals, conservation biology, landscape ecology, and regional planning provides information that can be used in managing habitats and human land use to maintain an environment suitable for all of New England's native birds.

The Cooperative Extension System is at the heart of University land grant outreach. This partnership, which links research knowledge and practical application, involves the U.S. Department of Agriculture, state universities and local counties. It is UMass Extension and its Natural Resources and Environmental Conservation (NREC) program that has published this book. NREC provides educational programs and materials that enable people to make informed decisions and take action to preserve or enhance the quality, productivity, and sustainability of natural resources and natural systems.

The program builds on the broad, multi-discipline research base of the University and uses the delivery system of University of Massachusetts Extension to focus on conservation of native fish and wildlife, habitats, biodiversity, water, and other natural resources. These programs promote bird conservation in the context of ecosystem management and the influence of human land use on wildlife populations and ecosystems. Extension programs provide information, training, and technical assistance in wildlife habitat assessment, land conservation and management, forest stewardship, and the protection of wetlands and other water resources. Recent efforts are focused on the use of satellite imagery, Geographic Information Systems (GIS), and computer modeling to identify priorities for conservation based on an area's ability to support birds, other wildlife, and biodiversity.

The future of grassland, shrubland, and forest birds in Massachusetts and throughout New England is dependent on the conservation and proper stewardship of habitats. Proceeds from the sale of this book will support UMass Extension's continuing efforts to protect critical habitats by providing information, technical assistance, training, and the development of new tools and approaches for land conservation. Contributions to land trusts or other conservation organizations will help ensure that birding in Massachusetts will be as exciting in the future as it is now.

Scott Jackson, University of Massachusetts Extension

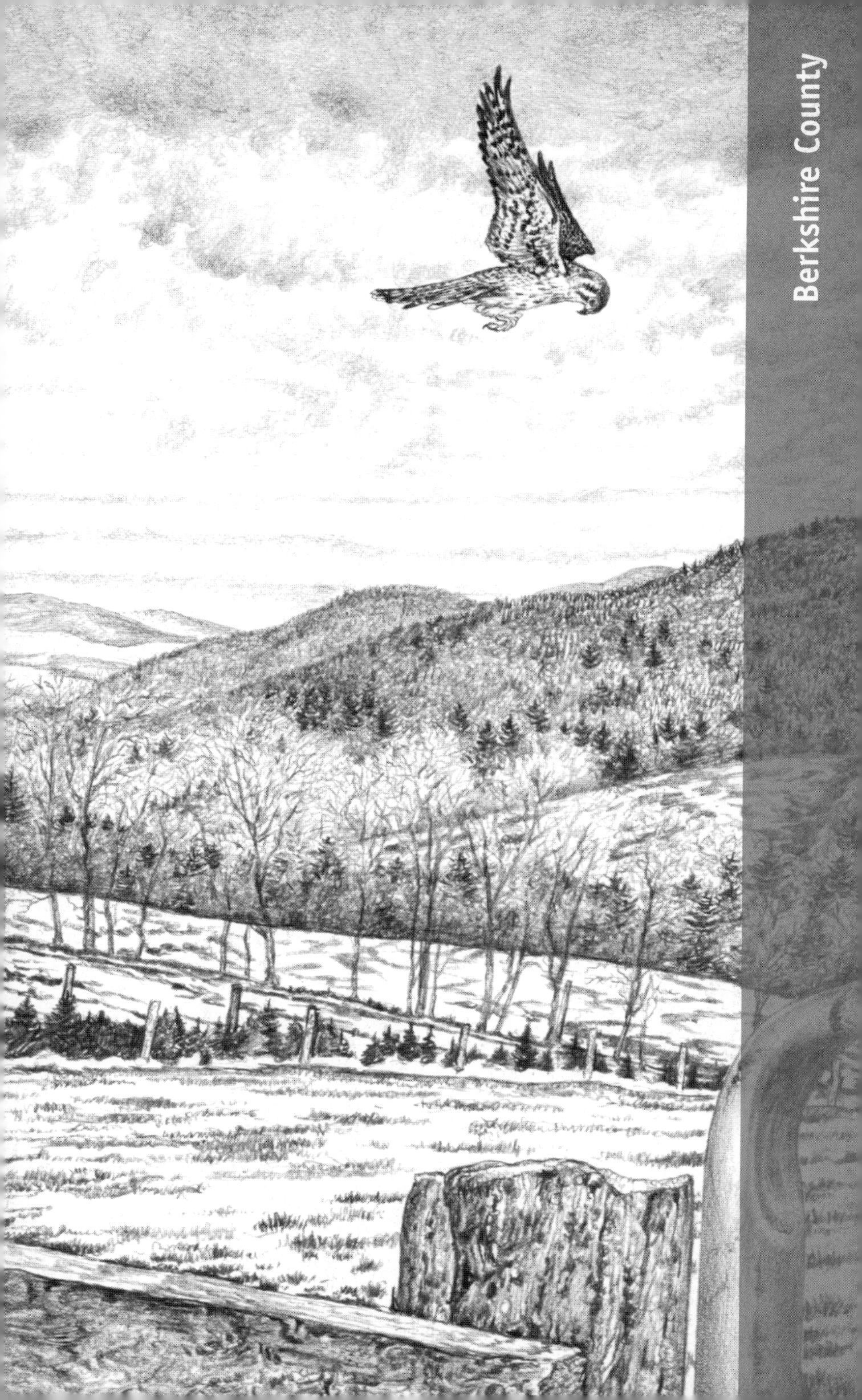

Berkshire County

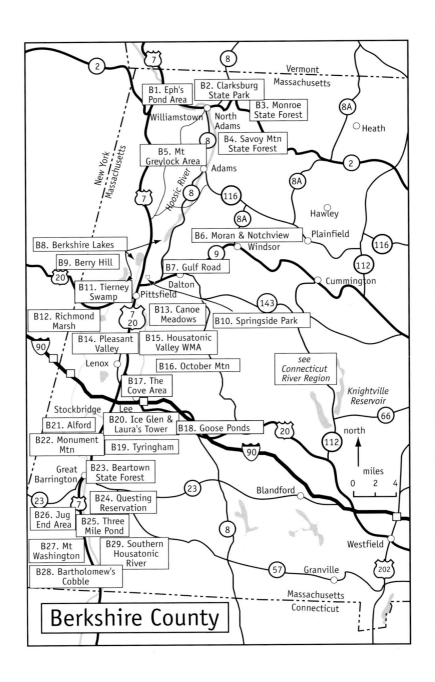

- 2
- 7
- 8
- Vermont
- Massachusetts
- B1. Eph's Pond Area
- B2. Clarksburg State Park
- B3. Monroe State Forest
- 8A
- Heath
- Williamstown
- North Adams
- B4. Savoy Mtn State Forest
- 8
- B5. Mt Greylock Area
- Adams
- 2
- Hoosic River
- 8A
- 7
- 8
- 116
- Hawley
- 8A
- Plainfield
- B6. Moran & Notchview
- Windsor
- 116
- B8. Berkshire Lakes
- B9. Berry Hill
- 9
- 112
- B7. Gulf Road
- Dalton
- Cummington
- 20
- B11. Tierney Swamp
- Pittsfield
- 143
- B12. Richmond Marsh
- 7 20
- B13. Canoe Meadows
- B10. Springside Park
- B14. Pleasant Valley
- B15. Housatonic Valley WMA
- 90
- Lenox
- B16. October Mtn
- see Connecticut River Region
- Knightville Reservoir
- B17. The Cove Area
- 66
- Stockbridge
- Lee
- B21. Alford
- B20. Ice Glen & Laura's Tower
- B18. Goose Ponds
- 20
- north
- B22. Monument Mtn
- B19. Tyringham
- 112
- 90
- miles
- Great Barrington
- B23. Beartown State Forest
- 23
- Blandford
- 0 2 4
- 23
- 7
- B24. Questing Reservation
- B26. Jug End Area
- B25. Three Mile Pond
- 8
- Westfield
- B27. Mt Washington
- B29. Southern Housatonic River
- B28. Bartholomew's Cobble
- 57
- Granville
- 202
- Massachusetts
- Connecticut

Berkshire County

Berkshire County

Introduction

Berkshire County encompasses approximately 950 square miles, with meadows, lakes, marshes, numerous bogs and fens, and thousands of acres of upland forest. There are over 125,000 acres of public forests, reservations, and wildlife management areas owned by the state. More than 6,000 additional acres are owned by private organizations such as Massachusetts Audubon Society and The Trustees of Reservations. The many country roads winding through forest and field and by lakes, ponds, and wetlands allow excellent roadside birding.

Two rivers flow through Berkshire County. The Housatonic River flows south through its valley creating approximately 70 miles of riparian corridor with many marshes and swamps. The Hoosic River flows northwest from Williamstown to the Hudson River. These river valleys are used as migration flyways. Lakes and ponds throughout the county also attract migrating waterfowl.

Berkshire County is bordered by the Hoosac Range and Berkshire Plateau on the east, and by the Taconic Range to the west. Greylock Mountain, in the northwest corner of the county, is the highest point in the state at 3491 feet above sea level. The lowest elevation is on the Hoosic River at 590 feet and the next lowest point is on the Housatonic River as it leaves the county to the south. The approximately 3000 feet of elevation relief allows for a large diversity of flora and fauna not found in other areas of the state. The average altitude in the county is 1500 feet.

The forests are mostly second-growth hardwoods: beech, hemlock, sugar maple, and yellow birch in the north; oaks, hickories, ash, and red maple in the south. At some higher elevations, areas of spruce-fir forest provide breeding habitat for northerly species and attract invasion species in winter.

Some of the species found in Berkshire County in the breeding season are Pied-billed Grebe, American Bittern, Common Moorhen, Wilson's Snipe, Olive-sided Flycatcher, Yellow-bellied Flycatcher, Swainson's Thrush, Blackpoll Warbler, Mourning Warbler, and Rusty Black-

Preceeding Pages: **AMERICAN KESTREL**

bird. In winter, species such as Snow Bunting, Pine Grosbeak, Red and White-winged Crossbills, Common Redpoll, Pine Siskin, and Evening Grosbeak can often be found.   *Noreen Mole*

B1. Eph's Pond Area
Williamstown

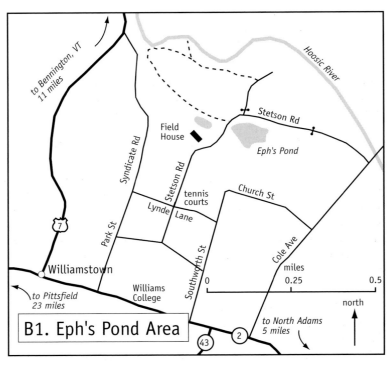

Eph's Pond

It is amazing that amidst the comings and goings of hundreds of students it is possible to see a migrant Osprey fishing for goldfish. Backed by an extensive swamp and ringed with snags, Eph's Pond has a surprisingly diverse population in all seasons. The best times for birding are early morning and late afternoon.

From the intersection of Routes 2 and 7 in Williamstown head 0.3 mile east on Route 2 and turn left on Park Street. Head north 0.2 mile to Lynde Lane, turn right, and go one block. At the four-way stop turn left and continue straight past the Williams College field house on the left and downhill to the playing fields. The pond is immediately on the right. Parking is available along the edge of the field.

Bird by walking along the edge of the pond on the drive. There are several places with good views of the pond. Check the shrubby edges as well. Wood Duck, Gadwall, American Black Duck, Blue-winged and Green-winged Teal, and Common Merganser are seen in early spring. Occasionally American Wigeon, Northern Shoveler, Northern Pintail, and Hooded Merganser also stop here.

Activity around the pond starts in early spring with the return of Swamp Sparrows and other early arrivals. Great Blue Heron and Belted Kingfisher, found along the Hoosic throughout the winter in some years, also visit in early spring.

The Osprey, a spectacular migrant, fishes the ponds and the river, perching in large cottonwoods. Other raptors here include Sharp-shinned, Broad-winged, and Red-tailed Hawk, American Kestrel, Eastern Screech-Owl, and Great Horned and Barred Owls. It is not unusual to find piles of feathers dotting the playing fields on early morning walks, evidence of these winged predators.

The pond and pond edge are very active in April. Shorebirds such as Semipalmated Plover, Greater Yellowlegs, and Solitary Sandpiper are spring visitors. American Bittern, Wilson's Snipe, and American Wood-cock are sighted occasionally. Virginia Rail has been reported. Green Heron is a warm-weather resident, often flying between the pond and the river. Look for Ruby-crowned Kinglet, Blue-gray Gnatcatcher, and Yellow-rumped, and Palm Warblers around the pond.

May is of course the jackpot for species. Watch for Wood Duck on the pond and Tree, Northern Rough-winged, Bank, and Barn Swallows over the pond. Eastern Kingbird, Warbling Vireo, and Baltimore Oriole nest in the shrubby perimeter. Killdeer, Eastern Bluebird, and American Robin stalk the field. Hermit and Wood Thrushes, Scarlet Tanager, Rose-breasted Grosbeak, and Indigo Bunting are in the woods. Willow and Least Flycatchers, Carolina and House Wrens, Cedar Waxwing, Black-and-white Warbler, and American Redstart add their songs to the cacophony.

A few shorebirds filter through in August. Three or four Great Blue Herons consider the pond their August home and expend significant energy chasing away the immature Little Blue Herons, Great and Snowy Egrets, and Black-crowned Night-Herons that disperse to fish here. Killdeer, Solitary and Spotted Sandpipers gather on muddy banks if the water is low. Chimney Swifts gather over the pond in great numbers at dusk.

In fall watch for American Black Duck and noisy blackbird flocks. Vireos, thrushes, warblers, and sparrows, including White-throated and

White-crowned, and other fruit-eating migrants gorge on fruits of the silky, red-panicled, and red-osier dogwoods, Japanese honeysuckle, and buckthorn. Walk slowly around the pond listening for the rustle of the underbrush as these birds prepare for migration.

Late fall and winter are the times to see the last waterfowl and returning winter residents. Cedar Waxwing flocks inhabit thickets around the pond; check for Bohemian Waxwing among them. Eastern Bluebird, American Robin, and Northern Cardinal are also common here. On the river, Common Mergansers congregate in the swifter areas through winter.

Hoosic River

From Eph's Pond, walk north along the drive to the large gate at the curve. Follow a paved road between the lower football field and the higher playing field until just past the large spruces. Turn left into the woods and follow the track west along the Hoosic River. In spring, look for both nuthatches, Carolina Wren, Black-and-white Warbler, and American Redstart in tangled understory along the path. Approach the lookouts above the river quietly and scan for Wood Duck, American Black Duck, Common Merganser, and, in migration, Osprey. The tall cottonwoods and other floodplain species attract Red-eyed Vireo, Rose-breasted Grosbeak, Indigo Bunting, Baltimore Oriole, and a variety of woodpeckers. The trail branches several times; follow the trail to the right to a sand and gravel bar along a curve of the river or continue through the floodplain forest to the bottom of the curve, the best place to look for Red-bellied and Pileated Woodpeckers. A left-hand turn at that point leads across a bridge and through the woods to a cleared sewer easement. The brushy edge here hosts many warblers in migration. Turn left and follow this cleared path back to the playing field and parking area, passing a smaller pond and its associated swamp on your right. *Leslie Reed-Evans*

B2. Clarksburg State Park
Clarksburg

In North Adams at the intersection of Routes 2 and 8, go north on Route 8. After 3 miles turn left on Middle Road in Clarksburg. The park entrance is 0.2 mile on your right. Park near the headquarters and pick up a trail map.

Birding Clarksburg State Park is best April through October. The walk on the paved park road heading east to the pond through a grove of towering white pines is usually productive. Great Horned Owls breed, and Yellow-rumped and Blackburnian Warblers are numerous. At the pond scan for waterfowl and Spotted Sandpipers. In spring you may have the whole

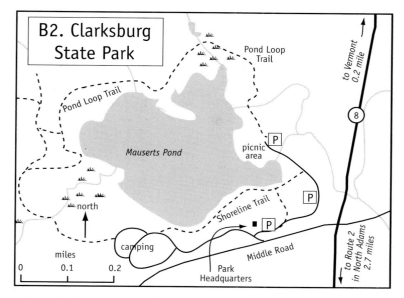

B2. Clarksburg State Park

Pond Loop Trail

to Vermont 0.2 mile

8

picnic area

P

Mauserts Pond

Pond Loop Trail

Shoreline Trail

P

north

P

camping

Middle Road

to Route 2 in North Adams 2.7 miles

miles

0   0.1   0.2

Park Headquarters

park and migrating waterfowl, Osprey, and songbirds to yourself. A trail encircles the pond, beginning at the far end of the picnic area. Magnolia, Black-throated Blue, Black-throated Green, Blackburnian, and Canada Warblers and Northern Waterthrush breed here. Red-shouldered Hawks frequent the marshy inlets, and Pileated Woodpecker is often encountered. This blue-blazed trail can be wet, especially during rainy periods and in spring. Bridges and boardwalks make it more accessible. You can also explore Shoreline Trail linking the camping area and parking lots and trails to the west of the pond loop. Watch in the park for Great Blue Heron, Hooded Merganser, Blue-headed Vireo, Common Raven, Red-breasted Nuthatch, Brown Creeper, Golden-crowned Kinglet, Purple Finch, and Evening Grosbeak.   *Ronald Rancatti*

B3. Monroe State Forest
Monroe

See map B3. Monroe State Forest

In North Adams at the intersection of Routes 2 and 8, go east on Route 2 crossing the top of the Hoosac Range at the Florida town line. After nearly 5 miles from the intersection turn left (north) on Tilda Hill Road at a green sign for Monroe and the Fire Department buildings. Drive roughly 4.2 miles on this road to a Monroe State Forest sign on your right shortly after a small bridge spanning Dunbar Brook. Ample parking is just beyond this sign. North Road is across the road. South Road and the Dunbar Loop are on the same side as the parking lot. Watch in appropriate habitat in this forest for Hooded Merganser, Pileated Woodpecker, and Evening Grosbeak.

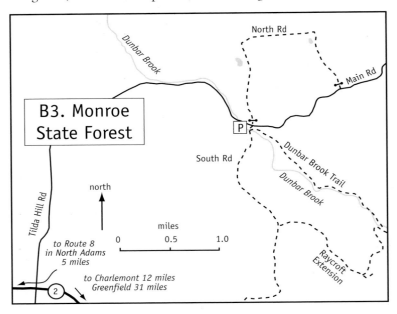

North Road

The best time to bird this area is May through July. North Road (closed to traffic) passes a metal gate and climbs steadily a short while before becoming an easy level walk. Swainson's Thrush, Hermit Thrush, and upland forest warblers can usually be heard singing from thick hemlock-covered slopes to your left on the lower portion of this road. Winter Wren is also regular here. These species continue as the road becomes more level. To the left a small beaver pond, obscured by vegetation except in the spring, offers excellent opportunities for Red-shouldered Hawk.

The road ascends gradually to a small clearing, an old farm site. Turn sharply right; you will immediately pass another beaver pond on your left with a white pine plantation on your right. Sharp-shinned Hawk, Northern Goshawk, and Red-shouldered and Broad-winged Hawks nest between this point and the next metal gate at the other end of this road. Barred and Northern Saw-whet Owls are present here in breeding season. Swainson's Thrushes are expected. Rusty Blackbirds have been observed near the beaver ponds in breeding season, but nesting is not confirmed. The area is remote and the road closed, allowing a quiet birding opportunity.

SWAINSON'S THRUSH

Dunbar Loop

This hike, nearly 4 miles long, has some steep ascents and descents. Numerous Swainson's Thrushes are expected, especially in the first half of July, when counts have reached 20 individuals. Start early to enjoy their beautiful song, Swainson's Thrush regularly sings until late morning in early July. From the moment you leave your vehicle be alert for their song. Walk down South Road toward the bridge over Dunbar Brook around the first bend. The rushing stream almost drowns out all bird song, but the road soon swings right and climbs away from the noisy stream.

Continue on South Road to Raycroft Extension Road, your first left. Swainson's Thrushes and numerous Blackburnian Warblers are found along this road. Follow the road about one mile to a footpath on your left, the third leg of this trip. It descends gradually at first but becomes increasingly steep. A three-sided shelter along this trail is a good spot to rest. From here to the bottom of the ravine the going is steep. Winter Wren is often found here, especially around toppled trees on the slope. Swainson's Thrush, also fond of hemlock ravines, is again found here. Cross Dunbar Brook over a footbridge and turn left.

You are now on the hike's fourth and final portion; Dunbar Brook keeps you company for awhile. Golden-crowned Kinglets can be present but are sometimes difficult to hear next to the stream. The trail ascends gradually, following the stream, but near the end it veers away and climbs the side of the ravine, where you usually encounter more Swainson's Thrushes. After the steep climb the trail levels out, and you are soon back on South Road near the bridge you crossed at the beginning. Turn right; your vehicle is only yards away.   *Ronald Rancatti*

B4. Savoy Mountain State Forest
Florida, North Adams, and Savoy

Spruce Hill

From Monroe State Forest (see previous account), return to Route 2, turn right (west), go 1 mile and turn left (south) on Central Shaft Road.

Alternatively, from the intersection of Route 8 north and Route 2 in North Adams, head east on Route 2, up through the hairpin turn, over the Hoosac Range into the town of Florida. After 4.2 miles past Route 8, just after a Savoy Mountain State Forest sign, turn right on Central Shaft Road.

Once on Central Shaft Road go 0.3 mile, bear right and go an additional 1.0 mile. Turn sharply right to stay on Central Shaft Road and continue another 1.5 miles. Park on the wide shoulder just after the Savoy Mountain State Forest Ranger Station on the right.

Before hiking to the summit, walk ahead a hundred feet from your vehicle to view Busby Swamp, where you may see moose. Listen for Alder Flycatcher and Swamp Sparrow in spring and summer. Wetlands such as these are favored areas for Barred and Northern Saw-whet Owls.

Return to your vehicle, walk to the woods road, and quickly take the first road to the right. There are signs for the blue-blazed Busby Trail to the Spruce Hill hawk lookout. It is 1.2 miles to the summit.

You almost immediately cross a power line, where Chestnut-sided Warbler is found. A second power line is good for Chestnut-sided Warbler and Eastern Towhee. The trail gradually ascends through several Norway spruce plantations. Watch for nesting Sharp-shinned Hawk. These spruce plantations are dependable for Blue-headed Vireo, Red-breasted Nuthatch, Golden-crowned Kinglet, Magnolia, Black-throated Green, and Blackburnian Warblers.

Hardwood forest takes over for the remainder of the journey. After the cellar hole of an old farm house the trail swings left and climbs steeply toward the summit. Stop and rest where an old stone wall straddles the trail. Hermit Thrush and Black-throated Blue and Canada Warblers are found here.

After this wonderful resting stop you climb steadily again. A loop hike is recommended from a fork in the trail where a steep ledge looms before you. Turn left; the trail soon scrambles up the ledge face. Beyond the top of the ledge the trail continues steadily uphill. After climbing the last small piece of ledge just below the summit you are treated to a view that makes your hard work worth it. Mount Greylock commands the Hoosic Valley yawning before you. But the birds are the main reason for being here so watch for Turkey Vultures and Common Ravens floating

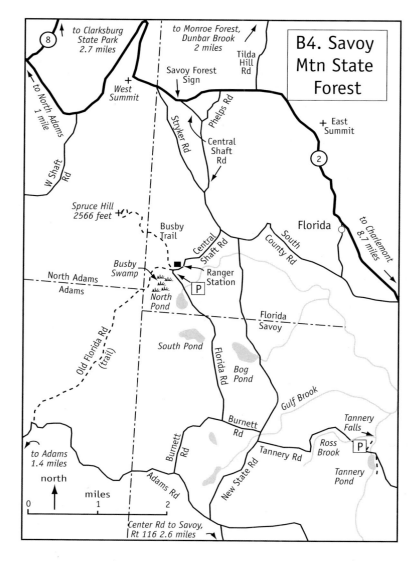

B4. Savoy Mtn State Forest

to Clarksburg State Park 2.7 miles

to Monroe Forest, Dunbar Brook 2 miles

Tilda Hill Rd

Savoy Forest Sign

West Summit

to North Adams 1 mile

Stryker Rd

Phelps Rd

Central Shaft Rd

East Summit

W Shaft Rd

Spruce Hill 2566 feet

Busby Trail

Florida

to Charlemont 8.7 miles

Busby Swamp

Central Shaft Rd

South County Rd

North Adams
Adams

Ranger Station

P

North Pond

Florida Savoy

Old Florida Rd (trail)

South Pond

Florida Rd

Bog Pond

Gulf Brook

Tannery Falls

Burnett Rd

Ross Brook

P

to Adams 1.4 miles

Burnett Rd

Tannery Rd

Tannery Pond

north

miles

0   1   2

Adams Rd

New State Rd

Center Rd to Savoy, Rt 116 2.6 miles

by. In fall, visit the full-time hawkwatch site on the north side of the summit, reached by following the blue-blazed trail a few hundred feet through stunted hardwoods to a large clearing.

In early September expect to see migrating Osprey, Bald Eagle, Northern Harrier, Sharp-shinned Hawk, American Kestrel, and a few early Broad-winged Hawks. Usually by September 10 the number of migrating Broad-winged Hawks swells dramatically, and peak numbers occur anytime between this date and September 24. High counts of Osprey also occur at this time. Close up views of passing hawks are common. By late September, usually after the Broad-winged Hawks depart, adult Sharp-shinned Hawks take over as the most common raptor. This is also an excellent time for Peregrine Falcon and good numbers of Osprey and American Kestrels. A few Northern Harriers, Cooper's Hawks, and Merlins add to the excitement. By mid-October the deciduous foliage disappears, and Red-tailed Hawk is the most common migrating raptor. From mid-October into November, sighting a magnificent Golden Eagle is possible. If you have never seen a Golden Eagle, you'll never forget your first. Other late-season migrants include Osprey, Bald Eagle, Northern Harrier, Sharp-shinned Hawk, Northern Goshawk, Red-shouldered Hawk, and American Kestrel.

Other migrants seen in good numbers include Snow Geese (October), flocks of Blue Jays and American Robins, and numerous Yellow-rumped Warblers. October brings occasional Northern Shrikes, Snow Buntings, Evening Grosbeaks, and other winter finches.

To return to the main trail, head north through the hawkwatch site clearing and follow the blue-blazed trail. Descend a stone staircase just before the terminus of the summit loop. The trail back to your vehicle is on the left.

Tannery Pond and Tannery Falls, Savoy

This is a heavily forested area with the possibility of raptors and Pileated Woodpecker along the roads and trails. Species found here include Wood Duck, American Woodcock, Barred and Northern Saw-whet Owls, Alder Flycatcher, Blue-headed Vireo, Common Raven, Brown Creeper, Black-throated Blue and Canada Warblers, Northern Waterthrush, and Purple Finch. The recommended time to visit is May through July. Tannery Road is not open in winter.

Continue south on Central Shaft Road (which becomes Florida Road), go left on Burnett Road, and turn sharply right over a small bridge on New State Road (about 2.5 miles from the ranger station). After about 0.2 mile turn left on Tannery Road and drive 2 miles to the parking lot at the trailhead to Tannery Falls.

The trail to the bottom of Tannery Falls and its ravine travels through heavy hemlock growth with Winter Wren, Swainson's Thrush, Black-throated Green, and Blackburnian Warblers, and Louisiana Waterthrush. Return to the parking lot and walk along Tannery Road just beyond. Turn left; Tannery Pond is soon on your right. Examine the pond for waterfowl and an occasional Great Blue Heron. To reach the marshy end of Tannery Pond walk beyond the pond. Turn right on an old woods road amidst a white pine grove, and walk past thick hemlocks on your right. Listen for Red-shouldered Hawk, Red-breasted Nuthatch, Golden-crowned Kinglet, Blackburnian Warbler, and Evening Grosbeak.

The forest thins after a few minutes of walking, and you gain an excellent view of the marshy end of the pond. Be alert for rare nesters such as Olive-sided Flycatcher, Lincoln's Sparrow, and Rusty Blackbird. These upland marshy areas are the favorite habitat of these three species.

Return to Tannery Road, walk past the parking lot, and cross the Ross Brook bridge. Continue walking on Tannery Road a short distance to a Norway spruce plantation on your left and hemlocks on your right, a dependable location to hear Golden-crowned Kinglet, Swainson's Thrush, and Magnolia and Blackburnian Warblers. Norway spruce plantations near openings such as Tannery Road are excellent nesting locations for Sharp-shinned Hawk. Noisy fledglings are usually found from mid-July into early August.   *Ronald Rancatti*

B5. Mount Greylock Area
Adams, Cheshire, New Ashford, North Adams, and Williamstown

See map B5. Mt Greylock Area

Mount Greylock is the highest spot in Massachusetts. The mountain and surrounding highlands host many northern species, and many of the boreal areas, including the summit, are readily accessible by car when the road is open (late spring through late fall). There are many options for hikes of various levels of difficulty. If you are planning to hike, carry one of the many excellent trail maps and guides available at the Visitors Center, park kiosks, and area bookstores.

From the north (Notch Road): From downtown North Adams head west on Route 2 over the overpass; after 1.2 miles turn left on Notch Road. Proceed on Notch Road to its junction with Pattison Road. Turn left and continue on Notch Road until small fields appear on both sides. Bear sharply right just beyond. You will pass a large Mount Greylock State Reservation sign on your right and go through a gate (closed in winter). Continue on Notch Road as it climbs the northern slope of Mount Williams. The Appalachian Trail (AT) crosses at roughly 6 miles. Continue to the junction of Notch Road and Rockwell Road at nearly 10 miles from North Adams. The Gould Trail starts at the parking lot directly across from the stop sign.

From the south (Rockwell Road): Driving north from Pittsfield on Route 7, watch in Lanesborough for the brown Mount Greylock State

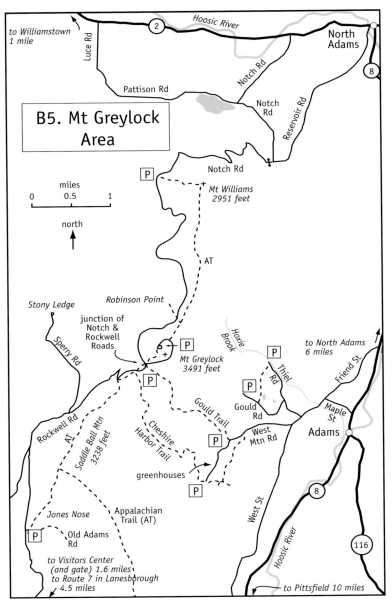

B5. Mt Greylock Area

miles
0   0.5   1

north

to Williamstown 1 mile

Hoosic River

Luce Rd

Pattison Rd

Notch Rd

Notch Rd

Reservoir Rd

North Adams

8

2

P

Mt Williams 2951 feet

AT

Stony Ledge

Robinson Point

junction of Notch & Rockwell Roads

Sperry Rd

Hoxie Brook

P

to North Adams 6 miles

Thiel Rd

Friend St

P

Mt Greylock 3491 feet

P

Gould Trail

Gould Rd

Maple St

Adams

P

Rockwell Rd

AT

Saddle Ball Mtn 3238 feet

Cheshire Harbor Trail

greenhouses

P

West Mtn Rd

P

West St

8

Jones Nose

Appalachian Trail (AT)

P

Old Adams Rd

to Visitors Center (and gate) 1.6 miles
to Route 7 in Lanesborough 4.5 miles

Hoosic River

116

to Pittsfield 10 miles

Reservation sign. Turn northeast on North Main Street. Drive nearly 0.7 mile and bear sharply right on Greylock/Quarry Road. Pass the Mount Greylock State Reservation maintenance building on your left. The road becomes Rockwell Road at this point and climbs past open fields to the

Mount Greylock Visitors Center on your right. The road is steep past the metal gate (closed in winter) but soon levels off. From the Visitors Center it is 7.4 miles to the junction with Notch Road.

Notch Road, Adams

Because this trip, which begins at the parking lot at the junction of Notch and Rockwell Roads, includes walking on Notch Road, it is best to begin at dawn when traffic is not a problem and bird song is at greatest intensity. Listen for Swainson's Thrush and Yellow-rumped and Blackpoll Warblers as soon as you leave your car. You may be surprised at the number of American Robins. Walk across Rockwell Road and head north on Notch Road. Thick spruce and balsam fir are on both sides of the road. After one mile the Robinson's Point trailhead on your left has been a dependable spot for Blackpoll Warbler. Continue a little farther to the sign marking the boundary of the War Memorial Park.

You can return to your vehicle or continue on a loop hike. For the loop hike take a spur trail on the opposite (east) side of the road a short distance south of the Robinson's Point trailhead. This spur leads quickly to the Appalachian Trail (AT). Turn right on the AT and ascend steadily through an excellent area for Winter Wren, Canada Warbler, Eastern Towhee, White-throated Sparrow, Dark-eyed Junco, and Indigo Bunting. The trail continues to Rockwell Road where the trail on the left heads downhill toward your vehicle less than half a mile away. Along the way you have a commanding view of the Hoosic Valley. Watch for Chimney Swifts and swallows, especially in late summer.

You may also encounter Barred and Northern Saw-whet Owls, Common Raven, Red-breasted Nuthatch, Golden-crowned Kinglet, Swainson's and Hermit Thrushes, Magnolia Warbler, White-throated Sparrow, Purple Finch, Evening Grosbeak, and, in some years, Red Crossbill and Pine Siskin.

Mount Greylock Summit, Adams

From the junction of Notch and Rockwell Roads, continue on the paved road about 0.8 mile to the parking area at the top. The summit, with its spruce-fir woods and large grassy openings, has a rich history of attracting rare nesters, migrants, and species unexpected at high altitude. Watch for Common Raven, Red-breasted Nuthatch, Golden-crowned Kinglet, Swainson's Thrush, Magnolia, Yellow-rumped and Blackpoll Warblers, White-throated Sparrow, and Purple Finch. Red Crossbills and Pine Siskins can occur at any time or not at all. Keep an eye to the sky for migrating raptors from late August through October. October is a good time to find Snow Buntings. Unusual sightings have included an Eastern Screech-Owl in June 1948, a Black-backed Woodpecker back in February 1928, a Northern Wheatear in October 1994, and 20 Lapland Longspurs in October 1985.

Bicknell's Thrush nested near the Mount Greylock summit up to about 30 years ago. It still nests on southern Vermont's higher peaks, so keep this species in mind at the summit, especially late May through mid-July.

Saddle Ball Mountain on the Appalachian Trail (AT), New Ashford

From the junction of Notch and Rockwell Roads, follow Rockwell Road downhill (south) 0.5 mile to the large AT sign. A short dirt road to the left of this sign leads to the parking lot. Walk back to the paved road, pass the sign, and enter the forest on the AT to the right of the sign. If you have two vehicles, leaving the second at the Jones Nose parking lot (2.8 miles farther south on Rockwell Road) eliminates the need to retrace your steps; the return hike, however, is often productive.

Mid-May through mid-August is the best time to visit Saddle Ball Mountain, its birds, and its forest of spruce-fir and northern hardwoods. After you enter the forest the trail ascends, crosses a small knoll, and then descends to a boardwalk across a sphagnum bog. Listen for Yellow-bellied Flycatcher, Common Raven, Winter Wren, Swainson's Thrush, and Nashville and Canada Warblers. Barred and Northern Saw-whet Owls occur here and at other locations on this ridge. The trail then ascends a series of small summits and passes other sphagnum bogs. Sharp-shinned Hawks have nested at one of these bogs. A few Blackpoll Warblers are usually found along this trail near bogs and small summits. A good day along Saddle Ball could yield four to six Blackpoll Warblers. One or two Yellow-bellied Flycatchers, closely associated with spruce bogs, are usually found each year. Mourning Warblers are found in recently disturbed, scrubby areas. One such place is on Old Adams Road which leads east from the parking lot below Jones Nose.

Nomadic Red Crossbills and Pine Siskins add excitement those years they occur. Common Raven, Golden-crowned Kinglet, and Swainson's Thrush can be heard almost anywhere along the ridge top. Swainson's Thrush occurs here in small numbers, so if you encounter one, take time to savor his beautiful song. Listen throughout this area for Red-breasted Nuthatch, Hermit Thrush, Magnolia and Yellow-rumped Warblers, White-throated Sparrow, Purple Finch, and Evening Grosbeak.

Greylock Glen (Gould/Thiel Roads Property), Adams

From the intersection of Routes 8 and 116 in the center of Adams, go north about 0.2 mile on Route 8, and turn left (west) on Maple Street

MOURNING WARBLER

(note large statue of President McKinley at the intersection). After about 0.2 mile turn left (south) on West Street where Maple ends. After 0.4 mile turn right (west) on Gould Road; apple orchards will be on both sides of the road. After 0.3 mile go left on Gould Road. Parking is available a few hundred feet farther on the right.

This area's many habitats, including mixed forest, spruce lots, weedy fields, and small wetlands, provide good birding year-round. This area is popular with town residents; you probably will not find yourself alone, although this 1000+ acre State Department of Environmental Management tract has plenty of elbow room. An ideal way to bird the center portion of this area is to use the paved roads that nearly circle it. You can also enter the center of this open area by various trails. Pick up a free map at the Greylock Glen regulations sign. It is hard to get lost if you use Mount Greylock's imposing mass to the west as a reference point.

From October to April, look for Red-tailed and the scarcer Rough-legged Hawks, American Kestrel, Northern Shrike, and Snow Bunting. Common Ravens often soar overhead or over Greylock's slopes. Cedar Waxwings frequent this area; their flocks should be checked carefully for Bohemian Waxwing. Some hardy Eastern Bluebirds and American Robins are seen here in mild winters. Quietly inspect the spruce lots for whitewash or pellets, evidence of recent owl roosting. With luck you may find the owl itself. Stay alert for American Crows mobbing Great Horned or Barred Owls and for Black-capped Chickadees mobbing Eastern Screech-Owls or Northern Saw-whet Owls.

In fall and spring, this site yields Northern Harrier and other migrating hawks looking for a meal. Northern songbirds such as Ruby-crowned Kinglet, Palm Warbler, and, less commonly, Wilson's Warbler and Fox Sparrow, frequent this area in migration. A 1995 breeding bird survey of this tract located 78 species. A Mourning Warbler was a rare find. Louisiana Waterthrushes are found along Hoxie Brook. Other species include American Woodcock, Sharp-shinned, Broad-winged and Red-tailed Hawks, and American Kestrel. Black-billed Cuckoo, Alder and Willow Flycatchers occur around the ponds.

Watch in appropriate habitat for Cooper's Hawk, Pileated Woodpecker, Red-breasted Nuthatch, Brown Creeper, Winter Wren, Blue-winged, Magnolia, Black-throated Blue, Black-throated Green, Blackburnian, and Canada Warblers, Eastern Towhee, Savannah Sparrow, and Indigo Bunting.

Greylock Glen (West Mountain Road Property), Adams

This is a less traveled portion of the Glen. Follow directions above to Greylock Glen, but continue south on West Street an additional 0.1 mile. Turn right on West Mountain Road immediately after the small Peck's Brook bridge. Proceed on West Mountain Road until you reach fields on both sides. At a sharp left corner (0.7 mile) there is parking on your right for the Gould Trail.

From here scan for Red-tailed Hawk and American Kestrel, and, from October to April, for Rough-legged Hawk and Northern Shrike. Then drive farther on West Mountain Road, passing Mount Greylock Greenhouses on your right. The road soon ends at parking for the Cheshire Harbor Trail. This is the trail of choice to hike to Mount Greylock's summit; be sure you have the necessary trail maps.

A different trail, and an excellent way to bird the varied habitat of highland meadows and forest, is to take a 2-mile loop which begins at the Cheshire Harbor Trail parking lot. Follow the footpath (old road) on the east side of the parking area through a brushy pasture. At a fork in the trail, continue straight through a row of trees and stone wall that separates this pasture from a smaller one, bear left on another footpath. Eastern Towhee and Indigo Bunting are common here. This footpath enters secondary growth and than descends to a field. Expect Alder Flycatcher here, and listen for the buzzy Blue-winged Warbler song in May and June. Veery, Hermit and Wood Thrushes, Nashville Warbler, and White-throated Sparrow occur in this upland area.

Just beyond the field and a small brook, bear sharply right, and follow a badly rutted trail along the edge of a field with a mature mixed-hardwood forest on your right. Views of Mount Greylock are impressive from this entire area of the Glen. Where the trail intersects another footpath near the end of the field, go right and enter the forest. Turn left at the next intersection. Turn left again back to West Mountain Road. At the road either retrace your route or take West Mountain Road past the Gould Trail parking lot and the greenhouses back to your vehicle.

Watch in appropriate habitat in this section for Northern Harrier (spring and fall), Sharp-shinned, Cooper's, and Broad-winged Hawks, American Woodcock, Black-billed Cuckoo, Great Horned and Barred Owls, Pileated Woodpecker, Willow Flycatcher, Common Raven, Red-breasted Nuthatch, Brown Creeper, Winter Wren, Eastern Bluebird, Magnolia, Black-throated Blue, Black-throated Green, Blackburnian, Palm (spring and fall), and Canada Warblers, and Savannah Sparrow.   *Ronald Rancatti*

B6. Moran WMA and Notchview Reservation
Windsor

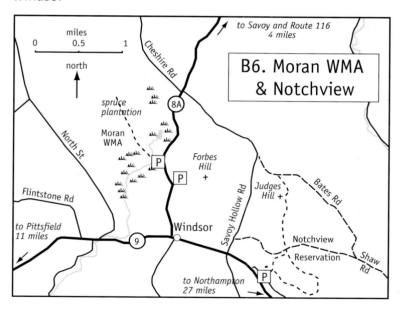

Eugene D. Moran Wildlife Management Area and North Street

Moran Wildlife Management Area. Often referred to as a "feast or famine" birding spot, Moran (1239 acres) offers beautiful views and the possibility of fine birding. Moran may be the most reliable place in the state for Northern Shrike, even in winters when this species is scarce, and Moran and nearby roads are one of the best areas for a chance of

WHITE-WINGED CROSSBILL

Rough-legged Hawk, Gray Jay, Boreal Chickadee, both crossbills, and other winter finches. In summer the chance of rare breeding records (e.g., Henslow's Sparrow, Lincoln's Sparrow, and Dickcissel have each summered on occasion) attracts observers. Fairly good fall hawk flights can occur. In spring migration, the abundant thickets are often havens for warblers. At least one pair of American Kestrels nest here. Barred Owls call from the woods. Avoid in hunting season.

From Route 9 in the center of Windsor go 0.9 mile north on Route 8A. Parking lots for Moran are on both sides of the road. The lot on the left (west) provides access to the easiest walking and most diverse habitats.

From the south end of the lower (west) parking lot, walk the dirt road winding to the right. Check the wetlands below (a scope helps) for Northern Harrier (a pair nested in 1999). Sedge Wrens have been found in the wetlands. Continue on the road; both sides have good cover. Farther down, the road crosses a brook, dammed in places by beaver, then leads upward with thick growth on either side. Farther up on the right, a field often has Bobolinks. It can be worthwhile to circumnavigate this field surrounded with thickets. To the north an overgrown portion of another road leads to a spruce plantation. In winter, both crossbills have occurred here, and it is the spot to look for Boreal Chickadee.

From the upper (east) parking lot, a walk up Forbes Hill can be good for migrating hawks. There are no trails on this side of Route 8A so the going can be rough!

North Street. North Street goes north from Route 9 in Windsor about a mile west of Route 8A. Winter and spring are the best times to visit. A slow drive on North Street in winter may reward you with Snow Buntings and other field species. Some feeding stations here have had large numbers of birds. About one mile in, a weedy field on the right can be productive. A drive through in spring sometimes produces many migrants. *Dave Charbonneau*

Notchview Reservation

Notchview Reservation, a 3,000-acre reserve owned by The Trustees of Reservations (TTOR), is a high elevation (largely above 2000 feet) mix of fields, wooded wetlands, farmland, hedgerow, ravine, deciduous, coniferous, and mixed woodlands with a northern flavor. Large parcels of forested land, especially Windsor State Forest, border the property, which offers four seasons of challenging birding with almost 15 miles of well-maintained trails.

The Notchview entrance is about one mile east of the intersection of Routes 9 and 8A in the center of Windsor. Turn at the green TTOR sign on the north side of Route 9 for parking, headquarters, and trail maps. A small fee may be charged to non-members.

Winter can bring northern species, such as crossbills, Pine and Evening Grosbeaks, Pine Siskins, and possibly a Gray Jay or Boreal Chickadee, attracted to the dense red spruce-fir habitat. Spring migrants often linger into early June, offering an extension of migration to the valley birder.

A brief list of summer species affirms the diversity of habitats available to hikers here. Open fields harbor Savannah Sparrow, Bobolink, and the occasional American Kestrel. Conifers are home to Red-breasted Nuthatch, Winter Wren, Golden-crowned Kinglet, Magnolia, Yellow-rumped, and Blackburnian Warblers, the ever-present White-throated Sparrow, Dark-eyed Junco, and Purple Finch. Mixed woods support Blue-headed Vireo, Canada Warbler, and, where logging has opened the forest, Mourning Warbler.

Wild Turkey, Black-billed Cuckoo, Yellow-bellied Sapsucker, Eastern Wood-Pewee, Veery, Wood Thrush, Black-throated Blue Warbler, Scarlet Tanager, and Rose-breasted Grosbeak prefer deciduous woodland. Black-throated Green Warbler favors streamside hemlocks. Eastern Towhee, Field Sparrow, and Indigo Bunting are regular at brushy fields. Eastern Bluebird nests around the buildings. With sightings of black bear, fisher, coyote, white-tailed deer, and moose possible, a Notchview trip is always an adventure. *Edwin J. Neumuth*

B7. Gulf Road
Dalton

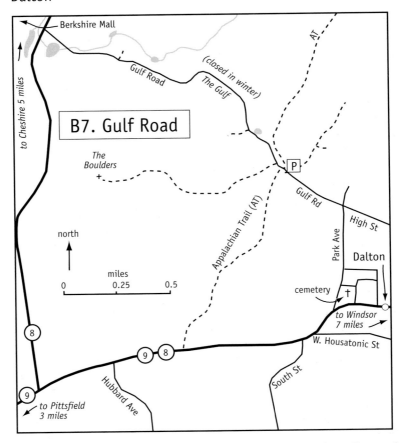

From Notchview (see previous account), go right (west) on Route 9 for 6.5 miles into Dalton. Just after a cemetery on the right, turn right (north) on Park Avenue.

Alternatively, from the Berkshire Museum in downtown Pittsfield, head north on Route 7 following signs to Dalton. At 0.7 mile turn right on Tyler Street (Route 9), and continue 4.0 miles just past the light at the intersection with West Housatonic Street in Dalton. Continue on Route 9 up a slight hill, and turn left (north) on Park Avenue just before a cemetery on the left.

Go to the end of Park Avenue (about a half mile), and turn left (west) on Gulf Road. A short distance down the road is a parking area on the right.

This area is best in late spring and early summer; the road is closed in the winter. At the parking area you should hear Blackburnian Warbler and may find Black-throated Blue and Black-throated Green Warblers, American Redstart, Ovenbird, and Eastern Towhee.

Walk the trail to the right of the parking lot near the chain-link fence, and listen for Black-and-white Warblers. Mourning Warblers have nested along this trail. A short distance up the trail, a path branches to the right toward a meadow, formerly a landfill. From this meadow look back at the treetops for potential spectacular views of Rose-breasted Grosbeak, Indigo Bunting, and Baltimore Oriole. Check the meadow's perimeter for Chestnut-sided and Magnolia Warblers. Watch for Bank Swallows, which nest in nearby sandbanks.

Return to the parking lot and walk northwest along Gulf Road. Be careful to avoid traffic. You can take side trips on marked trails from Gulf Road along the Appalachian Trail or to The Boulders hilltop. Continue along Gulf Road, where Yellow-bellied Sapsucker, Blue-headed Vireo, and Brown Creeper nest, to a small pond on your right, a favorite spot for Winter Wren and possibly a Canada Warbler. You may explore a trail into the woods to the left just after the pond. Gulf Road climbs through a wonderful set of boulders, with cold air, stately hemlocks, Ruffed Grouse, Blackburnian Warbler, and Dark-eyed Junco.

Return to your car, drive past the boulders, and park where there is room. Walk along the road to look for warblers. You may hear a Barred Owl. Retrieve your car and drive down the road, past a few houses, to a chained dumping/storage area entrance on the right. Park well off the road and walk into the dumping area. Look for Pileated Woodpecker, Nashville, Yellow, and Chestnut-sided Warblers, and Indigo Bunting. Belted Kingfishers sometimes nest in a sandbank on the right. Return to your car and drive to the pond on the left for a quick look for ducks. You should see Yellow-rumped Warblers in bushes along the road. Gulf Road runs into Route 8 near Berkshire Mall in Lanesborough.

Linda Brazeau

B8. The Berkshire Lakes
Cheshire, Lanesborough, Pittsfield, Richmond, and Stockbridge

See map B8. The Berkshire Lakes

Four major freshwater lakes and several smaller ponds and reservoirs have been focal points of the Hoffmann Bird Club's annual Waterfowl Count for over 50 years. The most rewarding of these lakes are in or partly in Pittsfield, with Hoosac Lake (also called Cheshire Reservoir) just to the north. South of Pittsfield, other lakes and ponds also attract birds and birders. The Berkshire Museum, just south of Pittsfield's Park Square (about 0.5 mile south of the intersection of Routes 9 and 7), is a good place to begin.

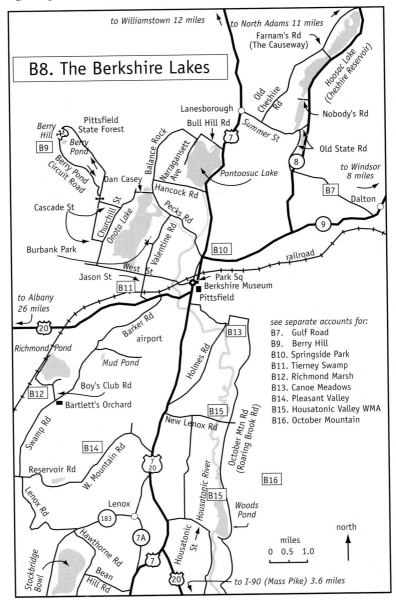

B8. The Berkshire Lakes

to Williamstown 12 miles

to North Adams 11 miles
Farnam's Rd
(The Causeway)

Hoosac Lake (Cheshire Reservoir)

Lanesborough
Bull Hill Rd
Old Cheshire Rd
Summer St
Nobody's Rd

Berry Hill
B9
Pittsfield State Forest
Berry Pond
Balance Rock
Narragansett Ave
7
Old State Rd
8

Berry Pond Circuit Road
Dan Casey
Hancock Rd
Pontoosuc Lake
to Windsor 8 miles
B7
Dalton

Cascade St
Churchill St
Onota Lake
Pecks Rd
Valentine Rd
9

Burbank Park
West St
B10
railroad

Jason St
B11
Park Sq
Berkshire Museum
Pittsfield

to Albany 26 miles
20

Barker Rd
airport
B13
see separate accounts for:
B7. Gulf Road
B9. Berry Hill
B10. Springside Park
B11. Tierney Swamp
B12. Richmond Marsh
B13. Canoe Meadows
B14. Pleasant Valley
B15. Housatonic Valley WMA
B16. October Mountain

Richmond Pond
Mud Pond
Holmes Rd

B12
Boy's Club Rd
Bartlett's Orchard

Swamp Rd
New Lenox Rd
B15
October Mtn Rd (Roaring Brook Rd)

B14
W. Mountain Rd
7 20

Reservoir Rd
Housatonic River
B16

Lenox Rd
Lenox
183
Housatonic St
B15
Woods Pond

north

Hawthorne Rd
7A

miles
0   0.5   1.0

Stockbridge Bowl
Bean Hill Rd
7
20
to I-90 (Mass Pike) 3.6 miles

Pontoosuc and Hoosac Lakes

From the Berkshire Museum, head 2.7 miles north on Route 7 to the dam at the south end of Pontoosuc Lake. Just past a set of stoplights, parking for the YMCA boathouse (called Ponterell) offers a good overview. A stop farther north at either Dunkin Donuts or Matt Reilly's Restaurant (4.2 miles) offers another view. Continue 0.5 mile farther to Bull Hill Road, and turn left (west) toward the north inlet of Pontoosuc. Before making this turn, you may want to visit Hoosac Lake (Cheshire Reservoir).

To reach Hoosac Lake, continue north on Route 7 about 1.1 miles from Bull Hill Road to the center of Lanesborough and turn right up Summer Street. A magnificent American elm is in a yard on the right as you go uphill. Go about 0.5 mile and turn left (north) on Old Cheshire Road. Check the farm on the immediate right for raptors and Wild Turkey. Travel 2.6 miles, and turn right on Farnam's Road, generally called "the causeway." Park at the dirt pull-off, usually the best vantage point. Other good views can be reached by continuing east on the causeway to Route 8 and then left (north) for 1.7 miles to the parking area at the north end of the lake. Many species of waterfowl visit Hoosac Lake, as do herons, egrets, and Osprey; Greater White-fronted Goose and Redhead have been seen recently. The view west may be productive for migrating hawks and nesting Common Raven.

For a final view return south on Route 8 for 3.1 miles passing the intersection with the causeway. Turn right on Old State Road and, in a short distance, where two ponds meet, bear right back on Summer Street (no sign). Pass the spring (drinking not recommended) and park where you can to search for Pied-billed Grebes, small herons, egrets, and other water birds.

To return to Pontoosuc Lake continue west on Summer Street to the end and turn left (south) on Route 7. In 2.1 miles turn right on Bull Hill Road. Stop at a dirt parking area on the right (north) side of Bull Hill Road, the north end of Pontoosuc Lake. In recent years, King Eider, Parasitic Jaeger, and Caspian Tern have been recorded. Gadwall, Northern Shoveler, and American Coot occur. Black Terns are possible from May into early June and again in late summer. When the lake is partially drained, mud flats can provide an array of shorebirds. On the north side of the inlet, cattails can conceal Virginia Rail and Sora, and the surrounding trees often harbor Rusty Blackbirds in early spring or late autumn.

Continue 0.7 mile west to where Bull Hill Road makes a sharp left and becomes Narragansett Avenue. Stop near the bridge (another causeway). Check both sides for Wood Duck, American Black Duck, and Hooded

Merganser. The open water of Pontoosuc sports a good variety of waterfowl, including loons, cormorants, and mergansers. Bald Eagles are occasionally spotted here.

Onota Lake

Turn around and head a short distance north on Narragansett. Turn left on Balance Rock Road and follow this as it turns sharply left (south), crossing back into Pittsfield, where it becomes Pecks Road. At 2.6 miles turn right (west) on Dan Casey Memorial Drive at the north end of Onota Lake. This part of Onota is popular, but there is usually ample space to park. Impressive concentrations of Gadwall, Wood Duck, Green-winged Teal, and others occur in late summer and early autumn. Carefully scan the north shore for shorebirds. This location has produced Tundra Swan, Hudsonian Godwit, Purple Sandpiper, and a Little Gull seen by Ludlow Griscom in the spring of 1946. We are still waiting for the next one! You may walk to a small, forested peninsula south of the road at the west end of the causeway. Hop over the guard rail, pass a small pond on the left (with a high density of eastern painted turtles), and follow the trail to the water. Ring-necked and other ducks work the edges. This small patch of forest can be productive for spring migrants, especially warblers.

For additional access to Onota, return to your car, turn around, and head east to the intersection. Turn right on Pecks Road. From the causeway (Dan Casey Drive) travel south 0.7 mile, and turn right on Valentine Road. Take this 1.7 miles, and turn right on Lakeway Drive at the sign for Burbank Park. In a short distance, the road splits; you'll eventually take both forks. First, bear right and wind around to the parking lot. Walk to the water; scan for waterfowl, shorebirds, gulls, and a magnificent view of the Taconics. Retrace your steps, turning right to the boat launch and fishing pier. In autumn, the wind can be brutal but the birding productive. Horned Grebes are common in spring and likely in autumn; other diving birds are possible.

Richmond Pond

Drive out the park entrance and turn right (south) on Valentine Road. In 0.8 mile you reach the stop light at West Street. Continue straight across on Jason Street. If you want to visit Tierney Swamp on the way (see B11. Tierney Swamp), park just before the railroad underpass.

To reach Richmond Pond, continue south on Jason Street beyond the parking lot until it ends. Turn left on Gale Avenue, which ends shortly at Route 20 (West Housatonic Street). Turn left (east) on Route 20 and go 0.4 mile to Barker Road. Turn right on Barker, and go just over 4 miles to Bartlett's Orchard. Turn right on Boys Club Road (Rich-

RING-NECKED DUCK

mond Shore Road), and in 0.5 mile take the left fork, a dirt road. A stop at the first swamp or near the bridge may reveal winter concentrations of waterfowl, raptors (including Rough-legged Hawk and Merlin), Cedar Waxwings, and blackbirds. Continue about half a mile to the parking lot and boat ramp, a prime location for Canvasback and Redhead; Brant are regular late autumn visitors. From the parking lot, walk north past the gate to a shallow cove that may produce more species. You may want to visit the marsh just southwest of Richmond Pond; see B12. Richmond Marsh for directions.

Stockbridge Bowl

If you have the time, visit Stockbridge Bowl (also known as Lake Mahkeenac). There are a few turns, so pay attention to the roads instead of the birds as you drive. When you come back out of Richmond Pond to Bartlett's Orchard, turn right. Barker Road is now called Swamp Road. Follow it south 2.4 miles, and turn left at the four-way intersection on Lenox Road. Lenox Road bears right just past the big farm and then left at the small Fairfield Pond, sometimes worth a brief stop. Lenox Road winds uphill 3.1 miles from the four-way intersection into Lenox and Stockbridge, coming out on Route 183 at Tanglewood. Turn right (south) on Route 183, and quickly (0.2 mile) turn left on Hawthorne Road at Gould Meadow Conservation Area. Follow Hawthorne Road even when it makes a sharp right for 1.3 miles to a widening of the road that serves as a parking space. Scan from here (you are on the east side of the lake) for loons, grebes, and swans. The wetland west of the road where Lily Brook comes in may produce herons, rails, and songbirds. Continue driving (0.8 mile) to the south end of Stockbridge

Bowl and turn right into the Public Town Beach (residents-only in summer). Among other surprises here have been Wilson's and Leach's Storm-Petrels following major coastal storms.

To return to the Berkshire Museum, continue south to the town of Stockbridge, where you can return via Route 7 North.

There are dozens of smaller, less-visited swamps, bogs, ponds, and pools, including Laurel Lake in Lee, Smiley's Mill Pond in South Egremont (see B26. Jug End Area), Lakes Buel and Garfield in Monterey, Otis Reservoir in Otis, Ashley Lake in Washington, and Ashmere Lake in Hinsdale. There is plenty of bird habitat and never enough birders to go around. Those who take the time to visit and lift their binoculars can add to our growing knowledge of Berkshire birds.   *Bartlett Hendricks and Tom Tyning*

Western Massachusetts lost one of its most ardent compilers of bird records with the death of Bartlett Hendricks (1910–2002). His Birds of Berkshire County *(1994 Hoffmann Bird Club) is one of his many contributions.*

B9. Berry Hill
Pittsfield

See map B8. The Berkshire Lakes

The north-facing hawkwatch at Berry Hill, in Pittsfield State Forest (SF) in the Taconic Range, is on an outcropping surrounded by hardwood forest, azalea fields, and mountain shrub. The ridge drops to the east into the Berkshire Valley and to the west into the Lebanon Valley. Trails (maps available at the SF entrance) allow access to the ridges, valleys, and their breeding thrushes and warblers.

From Park Square rotary in downtown Pittsfield go west on West Street. The Crown Plaza Hotel will be on the left. Continue 2.6 miles on West Street, turn right on Churchill Street (sign to Pittsfield State Forest). Continue 1.7 miles past the first entrance to Cascade Street to the north end of this semi-circular road and turn left. Continue straight, following the SF signs to the entrance. Bear right and continue up the mountain until the road leaves the trees and climbs steeply to the left, approximately 3 miles. At the top of this rise look for a turnoff on the right. This one-way road is frequently traveled in nice weather; be sure to pull completely off the road. The road is not passable from early winter until late spring.

The primary attraction here is fall hawkwatching. However, the surrounding forest is rich in other migrants. There are two hawkwatch sites. With east/northeast wind the better spot is about 75 feet up the trail from the parking turnoff and facing north (right). The trail continues, ascending slightly to the northwest for 200 yards. Look for a clearing on the right with exposed ledge facing due north; it is best in west/northwest wind.

Broad-winged Hawks migrate in good numbers in September. You can also expect Turkey Vulture, Bald Eagle, Northern Harrier, Sharp-shinned, Cooper's, and Red-tailed Hawks, American Kestrel, Merlin, Peregrine Falcon, and Common Raven. During late October, be alert for Golden Eagles. Listen for Barred Owls.

Chris Blagdon

B10. Springside Park
Pittsfield

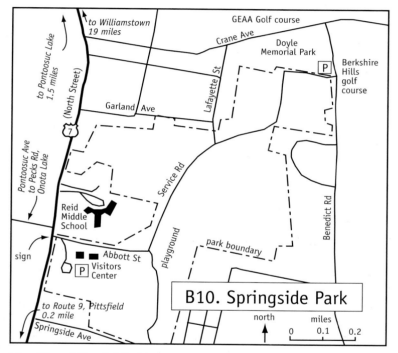

B10. Springside Park

The City of Pittsfield's 237-acre Springside Park, open every day year-round, is noted for springs and streams that attract many birds, including spring and fall migrants. Almost every songbird recorded in the county has been seen in this park. The Benedict Road entrance offers a panoramic view of the Berkshire hills and fall hawkwatching.

Route 7 (North Street) Entrance

From the Berkshire Museum at 39 South Street in Pittsfield, travel 1.4 miles north on Route 7. The park entrance is on the right, just before Reid Middle School (sign to the park and the Hebert Arboretum). A trail map is posted at the visitors center to the right of the park entrance. Park here and walk east in front of the Springside House to the Butterfly

EASTERN PHOEBE

and Hospice gardens, where Ruby-throated Hummingbirds visit regularly when the flowers are in bloom and Prairie Warbler may be found.

From the parking lot, follow the main road into the park. Scan the pines near the garages for Pine Warblers. In wet thickets along the road Carolina and House Wrens, and Yellow, Chestnut-Sided and Black-and-white Warblers are often present in spring and summer. Scan the trees bordering the large playground parking area for Eastern Screech-Owls. Look for Least Flycatcher, Eastern Phoebe, and Eastern Kingbird.

The service road leading south from the playground goes through mixed woods to a former wading pool on Springside Avenue where Great Blue Herons have been seen. In spring migration, Eastern Wood-Pewee, Great Crested Flycatcher, Swainson's and Hermit Thrushes, and a variety of vireos and wood warblers occur in this vicinity. Black-billed Cuckoo, Red-bellied Woodpecker, and, rarely, Red-headed Woodpecker have been recorded here. A Pileated Woodpecker is sure to be heard if not seen.

The service road north from the playground goes past playing fields and through open weedy fields. In spring, scan the playing fields for Northern Flickers. In the open fields, migrant Vesper, Savannah, Lincoln's, White-throated, and White-crowned Sparrows are often present. Field Sparrows nest here. You may follow any of the paths that cross and circle the fields. Watch for soaring Broad-winged and Red-tailed Hawks. Sometimes Cooper's and usually Sharp-shinned Hawks are present. Fish Crow has been heard here. Chimney Swifts and Tree Swallows are often in the air.

Blue-winged Warblers, Rose-breasted Grosbeaks, and Indigo Buntings are often active in trees and bushes west of the service road. In a small pine grove just past the fields are many warblers including Magnolia,

Black-throated Blue, Black-throated Green, Blackburnian, Pine, Palm (migration), Black-and-white, American Redstart, Ovenbird, and an occasional Wilson's Warbler (migration). Kinglets pass through in fall. The service road ends at Benedict Road.

You can also enter the park from Benedict Road, parking at the Doyle Memorial Park (see map). In the southeast corner of the park between the playing fields look for Northern Mockingbird, Eastern Towhee, Indigo Bunting, and Baltimore Oriole. In the fall look northwest over the golf course for migrating hawks, especially Broad-winged Hawks in mid-September.

Noreen Mole

B11. Tierney Swamp (Jason Street Swamp)
Pittsfield

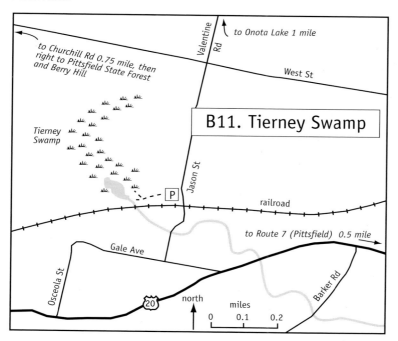

Tierney Swamp, managed by the Pittsfield Conservation Commission, is a gem of birding potential near downtown Pittsfield. A short brook, originally impeded by a railroad bed to form a modest wetland, was expanded by beavers to a multi-acre marsh. A mature white pine forest constitutes the marsh's eastern margin.

From the intersection of Routes 7 and 20, just south of Pittsfield center, go 1.2 miles west on Route 20 past a McDonald's on the left. Take the next right (west) on Gale Avenue, and then the next right (north) on Jason Street. The well-marked Tierney Swamp parking is immediately on the left after the railroad overpass. Follow the trail straight from the lot several hundred feet to the marsh. A side trail veers north allowing limited access to the area's upper reaches.

Pied-billed Grebe, Least Bittern, King Rail, and Marsh Wren have recently been found throughout the summer, suggesting breeding. Common Moorhens have declined from the 37 seen in 1978 to a single pair in 1999. Great Blue and Green Herons are regular. An occasional American Bittern may call from cattails at the rear of the marsh. Hooded Merganser is a common, but secretive, breeder. Virginia Rail and Sora are regular here, and sometimes in fall migration their numbers, especially of Sora, may be impressive. Alder and Willow Flycatchers occur here. In summer, the wetland is a staging area for herons and egrets. Wilson's Snipe, especially apparent in April and early May, breed here. In migration, passerines are often abundant on the trail into the wetland, while most species of dabbling ducks are possible in the open water. Barred Owls occur in the evergreens across the wetland.   *David P. St. James*

B12. Richmond Marsh
Richmond

Take Route 20 west from Route 7 just south of the center of Pittsfield. After 0.8 mile turn left on Barker Road. Go 4.3 miles and turn right on Boy's Club Road (Richmond Shore), opposite Bartlett's Orchard. Follow Richmond Shore Road approximately 0.75 mile, always bearing left. At a 90 degree right-hand turn at the railroad tracks, pull off and park to the left. In early spring this road may be a muddy quagmire.

This area is best in late spring and early summer. Proceed south (left) on the path that parallels the railroad. **Use extreme care; keep off the tracks, which are heavily used.** After about 0.2 mile, the marsh opens up on the left.

There is good birding along the path. In spring look for Ruffed Grouse, Yellow-bellied Sapsucker, Willow and Least Flycatchers, Veery, American Redstart, and migrating warblers.

The marsh is a sure bet for nesting Marsh Wrens. Early morning is best for spotting American Bitterns. Evening is better for Virginia Rail and Sora. Swamp Sparrows are abundant. Great Blue Herons hunt along the water's edge.

In fall, it is not uncommon to see a flock of a thousand or more Red-winged and Rusty Blackbirds, Common Grackles, and Brown-headed Cowbirds in trees edging the swamp. Watch for hunting Sharp-shinned

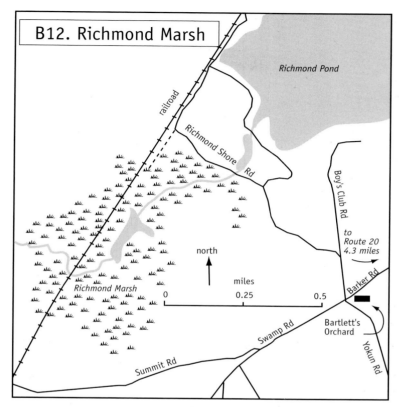

B12. Richmond Marsh

Richmond Pond

railroad

Richmond Shore Rd

Boy's Club Rd

to Route 20 4.3 miles

north

Barker Rd

miles

Richmond Marsh

0   0.25   0.5

Bartlett's Orchard

Swamp Rd

Yokun Rd

Summit Rd

Hawks. In winter there is little activity, although the wood edges harbor woodpeckers, Cedar Waxwings (and at least once a Bohemian), and American Tree Sparrows.

Chris Blagdon

B13. Canoe Meadows Wildlife Sanctuary
Pittsfield

See map B13. Canoe Meadows Wildlife Sanctuary

The best seasons for birding this 262-acre Massachusetts Audubon Society sanctuary are spring and fall, although its varied plant communities make for fine year-round birding. A sanctuary bird checklist is available from the Berkshire Wildlife Sanctuaries office in Lenox, (413) 637-0320. Canoe Meadows is open year-round, 7 a.m. to dusk, except Mondays and major holidays. There is a small fee for non-members.

From Exit 2 (Lee) of the Massachusetts Turnpike turn right (north) on Route 20. Follow Route 20 for 8 miles through Lee and Lenox to Holmes Road (at the traffic light and gas station about a half-mile south of the Pittsfield town line). Turn right on Holmes Road, and go 2.7 miles to the sanctuary entrance on the right.

Alternatively, from the Berkshire Museum, go south on Routes 20 and 7 for 3.2 miles to Holmes Road on your left just after the Lenox town line. Go 2.6 miles to the sanctuary entrance on your right.

There is a large trail map and portable toilet at the parking area. The area immediately beyond the kiosk can be productive in spring and fall when a variety of sparrows, such as Fox and White-crowned, and other passerines can be found there.

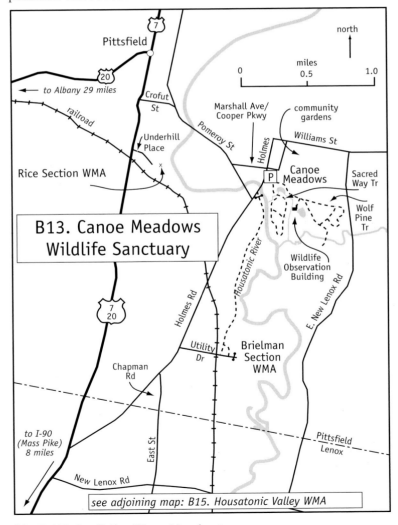

NORTHERN SHRIKE

Two loop trails, totaling three miles, offer different opportunities. For the Sacred Way Trail walk one hundred feet down the gravel service road, turn right past a bench, and follow the trail through the brushy field. The trail traverses wet meadows, shrub meadows, and beaver pond edges. Most of the trail is in the Housatonic River floodplain migration corridor. This mile-long loop yields about 50 species in peak spring migration and takes one to two hours to bird. Due to flooding, access to this trail during spring, and sometimes fall, may be impossible; call ahead for current conditions.

Nesters along the loop include Wood Duck, Alder and Willow Flycatchers, Eastern Kingbird, Warbling Vireo, House Wren, Veery, Yellow and Chestnut-sided Warblers, American Redstart, Eastern Towhee, Swamp Sparrow, Northern Cardinal, and Baltimore Oriole. Occasional visitors are Red-bellied Woodpecker and Fish Crow. Belted Kingfisher is a regular visitor. Migrants include Osprey, Olive-sided Flycatcher, and Palm, Wilson's, and other warblers. A Great Egret occurs some years. This is an excellent place to find wintering species; Northern Shrike, Pine Grosbeak, wre, and Pine Siskin appear in flight years. Yellow-crowned Night-Heron, Blue-winged Teal, White-eyed Vireo, and Yellow-breasted Chat have occurred along this trail.

To reach Wolf Pine Trail from the parking area follow the service road around to the right under red and white pines where Red-breasted Nuthatch, Brown Creeper, kinglets, and Pine Warbler are found. The trail begins on the left just past two portable toilets. Passing through mixed woodlands and white pine and eastern hemlock stands, it hosts a variety of woodland avifauna. Two short side trips are described first.

To examine the large beaver pond from the Wildlife Observation Building, turn right at the end of the pines and follow the boardwalk about 50 yards to the blind. From this blind, Wood and American Black Ducks can be seen. Also watch for Great Blue and Green Herons, Gadwall, Northern Shoveler, Green-winged Teal, Hooded Merganser, and Belted Kingfisher. Look for Rusty Blackbirds in early April and mid-October. A bit farther ahead the service road bisects the wetland. Northern Waterthrush nests regularly in the smaller swamp on the left.

Another side-trip goes up the dirt farm road (opposite the path to the blind) to hayfields. Scan for American Kestrel, Field Sparrow, Indigo

Bunting, and Bobolink. In late fall and winter Horned Larks, American Pipits, and Snow Buntings are possible.

Wolf Pine Trail can be covered in an hour. Ruffed Grouse, Great Horned and Barred Owls, Cooper's Hawk, Yellow-bellied Sapsucker, Pileated Woodpecker, Blue-headed and Red-eyed Vireos, nuthatches, Veery, Wood Thrush, Black-throated Green and Blackburnian Warblers, Ovenbird, Scarlet Tanager, and Rose-breasted Grosbeak breed here. Winter Wren haunts the wet hemlock woods in spring and fall. When you reach the service road at the trail's other end, turn right to return to the parking area. Wild Turkeys frequent the hayfield here and roost in the tall trees. You can also turn left and follow the service road a few hundred yards to the gated border with Tweenbrook Farm (private property). Eastern Bluebird and Tree Swallows use nest boxes along the fence. Follow the service road back to your vehicle.

In fall visit scenic Canoe Meadows community gardens, open May through October. From the sanctuary entrance, continue north on Holmes Road 0.35 mile past the sanctuary entrance to Williams Street at a light. Turn right and follow Williams Street another 0.35 mile to a gravel driveway on the right (note split-rail fence). This is a fine location in September and October for sparrows including Lincoln's, White-throated, White-crowned, and even Vesper. The Hoffmann Bird Club conducts its nighthawk watch here late August to early September. *René Laubach*

B14. Pleasant Valley Wildlife Sanctuary
Lenox

The most productive periods for birding this heavily wooded Massachusetts Audubon Society property, also popular for its easily observed beaver population, are May through early July and late August through early October. A well-marked, well-maintained 7-mile trail system (a delightful walk) affords easy access to woodlands, wetlands, and fields. For the greatest variety of birds, walk a combination of trails around the numerous beaver ponds (beavers are most reliably observed at dusk), and one of two trails ascending steep slopes through northern hardwood forest to Lenox Mountain summit. Bird feeders are at the office and a bird checklist is available there. The sanctuary is open year-round, dawn to dusk, but is closed Mondays except July through Columbus Day. There is a small non-member fee.

To reach Pleasant Valley, turn west from Routes 7 and 20 on West Dugway Road, 6.6 miles north of Exit 2 (Lee) from the Massachusetts Turnpike or 4.7 miles south of the Berkshire Museum in Pittsfield center. The turn is across from a Quality Inn, and there is a Massachusetts Audubon sign. Follow West Dugway Road 0.75 mile; then bear left on West Mountain Road and continue for 0.8 mile to the Pleasant Valley parking lot.

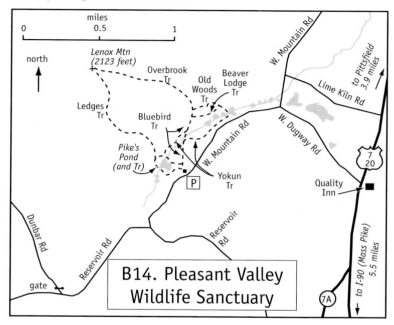

By mid-April, male American Woodcock perform at dusk in fields near the sanctuary buildings. In addition to about 65 nesting species, spring migrants passing through include Swainson's Thrush (sightings seem to be diminishing) and Palm, Bay-breasted, and Blackpoll Warblers. By the third week of May, most nesters are back on breeding territories. Eastern Wood-Pewee is often one of the last to return.

Wood Ducks and Hooded Mergansers use nest boxes along the beaver ponds. Winter Wren is partial to shady hemlock ravines along Overbrook Trail and the lower reaches of Trail of the Ledges. Yellow-bellied Sapsucker, a common summer resident easily found from the valley trails, seems to prefer white and gray birches here for nest sites. Pileated Woodpecker is more often heard than seen at Pleasant Valley.

Barred Owls are the most common owls here; their calls reverberate from the wooded slopes year-round. Great Horned and Northern Saw-whet Owls are much less common. Broad-winged Hawks commonly nest in these woodlands. Cooper's Hawk seems to be increasing. Common Ravens are seen year-round.

The most abundant woodland nesters are Red-eyed Vireo, Veery, and Ovenbird. Yellow-throated Vireo is usually found in tall deciduous trees at field edges, e.g., along portions of Bluebird Trail. Least Flycatcher is very common along Pike's Pond Trail, Yokun Trail, and other trails bordering water. Hermit and Wood Thrushes are common nesters. The 15 breeding species of wood-warblers here include Magnolia, Black-throated Blue, Black-throated Green, and Canada. Check tall eastern hemlocks on Lenox Mountain's slopes for Blackburnian Warbler in June, Yokun Brook for Louisiana Waterthrush, an early returnee in late April, and the upper slopes of the mountain for Yellow-rumped Warbler. A seemingly out-of-place male Mourning Warbler has established territory near the sanctuary parking lot in recent summers.

Gaudy canopy nesters such as Scarlet Tanager and Rose-breasted Grosbeak are most easily observed in early July feeding on the ripe mulberry fruits adjacent to the office, along with American Robin, Veery, Gray Catbird, Cedar Waxwing, Baltimore Oriole, and other fruit eaters. Alder Flycatcher and Blue-winged Warbler sing in shrubby wet meadows and adjacent beaver flowage and can be heard and sometimes seen from West Mountain Road, 200 yards north of its intersection with West Dugway. Park at the intersection and walk along the road. There are no trails on this part of the property and entry is not permitted.

American Kestrels have used a nest box in the fields for the past few seasons. There have been no sightings here of the declining Golden-winged Warbler since 1995.

Fall warbler migration is quite strong; the same species seen in spring usually reappear. Fox Sparrow is a regular spring and fall migrant seen most easily near the feeders.

Winter birds include Golden-crowned Kinglet, which favors eastern hemlocks; foraging flocks are often numerous near the intersection of Beaver Lodge Trail and Old Wood Road. Red-breasted Nuthatch nests in mixed woodlands but is prone to irruptive population fluctuations. Visiting winter finches include Evening Grosbeak, usually appearing in alternate years. Common Redpoll is an irruptive winter visitor. Pine Siskin is often present from late winter to early summer. Purple Finch is most often found in spring and summer. The sanctuary feeders, attracting up to 15 species, usually offer the most productive winter birding.   *René Laubach*

B15. Housatonic Valley Wildlife Management Area
Lee, Lenox, and Pittsfield

The state Housatonic Valley Wildlife Management Area (WMA), an 850-acre corridor along the Housatonic River, contains floodplain, northern deciduous woods, agricultural lands, swamps, and marshes associated with the river. Watch in the woods for Yellow-bellied Sapsucker, in wetland edges for Alder and Willow Flycatchers, and in winter for winter finches including crossbills.

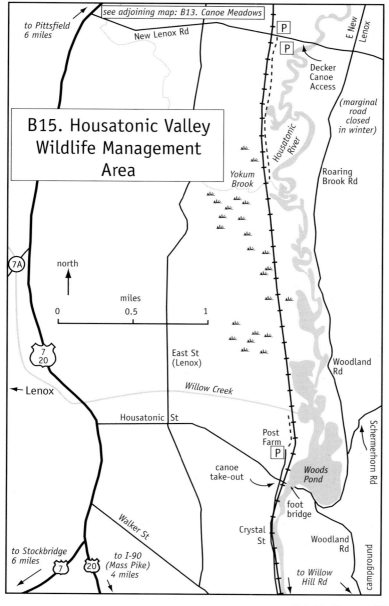

B15. Housatonic Valley Wildlife Management Area

To reach the Housatonic Valley WMA, turn east from Routes 7 and 20 on New Lenox Road in Lenox, 7.6 miles north of Exit 2 (Lee) from the Massachusetts Turnpike or 3.7 miles south of the Berkshire Museum in Pittsfield center. New Lenox Road is just south of Holmes Road (the turn for B13. Canoe Meadows Wildlife Sanctuary) and just north of West Dugway Road (the turn for B14. Pleasant Valley Wildlife Sanctuary.)

Drive east approximately 1.2 miles past East Street and across the railroad tracks to the Decker Canoe Access, a central reference point for locating other sections of the WMA. The property is divided into several subunits with diverse habitats.

Daly Section, Lenox

This area is bordered by the railroad to the west, the Housatonic River to the east, Woods Pond to the south, and a high voltage experimental transmission station to the north. Parking lots along New Lenox Road and the Decker Canoe Access offer easy access to this section of the WMA. Rewarding birding can be found by walking south along an overgrown road parallel to the railroad. A leisurely walk of about 1.5 miles to the confluence of Yokun Brook and the Housatonic River can yield many species.

Shorebirds and waterfowl can, in season, be abundant in Yokun Brook, swollen into a broad marsh by beavers. Nesting American Bittern, Virginia Rail, Wilson's Snipe, Winter Wren, Blue-gray Gnatcatcher, and waterthrushes are regulars here, with summer records of King Rail and Rusty Blackbirds suggesting breeding. Whip-poor-wills, increasingly rare in the Berkshires, have until recently been heard in these fields. In winter, Rough-legged Hawks frequently feed over the fields, and Northern Shrikes often tee up looking for a careless mouse. Watch for Northern Harriers in the fields. This area is rich in owls. Up to eight Great Horned Owls have been heard calling at one time. Barred Owls are common; both Eastern Screech-Owl and Northern Saw-whet Owl have been recorded in this section. A Short-eared Owl has been seen from New Lenox Road.

Pine Siskins and Evening Grosbeaks, seen throughout the summer on the WMA, may breed in adjacent October Mountain State Forest. Barn Swallows and fifteen to twenty pairs of Cliff Swallows breed beneath the river bridge on New Lenox Road. The river is a flyway for migrating Common Nighthawks; large numbers are noted at sunset in late August and early September.

Canoe Trip from Decker Canoe Access to Woods Pond. The most pleasurable mode of birding is by canoe with opportunities to observe birds and other wildlife normally too shy to be seen closely.

About 6 miles of flat water river paddling begin at the Decker Canoe Access on New Lenox Road. Anticipate a 3 to 4 hour canoe trip from Decker to Woods Pond allowing for birding and backwater exploration. From September 15 to May 15, canoeists must wear a Coast Guard-approved personal floatation device.

To reach Woods Pond to leave a second car, return west on New Lenox Road to the first intersection and turn left. Proceed approximately 2.8 miles south on East Street to Housatonic Street. Turn left on Housatonic Street. After 0.8 mile, the road veers sharply to the right and the pond and footbridge are visible straight ahead. Park judiciously; do not block the private drive on the left.

From the Decker Canoe Access look for American Bittern, Virginia Rail, and Sora that have nested near the access. Throughout spring Osprey fish for foot-long goldfish, unwanted "pets" grown to prodigious size.

Canoe south from the access through varied habitats. Pastures in the journey's first third yield Bank Swallow, Bobolink, Eastern Meadowlark, and an occasional Spotted Sandpiper. American Bittern, heard pumping on early summer mornings, has nested just south of the access for many years. The winnowing of Wilson's Snipe is a common summer sound here.

The fields yield to woods of silver maple, basswood, American elm, and white ash. An occasional willow arches over the bank, and willow and dogwood make an impenetrable understory. Yellow-throated and Warbling Vireos add to the sound of thrushes, warblers, Scarlet Tanager, and Baltimore Oriole. Green Herons commonly flush before the canoe. Blue-gray Gnatcatchers nest along the river. The trees then cede to broad marshes with many backwaters where Common Moorhen has recently nested. In fall, large numbers of ducks and geese use this staging area.

Woods Pond. The canoe trip ends at Woods Pond (see directions above). The pond was produced by a nineteenth century mill dam on the river. Great Blue Herons commonly fish its banks. In early spring Ringed-necked Ducks, Common Goldeneyes, and Hooded Mergansers are often found in surprisingly large numbers for such a small body of water. In late fall the pond often remains largely ice free when other regional lakes are completely locked in, and thus serves as a sanctuary to late waterfowl. In recent years Bald Eagles have wintered here. At the southern end of Woods Pond a footbridge crosses the river, where, on the western abutment, most people take out their canoes.

RUSTY BLACKBIRD

Post Farm. Following the directions to Woods Pond, turn north at the canoe take-out. The road terminates in about 0.5 mile at a small parking lot. This 200-acre former dump was recently reclaimed as a wildlife area administered by the Lenox Conservation Commission; it affords magnificent vistas. October Mountain directly to the east is mirrored in Woods Pond. The Housatonic Valley stretches to the north. At fall foliage peak this is one of the most scenic of the Berkshire's many spectacular backdrops.

This glacial area has little mature woodland, and its plants and associated wildlife differ from those of the alluvial WMA. In fall, this area attracts many migrating warblers, vireos, and especially Lincoln's, White-crowned, and other sparrows. Extremely large flocks of American Robins and Cedar Waxwings linger into winter. The parking lot and the slope immediately to the west are excellent observation points for migrating raptors following the Housatonic River. In recent years Bald Eagles have been sighted somewhat regularly.

Follow the road (an old trolley line) north from the parking lot to an extensive cattail marsh at Willow Creek. Focus on rails, Marsh Wrens, and other wetland species here. Willow Creek Road veers to the west (left) just prior to the marsh and may be followed about 0.2 mile to a field on the left. The trail continues through this field and adjoining woodland to power lines, which eventually lead back to the parking area.

Roaring Brook Road/Woodland Road. Proceed east along New Lenox Road from the Decker Canoe Access about 0.3 mile to the intersection with Roaring Brook Road (south) and East New Lenox Road (north). Evening Grosbeaks occur every summer at this intersection. Turn right on Roaring Brook Road and drive one mile south through sparse housing, after which the road becomes dirt, **passable only seasonally and only to high-clearance vehicles.** The road roughly parallels the Housatonic. October Mountain State Forest rises to the east (see B16. October Mountain). At the Lee town line Roaring Brook Road becomes Woodland Road. The road continues along the river, with many access points to observe the river and the east shore of Woods Pond. The road ends at a T 3.5 miles south of New Lenox Road. Turn left and go past the campground at October Mountain State Forest. At 1.0 mile from the T, go straight on Willow Hill Road and right at the next junction on Crystal Street to the Woods Pond canoe take-out.

The habitat here is different from that of the rest of the area. The steep slopes of October Mountain abutting the road bring more boreal plants and birds. Winter Wren, Hermit Thrush, Blackburnian Warbler, and Scarlet Tanager claim the woods. Ruffed Grouse range the deciduous woodlands, and Wild Turkeys are common. Sightings of black bear are also common. In the early spring, wildflowers abound and the sides of the road feature magnificent patches of Dutchman's breeches, spring beauty, trillium, and hepatica.

Brielman Section, Pittsfield

See map B13. Canoe Meadows Wildlife Sanctuary

From the canoe take-out at Woods Pond go west on Housatonic Street and turn right (north) on East Street. Go 3.7 miles on East Street, crossing New Lenox Road and the Pittsfield town line (East Street becomes Chapman Road). Turn right on Holmes Road, go 0.2 mile, and turn right on Utility Drive. The wetland on the left (north) beyond the railroad underpass affords most of the interesting birding in this section. Park by the second gated dirt road to the left just before the wastewater treatment plant gate. Areas beyond here are inaccessible to vehicles.

This small wetland hosts an interesting array of birdlife. American Bittern, Virginia Rail, Sora, Wilson's Snipe, and Marsh Wren breed here. King Rail and Common Moorhen have nested here and should be watched for.

The gravel road forks almost immediately into left and straight branches. Walk along the left fork approximately 1.5 miles along the river. The road comes near houses with associated feeder birds. In recent years this location has hosted wintering holdovers such as Ruby-crowned Kinglet, Gray Catbird, Brown Thrasher, and Eastern Towhee. *David P. St. James*

B16. October Mountain State Forest
Becket, Lenox, Washington, and Lee

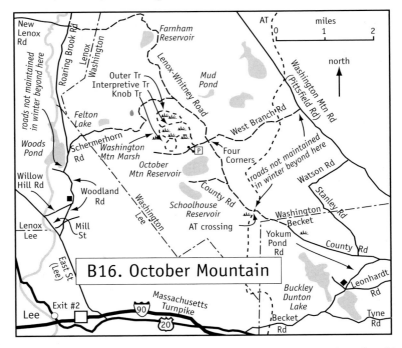

October Mountain State Forest is a fairly high elevation (much of it above 1,500 feet) extensive tract of undeveloped land primarily in the town of Washington with spruce-fir, mixed, and deciduous forest, beaver ponds and meadows, and lakes. Numerous trails provide access to some of the more intriguing habitat. Maps are available from forest headquarters (413-243-1778; see directions below).

Since roads are not maintained in winter, avoid driving the area between the first snowfall and the beginning of April. The rest of the year, the gravel roads are not regularly maintained, so **make sure your vehicle has reasonable clearance.** That said, in late spring, summer, and fall, this area offers excellent opportunities for discovering Canadian Zone breeders in a wild setting with better than average chances of spotting mammals such as black bear, moose, mink, beaver, porcupine, and fisher. In addition to the route described below, you can also enter by Schermerhorn Road or West Branch Road.

From Exit 2 (Lee) of the Massachusetts Turnpike follow signs for Route 20 east and proceed 3.9 miles to Becket Road on the left, across from Belden Tavern. Follow Becket Road, which becomes Yokum Pond Road, uphill for 2.5 miles to the road just before a state maintenance building on the left across from Leonhardt Road. Turn left and follow the paved road to the end (approximately 0.5 mile) to Buckley Dunton Lake, the largest body of open water in the forest. This pristine lake offers wonderful canoeing and is a spring and fall stopover for migrant waterfowl.

Backtrack to Yokum Pond Road, turn left, and proceed 1.0 mile. Take a hard left on County Road. Stop after 0.8 mile to check out a small wetland on the right, good for Northern Waterthrush and Canada Warbler. Scope another wetland on the left, in another 1.3 miles, for Great Blue Heron, Wood Duck, American Black Duck, and Hooded Merganser. Drive slowly over the next 2 miles of rough road and check dense spruce stands for Winter Wren, Golden-crowned Kinglet, Magnolia, Yellow-rumped, and Blackburnian Warblers, Purple Finch, and Evening Grosbeak. Logged areas grown up to blackberry and striped maple are the favorite haunt of Mourning Warbler. Mixed woods favor Wild Turkey, Yellow-bellied Sapsucker, Pileated Woodpecker, Eastern Wood-Pewee, Hermit Thrush, Black-throated Blue Warbler, and White-throated Sparrow. Listen all the while for Common Raven and, around wetlands, Red-shouldered Hawk. An interesting diversion along this section is to follow the Appalachian Trail south (left) to a beaver pond and meadow about 0.5 mile in, where Red-shouldered Hawk has nested.

At an obvious fork County Road bears left (no sign), becomes narrower and a bit rougher, and ends after 0.4 mile at the bottom of the hill in a complex wetland. There is room to pull off and park on the right. This area should be explored on foot. October Mountain Reservoir is on the right, a wooded swamp is on the left, and Schoolhouse Reservoir is farther ahead at the end of the road. Search the swamp for Great Blue Heron, Wood Duck, American Black Duck, Green-winged Teal, Virginia Rail, Alder Flycatcher, Eastern Kingbird, Northern Waterthrush, and Rusty Blackbird (seen here in July). Spotted Sandpipers nest along these reservoirs. Wild Turkey, Killdeer, and Indigo Bunting are found in open areas where material was excavated for the dams. Sharp-shinned Hawks are occasionally seen entering the dense spruce thickets in summer.

Return uphill to the fork in County Road and turn left on the other fork, Lenox-Whitney Road (no sign). After 1.2 miles you are at the Four Corners at the center of the forest. Listen by the spruce and red pine grove for Red-breasted Nuthatch, Golden-crowned Kinglet, and Blackburnian Warbler. Check forest clearings with saplings for the regularly present Mourning Warbler. West Branch Road goes right (east) at the Four Corners and comes out at Washington Mountain Road (Pittsfield Road).

Turn left (west) at the Four Corners and go 0.5 mile on the dead-end Meadow Trail (the west extension of West Branch Road) to the Washington Mountain Meadow Interpretive Trail and parking area. The scenic hiking trail, boardwalk, and handicapped-accessible hardened walkway on the first section of trail represent an endeavor by the state to use creatively what was to be Washington Mountain Lake; the planned flooding of a complex of beaver meadows never took place. The result, after years of disturbance, is a marvelous trail almost 3.5 miles long allowing close study of wildlife in the Washington Mountain Marsh. This wetland may hold surprises for the birder. Trail maps should be available at the trail entrance.

For another view of the marsh continue on Meadow Trail Road beyond the parking area, bearing right until the road ends in about a mile. Here you encounter evidence of another planned impoundment that now offers an elevated overview of the extensive wetland.

Return to the Four Corners, turn left (north) on Lenox-Whitney Road (no sign), and proceed 0.7 mile to a spruce thicket on the right. From here **with map and compass** the intrepid may attempt to locate Mud Pond 2500 feet northeast of the road. This sphagnum bog with wet spruce-fir border and associated vegetation has a north woods flavor, perfect habitat for Yellow-bellied Flycatcher. The walk will be wet and buggy.

Follow Lenox-Whitney Road another 0.7 mile and bear left on Schermerhorn Road (no sign) toward the State Forest's western border. After 0.7 mile stop at a scenic pull-off on the right with a view of Mount Greylock to the north. A mile farther, as the road descends from the plateau to the Housatonic River, listen for Winter Wren, Black-throated Green Warbler, and Louisiana Waterthrush in dense hemlocks on the left. On the red oak hillside to the right, check for Eastern Wood-Pewee, Black-throated Blue Warbler, Scarlet Tanager, and Rose-breasted Grosbeak. Just after the road becomes paved, a short road to the right leads to Felton Lake, a popular picnic area in summer but worth a look in the off-season.

Continue down to the intersection with Roaring Brook Road (no sign) at the base of the forest. Turn left here and bird along the Woods Pond section of the Housatonic River to Woodland Road (no sign) and turn left (see B15. Housatonic Valley Wildlife Management Area). The State Forest headquarters and camping area are about one mile down Woodland Road.

To return to Route 20, pass the forest headquarters on the right and the campground on the left. Turn right on Willow Hill Road. Take the first left (Mill Street) and follow it to its end at East Street. Bear left on East Street and continue on East Street 2.3 miles to Route 20. You can then turn right (west) on Route 20 to return to the Massachusetts Turnpike (I-90) or turn left on Route 20 to return to Becket Road where you entered the forest.
Edwin J. Neumuth

B17. The Cove Area
Lee

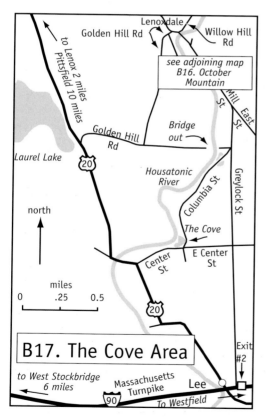

Three small ponds, close to downtown Lee, can be checked quickly from your vehicle; the fields of Golden Hill require a brief detour across the Housatonic.

The Cove and Associated Ponds

From Exit 2 (Lee) of the Massachusetts Turnpike, turn right and travel 1.3 miles north on Route 20 through downtown Lee. Turn right on Center Street, and drive 0.3 mile to the pond on the left known as "the Cove."

From late July to early October migrant shorebirds such as Greater Yellowlegs and Solitary Sandpiper, stop along the Cove's muddy perimeter. Great Blue Herons are most common in September. Post-breeding Green Heron is less regular, from mid-August to mid-September. Look for Great Egrets from August through early October. As summer yields to fall, the water level usually drops. Occasionally the Cove dries up. Look for dabbling ducks whenever there is open water. Wood Duck is more likely on the river, but sometimes immature Wood Ducks grace the Cove. Blue-winged Teal have appeared in early September. Watch for Belted King-fishers especially from late July to mid-September.

To view the two small ponds to the north that harbor some of the same species, continue for 0.7 mile north on Center Street (which becomes Columbia Street). Look for American Black Duck and others.

Between the Cove and these ponds, pull off the pavement where you can to scan the Housatonic for the species mentioned above and Common Merganser, found in all seasons except summer. Watch for Hooded Merganser in late March. Common Goldeneyes occasionally visit in early spring. Up to 26 Turkey Vultures have been tallied in a large dead roost tree to the west on Golden Hill. Look for Osprey following the Housatonic April through early May and again late September through early October.

Golden Hill

To reach Golden Hill, travel north on Columbia Street as it becomes Grey-lock Street, and continue on what is now Mill Street for a total of 1.1 miles beyond the two ponds. Cross the Housatonic River into Lenox (Village of Lenoxdale sign), turn immediately left, and then immediately bear left at the fork on Golden Hill Road. Follow Golden Hill Road uphill 0.8 mile to a T junction and then turn left toward the river.

Golden Hill's pastures yield different birds and a panoramic view. Flocks of Killdeer find the fenced pastures to their liking in late March and late September. Eastern Bluebirds nest along utility lines, which should be checked, especially in late September, for American Kestrel and passing Sharp-shinned Hawks. American Robins and Cedar Wax-wings seek fruiting shrubs in winter. Northern Mockingbird is some-times present. Brown Thrasher, an uncommon breeder, prefers brushy margins south of Golden Hill Road. Drive to the river, where the historic iron Golden Hill Bridge is closed. Scan for waterfowl. My most exciting observation here was a Red-headed Woodpecker.

Return to the T and go straight (still Golden Hill Road) to its end at Route 20. Turn right (north) to Lenox and Pittsfield or left (south) to Lee.

René Laubach

B18. Goose Ponds
Lee, Tyringham

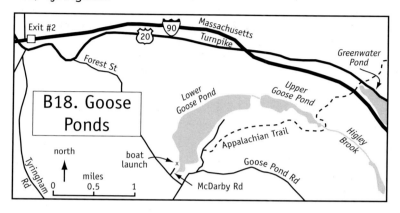

Two artificial bodies of water linked by a narrow channel, the Goose Ponds cover nearly 300 acres at about 1500 feet elevation. Lower Goose, the larger at 245 acres, is lined by vacation homes except The Trustees of Reservations' Goose Pond Reservation in the northeast corner. The shores of Upper Goose, held as conservation land by the National Park Service, the state, and the town of Lee, are nearly undeveloped.

Hills rise 300 feet above the ponds, clothed in dense regenerating northern hardwood forest: birch, beech, and maple, with some eastern hemlock and white pine, and an understory of striped and mountain maples, mountain laurel, and hobblebush. Upper Goose's shoreline is rocky; a couple of picturesque bedrock islets help impart a north woods atmosphere. Higley Brook feeds the ponds, with lush wetland vegetation at its upper end. Beavers have constructed dams and lodges in this still water.

Upper Goose Pond is not reached without effort. There are two approaches: overland via the AT and over water from the public boat ramp on Lower Goose. For the land approach from Exit 2 (Lee) of the Massachusetts Turnpike, drive east on Route 20 for 4.5 miles. Just beyond the Becket town line there is a wide, paved pull-off on the right (south); park at the far end. Walk easterly along the shoulder a short distance, and turn right (south) at the wooden sign for the AT. Follow the AT over the turnpike, and continue about 2 miles to Upper Goose Pond.

To reach the boat launch in Tyringham, drive 0.75 mile east from the turnpike exit on Route 20, and turn right on Forest Street. Continue uphill for 2.1 miles to the last turn before Goose Pond Road. Turn left on McDarby Road, go to the boat ramp on the right, and park along the right shoulder.

The AT excursion provides exercise and birding. After leaving Route 20, the trail winds through damp, brushy areas with Gray Catbird, Yellow and Chestnut-sided Warblers, and Eastern Towhee in late spring and summer, and then crosses a bridge over the turnpike. The trail enters hardwood forest and goes uphill through white pine stands where Red-breasted Nuthatch and Black-throated Green Warbler are abundant. After cresting the ridge, you descend to Upper Goose. The trail forks east and west along the shore.

Turning left takes you to the Higley Brook crossing within about 0.25 mile. Turning right takes you along the lakeshore through northern hardwoods with hemlocks. Listen for breeding Alder Flycatcher, Warbling Vireo, Canada Warbler, Swamp Sparrow, and other wetland species. An old stone chimney is a good place from which to scan the water and the best location to take out a canoe.

In breeding season, the moist deciduous woodlands reverberate with songs of Eastern Wood-Pewee, Yellow-throated, Blue-headed, and Red-eyed Vireos, Winter Wren, Veery, Hermit and Wood Thrushes, Black-throated Blue and Black-and-white Warblers, American Redstart, Ovenbird, Canada Warbler, Scarlet Tanager, and Rose-breasted Grosbeak. Yellow birch is a favorite source of sweet sap for the numerous Yellow-bellied Sapsuckers. Ruby-throated Hummingbird also relies on these sap wells early in the season.

On Upper Goose itself, be alert for Great Blue Heron and Wood Duck. Spotted Sandpiper nests along the shores, and Belted Kingfisher is fairly reliable in all seasons but winter.

There are few water birds on busy Lower Goose at any time. Carolina Wren has been found near the boat launch in summer, but is highly sporadic. You'll probably want to paddle your canoe to the far end of the lake and enter Upper Goose as quickly as possible. Along the way, stay alert for Common Loon, Double-crested Cormorant, and Osprey in migration. Northern Goshawk is seen occasionally. One of the oddest sightings in the annals of inland Massachusetts birding took place here in November 1970: an Atlantic Puffin!

Pileated Woodpecker, Common Raven, Red-breasted Nuthatch, and Brown Creeper are year-round inhabitants. Magnolia and Blackburnian Warblers breed in the area. Golden-crowned Kinglets forage among the hemlock boughs in winter, but reaching Goose Ponds in the snow and ice can be problematic. *René Laubach*

B19. Tyringham Valley and Tyringham Cobble

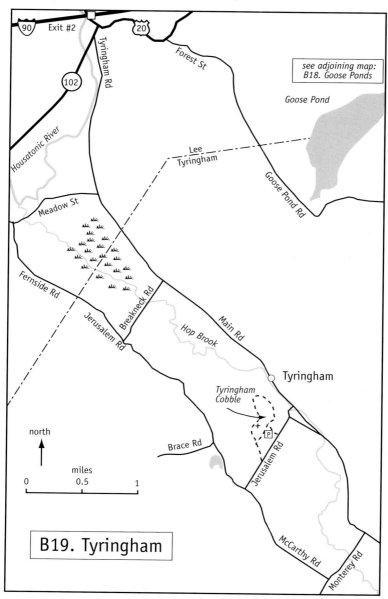

The Tyringham Valley offers diverse habitats in one of the most scenic pastoral areas of Berkshire County. The vista from Tyringham Cobble

WILSON'S SNIPE

summit is extraordinary, and the birding can be rewarding, especially in spring and fall migration.

Take Route 102 southwest from Route 20 at Exit 2 (Lee) of the Massachusetts Turnpike (I-90). After about 0.1 mile turn left (southeast) on Tyringham Road. After about 1.5 miles turn right on Meadow Street. The loop starts here.

Once on Meadow Street, pull off the road just beyond the barn as the fields open up. Search the barnyard for Eastern Kingbird, swallows, and Eastern Bluebird. In spring, listen for Savannah Sparrow, Bobolink, and Eastern Meadowlark in the field on the right. Look in spring or fall for Killdeer, both yellowlegs, Solitary, Semipalmated, and Least Sandpipers, and Wilson's Snipe in flooded areas. This field, if left to grow, provides cover for a variety of sparrows in fall. Check the left side of the road here, usually planted with corn, in spring for dabbling ducks in pools, and in fall and winter for Horned Lark and Snow Bunting. Check the far end of the field past the auto graveyard; then cross Hop Brook. Pull off the road after the bridge and walk back to the brook. American Bittern and Wilson's Snipe are occasionally heard here and Red-bellied Woodpecker, Alder and Willow Flycatchers, and Yellow-throated and Warbling Vireos are found.

A few hundred yards farther take the first left on Fernside Road. This narrow, lightly-traveled road paralleling the valley offers only a few spots to pull over safely, but affords an opportunity to drive slowly. As you pass through mixed woods on the steep hill, listen for Ruffed Grouse, Winter Wren, Hermit Thrush, and Dark-eyed Junco. After about a mile, a small pull-off on the left permits exploration on foot. Fernside changes to dirt and becomes Jerusalem Road at the Lee town line.

Continue on Jerusalem Road to the first left, aptly named Breakneck Road. This short (0.4-mile) trip to Hop Brook is worthwhile **if your brakes are reliable.** Park at the Hop Brook bridge on Breakneck to look for American Bittern, American Kestrel, Warbling Vireo, and Bobolink.

Return to Jerusalem Road and turn left to proceed again along the hillside 1.3 miles to a fork (Brace Road goes right). Bear left on Jerusalem Road, proceed 0.2 mile, and pull over on the right at a pond. In winter there is usually a fair amount of activity here with a diversity of birds attracted to feeders at the house across the street. Red-bellied Woodpecker is found here.

When the pond is open, search for herons, ducks and Belted Kingfisher. Walk a few hundred feet to a dense hemlock grove where the stream leaves the pond. This spot often produces Red-breasted Nuthatch, Brown Creeper, and Golden-crowned Kinglet in winter and a variety of warblers in spring.

Continue 0.3 mile to where Jerusalem Road bears left and the dirt McCarthy Road proceeds straight ahead. To go directly to Tyringham Cobble (described below) turn left on Jerusalem Road; the entrance is 0.7 mile on the left.

To continue the loop take McCarthy Road and check the area around the intersection for Yellow-bellied Sapsucker, Pileated Woodpecker, and Eastern Bluebird. Pass between two open fields, where Bobolinks are found in the summer, go 0.3 mile, and park just before a stream. Listen here for Blue-headed Vireo, Brown Creeper, Winter Wren, and Black-throated Green Warbler in the hemlocks to the left.

Continue to the T at Monterey Road. Turn left here to cross the valley. A consistent spot for Wilson's Snipe is where Monterey Road crosses the wet meadow on the right.

Turn left on Main Road, the Tyringham counterpart of Tyringham Road in Lee. Follow Main Road 1.4 miles into the village and turn left on Jerusalem Road to reach The Trustees of Reservations' Tyringham Cobble. There is a sign and parking on the right; the kiosk should have trail maps and a bird list.

From the parking area take the trail through field and woodland to the outcrop with a spectacular view at the cobble summit. The hike is not particularly strenuous. Along the way listen for Least Flycatcher, Hermit Thrush, Brown Thrasher, Cedar Waxwing, Magnolia Warbler, Prairie Warbler, Eastern Towhee, Field Sparrow, and Indigo Bunting. Continue on the trail over the summit to the other side and down to Jerusalem Road where you can walk downhill to the parking area. Birding the Cobble is a pleasure in any season, but early mornings in migration can be outstanding.

To complete the Tyringham Valley loop, go back to Main Road and turn left. Follow the road with the valley on your left 2.6 miles back to the starting point, the corner of Meadow Street and Tyringham Road. This side of the valley lacks the observation opportunities of the other side because, although the view is more open, the road is substantially busier.

Edwin J. Neumuth

B20. Ice Glen and Laura's Tower
Stockbridge

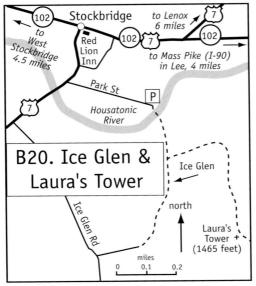

Ice Glen is a shadowy hemlock gorge with a primeval atmosphere. Huge angular fern and moss-covered boulders litter this defile. Enormous old growth white pines and eastern hemlocks tower above. This spot is cool year-round; pockets of ice sometimes linger into June. Laura's Tower sits atop a hill clothed in birch, beech, maple, oak, and sunshine. Climbing the sturdy 25-foot observation tower provides panoramic views and an acceptable hawkwatch site (nearby Monument Mountain is better, see B22). The usually languid Housatonic River loops around the base of the promontory.

From the intersection of Routes 7 and 102 at the Red Lion Inn in Stockbridge center follow Route 7 south 0.2 mile, then turn left on Park Street. Do not cross the Housatonic River. Follow Park Street 0.1 mile to a parking lot. Cross the river on a footbridge, and pick up the trail on the far side. Soon the trail splits. The right fork descends steeply through the Glen; the left fork leads up to Laura's Tower.

Alternatively, to ascend the Glen drive south 0.4 mile from the Red Lion Inn on Route 7, cross the Housatonic, and turn left on Ice Glen Road. Follow it 0.5 mile to a small "Ice Glen Walkers Welcome" sign at a private drive on the left. Park along the road, not the private drive. Follow the drive to the trailhead on the left. **Caution: Winter footing in the Glen can be icy and hazardous.**

The most auspicious seasons to visit the Glen are late spring and early summer when warblers such as Black-throated Green, Blackburnian, American Redstart, and Canada hold territories. Spotting canopy-inhabiting Blackburnians can be a challenge in the impressive evergreens. Ethereal Hermit and Wood Thrush songs sound through the chasm, especially early and late in the day in June and early July. Eastern Wood-Pewee and Blue-headed Vireo are common breeders, and sometimes the sweet trill of Pine Warbler is heard.

In hardwood forests above Ice Glen, from May through August, listen for Red-eyed and the less common Yellow-throated Vireos, Veery, Black-throated Blue and Black-and-white Warblers, Ovenbird, Scarlet Tanager, and Rose-breasted Grosbeak. From Laura's Tower in late spring scan the skies for Sharp-shinned Hawk, Chimney Swift, and Northern Rough-winged Swallow. In woodland edge or vines near the Housatonic, Least Flycatcher, Warbling Vireo, Gray Catbird, Chestnut-sided Warbler, and Eastern Towhee hold forth.

Year-round residents of the Glen include Red-breasted Nuthatch, Brown Creeper, and the shy Pileated Woodpecker. Cedar Waxwing flocks can occur at any season. Carolina Wren has occasionally occurred in tangles along Ice Glen Road.

In spring and fall migrations, all the area's diurnal raptors are possible from the tower. In fall, winter, and early spring listen for American Goldfinch and, in some years, the buzzy refrain of Pine Siskin, both often feeding on yellow birch seeds.

In winter Golden-crowned Kinglets, those high-wire acrobats, flutter about hemlock boughs. In thickets and woodland/field edges bordering the river, the pleasant tinkling notes of American Tree Sparrow are heard from November into April. When crossing the footbridge, be alert for Belted Kingfisher as long as open water persists. American Black Ducks and Dark-eyed Juncos feed in adjacent fields.   *René Laubach*

B21. Alford

See map B21. Alford

Alford nestles along the New York border. The town center, with a small schoolhouse, church, and town hall, boasts no commercial enterprises. Between Tom Ball Mountain dominating the eastern boundary and the Taconic Mountains on the western edge, Alford Brook winds southward, bisecting hay fields and pastures before it flows into Seekonk Brook just southeast of town. Two roads paralleling the brook afford beautiful vistas.

By Berkshire County standards, temperatures here are moderate, with more southern bird species found in the town. Red-bellied Woodpecker and Carolina Wren are frequently found along roadsides. Eastern Bluebirds have recently become common year-round. Listen for Blue-gray Gnatcatcher in woods and for Blue-winged and Prairie Warblers in second-growth woodlands.

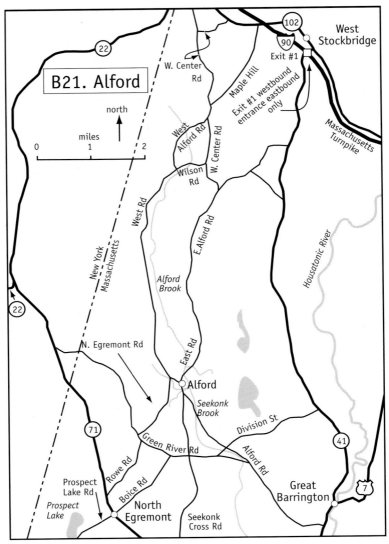

B21. Alford

north

miles

0   1   2

From the center of West Stockbridge proceed west on Route 102 approximately one mile. Turn left on West Center Road, and after approximately 3 miles turn right on West Alford Road which becomes West Road at the town line (2.5 miles).

Continue south on West Road. Pastures and cornfields dominate the valley. The thread of Alford Brook can be seen from the road. Turkey Vultures and Common Ravens often soar above the ridges. Be alert for occasional Black Vultures, increasingly seen in South Berkshire towns. Flocks of up to 300 Wild Turkeys have been recorded in winter throughout the valley. Breeding grassland species such as Field and Savannah Sparrows, Bobolink, and Eastern Meadowlark are common, and Horned Larks occur in winter.

From the town line, West Road continues approximately 4 miles to the town center. Immediately after Alford's center turn left on East Road, parallel the route just taken, with the opposite view of the valley. Stop at a small stone bridge over Alford Brook in summer for Yellow-throated and Warbling Vireos and Northern Rough-winged Swallow. East Road (which becomes East Alford Road at the West Stockbridge town line) rejoins West Center Road 4 miles north of Alford center.

David P. St. James

B22. Monument Mountain Reservation and Fountain Pond
Great Barrington

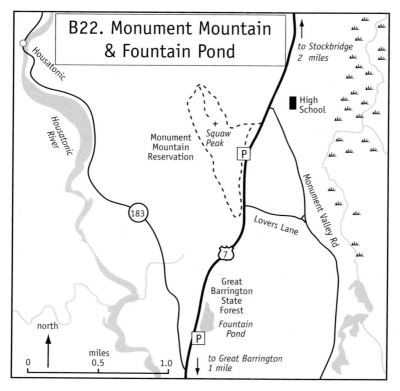

WOOD DUCK HATCHLING

Monument Mountain Reservation

Take Route 7 south from Stockbridge to Great Barrington. The Trustees of Reservations' Monument Mountain Reservation is on the right about 1 mile south of the Great Barrington town line. A three-mile loop trail goes to the top of the mountain.

Monument Mountain has incredible views from steep cliffs, a walk through New England mixed forest, and good hawkwatching. Around mid-April, with the right weather, you can pick up Sharp-shinned Hawk, Cooper's Hawk, Merlin, and American Kestrel. Monument Mountain is even better noted as a fall hawkwatch site.

At the peak, locally nesting Turkey Vultures and Common Ravens fly by at eye level, often only a few feet away. Quite a spectacular sight! Monument Mountain was the last Peregrine Falcon nest site in Berkshire County. Expect a great diversity of woodland birds on the trail through the forest, including Blue-headed and Red-eyed Vireos, Brown Creeper, Hermit and Wood Thrushes, Black-throated Blue, Black-throated Green, and Blackburnian Warblers, Ovenbird, and Scarlet Tanager. Winter Wrens often nest along the small stream on the trail near the waterfall. *Don Reid*

Fountain Pond

Fountain Pond, a small pond with emergent vegetation along Route 7 in Great Barrington State Forest, is an easy, quick stop that should be checked. A short trail leads through good mixed forest. The whole area is great for odonates. Dawn is the time to see the most activity on the pond.

Wood Ducks (regularly) and Hooded Mergansers (occasionally) breed on the pond. Egg dumping can produce mixed broods. In 2002 we witnessed a Wood Duck brood emerge from a nest box with a single Hooded Merganser duckling, which the female Wood Duck proceeded to peck. Common Moorhen is a rare migrant and may rarely breed here. Migrants include Solitary and Spotted Sandpipers. Great Blue and Green Herons and American Black Duck visit in spring, summer, and fall. The forest holds breeding Yellow-bellied Sapsucker, Pileated Woodpecker, Eastern Wood-Pewee, Yellow-throated, Blue-headed, and Red-eyed

Vireos, Brown Creeper, Winter Wren, Veery, Hermit Thrush, Black-throated Green and Blackburnian Warblers, and Ovenbird.

From the Monument Mountain picnic area, drive 1.3 miles south on Route 7 to the Great Barrington State Forest rest area on the left (east) at the southern end of Fountain Pond (about 0.2 mile north of the intersection of Routes 7 and 183). Be careful pulling in and out; traffic really speeds along Route 7.

Carefully scan all vegetated edges (a scope helps). Birds come and go in the cattails often; give them time. Many times my first look finds no birds, and only continual searching reveals the ducks. Follow the obvious trail along the southern edge of the pond that eventually swings south around the base of the hill through mixed forest great for Yellow-bellied Sapsucker, vireos, thrushes, and warblers. It is not necessary to hike far.

Return to Route 7 and drive north a short distance to the pull-off at the north end of the pond. Scan all muddy islands and cattail edges for Wood Ducks, shorebirds, and, with a lot of luck, Common Moorhen. Do **not** play tapes, which might disrupt the breeding of this state endangered species! *Mark C. Lynch*

B23. Beartown State Forest
Great Barrington, Lee, and Monterey

See map B23. Beartown State Forest

The miles of roads and trails in Beartown State Forest can be birded by vehicle or on foot. On weekdays throughout the year you may have the forest to yourself. On weekends you will see few other people, although many trails are open to ATVs and snowmobiles. In winter most roads are closed, so skiing or snowshoeing may be the best way to visit. Late spring and early summer are perhaps the best seasons to ramble the trails. Nesting birds include Ruffed Grouse, Wild Turkey, and all three accipiters. Two walking loops and a road through the forest are described here, among many possible routes. A Beartown State Forest Trail Map available at the forest headquarters and a Great Barrington USGS topographic map help in this extensive forest.

From Monument Mountain Reservation go south on Route 7 for 3.1 miles to Route 23. Turn left (east), continue on Route 23 for 5 miles and turn left (north) on Blue Hill Road. The forest headquarters will be on your left if you want to pick up a free map. After 2.2 miles on Blue Hill Road, turn right on Benedict Pond Road to Benedict Pond on the right (0.4 mile).

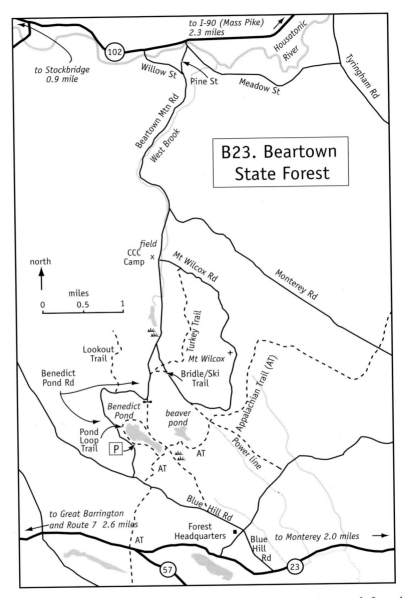

to I-90 (Mass Pike)
2.3 miles

Housatonic River

102

Tyringham Rd

to Stockbridge
0.9 mile

Willow St

Pine St

Meadow St

Beartown Mtn Rd

West Brook

B23. Beartown State Forest

field
CCC Camp ×

Mt Wilcox Rd

Monterey Rd

north

miles
0   0.5   1

Lookout Trail

Turkey Trail

Benedict Pond Rd

Mt Wilcox

Bridle/Ski Trail

Benedict Pond

beaver pond

Appalachian Trail (AT)

Pond Loop Trail

P

AT

AT

Power line

to Great Barrington
and Route 7 2.6 miles

AT

Blue Hill Rd

Forest Headquarters

Blue Hill Rd

to Monterey 2.0 miles

57

23

Alternatively, from the Massachusetts Turnpike Exit 2, turn left and almost immediately turn right (west) on Route 102. Continue on Route 102 for 2.5 miles and turn left on Meadow Street. After about 0.1 mile, immediately after the bridge, turn right on Pine Street, which becomes Beartown Mountain Road. At the fork bear right on Benedict Pond Road (no sign). Benedict Pond is about 4 miles farther on the left.

Benedict Pond to Mount Wilcox Road Loop

A 4.5-mile walking loop from the Benedict Pond parking area samples many habitats. From the parking area, turn right (east) on the Pond Loop Trail.

Benedict Pond often has Great Blue Heron, Wood and American Black Ducks, and Belted Kingfisher. Along the southeast shore you enter a wet area where Least Flycatcher is often found. Look in dead trees and on snags for woodpeckers, including Yellow-bellied Sapsucker and Pileated Woodpecker, present throughout the forest.

The Appalachian Trail (sign for AT South) will join the Pond Loop Trail. Continue on Pond Loop across two small bridges and, where the trails divide, you can either go left continuing around to the pond back to your car or go right on the AT for the longer loop. If you bear left on Pond Loop, you go along an old road with rocky slopes. Worm-eating Warbler has been seen here, particularly near Benedict Pond Road.

The right-hand trail, the Appalachian Trail, soon ascends a short steep section at the top of which is a large beaver pond where, in spring and summer, Great Blue Heron, American Wood Duck, and Belted Kingfisher are common. This trail continues to ledges with a great view to the east. Turkey Vulture, Common Raven, and Red-shouldered, Broad-winged, and Red-tailed Hawks may be seen soaring.

The trail descends into a small ravine with breeding Magnolia, Black-throated Blue, and Black-throated Green Warblers, Scarlet Tanager, and Rose-breasted Grosbeak. Ascend out of the ravine and continue uphill to a junction with a power line. Turn left on the powerline and follow it uphill to unpaved Mount Wilcox Road. Turn left, walk down the road about 0.4 mile, and turn left on a Bridle/Ski trail. When you reach the junction with the Turkey Trail, turn left (downhill) and continue through areas with breeding woodland warblers. Northern Parulas have been heard here in June and July. Descend the trail to paved Benedict Pond Road, turn left, and then turn left again at a gate on a wide trail. Continue until you meet the Pond Loop Trail, described at the beginning of this section. You can follow the trail in either direction to your car.

Turkey Trail/Benedict Pond Road Loop

This 3-mile loop is mostly easy walking along Benedict Pond Road and Turkey Trail through coniferous stands and mixed hardwood forest. It is a fine trail to combine skiing or snowshoeing with birding.

BELTED KINGFISHER

This loop begins at the northern of the two intersections of Benedict Pond and Mount Wilcox Roads. Find a suitable parking place. Follow Mount Wilcox Road east, over West Brook. After approximately 0.25 mile turn right (south) on Turkey Trail. Immediately the trail crosses a small stream. In some years Louisiana Waterthrushes are along this and other streams crossing the trail. The trail crosses spruce and pine patches with Chestnut-sided, Magnolia, Yellow-rumped, and Blackburnian Warblers. In upland deciduous forest you may hear Blue-headed and Red-eyed Vireos, Veery, Hermit and Wood Thrushes, Scarlet Tanager, and Rose-breasted Grosbeak. The trail runs about 1.5 miles through woods to the southern end of Mount Wilcox Road. Turn right and head downhill (west), and then turn right (north) along Benedict Pond Road back toward your vehicle, past many beaver ponds where Wood and American Black Ducks and Least Flycatcher nest. Spruce groves along the road hold both nuthatches and Golden-crowned Kinglet. These areas are likely winter habitat for both crossbills, Common Redpoll, and Evening Grosbeak.

Benedict Pond Road

Benedict Pond Road (paved) traverses the forest. Starting near Benedict Pond it ascends to the upper portions of the forest. At 1.1 miles from the pond, the Outlook Trail leads west to an overlook about 15 minutes from the road with a spectacular view to the Catskill Mountains on the western horizon and Monument Mountain to the northwest. In autumn, hawks can be seen flying south along the valley.

Continue north by car along Benedict Pond Road past beaver ponds and mixed forest. Park at the old CCC camp and walk a short distance along Benedict Pond Road to a large field on your left, one of few open areas in the forest. Red-shouldered and Red-tailed Hawks patrol the area, and the small pond attracts swallows and flycatchers. This field can be good for Great Crested Flycatcher and Baltimore Oriole.

Continue to drive north on Benedict Pond Road as it descends to the Housatonic River valley. This portion of West Brook has nesting Louisiana Waterthrush.

The forest is public land and walking off established trails is not only allowed but encouraged. A little bushwhacking helps you find the secluded places that wild animals and birds prefer over areas frequented by humans. *Myles and Kathy Conway*

B24. Questing Reservation
New Marlborough

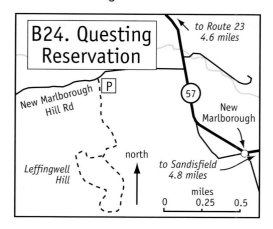

To get to Questing, a 400+ acre reserve owned by The Trustees of Reservations, take Route 57 southeast from Route 23 near the Great Barrington/ Monterey town line. After 4.6 miles turn right on New Marlborough Hill Road (dirt). Go about a mile to the Questing parking area on the left.

A two-mile loop trail leads through New England transitional forest and some field edge. The large forest at Questing offers an abundance of woodland species including Pileated Woodpecker, Least Flycatcher, Great Crested Flycatcher, Veery, Hermit and Wood Thrushes, Black-throated Blue, Black-throated Green, and Blackburnian Warblers, Ovenbird, and Scarlet Tanager. A 17-acre field offers spring American Woodcock courtship and a mid-summer butterfly and dragonfly spectacular. Ruffed Grouse and Wild Turkey are often found in spring and fall.   *Don Reid*

B25. Three Mile Pond Wildlife Management Area
Sheffield

See map B25. Three Mile Pond

The Three Mile Pond Wildlife Management Area has a rich variety of habitats with many fine birds. Once farmland, this 875-acre state-owned tract holds a large shallow pond and a dirt road through woods with aged apple trees and shrubby pastures. Stone foundations and an old cemetery enhance the quiet beauty. Birders should avoid this area in hunting seasons.

Start measuring mileage from the intersection of Routes 7 and 23 in Great Barrington, and go south 0.9 mile on Route 7. Turn left (east) on Brookside Road (which becomes Brush Hill Road and then Home Road) at the sign for Camp Institute of Living Judaism. At 5.1 miles turn left on a different Brush Hill Road (you are now in Sheffield). At 5.3 miles there is an excellent stop for spring warblers. At 5.9 miles the wildlife management area begins. A small turnoff is at 6.4 miles, after which you may drive or walk the last 0.5 mile of road.

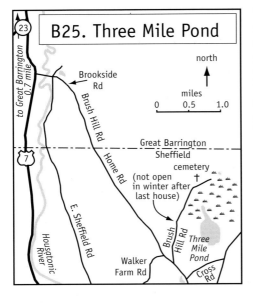

B25. Three Mile Pond

north

Brookside Rd

Brush Hill Rd

to Great Barrington 0.7 mile

miles
0   0.5   1.0

Great Barrington
Sheffield
cemetery †
(not open in winter after last house)

Home Rd

E. Sheffield Rd

Housatonic River

23

7

Walker Farm Rd

Brush Hill Rd

Three Mile Pond

Cross Rd

There are several places on Brush Hill Road to stop and explore woods or brushy fields. Observe the private property signs; there are private homes along the first section, but you are soon on state land. You may see Yellow-bellied Sapsucker, Pileated Woodpecker, Great Crested Flycatcher, Blue-headed and Red-eyed Vireos, Common Raven, Brown Creeper, both kinglets (migration), Blue-gray Gnatcatcher, Cedar Waxwing, Tennessee (migration), Yellow, Chestnut-sided, Magnolia, Yellow-rumped, Black-throated Green, Blackburnian, Palm (migration), and Black-and-white Warblers, American Redstart, Canada Warbler, Scarlet Tanager, Rose-breasted Grosbeak, and Baltimore Oriole. Check old fields for migrating sparrows and breeding Ruby-throated Hummingbird, Least Flycatcher, and Blue-winged Warbler.

After the cemetery on your left (a good spot to check) look for Eastern Wood-Pewee, Veery, and Fox Sparrow (in migration); Ring-necked Pheasant and Wild Turkey may occur here. Migrant Solitary Sandpipers may be at the water's edge at the end of the road. Watch for beavers, Great Blue Heron, waterfowl, Belted Kingfisher, Yellow and Chestnut-sided Warblers, Swamp Sparrow, and, in migration, Osprey and Bald Eagle.   *Jill Barrett Johnson*

B26. Jug End Area
Egremont
Jug End State Reservation and Wildlife Management Area, Egremont

An underused area for bird study, the 1170-acre Jug End property is administered by both the Department of Environmental Management and Division of Fisheries and Wildlife. Once a resort, the area has largely reverted to its natural state, though ski slope and golf course remnants persist. The fields are mown yearly for grassland species. There is a small riparian margin along Fenton Brook, which bisects the area. Mature northern deciduous forests rise east from the valley (900 feet) to Jug End (1520 feet), which hosts the Appalachian Trail. The Taconics to the west rise to over 2000 feet.

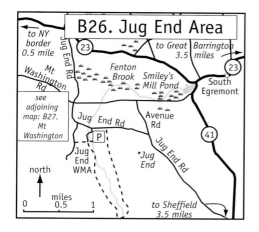

From the center of Great Barrington, drive south about 0.7 mile on Route 7, and turn right (southwest) on Routes 41 and 23. Continue approximately 4 miles through the village of South Egremont to the small Smiley's Mill Pond (also called Mill Pond or Egremont Pond; see below). At this point Route 41 heads south to Sheffield and Connecticut while Route 23 leads west to New York. The small Mount Washington Road turns off of Route 41, hugs the south side of Egremont Pond, and goes approximately 1.5 miles to Jug End Road. Turn left and take Jug End Road about 0.5 mile to the parking area.

The meadows abound in Eastern Bluebird, Savannah Sparrow, Bobolink, and Eastern Meadowlark. American Kestrels nest in boxes on trees in the meadow. The pleasant vistas allow an excellent view of migrating Turkey Vulture and increasingly observed Black Vulture, as well as migrant and resident raptors including Sharp-shinned, Red-shouldered, Broad-winged, and Red-tailed Hawks. Northern Harriers and both Bald and Golden Eagles have been observed migrating down the valley in the fall.

From the parking lot, a trail leads over Fenton Brook to the west where the fields may be explored. Another trail leads directly south to upper meadows and the forested east slope.

Bird species in the more elevated woodlands are drastically different. Waterthrushes sing along waterways. Black-throated Blue Warbler hides in mountain laurel; an occasional Worm-eating Warbler occurs on wooded slopes. Winter Wrens and Hermit Thrushes heard in early summer mornings bespeak our northern climate, yet Red-bellied Woodpecker, Tufted Titmouse, Carolina Wren, and Blue-gray Gnatcatcher show a southern influence. This area pleads for a more determined birder's presence. *David P. St. James*

Smiley's Mill Pond (Mill Pond, Egremont Pond), South Egremont

See the directions to this pond above. There are turn-offs for the pond on Route 41 and on Mount Washington Road.

Wood Duck, Gadwall, American Wigeon, American Black Duck, Ring-necked Duck, Bufflehead, Common Goldeneye, and Hooded and Common Mergansers are regulars at this pond in early spring and fall. Because the pond is small, good views are available. Greater White-fronted Goose and American Coot have occurred. Pied-billed Grebe and Common Moorhen have nested. Great Blue Heron may be seen and Mute Swans visit. In late spring, Black Terns have been seen. One can observe beaver and muskrat year-round.

In May Virginia Rail nest; sometimes their young cross the highway to a marsh area where Willow Flycatchers can be seen. It is a pleasure to watch foraging Red-winged Blackbirds turn over the lily pads. Baltimore Orioles nest near the pond, and on the road toward Mount Washington. Look for their nests a short distance west of the wet area. American Tree, Savannah, and Fox Sparrows occur.

Prospect Lake, North Egremont
See map B21. Alford

From the intersection of Route 7 with Routes 23 and 41 in Great Barrington, take Routes 23 and 41 south 1.5 miles; bear right on Route 71 toward North Egremont. Continue 2.8 miles to the center of North Egremont and turn left on Prospect Lake Road; follow signs for the lake.

This small lake, busy in summer but relatively quiet in spring and fall, has excellent views of migrating ducks including Wood Duck, Blue-winged Teal, Ring-necked Duck, White-winged Scoter, Bufflehead, Common Goldeneye, and Common Merganser. Migrating Osprey also occur here.

Jill Barrett Johnson

B27. Mount Washington Area
South Egremont, Mount Washington

Mount Washington State Forest

Take Mount Washington Road west from Route 41 at Smiley's Mill Pond (Egremont Pond; see B26. Jug End Area) in South Egremont. This road enters the State Forest and gains elevation quickly with very few places to pull off. Mount Washington Road becomes East Street at the Mount Washington town line. At 4.5 miles from Smiley's Mill Pond, turn right on an unnamed dirt road. The paved road bearing left is East Street (no sign). The field across the road occasionally has Wild Turkeys. Measure mileage from this intersection.

After 0.25 mile turn left at the T onto West Street, which has mixed forest with good mountain laurel understory. Pull off the road wherever possible for Yellow-bellied Sapsucker, Eastern Wood-Pewee,

Black-throated Blue, Yellow-rumped, Black-throated Green, Blackburnian, and Canada Warblers, Scarlet Tanager, Dark-eyed Junco, and Rose-breasted Grosbeak. The road climbs and suddenly descends on a winding stretch. After 2 miles turn right on Falls Road at an almost hairpin turn. Look for a deteriorating sign for Bash Bish Falls.

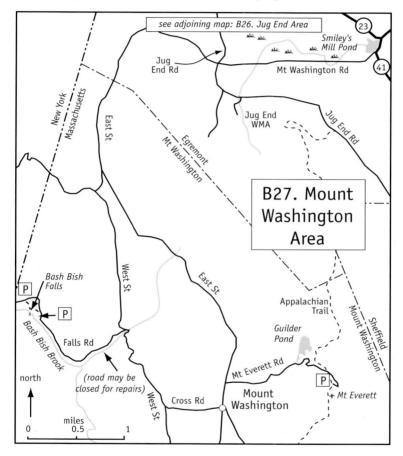

It is possible that Falls Road will be closed for badly-needed repairs. Check with DEM (413-442-8928) for an update and an alternative route through Copake Falls, New York.

Bash Bish Falls State Park

Narrow, winding Falls Road is usually in poor condition; drive carefully. Bash Bish Mountain to the south and Cedar Mountain to the north rise over 600 feet above the road, which runs along Bash Bish

Brook, a Hudson River tributary. The steep conifer-covered hillsides have many Black-throated Green and Blackburnian Warblers. Winter Wren and Louisiana Waterthrush breed along the stream. There are a few pull-offs, but sometimes song is difficult to hear over the roaring water. After 1.4 miles on Falls Road, park in the lot on the left, the trailhead for the long, steep hike down to the falls. Other trails to the falls are reached by continuing on Falls Road into New York. Bird around the parking area, then climb the short, steep distance to the lookout atop the rocks with commanding views of the Taconics and New York. The sky is often alive with Turkey Vultures, occasional Black Vultures, and other raptors. The scenery alone is worth the trip.

Mount Everett State Reservation

To get to Mount Everett, return to the intersection of Falls Road and West Street, and drive right (south) on West Street. This road climbs and winds steeply through a somewhat residential stretch. At a fork (almost a T) after 1.1 miles on West Street, go left on Cross Road (no sign). Where Cross Road ends, after little less than a mile, turn left on East Street. After 0.3 mile on East Street, turn right on the Mount Everett entrance road. This dirt road is usually open almost to the summit in summer, though it may be gated part way up. Bird all along the road for the typical neotropical migrant breeders. Guilder Pond on the left is spectacular when the mountain laurel is blooming. The road ends at a stone shelter near the summit (2594 feet) and the Appalachian Trail. Park and get out your scopes and picnic lunch. The stunning, unobstructed view at this great hawkwatch looks north past Mount Greylock. Black Vultures are often here in mid-summer, sometimes quite close, though it may take some waiting for them to show up.

From the intersection of the Mount Everett Road and East Street, it is 4.2 miles north on East Street to the Mount Washington/Egremont town line where East Street becomes Mount Washington Road. Watch fields in this area for Wild Turkey.   *Mark C. Lynch*

B28. Bartholomew's Cobble Reservation
Sheffield

Bartholomew's Cobble, a 300-acre reserve owned by The Trustees of Reservations (TTOR), is a premier birding area, "the place" in Berkshire County to expect the unexpected. With the Housatonic River, a mix of hardwood/conifer forest and fields, and the Housatonic Valley hawk migration route, you can't go wrong here in any season. There are approximately 5 miles of trails.

From Sheffield center, take Route 7 south 1.5 miles. Turn right on

Route 7A (sign to Ashley Falls). At 0.5 mile, turn right on Rannapo Road. After 1.5 miles turn right on Weatogue Road. The TTOR visitors center (with museum, maps, and rest rooms) and parking area are just ahead on the left. Bartholomew's Cobble has a small entrance fee.

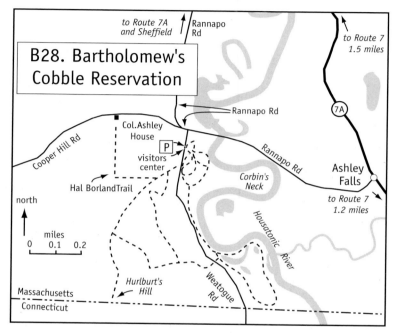

The west side of Weatogue Road offers trails through mixed forest, large fields, and edge habitat to spectacular vistas and hawkwatch sites at Hurlburt's Hill. The east side of Weatogue Road, with the visitors center, offers trails around rocky outcrops called cobbles and along the Housatonic with its diverse riparian, floodplain forest, oxbow pond, and field habitats. All are good areas for Red-bellied Woodpecker, Least Flycatcher, Yellow-throated and Warbling Vireos, Northern and Louisiana Waterthrushes, and perhaps a glimpse of nesting Red-shouldered and Broad-winged Hawks.

Most fields at Bartholomew's Cobble are managed for grassland birds. Expect Eastern Bluebird, Field and Savannah Sparrows, Eastern Meadowlark, and one of the largest nesting populations of Bobolink (mid-May through June) in the state. Black Vultures are regular visitors to the area.

Wildflowers are abundant in April and May at the Cobbles, especially on the Ledges Trail. The reservation boasts over 900 species of vascular plants and the greatest diversity of ferns in any one area in North America.

BLACK VULTURE

Around mid-May one might observe well over 100 bird species in a few hours at Bartholomew's Cobble. Keep to the river trails, especially Ledges Trail, Bailey Trail, and Spero Loop, for most warblers. From Corbin's Neck, off Ledges Trail, you can observe Belted Kingfishers, Northern Rough-winged Swallows, and hundreds of Bank Swallows nesting in riverbanks. Fish Crows nest in the trees at the eastern end of Corbin's Neck. In July check mud flats along the river for flocks of Least Sandpipers and numbers of Solitary Sandpipers, both yellowlegs, and others. Check the river in late summer and early fall for Little Blue Heron (usually one each year), Great Blue Heron, Great and Snowy Egrets, and occasionally a Black-crowned Night-Heron.

From August 21 through September 5, Common Nighthawks use the Housatonic River as a flyway. Data are collected just west of Rannapo Road Bridge. It is not unusual to observe several hundred nighthawks in one evening.

In fall, think hawks. Hurlburt's Hill can produce thousands of Broad-wings in mid-September and a flow of Bald Eagles, Northern Harriers, accipiters, and falcons. You might not get closer views of hawks in all of Western Massachusetts.   *Don Reid*

B29. Southern Housatonic River

See Berkshire County map at the beginning of this chapter

Berkshire County south of Stockbridge offers productive birding in diverse habitats, including vast riverine habitats near the Housatonic River, one of the state's most scenic rivers, bordering Route 7.

The Housatonic from Great Barrington south offers great birding. Because of difficulty reaching it through private property a canoe is a must. Pleasant Valley Wildlife Sanctuary (413-637-0320) and Bartholomew's Cobble Reservation (413-229-8600) offer canoe trips with all necessary equipment for reasonable fees (see accounts B14 and B28). Several moderately priced companies in southern Berkshire County rent canoes, provide livery service, and give advice about put-ins and take-outs. The birding is up to you. This section of the river is flat water, relatively shallow, and thirty to fifty feet wide. The best time for canoe birding is early morning or at sunset in late spring, late summer, or fall.

In late spring to early summer expect nesting Belted Kingfisher, Northern Rough-winged Swallow, and thousands of Bank Swallows. Check under bridges for Cliff Swallow. Other nesters or spring migrants include Green Heron, Osprey, Bald Eagle, Red-shouldered Hawk, Killdeer, Spotted Sandpiper, Willow and Least Flycatchers, Yellow-throated and Warbling Vireos, a diversity of warblers, Scarlet Tanager, Rose-breasted Grosbeak, and Indigo Bunting. Check grasslands along the river for American Kestrel, Eastern Bluebird, sparrows, and Bobolink.

July through September expect Little Blue Heron (usually one per year), Great Egret, Green Heron, and possibly American Bittern or Black-crowned Night-Heron. Mud flats may have Greater and Lesser Yellowlegs, Solitary, Semipalmated, Least, and possibly White-rumped Sandpipers. Black-bellied Plover is occasional.

Do not overlook this area in winter (just trade the canoe in for a car). Snow Goose, Tundra Swan, Ring-necked Duck, Bufflehead, Common Goldeneye, and Common Merganser can occur when the river is open. Bald Eagles are possible.

Don Reid

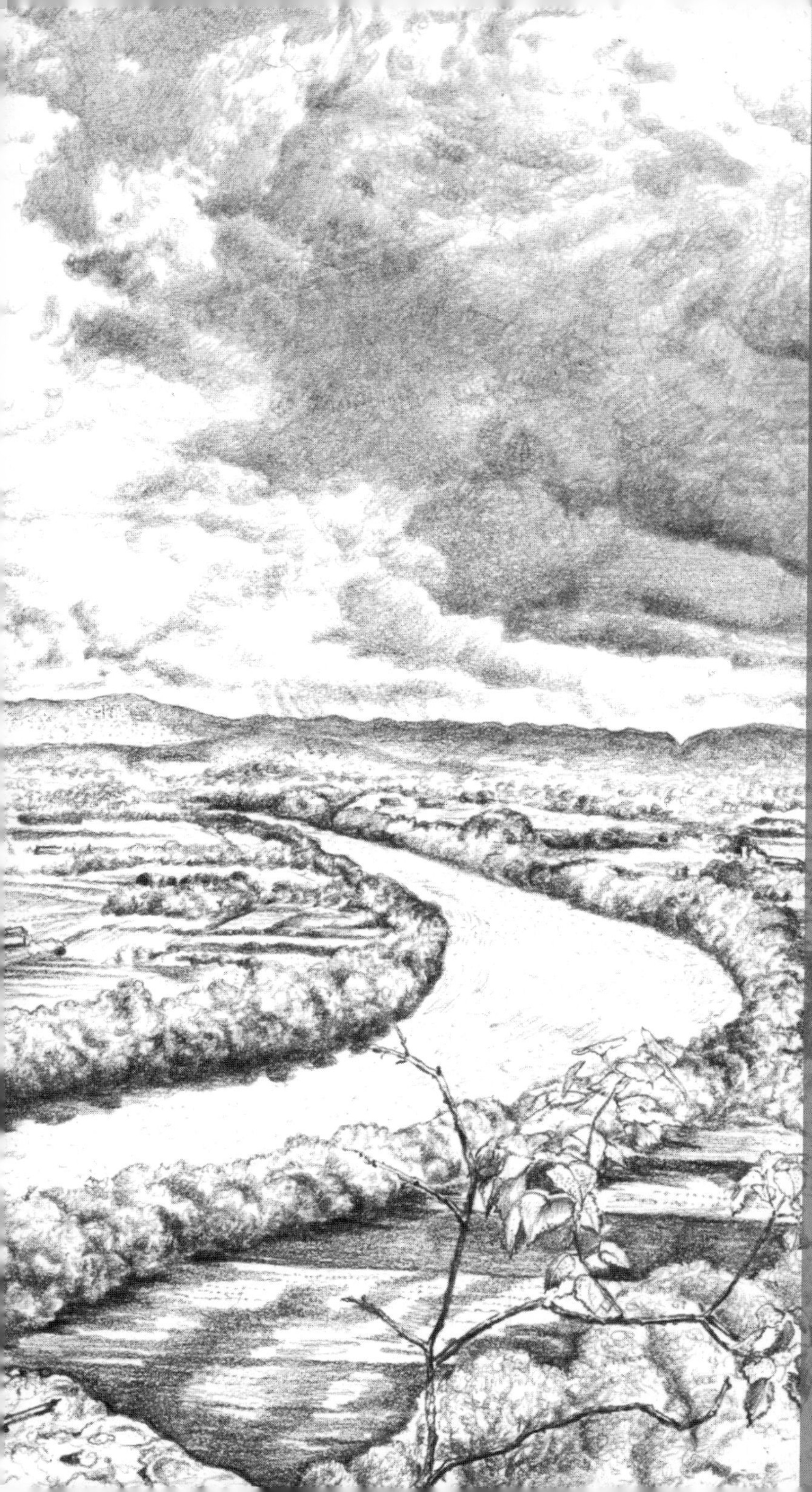

Connecticut River Valley

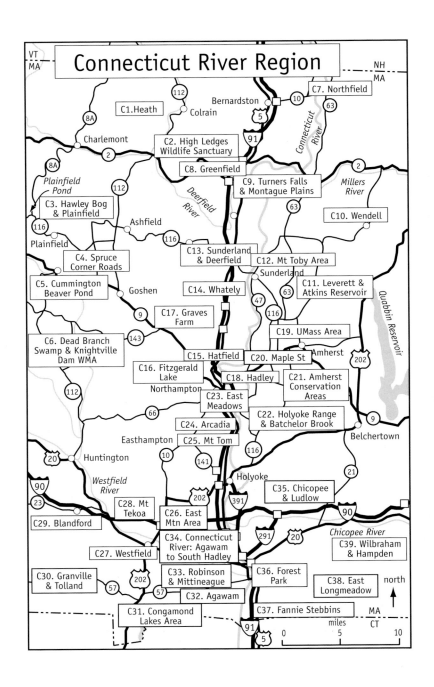

Connecticut River Region

VT / MA   NH / MA

C7. Northfield

C1. Heath

Bernardston

Colrain

Charlemont

C2. High Ledges Wildlife Sanctuary

C8. Greenfield

C9. Turners Falls & Montague Plains

Millers River

Plainfield Pond

C3. Hawley Bog & Plainfield

Ashfield

C10. Wendell

Plainfield

C4. Spruce Corner Roads

C13. Sunderland & Deerfield

C12. Mt Toby Area

Deerfield River

Sunderland

C5. Cummington Beaver Pond

Goshen

C14. Whately

C11. Leverett & Atkins Reservoir

C17. Graves Farm

C19. UMass Area

Quabbin Reservoir

C6. Dead Branch Swamp & Knightville Dam WMA

C15. Hatfield

C20. Maple St

Amherst

C16. Fitzgerald Lake

C18. Hadley

C21. Amherst Conservation Areas

Northampton

C23. East Meadows

C24. Arcadia

C22. Holyoke Range & Batchelor Brook

Easthampton

C25. Mt Tom

Belchertown

Huntington

Holyoke

Westfield River

C35. Chicopee & Ludlow

C28. Mt Tekoa

C26. East Mtn Area

C29. Blandford

Chicopee River

C34. Connecticut River: Agawam to South Hadley

C39. Wilbraham & Hampden

C27. Westfield

C30. Granville & Tolland

C33. Robinson & Mittineague

C36. Forest Park

C38. East Longmeadow

north

C32. Agawam

C31. Congamond Lakes Area

C37. Fannie Stebbins

MA / CT

miles

0   5   10

Connecticut River Valley

Introduction

Much of the Connecticut River Valley's story can be read from a map. The river runs roughly north-south, providing an active migratory flyway. In early spring songbirds seek the relative warmth of the river corridor. In the spring and fall hawks soar on the thermals rising off the valley floor and use the updrafts from the mountain ridges to propel them onward. Thousands of Common Nighthawks pour through the valley in late August, impressing observers with their numbers and agile flight.

The river meanders through the flat parts of the valley, offering birds old river channels, marshes, and agricultural fields, rich habitats that sustain many during nesting, migration and winter. Waterfowl find the river, ponds, and fields a welcome respite in migration. The river itself hosts a variety of birds, and occasionally even such oddities as Northern Gannet, Arctic Tern, and harbor seal. Several pairs of Bald Eagles nest along the river.

In Massachusetts four major drainages join the Connecticut River. The Deerfield and Westfield Rivers flow from the Berkshire Hills. The Millers and Chicopee River systems drain most of the eastern hills. The water has served as a corridor of transportation and settlement for thousands of years. The industrial and demographic history of the valley since the nineteenth century is linked to waterpower. Today the power dams, the pump storage facility in Northfield, and the flood control dams on tributaries have an almost tidal effect on portions of the river, providing migrating shorebirds with mudflats in spring and late summer.

The flat-bottomed valley and the sculpted north-south hills on either side are the work of glaciers over a number of different glacial eras. The melting of the most recent glacier left an enormous lake, Lake Hitchcock. When the lake drained, it left dunes and big deltas along the former shoreline, which, when not mined for sand and gravel, produce pitch pine barrens such as the Montague Plains. Of the formerly extensive floodplain forests, only a few such as Fannie Stebbins Wildlife Sanctuary and Arcadia Wildlife Refuge remain.

Much of the floor of glacial Lake Hitchcock was cleared for agriculture. Weedy fields are excellent for migrant sparrows. Barren fields

Preceeding Pages: **COMMON RAVEN**

attract Horned Larks, American Pipits, and Snow Buntings, and, especially when wet and manured, shorebirds, geese, and gulls. Westover Air Reserve Base has the largest population of Grasshopper Sparrows and most of the remaining breeding population of Upland Sandpipers in the valley. The fields along the river also host raptors, including the occasional wintering Gyrfalcon or Great Gray Owl.

Difficult as it is to visualize glaciers here, it is even harder to imagine the valley's origin as a rift valley parallel to the rift that opened the Atlantic Ocean about 180 million years ago. Later volcanic activity produced ridges such as Poet's Seat in Greenfield, Mount Tom, and the Holyoke Range. The local portion of the rift valley became the Connecticut River Valley, and the steep cliffs became nesting places for Peregrine Falcons and Common Ravens. Today's peregrines, successfully introduced after DDT destroyed the native population, had chosen artificial urban "cliffs" until 2002 when a pair nested on cliffs in Erving for the first time in more than 50 years. Some of the ridges provide an opportunity to hear the songs of Dark-eyed Juncos and Worm-eating Warblers at the same time, symbolizing the meeting of northern and southern species here in New England.

The accounts in this chapter begin in the northwest and are clustered by habitat. One last tip for visitors: the "h" is not pronounced in Amherst ("Amerst"), compensated by the extra "h" articulated in Northampton ("North-hampton").

Jan Ortiz, David A. Spector, and Mary Alice Wilson

C1. Heath

Heath is largely mixed deciduous forest with dense hemlock stands in ravines and on north facing slopes. The town has pristine streams, some disturbed wetlands, and pockets of open land. Burnt Hill, a cleared area with rugged blueberry barrens, overlooks the Deerfield River watershed.

You CAN get to Heath, but it takes effort. The best road into town is Route 8A. Don't try to get there from Oxbow Road in Charlemont, as some maps would have you do, unless you love long walks.

From Route 2 in Charlemont, follow Route 8A north for 2.5 miles across the town line into Heath. Almost immediately you enter The Dell with a small mill pond and several homes. Continue on Route 8A for 2.0 miles to a small dirt pull-off area on the west side, across from a red farm house, just after Rowe Road on the left. Hazel Porter and Alastair Maitland own the home and have set aside a beautiful mixed deciduous-white pine woodland as a preserve with miles of trails and nesting Red-shouldered Hawk and Barred Owl. There is a large vernal pool along the main trail.

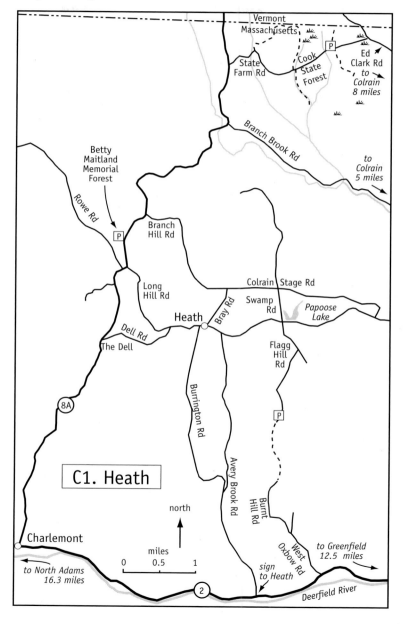

Continue north 4.0 miles on Route 8A to State Farm Road. If you reach Vermont you have gone about 0.5 mile too far. Turn right onto State Farm Road, past the last home and into the woods of the H.O. Cook State Forest, with extensive red pine and Norway spruce plantations, some of which are being logged. Both crossbills, Pine and Evening Grosbeaks, and Pine Siskins can be found in these conifers in some winters. Barred Owl and Common Raven occur. Breeding birds include Brown Creeper, Winter Wren, Swainson's Thrush, White-throated Sparrow, and a good variety of warblers. The State Forest roads are not plowed, so go before the first snow or plan to use winter footgear. The State Forest roads are fairly well maintained in seasons other than winter, but be careful as one can easily get lost in the maze of forest roads. You can return to 8A and Route 2, or continue through the forest, turn right (south) on Ed Cook Road, left (east) on Thompson Road, and right (south) on Route 112 to Colrain. *Ted Watt*

C2. High Ledges Wildlife Sanctuary
Shelburne

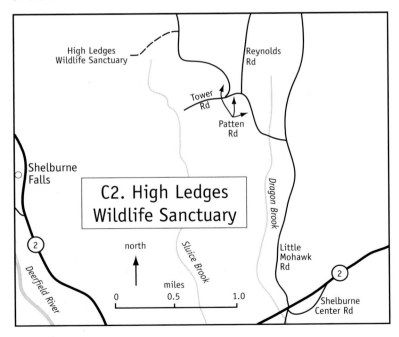

This Massachusetts Audubon Society Sanctuary donated to MAS by Ellsworth and Mary Barnard consists of rich mesic forest with beech, maple, oak, hickory, pine, and hemlock stands, hemlock ravines, dense

OVENBIRD

mountain laurel understory, a small bog, woodland stream, alder swamps, steep rocky cliffs, and scattered old-field clearings.

From the I-91 rotary in Greenfield, go west on Route 2 for 5.5 miles. Turn right (north) onto Little Mohawk Road, just across from the west end of Shelburne Center Road. In 1.3 miles bear left on Patten Road. For 0.9 mile, stay on Patten Road turning left and then right as you continue uphill; at each turn there are signs to High Ledges. Turn left at the dirt entrance road (road closed November to April) which leads down and then uphill to a small parking area by a gate and information kiosk. Take a trail map.

In old fields along the entrance road, Eastern Bluebirds use the nest boxes; listen for Chestnut-sided Warbler in shrubby edges. The trail beyond the gate leads to a scenic vista atop the ledges where Eastern Phoebe, Winter Wren, and Dark-eyed Junco breed. Continue on the trail into deep forest, where Black-throated Blue and Canada Warblers are common in dense understory; Magnolia, Black-throated Green, and Blackburnian Warblers breed in hemlock stands; Pine Warbler inhabits white pine stands; and Black-and-white Warbler and American Redstart nest in hardwood stands. The trail system provides several loops. Throughout the forest Eastern Wood-Pewee, Blue-headed and Red-eyed Vireos, Veery, Hermit and Wood Thrushes, Ovenbird, and Scarlet Tanager are common. Louisiana Waterthrush breeds along the forested stream that parallels some of the trails, while Northern Waterthrush sometimes nests in the alder swamp. When Yellow-bellied

Sapsuckers visit their array of sap trees, Ruby-throated Hummingbirds sometimes follow closely behind for a free meal of sap and insects. Northern Goshawk, Barred Owl, Pileated Woodpecker, Great Crested Flycatcher, Yellow-throated Vireo, Brown Creeper, and Rose-breasted Grosbeak also breed here. *David McLain*

C3. Hawley Bog and Plainfield
Hawley, Plainfield

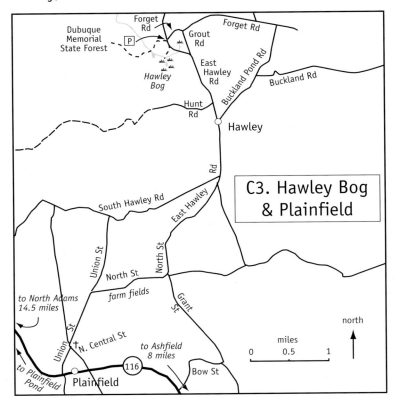

Plainfield Farm Fields

Begin in Plainfield Center on Route 116. Turn right (north) on North Central Street and continue 0.4 mile to the cemetery at the corner of Union Street. Turn right on Union Street and follow it 0.8 mile around the cemetery to the intersection with North Street. Turn right on North Street.

Along the next mile on North Street, **pull your car completely off**

the road to bird the **privately owned** farm fields on your right. Please do not enter the farm fields.

Birds here include Eastern Bluebird, Field and Savannah Sparrows, Indigo Bunting, and Eastern Meadowlark. Vesper Sparrow breeds sparingly in the northern sector of the property just south of North Street. The species is listed as state endangered; **do not play tapes,** which may disrupt breeding. Turkey Vulture, American Kestrel, and Common Raven occur here. *Charles B. Quinlan*

Hawley Bog

Hawley Bog, a National Natural Landmark, is owned by Five Colleges, Inc., and The Nature Conservancy (TNC), which manages the preserve. **Note:** Any organized group use of Hawley Bog requires permission from the TNC's Boston Office at (617) 227-7017. Hawley Bog is an approximately 100-acre peatland perched in a high-elevation glacial lake basin. The peat is 40 feet deep in the middle! Valued as a botanical preserve, it is also great for birds. Spring and early summer are the best times to visit.

Continue on North Street as it turns sharply to the left and becomes East Hawley Road at the Plainfield/Hawley town line. It is 3.3 miles from the Union Street/North Street junction to the center of Hawley. Continue through Hawley, noting Hunt Road on your left at 0.3 mile. In another 0.7 mile, stay on East Hawley Road as it goes left (Grout Road bears right). Stay on East Hawley Road 0.3 mile farther to a small grassy pull-off and memorial stone to the First Church of Hawley on your left. Hawley Bog is called Cranberry Swamp on the USGS Plainfield Quadrangle topographic map.

After parking, the next challenge is to find the trail to the bog. The unmarked trail enters the forest on the southeast side of the small clearing (the trail at the northwest side of the clearing goes into the Dubuque Memorial State Forest). Walk gently through mixed deciduous woodland rich with spring wildflowers. Near the bog the water table rises to meet the trail. The trail is usually well maintained, but beaver activity along the east edge of the bog can make footing treacherous. The boardwalk, where footing improves, winds through shrub swamp gradually working its way out to the sphagnum mat. Black-throated Blue and Canada Warblers breed in the shrub swamp.

Visitors to Hawley Bog absolutely must not step off the boardwalk in the sphagnum mat area. The habitat is fragile and has suffered significant deterioration over the past decade. Listen for Olive-sided Flycatcher (has bred, but not recently) singing from a snag around the edge of the mat. Ruby-throated Hummingbirds often perch on dead branches. Watch for Common Raven and Evening Grosbeak flying over. Red-shouldered Hawk, Barred Owl, Alder Flycatcher, and Northern Waterthrush breed. After inspecting the bog return along the boardwalk.   *Ted Watt*

Plainfield Pond

See Connecticut River Region map at the beginning of the chapter

From Plainfield center at the junction of Routes 116 and North Central Street, go west along Route 116 for 3.4 miles. Just before Plainfield Pond, you will pass beaver ponds on both sides of the road and the turn for Route 8A north on your right. **Pull your car completely off the road** on the pond side. While a scope is helpful, the pond and the extensive marsh at the north end are best birded by canoe. Floating heart and meadow beauty are scarce plants that occur here.

The open pond, at an elevation of about 1700 feet, attracts a rich array of waterfowl. Common Merganser frequents the pond; Pied-billed Grebe and all three scoters occur in passage. American Bittern occurs in breeding season. Mourning Warbler has been heard singing from azalea bushes on the shoreline in breeding season. The beaver ponds to the east had breeding Olive-sided Flycatcher in recent times. This is also a good area to find American Bittern and possibly Least Bittern, both State Endangered.   *Charles B. Quinlan*

C4. Spruce Corner Roads
Ashfield, Goshen

You can reach the diverse habitats of Spruce Corner and Watson-Spruce Corner Roads from Route 9 in Goshen. In difficult driving conditions access might be easier from Route 116, which heads west from Route 112, 1.5 miles south of Ashfield or 4.5 miles north of Route 9. From the intersection of Routes 112 and 116 it is 1.9 miles on Route 116 to Watson-Spruce Corner Road and another 0.2 mile to Spruce Corner Road.

There are places to park along both Spruce Corner and Watson-Spruce Corner Roads. Be sure to pull your car completely off the road. **Do not walk down private drives or on private land.** You can easily bird the entire area from the edge of the road.

Birds are found in appropriate habitat all along the 6 miles of these two roads. At any time, watch for all three accipiters and Common Raven. In summer, Yellow-bellied Sapsucker is the most common woodpecker, and Blue-headed Vireo (in mixed woods) and Red-eyed Vireo (in deciduous woods) are widespread. And there are warblers: Northern Waterthrush by marshes and Louisiana Waterthrush by running water; Black-throated Green and Black-and-white Warblers, American Redstart, and Ovenbird in deciduous woods; Nashville, Magnolia, and Black-throated Blue Warblers in higher, mixed woods; and Canada Warbler in wet, mixed woods. There are Purple Finches all year, and Evening Grosbeaks can be found occasionally as breeding pairs in summer and in flocks in winter.

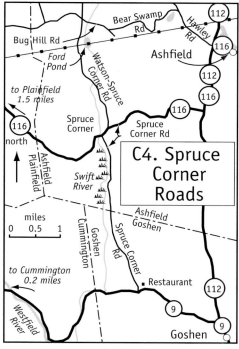

C4. Spruce Corner Roads

Starting from Route 9, 2.2 miles west of the town of Goshen and 4.2 miles east of Cummington, Spruce Corner Road goes uphill through lovely deciduous forest with breeding Veery, Wood Thrush, and Louisiana Waterthrush (along the stream below). At 0.6 mile from Route 9, the road levels off into farmland. Look for Savannah Sparrow and other grassland birds in summer and Snow Bunting in winter. After the farm are houses with winter bird feeders often visited by Purple Finch, Pine Siskin and, occasionally, Evening Grosbeak. Near the Goshen/Ashfield town line (1.8 miles), the wet woods have breeding Winter Wren, Magnolia Warbler, Northern Waterthrush, and Canada Warbler. This is a likely place for a Northern Saw-whet Owl.

Just beyond the town line, a flat marshy area on the left (west) side is a good place to pull off the road to walk all or part of the 3/4 mile to the lumberyard. Watch for log trucks on the road. Listen for breeding Alder and Willow Flycatchers and Swamp Sparrow. Mixed woods on the right (east) side of the road have breeding Red-shouldered and Broad-winged Hawks, and Magnolia, Black-throated Green, Pine, and Black-and-white Warblers, American Redstart, and Ovenbird.

WHITE-THROATED SPARROW

Past the lumberyard, there is a big wet meadow just before Route 116. In early summer the singing birds are almost overwhelming, with Indigo Bunting, Bobolink, and Eastern Meadowlark among many other voices. Watch for American Kestrel on the phone lines. **Please respect private property; the roadside provides ample views of breeding species.**

Turn right on Route 116 at Spruce Corner (3.4 miles from Route 9), and then, in 0.2 mile, take the next left on Watson-Spruce Corner Road. The road begins in a maple grove, good for Scarlet Tanager, and in 1.0 mile enters dense spruces, a likely place to look for Golden-crowned Kinglet (winter), Ruby-crowned Kinglet (in migration and probably as a breeder), White-throated Sparrow, Dark-eyed Junco, Purple Finch, White-winged Crossbill (especially in winter), Pine Siskin, and American Goldfinch.

Beyond the spruces (1.3 miles from Route 116), the road crosses South Face Maple Farm; when they are sugaring, stop for pancakes. The fields and pond before the farm are good places for Common Merganser (in migration), breeding Hooded Merganser, Wild Turkey, and Bobolink. The road passes through the sugar bush (sugar maple trees) into a mixed forest with Pileated Woodpecker, Red-breasted (less common) and White-breasted Nuthatches, Veery, Hermit Thrush, and Nashville, Magnolia, and Black-throated Blue Warblers.

At the power line (2 miles from Route 116), you can look down to the right (east) on Ford Pond where Hooded Mergansers nest. In winter look in the fields after the power line for Northern Shrike and flocks of Horned Larks and Snow Buntings.

At 2.6 miles from Route 116, Watson-Spruce Corner Road ends at a four-corners, called Watson, where this road meets Watson Road (to the west), Old Stage Road (to the north), and Bug Hill Road (to the east). It is easiest to backtrack to Route 116. You can, however, turn right on Bug Hill Road and follow it through a series of farm fields. At the fork (0.6 mile), turn left (north) on Bear Swamp Road. The road bends northward along more farm fields, zigs past a boggy area (potentially excellent birding), and under a power line (1.0 mile from the corner). It then heads downhill in spruce forest past a small reservoir on the right (1.6 miles), and shortly one of the most beautiful views in western Massachusetts opens northwestward into the Apple Valley section of Buckland. A right turn on Hawley Road returns you to the Route 116/112 junction just west of Ashfield center. *Geoff LeBaron*

C5. Cummington Beaver Pond
Cummington

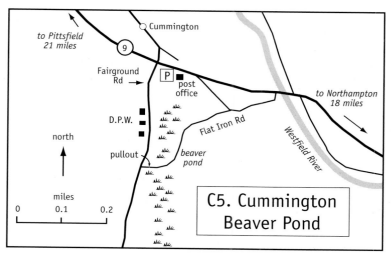

Approaching Cummington from the east on Route 9, cross a steel bridge over the Westfield River and just beyond the post office turn left on Fairground Road. The pond and associated wetlands will be on your left. There will be signs for the Department of Public Works (DPW) and the Cummington Fairgrounds. If you stop near the gray DPW buildings, pull completely off this busy road, out of the way of town trucks. It is wiser to drive on and walk back. Turn left onto the dirt Flat Iron Road (no sign), pull completely off the road, and park. You can also park at the Post Office on Route 9 and walk from there.

Water levels vary with beaver activity; sometimes the area across from the DPW is a swamp, sometimes a wet meadow. Flat Iron Road is not busy and one can stand (or bring a chair) and watch the wonderful activity and light.

This area is in a north-south valley used by hawks in spring and fall; a sky watch is often rewarding. A Gyrfalcon was seen late one fall; Merlin is often seen. Lincoln's Sparrow usually occurs near the corner of Fairgrounds and Flat Iron Roads in migration.

In late May and June, early risers may hear American Bittern, Virginia Rail (usually at the south end), and perhaps Great Horned and Northern Saw-whet Owls from wooded hills to the west. Eastern Kingbird, Alder and Willow Flycatchers (at the south end), Cedar Waxwing, Yellow, Chestnut-sided, and Black-and-white Warblers, Swamp Sparrow, and Baltimore Oriole breed here. American Kestrel, Northern Mockingbird, and Brown Thrasher breed on the shrubby, pastured hills to the east. A walk along Flat Iron Road returns you to the Route 9 bridge where Cliff Swallow nests. Common Merganser nests along the river, usually upriver behind the school.

In late fall and winter, check this area for Northern Shrike.

Charles B. Quinlan

C6. Dead Branch Swamp and Knightville Dam WMA
Chesterfield, Huntington

Dead Branch Swamp (Fisk Meadow Wildlife Management Area)

Dead Branch Swamp, with its slow stream, beaver swamp, laurel thickets, and conifer stands, has good birding from April thaw to October. Mink, otter, and moose occur here; if you do see a moose, steer clear!

From Williamsburg center take Route 9 west 0.5 mile to Route 143. Take Route 143 west 4.2 miles and park under the pines on your right, across from Bisbee Road. If you go too far you will see the huge swamp on your right. There is a small one-car parking lot across the road.

Scope the area from the Route 143 bridge; check the south side of Route 143 in the tall sedges and grasses for Swamp Sparrow, and check the alders along the stream for Alder and Willow Flycatchers. You can reach the middle of the swamp by driving back (east) on Route 143 0.5 mile and taking Sugar Hill Road on your left for 0.75 mile to Old Chesterfield Road. Park and walk to the left (west) 0.5 mile to a rickety pallet bridge to scan up and down the swamp.

With a canoe you can get the feel of this beautiful wetland. Put in at the Route 143 roadside pull-off. Paddle left (west) almost to the bank. From here you can paddle north by following the main channel, or if beavers rebuild the dam you can paddle along the shallow edges.

Along the edge in summer you should see many Eastern Kingbirds and Cedar Waxwings and a few Great Blue Herons, Wood Ducks, Belted King-fishers, and beavers. Check the woods for Broad-winged Hawk, Yellow-bellied Sapsucker, Eastern Wood-Pewee, Great Crested Flycatcher, Blue-headed Vireo, Brown Creeper, Winter Wren, Veery, Hermit and Wood Thrushes, Black-throated Blue, Yellow-rumped, Black-throated Green, and Black-and-white Warblers, American Redstart, Scarlet Tanager, and Dark-eyed Junco. Breeding Red-shouldered Hawks often scream from the forest edge. Listen for Northern Waterthrush, frustratingly hard to locate, that inhabits the small islands and thick laurels along the forest edge.

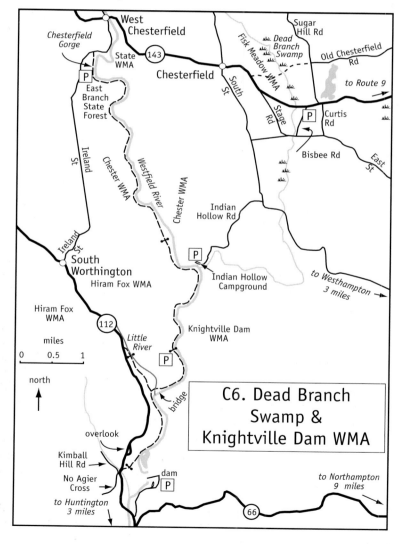

C6. Dead Branch Swamp & Knightville Dam WMA

About a mile from Route 143, at the pallet bridge accessible from Sugar Hill Road, pull your canoe across the grass on the left and continue. Winter Wren is often heard here. About 0.5 mile farther a wider shrub swamp with small cattail patches opens up. In this area you should find Great Blue Heron, Wood Duck, Belted Kingfisher, Swamp Sparrow, and sometimes Hooded Merganser or Virginia Rail. Barred Owls sometimes call here during the day. In late summer and early fall this section usually has hundreds of Tree and Barn Swallows, with a few Northern Rough-winged, Bank, and Cliff mixed in. In late spring and late summer a few shorebirds drop in, mostly Solitary and Least Sandpipers. In spring and fall check the edges for migrating warblers, especially in the dead conifers in the southern half.

Knightville Dam Wildlife Management Area (WMA)

This big, beautiful, wild area with many breeding and migrant birds can be visited for an hour or an entire day. It connects on the north with the Hiram H. Fox WMA, Chester WMA, Indian Hollow, and eventually The Trustees of Reservations' Chesterfield Gorge. A good all-day strategy is to park a car at each end and walk all the way through.

The area is open all year to hiking but the gates are usually closed from December (after deer hunting season) to mid-April (after the Westfield River canoe races) when the valley is flooded. It would take major bushwhacking to reach good birding areas during this time. You might try the overlook on Route 112 about 0.5 mile north of the main entrance to check the valley for ducks (usually not very productive), or the ridges in April for migrating raptors (can be excellent). Check below this overlook for possible breeding Mourning Warblers.

From Dead Branch Swamp, continue west on Route 143 for 7.2 miles to Worthington Corners. Turn left (south) on Route 112 and continue 9.5 miles to the dam entrance on your left. Alternatively, from Northampton take Route 66 (West Street) 14 miles west until it ends at Route 112 in Huntington. Turn right on Route 112, and at 0.3 mile the dam entrance is on your right. Usually not very birdy, the dam is good nevertheless for Common Raven all year, Turkey Vulture, and migrating raptors in spring and fall. Osprey and Bald Eagle usually come through in good numbers.

One mile north on Route 112, just after two roads branch off to the left and you cross a stream, the dirt entrance to the main area behind the dam is on your right (not well marked, but with a yellow Army Corps of Engineers gate). This is the best place to start. You can drive (if the gate is open) 2.8 miles up the Westfield river. The roads are usually good, even just after the valley is drained, but **be careful of deep**

mud and large puddles. This is a perfect place for those who like to combine birding with bicycling on dirt roads.

From Route 112 go through the short wooded section listening for Eastern Wood-Pewee, vireos, thrushes, and warblers. When it opens up exposing the valley, immediately pull over and park next to an old road before the old dam. The open brushy area on the right usually holds breeding Cedar Waxwing, Chestnut-sided Warbler, and Indigo Bunting. Proceed to the river and a pull-off at an old dam structure. Northern Rough-winged and Cliff Swallows are present in summer. Dabbling ducks are often across the river in the shrub swamp.

Follow the road north checking small pools on the left for shorebirds (usually only Killdeer and Solitary Sandpipers), and the hillsides for migrant and breeding flycatchers, vireos, warblers, and Rose-breasted Grosbeak. Listen in this area for breeding Alder and Willow Flycatchers. Where the hillside approaches the river, look and listen for Yellow-bellied Sapsucker, Yellow-throated Vireo, and Cerulean Warbler (rare) in summer. These hillsides can be great in migration for warblers.

At 1.7 miles from the entrance turn right onto a dirt road over a cement bridge. (Going straight returns you to Route 112.) The hillside here is good for Yellow-throated Vireo, Chestnut-sided, Black-throated Blue, Black-throated Green, and Black-and-white Warblers, and American Redstart. Ruby-throated Hummingbirds feed on jewelweed in late summer. The river and stream are good for Common Merganser and Spotted Sandpiper. Continue across the bridge and stop before the road curves left. Across the river Belted Kingfisher and Northern Rough-winged Swallow nest in a dirt bank. Across the road is a small viney copse where a Black-billed Cuckoo has resided the past couple years.

Continue on this road around a corner to large weed fields, good for fall sparrows such as Lincoln's and White-crowned. The hillsides here have the same vireos and warblers mentioned earlier. Check the river again for Common Merganser, Spotted Sandpiper, Cedar Waxwing, and swallows. When you come to a yellow gate, park in the small lot on the

BARN SWALLOW

left and walk as far upriver as you like. At the gate is a large pool popular with fishermen, Great Blue Herons, Spotted Sandpipers, Belted Kingfishers, and Eastern Phoebes. The young swampy wood just north of the gate on the left is good for Least Flycatcher, Cedar Waxwing, Chestnut-sided Warbler, migrant warblers, and Purple Finch.

After more fields you veer left into woods. Just ahead on the left are beaver ponds with Swamp Sparrow and possibly Wood Duck, American Black Duck, or Hooded Merganser. On the left are small fields where Tree Swallow and Eastern Bluebird nest in the boxes. Farther north you enter deeper forest with Pileated Woodpecker, Eastern Wood-Pewee, Blue-headed Vireo, Black-throated Blue, Black-throated Green, and Black-and-white Warblers, American Redstart, Ovenbird, and Scarlet Tanager. Check along rocky streams for Winter Wren and Louisiana Waterthrush. About 1.5 miles from the gate Indian Hollow Campground is across the river.

Continuing on the west side of the river the road rises into Chester WMA and a large conifer grove where Common Raven is often found, Blackburnian Warblers sing from treetops, and Yellow-rumped Warblers forage. On your right are beaver swamps where Cedar Waxwing, Swamp and White-throated Sparrows can be found. From here north, deep woods lead into rocky coniferous woods at the impressive Chesterfield Gorge where Blackburnian Warbler and Dark-eyed Junco nest. If you parked another car here, you can return by turning left after leaving the gorge and following Ireland Street to Worthington. Take a left onto Route 112 south 1.8 miles to the northern entrance to the WMA, which leads back to the road with the concrete bridge.   *Bob Packard*

C7. Northfield

Northfield is bisected by the Connecticut River and its valley with large, narrow tracts of farmland, primarily planted in corn. Main Street (Routes 10 and 63) goes through Northfield's beautiful historic village. East of the river, the town rises to a mountainous region. The large Satan's Kingdom swamp is west of the river.

Hell's Kitchen and vicinity

From Interstate 91 take the Northfield Exit (#28); follow Route 10 north 2.3 miles; turn left on Route 142. After 1.1 miles on Route 142 turn left on Old Vernon Road. Take this road 0.7 mile, checking ponds on both sides and a small swamp on the right, to a large swamp, Hell's Kitchen, on the right (east). At 1.2 miles there is a pull-off and places to park on the left (west), marked by a sign for the Satan's Kingdom Wildlife Management Area (WMA). From here the road is unpaved, but good for another 0.4 mile to a turnaround (limited parking with a private drive on the left). Beyond that, the road becomes increasingly primitive.

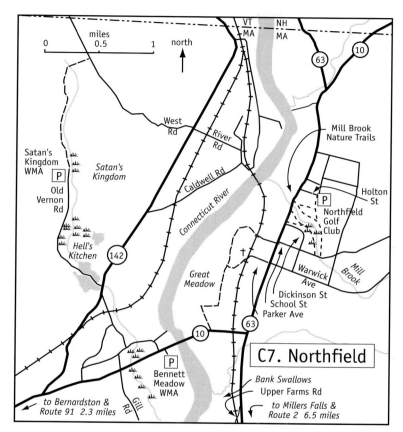

Hell's Kitchen is the largest of several connected tracts of swampland along Old Vernon Road. This area, part of Satan's Kingdom WMA, also contains large sections of upland deciduous woods. On the tops of dead trees here I have reliably found Olive-sided (migration) and Great Crested Flycatchers. Several Great Blue Heron nests are visible from the road. Red-shouldered and Broad-winged Hawks can be heard or seen here regularly.

Hell's Kitchen is productive for a variety of birds including Snow Goose (migration), American Black Duck, Hooded Merganser, Belted Kingfisher, Pileated Woodpecker, Eastern Wood-Pewee, Least Flycatcher, Northern Rough-winged and Bank Swallows, Blue-headed and Warbling Vireos, Veery, Hermit and Wood Thrushes, Northern and Louisiana Waterthrushes, Scarlet Tanager, and Swamp Sparrow.

Opposite Hell's Kitchen, a small hillside meadow with several overgrown apple trees offers a nice open area to observe Yellow-throated Vireo, Blue-gray Gnatcatcher, and Baltimore Oriole among others. Continue down this road 0.5 mile with swampland to the right and woodland to the left. Look and listen for the Yellow-bellied Sapsuckers that nest near the Satan's Kingdom WMA sign. At the end of the good road (0.4 mile from the WMA sign), listen for Louisiana Waterthrush in the spring.

Continuing down Old Vernon Road on foot or with an appropriate vehicle can be rewarding. This area has nesting Black-throated Blue and Black-throated Green Warblers, and another large snag-filled swamp on the west side, 1.0 mile from the WMA sign.

Caldwell and River Roads

Return south on Old Vernon Road, turn left (north) on Route 142 and continue for 0.7 mile. Turn right on Caldwell Road. First the road goes though a large expanse of cornfields where you can watch for Horned Lark and American Pipit. Tree, Bank, Cliff (rare) and Barn Swallows are possible here. As the road drops away from the fields, it comes to the intersection with River Road (0.9 mile from Route 142); pull off the road and start to bird. The large willow trees seem to be magnets for warblers, Warbling Vireo, Blue-gray Gnatcatcher, and Baltimore Oriole. I seem always to find my first Yellow Warbler of the year, loudly presenting himself for a mate, at this location. A shallow wetland between a raised railroad bed and the road has held Green Heron and Northern Waterthrush. Bird both sides of this short section of road to the railroad trestle and back. As the road continues along the river, the habitat on both sides is good and should be checked. Lincoln's, Swamp, and White-crowned Sparrows occur.

Bennett Meadow Wildlife Management Area

Return south on Route 142 to Route 10, turn left on Route 10, and head east 1.1 miles. Bennett Meadow is on the right (south) just before the bridge across the Connecticut River. The entrance is marked by an easily missed brown wooden "Bennett Meadow WMA" sign. Park at the bottom of the access road.

Bennett Meadow is a large cornfield bordered by wet areas with alders and large willows on the west, and a long line of locust trees along the river. This area is used for pheasant stocking and hunting in the fall. From the parking area in mid-May though mid-summer, Yellow-throated Vireos can usually be heard and sometimes seen on their nests on willow branches. Willow Flycatcher and Baltimore Oriole nest near-by. Bank Swallows are a common sight over these fields and take advantage of the tall riverbanks and other areas for nests. Farm roads run on both sides of the main field, making it accessible for walking along the perimeters. Watch for Bald Eagle perched along the river, Great Horned Owl at dawn or dusk, and breeding Eastern Kingbird, Field and Savannah Sparrows, Bobolink, and Orchard Oriole (rare).

There is a large Bank Swallow colony across the river from Bennett Meadow, in a gravel and loam bank in a farm field near Route 63 and Upper Farms Road, 0.7 mile south of the intersection of Routes 10 and 63.

Northfield Center Cemetery and the Old Dump

From the junction of Routes 10 and 63 on the east side of the Connecticut River, drive north on Main Street (Routes 10 and 63) for 0.6 mile toward the center of town. On the left, at a pedestrian crossing, is Parker Avenue, just before the IGA grocery store. Take this street a short distance to the cemetery and park either before the railroad tracks or in the cemetery itself. Walk down the road, which drops past the cemetery entrance to the area known as the Old Dump and a cattail wetland, opening to a large expanse of corn fields.

This area is an excellent spring warbler trap. From the large locust, maple, white pine, hemlock, and arbor vitae trees that surround the cemetery, to the vine-covered area of the Old Dump, to the cattail wetland, alder swamps, and cornfields, you'll find no better all-around area for birds. Blossoming, overgrown apple trees along the wet edge of the cornfields occasionally attract Orchard Orioles. The willows here invariably have Willow Flycatchers offering their "fitz-bew!" song. This section is also a good place to observe a variety of sparrows, particularly in the fall.

Generally, I start by birding the cemetery loop to search for warblers in the tall trees. This is a good area to look for breeding Red-bellied Woodpecker, Scarlet Tanager, Rose-breasted Grosbeak and Baltimore Oriole. Once back to the entrance to the cemetery, follow the road down to the Old Dump, which shows no resemblance to one now. Sumacs and alders are interspersed in this dump area with a somewhat crude path between them, and it is a good place to find Blue-winged Warbler. From the edge of the dump, scan the cattail wetland and thickets below. The embankment is a good place to look for skulking bird species; Wilson's and Canada Warblers occur most years. From the point where you entered the dump, walk down the road past the cattails on the left and alders on the right. The sound of Red-winged Blackbirds greets you here, and if you're lucky, the booming of an American Bittern. This section has been great for Wood Duck, Virginia Rail, Sora, Wilson's Snipe, swallows, and Lincoln's (migration), Swamp, and White-crowned (fall) Sparrows. In the cornfields, a left or right turn takes you along more prime bird habitat. Watch for American Kestrel, Killdeer, Willow Flycatcher, Eastern Kingbird, Horned Lark, and American Pipit (migration). The remnant of an old brook blocked by agriculture is now wetland along the east side of the fields.

Northfield Public Golf Course

Return to Main Street (Routes 10 and 63) and continue north 0.7 mile to Holton Street on the right just after a church. The entrance to the golf course, a "must bird" spot in the spring, is a short drive down Holton Street.

The parking area is under a canopy of large maple trees; the western edge of the parking lot includes thick tangles of bittersweet, lilacs, and sumacs. From the perimeter, the land drops off to a dell-like brook area which, in turn, opens into a wet meadow, perhaps the best location in Northfield to find nesting Blue-winged Warblers. The hybrid Lawrence's Warbler is a rare visitor.

From the south end of the parking lot, near the putting green, an old cart road goes down through vine thickets to a large wetland and brook known as the Millbrook Wetland Area. This area has a trail system developed and maintained by students and faculty from North-field Mount Hermon School, with a map box at the beginning of the road. The main cart path is perhaps the easiest walk, although all the trails are relatively flat. The area is mostly wooded, with the golf course visible on the left and wetland on the right. Hermit and Wood Thrushes are easy to find, and you should at least hear a pair of Pileated Woodpeckers. Marked trails branch off of this road, but if you are short on time, this abbreviated walk will still be rewarding. Black-throated Blue (less common), Black-throated Green, and Pine (common) Warblers breed. In less than a mile, the road comes to a cornfield and overgrown meadow where you can check the thickets along the edges. The meadow is reliable for Blue-winged Warbler.

This is not a loop, so you need to retrace your steps to the parking lot. If you have the time, it is worth spending a morning birding the entire trail system. Ruffed Grouse are often heard drumming along the wooded section. Solitary and Spotted Sandpipers are a good bet along the more open brook area. Chimney Swifts are a common sight overhead. Wood Ducks flush out of the stream every time I walk the trail, and mobbing American Crows signal the presence of a Great Horned Owl that usually roosts in the tall white pines. Birds likely to be encountered here also include Great Blue and Green Herons, American Woodcock, Ruby-throated Hummingbird, Belted Kingfisher, Eastern Wood-Pewee, Least Flycatcher, Blue-headed and Red-eyed Vireos, Blue-gray Gnatcatcher, Veery, Hermit and Wood Thrushes, Brown Thrasher, Nashville, Chestnut-sided, Magnolia, Yellow-rumped, Blackburnian, and Black-and-white Warblers, Ovenbird, American Redstart, Louisiana Waterthrush, Swamp Sparrow, and Indigo Bunting.

Mark Taylor

C8. Greenfield

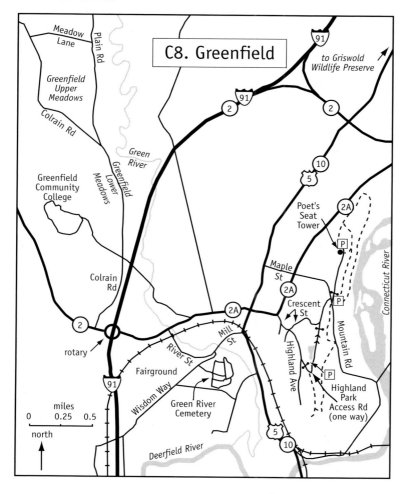

Greenfield Community College

From the I-91 Rotary, take Route 2 (the Mohawk Trail) west and immediately turn right on Colrain Road before the shopping malls; there is a sign to Greenfield Community College (GCC). The entrance to GCC is 0.6 mile on the left. Follow the driveway to the visitors' parking area. Park and walk around the campus.

The awesome habitats at GCC support a variety of migrant and nesting species. As you enter campus on your left there are some nice swampy, brushy areas. Eastern Bluebird nests in the trees in the parking lot islands. It's possible to sit in your car with bluebirds flycatching around you.

To the right of the building behind the duck pond, several paths lead into the back woods of GCC, where magic can happen! Many warblers are seen in migration, including, in recent years, Lawrence's and Cape May. Eastern Screech-Owl and Great Horned, Barred, and Northern Saw-whet Owls have all occurred. Common Nighthawks migrate by here on late August evenings.

From GCC continue north on Colrain Road (see map) searching for species of open fields.

Highland Park

Highland Pond. Highland Pond and Poet's Seat are part of the Town of Greenfield's Highland Park, a ridge bordering the Connecticut River. Return to Route 2, go east around the I-91 rotary and continue straight ahead on Route 2A into downtown Greenfield. Cross the intersection with Routes 5 and 10 and continue east 0.2 mile on Route 2A to the corner where 2A turns left. At that corner, turn right on Crescent Street. Stay on Crescent Street for 0.1 mile to a 3-road fork. Take the middle road, Highland Avenue, and continue for 0.2 mile. Bear left on the one-way Highland Park Access Road 0.2 mile to the large dirt parking lot.

Once at the parking area, Highland Pond is directly on your left. Great Crested Flycatcher and Scarlet Tanager can be seen in the canopy. Check the underbrush around the parking lot and the pond for migrating sparrows, including White-crowned.

When driving into the parking area, look to your right for a large dirt path that begins the trail system. The highest area at this south end on the ridge is Sachem Head. Paths run in front, behind, and on top of these large cliffs, home to many birds, the most exciting of which is a pair of Common Ravens that nest on the cliffs. Listen for their croaking. Late winter when they court and build nests is the most entertaining time to see the ravens.

Poet's Seat Tower. You can reach Poet's Seat on the Highland Park trails or you can drive. If you drive, continue on the one-way Highland Park Access Road until it ends at Crescent Street. Turn right on Crescent Street for 0.2 mile to Mountain Road. Turn right on Mountain Road and, almost immediately, the Poet's Seat parking area is on your left. **Caution:** this is a difficult turn at the crest of the hill; **use care when turning.** When the gate is open, you can drive to the top or you can park and walk to the tower. If you walk, you can choose the lower, deep woods trails or walk the road to the tower.

The lower path has mainly deciduous trees and supports many warbler species. Sharp-shinned and Cooper's Hawks, Eastern Screech-Owl, Great Horned Owl, Pileated Woodpecker, Scarlet Tanager, and Northern Cardinal breed. Great Crested Flycatcher nests and, because of the path's elevation, you can get awesome looks at this treetop dweller! This path is likely to be icy in winter.

The area around a radio tower on the left side of the upper trail (road) is a favorite spot for migrating warblers and thrushes. There are several spring records of Mourning Warbler, as well as Golden-winged and Cape May Warblers. The tower itself is a great place to enjoy views of the Connecticut River to the east, the Green River Valley to the west, and the Deerfield River Valley to the south. The tower is sometimes great for migrating hawks.

If you walk north to the paths beyond the tower, you do some ridge walking and enter mixed forest. Boreal Chickadee and hundreds of Common Redpolls have occurred in this area. In winter, it can be fun to walk through the roost of hundreds to thousands of crows along this ridge, although I'd suggest an umbrella!

Griswold Wildlife Preserve

An additional interesting but little explored area owned by the Town of Greenfield is the Griswold Wildlife Preserve, which includes deciduous and coniferous forest, swamp, and fields. To reach this area from the junction of Route 2A and Routes 5 and 10, go north on Routes 5 and 10 for 4.7 miles, turn right at a car dealer onto Log Plain Road for 0.6 mile, and turn left at the T onto Lampblack Road. A parking area with a trail map is 1.2 miles farther on the left. This area begs for more birders and documentation of its diverse breeding and migrant birds.

Green River Cemetery

A good, easily accessible spot for migrating song birds is the Green River Cemetery, just south of Greenfield center. See map for directions.

Zeke Jakub

C9. Turners Falls and Montague Plains
Gill, Montague

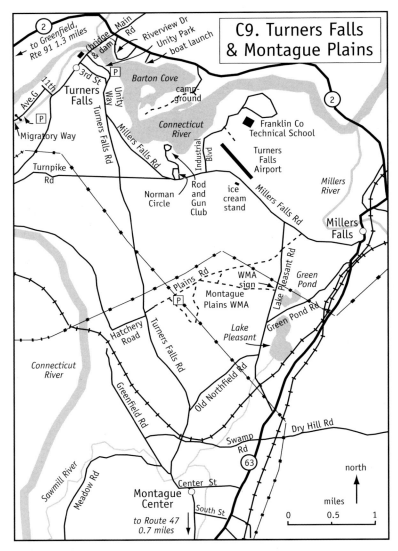

Barton Cove, Gill

Depending on the controlled water level, the Connecticut River impoundment here, behind the dam at Turners Falls, ranges from deep unbroken water to shallows with extensive mudflats. The cove is oriented almost east-west, so consider the sun for best early morning and late afternoon viewing from the sites listed below.

Just east of the bridge between Turners Falls and Gill, at the intersection of Route 2 and Main Road in Gill, is Riverview Drive. If you cross the bridge from Turners Falls, take a hard right at the end of the bridge back toward the river. After a sharp left you have an ideal view of the mouth of the cove. Riverview Drive provides access to the river and then loops back to Route 2. Turn right onto Route 2, and after about 300 yards turn right into the public boat ramp, closed to vehicles in late fall and winter, but open and busy the rest of the year. When the ramp is closed, there is room to park between the road and gate. This spot offers a good view of Barton Island, where Bald Eagles nest in a large tree. Dabbling ducks are seen mostly at or near the stump-cluttered shoreline of the island. From the boat ramp, turn right and proceed 0.25 mile to the Northeast Utilities Barton Cove Campground on the right. Follow the campground entrance road along the edge of the cove, park at the campground parking lot, and walk back for excellent views of the cove, especially in the morning with the light at your back.

The campground service road beyond the parking area runs the length of the peninsula through largely undisturbed woodland, with breeding Pileated Woodpecker, Eastern Wood-Pewee, Great Crested Flycatcher, and Pine Warbler.

In winter the cove freezes, leaving the main channel open. From January through ice-out, gulls gather in late afternoon on the ice edge. Riverview Drive near the old bridge abutment provides excellent views of mixed flocks. Iceland and Glaucous Gulls are annual, and Lesser Black-backed Gull nearly so. By late February Hooded and Common Merganser numbers build, and by early March Canvasback, Ring-necked Duck, and Common Goldeneye appear. Early April is usually the high point of spring migration here. Nearly every species of waterfowl expected on this inland flyway may appear, including Common Loon, all three local grebes, teal, Northern Shoveler, scaup, all three scoters, and Long-tailed Duck. From late April through May, Bonaparte's Gull is annual, and both Common and Black Terns are nearly so, especially in rain. All six swallow species, including an occasional Purple Martin, feed over the water.

In summer the river is used heavily for recreation; bird activity is spotty. Swallow numbers peak in August. In fall Double-crested Cormorant numbers build, with Great Cormorant occasional. Red-throated Loon, Black Scoter, and American Coot are more likely in fall. By late September, south-bound ducks appear. In October geese arrive and gulls trickle in.

Turners Falls

Near the dam in Turners Falls, the Great Falls Discovery Center, due to be fully open in 2004, and the nearby office of the S.O. Conte National Fish and Wildlife Refuge have live video feed from the Bald Eagle nest on Barton Island and natural history information. Unity Park in Turners Falls provides another view of Barton Cove. In downtown Turners Falls, ornamental fruit trees along Avenue A (the main street in town) and 3rd through 6th Streets off Avenue A sometimes attract large flocks of waxwings, including Bohemian Waxwings in invasion years.

Migratory Way and the Power Canal. From the Great Falls Visitors Center, drive south on the main street (Avenue A) for 0.7 mile. Turn right on 11th Street, cross the power canal, and turn left on Avenue G. Avenue G ends at a small park and the gated Migratory Way, which leads to the generating plant and the USGS Research Facility. The gate is usually open only on weekdays, but there is always parking to the left of the gate. This brief detour can be rewarding. A variety of waterfowl including Common Loon, Northern Pintail, Canvasback, Common Goldeneye, Hooded Merganser, and American Coot may be found in the canal. The habitat bordering the canal can harbor spring and fall migrants.

Turners Falls Rod and Gun Club. Return on Avenue A to the center of town (0.5 mile) and turn right (east) on 3rd Street. Continue on 3rd Street as it goes uphill and becomes Unity Way. Just after the stop sign (0.7 mile from Avenue A), bear left on Millers Falls Road (follow the sign to the airport). Turn left on Norman Circle (2 miles from Avenue A). A small brown and yellow "Turners Falls Rod and Gun" sign is at the corner. Go straight on Norman Circle and then downhill to the clubhouse area. Bear right to the water near the gravel boat launch.

The Rod and Gun Club is on the Connecticut River on the other side of the peninsula from Barton Cove. This area, strongly affected by the downstream dam and the upstream pump storage station, varies from unbroken water to acres of mudflats, and it can do so as fast as tidal changes at the seashore. Great Blue Heron and dabbling ducks occur here especially in the extensive shallow to the right, known as Deep Hole. Heavy rains occasionally ground many migrating shorebirds. The edge of the clubhouse lawn and the gravel boat landing provide views of the entire area. Birders should note that this location is **private property;** we are allowed to bird here with the club's permission. **Please be very considerate; park on gravel and do not block the boat ramp.**

The main channel attracts Bufflehead, all three mergansers, and every fall one or more tight flocks of Black Scoter. Check trees for Osprey, Bald

Eagle, and Pileated Woodpecker. Check the brush in front of the club for sparrows; Lincoln's and White-crowned are regular in fall. The ravine along the access road often hosts Louisiana Waterthrush in spring. The trees around the grounds may host a migration wave in May.

Turners Falls Airport. From the Rod and Gun Club go back to Millers Falls Road and turn left (east). After about 500 yards turn left onto Industrial Boulevard, which goes past the west end of the airport runway. Where a sand road turns onto airport property just past the runway, pull in and park on the side. Most of the grounds north of the runway away from the hangars can be reached on foot from here. For a second view of the airport, return to Millers Falls Road and go left a short distance to the main airport entrance, opposite an ice cream stand. Drive to the edge of the paved area and park.

Two cautions: First, please **stay on the well-marked access road** or in the parking lots. Grassland species nest in grass, and you could step on a well-camouflaged nest without knowing it. Foxes are common here; drawing attention to a nest could lead to predation of these increasingly uncommon birds. Secondly, do not go on or near the runway or otherwise interfere with airport operation. Birders are allowed on airport grounds only as long as they **do not become a nuisance or hazard.**

The airport features about ten nesting Grasshopper Sparrow pairs; the males sing from scattered saplings rising out of the bluestem grass or from runway lights and signs. Follow the sand track to the model airplane area by the small building tucked off in the northeast corner of the grounds. Vesper Sparrow is most reliably found singing from the edge of the adjacent tree belt. Savannah Sparrow may be found closer to the runway. Killdeer nest in open gravel on the edge of the parking lot and on any large patches of exposed earth. One or two pairs of Horned Lark nest here.

From early spring into summer American Woodcocks perform their spiraling courtship display over fields near the surrounding trees. In May they are joined after dark by Whip-poor-wills calling loudly from adjacent pine-oak forest. Upland Sandpiper occasionally occurs in spring and fall, and Northern Shrike can occur in winter.   *Mark Fairbrother*

Montague Plains

The Montague Plains is a pitch pine and scrub oak sand plain of nearly 2,000 acres. In the past, fires started by passing trains maintained this habitat. With diesel engines and increased fire suppression, the area is succeeding to a mixed species forest with more deciduous and fewer coniferous trees.

GRASSHOPPER SPARROW

From the Turners Falls Airport, return to Millers Falls Road, continue left (east) 1.2 miles from Industrial Boulevard. Turn right on Lake Pleasant Road to the Montague Plains Wildlife Management Area (WMA) sign 0.8 mile on the right. **The road through the Plains is unpaved and not maintained and should be traveled with considerable caution.**

If Plains Road is passable, one can enter at either end and drive slowly, listening for birds and stopping periodically. Additional portions of the area can be traversed on foot along side roads and a powerline. Breeding species routinely expected are American Woodcock, Whip-poor-will, Hermit Thrush, Pine and Prairie Warblers, Eastern Towhee, and Field Sparrow. In summer a flight of Great Blue Herons occurs late in the day, apparently to a rookery to the northeast. On at least two occasions in recent years, Chuck-will's-widow has been heard. In years when Gypsy Moth numbers are high, the area can be good for cuckoos. In winter finch invasion years, watch for Purple Finch, both crossbill species, and lesser numbers of Pine and Evening Grosbeaks.

The Whip-poor-will population is one of the main attractions, with numbers often exceeding 30-50 individuals. The Whip-poor-wills can be heard from the main roads surrounding the Plains. Prior to the recent change in ownership, the interior areas of the Plains were off-limits after dark, but current signs do not indicate such restrictions.

An area adjacent to the Plains, where access is allowed after dark, is Green Pond Road, 0.4 mile south of the WMA sign on the opposite side of Lake Pleasant Road (1.0 mile north of the junction of Lake Pleasant

Road and Route 63). Take Green Pond Road to the bottom of the hill (0.2 mile) to where the road passes between two ponds. The pond on the left is clearly visible from the road. This locale is one of the areas where Chuck-will's-widow has been heard. The odd sheep-like calls of Fowler's toads contribute to the chorus here.   *Al Richards*

C10. Wendell

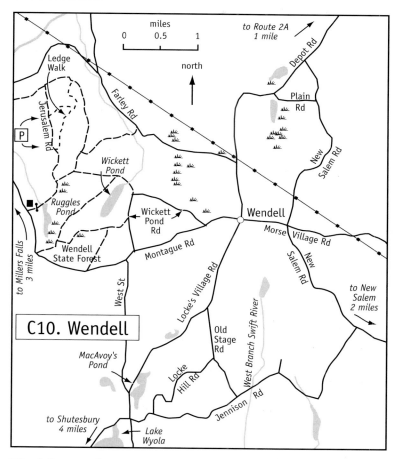

Wendell, at an elevation of 800 to 1200 feet, is over 90 percent forest, ranging from hemlock swamps to hardwood-studded dry hillsides. White pine, oaks, and maples prevail. Approximately one third of the town is state forest land. If you like the mystery of hidden ponds, wetlands, and other beautiful tucked-away places far from the sound of traffic, you will find Wendell enchanting.

All main roads into Wendell eventually lead to its center, which has the largest section of open land in town and a chance to view birds atypical of the town as a whole such as Killdeer, Barn Swallow, Northern Cardinal, and House Finch. In the fields around the town center you might hear American Woodcock courting on a spring evening, or watch Bobolinks establishing territory. Just south of the town center on Lockes Village Road is the Wendell Country Store and Post Office, a good place to ask for directions or make phone calls.

Check roadside wetlands throughout Wendell. MacAvoy's Pond on the east side of Lockes Village Road as you enter the town from Shutesbury can be great in spring for Wood Duck, American Black Duck, Green-winged Teal, Bufflehead, Common Goldeneye, and Hooded and Common Mergansers. At the edges of ponds and wetlands you may find Solitary or Spotted Sandpiper in spring and especially in autumn.

Check woodlands throughout the town for breeding Red-shouldered Hawk, Wild Turkey, Yellow-bellied Sapsucker, Great Crested Flycatcher, Blue-headed Vireo, Brown Creeper, Winter Wren, Veery, and White-throated Sparrow. Winter offers a chance to focus on residents like Pileated Woodpecker, Common Raven, and Red-breasted Nuthatch, or on winter visitors such as Golden-crowned Kinglet and irruptive winter finches.

Wendell State Forest Ledge Walk

The Ledge Walk, with mountain laurel, oaks, maples, beech, hemlock, and white pine, is a small section of the Metacomet-Monadnock (M-M) Trail that passes through Wendell State Forest (SF). From the center of town take Montague Road west 3.6 miles to the Wendell SF main entrance. Walk or drive 0.6 mile down the hill, past Ruggles Pond (with good trails), and uphill again into the woods. Bear left on Jerusalem Road. Watch for the blue triangular markers and white blazes on the trees marking the M-M Trail on the east side of Jerusalem Road.

The trail runs parallel to Jerusalem Road along a ridgetop and offers two beautiful overlooks. It loops back down to Jerusalem Road whether you follow the trail northward toward the overlooks or southward into hemlocks. Black-throated Blue and Canada Warblers, and Eastern Towhee are usually easy to find along this trail. Ruffed Grouse occurs in the woods. The overlooks offer wonderful views and a chance to observe birds such as Scarlet Tanager at and above treetop level.

Marcy Marchello

C11. Leverett and Atkins Reservoir

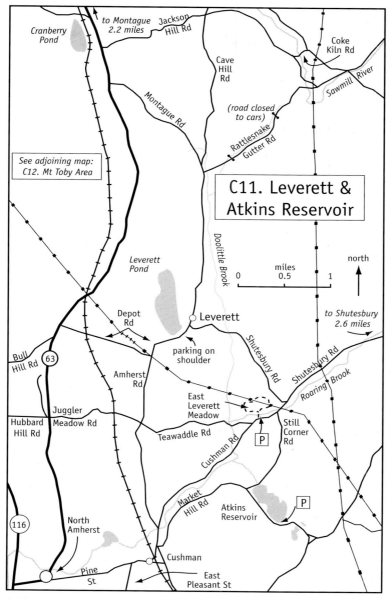

C11. Leverett & Atkins Reservoir

to Montague 2.2 miles

Cranberry Pond

Jackson Hill Rd

Coke Kiln Rd

Cave Hill Rd

Sawmill River

Montague Rd

(road closed to cars)

Rattlesnake Gutter Rd

See adjoining map: C12. Mt Toby Area

Doolittle Brook

Leverett Pond

miles
0   0.5   1

north

Depot Rd

Leverett

to Shutesbury 2.6 miles

Bull Hill Rd (63)

parking on shoulder

Shutesbury Rd

Amherst Rd

East Leverett Meadow

Roaring Brook

Juggler Meadow Rd

Hubbard Hill Rd

Still Corner Rd

Teawaddle Rd

P

Cushman Rd

(116)

North Amherst

Market Hill Rd

Atkins Reservoir

P

Cushman

Pine St

East Pleasant St

Rattlesnake Gutter, Leverett

From the corner of Route 63 and Montague Road (6 miles north of

WINTER WREN

North Amherst), turn right (east) on Montague Road, go 1.4 miles, and turn left on Rattlesnake Gutter Road. The road beyond the houses is closed to cars. Park and walk beside the steep gorge with its red maples, hemlock, and mountain laurel. Much of the land along the gorge is preserved by the Rattlesnake Gutter Trust.

Although a small stream now runs through the gorge, it was water overflowing from a prehistoric glacial lake that formed this mini-canyon.

The short, scenic walk through Rattlesnake Gutter can be very birdy. Pileated Woodpecker, Winter Wren, and Veery nest here and Common Raven nests in the cliffs near the upper end of the gorge. You can find Red-breasted Nuthatch, Golden-crowned Kinglet and Dark-eyed Junco among the hemlocks. Black-throated Blue Warbler frequents dense forest understory of mountain laurel. Northern Saw-whet Owl and Acadian Flycatcher have been found. Watch for pink moccasin flower and red trillium in the spring. At the top of the gutter in the spring, birding along the road bearing to the left up to Coke Kiln Road may produce more thrushes and warblers.   *Eric Marcum*

Leverett Pond

Return to Montague Road, turn left and continue 1.7 miles to the center of Leverett (town hall, church, and post office). Bear right on Depot Road. In 0.1 mile you will come to the public access to the pond. Pull completely off the road.

This picturesque 33-acre lake, surrounded by low, wooded hills, attracts many migrants and a variety of nesters. The south end of the pond, the best area for birding, offers the only public access. Although binoculars will do, a scope or canoe is helpful. Check the tall trees straight across the water from the path for herons, Osprey, and Belted Kingfisher.

Visitors in spring and fall include Ring-necked Duck, Bufflehead, Hooded and Common Mergansers, and an occasional Common Loon, Pied-billed Grebe, or Double-crested Cormorant. The waterfowl that use Leverett Pond often also use Atkins Reservoir, so if boaters flush birds here you might find them a few minutes later at Atkins Reservoir (see directions below). Migrant shorebirds include Killdeer, yellowlegs, and Solitary Sandpiper. Bald Eagles visit occasionally.

The heavy aquatic vegetation and cattail marsh support a variety of nesting birds. Virginia Rail and Sora have been found. Great Blue and Green Heron occur frequently. Wood Duck is resident most of the year. American Bittern, Purple Gallinule (1985), Common Moorhen (1993), and Marsh Wren have occurred.

Check the trees and shrubs near the entrance for Pileated Woodpecker, Ruby-crowned Kinglet (migration), Cedar Waxwing, Eastern Towhee, Rose-breasted Grosbeak, and Baltimore Oriole. Rusty Blackbirds can be seen in the fall.   *Barbara Alfange*

East Leverett Meadow

From Leverett Pond, continue on Depot Road around a sharp left-hand corner. When Depot Road goes right, continue straight ahead on Amherst Road 1.3 miles to the intersection with Teawaddle and Juggler Meadow Roads. Turn left on Teawaddle. When it ends (1.2 miles from the intersection), turn left (north) on East Leverett Road for 0.1 mile to the pines on the left. There is a gravel parking area on the left (north) side of the road. Pull completely off this busy road. The Rattlesnake Gutter Trust recently acquired this wonderful habitat.

The trail begins in a young stand of old-field pine, crosses Roaring Brook, and continues into the meadow. Before entering the meadow, check the edges, especially to the left (west) along the floodplain. Once into the meadow please stay on the path around the meadow to protect nesting species and vegetation. There is often a beaver pond directly across the meadow from the bridge and an old orchard along the northeast corner.

In winter the meadow's edges shelter mixed flocks, with the largest concentrations in the first old-field pine area and the orchard on the north edge. Cedar Waxwings and Golden-crowned Kinglets sometimes join these flocks. American Tree, Song, and White-throated Sparrows move through the shrubs. Northern Shrike occurs occasionally.

In migration, birds are everywhere. The shrubby areas host Black-billed Cuckoo and Fox Sparrow in season. Philadelphia Vireo and Northern Waterthrush have been seen at the pond. Killdeer, huge numbers of American Robins, and occasional Eastern Meadowlarks are seen in the meadows. American Woodcocks display on the south edge of the meadow, although on warm April nights their peenting is almost drowned out by the peeper and wood frog chorus. In late August just after sunset, the meadow is a good place to watch Common Nighthawks swoop for food as they fly south.

The best-known breeding birds are the 7+ male and 14+ female Bobolinks (western half of the meadow). The edges provide homes for Ruby-throated Hummingbird, Eastern Wood-Pewee, Willow and Least Flycatchers, Cedar Waxwing, and Field Sparrow. Beaver pond and orchard nesters include Eastern Phoebe, Eastern Kingbird, Warbling Vireo, Blue-winged Warbler, Louisiana Waterthrush, Rose-breasted Grosbeak, and Baltimore Oriole. Green Heron, Wood Duck, and Belted Kingfisher visit the pond daily.   *Mary Alice Wilson*

Atkins Reservoir, Amherst, Shutesbury

From East Leverett Meadow, continue east 0.1 mile to a sharp right turn on Still Corner Road. Continue on this road 1 mile over the dam until it ends at Market Hill Road. The reservoir will be on your left.

Alternatively, from downtown Amherst take East Pleasant Street northeast until it ends at Pine Street. Turn right and continue on Pine Street as it turns sharply to the left and crosses the railroad tracks. Just beyond the tracks, turn right onto Market Hill Road. Continue up Market Hill 1.3 miles to the reservoir.

Atkins Reservoir, on the Amherst-Shutesbury line, is part of the Amherst water system. In spring and fall, when the water is low, Killdeer and several species of sandpipers occur. Great Blue Herons visit frequently, and migrating Osprey often linger for a day or two. In late August, watch at dusk for dozens to hundreds of graceful Common Nighthawks moving southward.

Waterfowl numbers can be good, especially in spring. In fall, the DPW sets off charges when flocks of Canada Geese settle, which also keep other waterfowl away. Migrating Pied-billed Grebe, Wood, American Black, and Ring-necked Ducks, Bufflehead, Common Goldeneye, and Hooded and Common Mergansers regularly use the reservoir. Common Loon, American Wigeon, Green-winged Teal, and both scaup are seen less frequently. Occasionally, Horned Grebe, Long-tailed Duck, Red-breasted Merganser, or a flock of Black Scoters turn up. A scope is helpful.

Just beyond the earth dike at the east end of the reservoir is a scrubby area with white pine; beyond this are two ponds worth checking. A Common Moorhen was found here one September.

In spring, waves of songbirds can be found along Market Hill Road. Some of the species known to nest in the area include Cooper's Hawk, Northern Goshawk, Red-shouldered and Broad-winged Hawks, Barred and Northern Saw-whet Owls, Pileated Woodpecker, and a number of songbirds including Blackburnian Warbler and Louisiana Waterthrush. Other birds of interest that have been found here are Olive-sided Fly-catcher, Orange-crowned Warbler, Fox Sparrow (numerous at times), and both crossbills.

Jan Ortiz

C12. Mount Toby Area
Leverett, Sunderland

See map C12. Mt Toby Area

Mount Toby is a large area of mostly unbroken woods with cliffs, ravines, waterfalls, occasional clearings and experimental clearcuts, and adjacent farmland. It has a great variety of ferns, flowering plants, and herptiles. The more than 700 plant species recorded here include many rare and vulnerable flowering plants such as ginseng and climbing fumitory, and ferns like narrow-leaved spleenwort, Goldie's fern, slender cliffbrake, wall rue, and walking fern.

Much of the mountain and surrounding farmland are public, managed by the University of Massachusetts, the State Department of Environmental Management, and the State Division of Fisheries and Wildlife. The southern end of Mount Toby, however, is mostly privately owned. The Robert Frost Trail (RFT) crosses private lands by permission of the owners, and various side paths and woods roads are also in regular use as trails.

Breeding birds in Mount Toby's woods include Sharp-shinned Hawk, Ruffed Grouse, Wild Turkey, Eastern Screech-Owl, Great Horned and Barred Owls, Yellow-bellied Sapsucker, Pileated Woodpecker, Eastern Wood-Pewee, Great Crested Flycatcher, Red-breasted Nuthatch, Brown Creeper, and Veery. Other species are noted at specific locations below.

From North Amherst center, take Route 63 north 6.5 miles. Turn left (west) on Reservoir Road just past the Leverett/Sunderland town line. (This is a dirt road; the only sign says Road Not Maintained in Winter.) Go down the road, **use caution crossing the railroad tracks (this is an active line),** and continue to Cranberry Pond on the left. The road then goes uphill, becomes paved and shortly there will be a white building on the left and just beyond it a parking area and information kiosk.

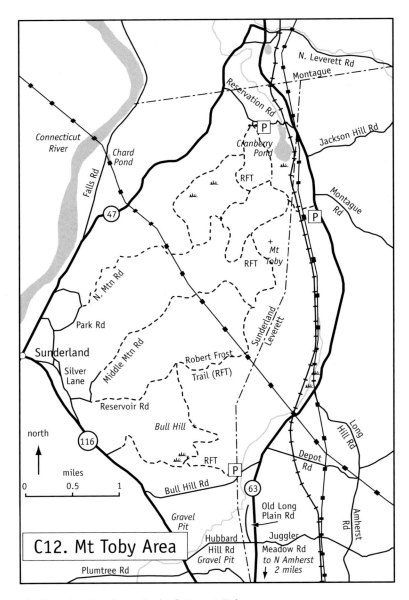

Birding the Northern End of Mount Toby

Cranberry Pond is good in migration for Pied-billed Grebe, Common Goldeneye, Common Merganser, Osprey, and Least Sandpiper. Check the wet seeps and thickets southwest of the pond for vireos and warblers.

The Robert Frost Trail enters Mount Toby at Reservation Road west of Cranberry Pond at the maintenance building and parking lot. It leads through excellent deep-woods birding, then joins the brushy electric line to the summit fire tower. There are a number of shorter trails leading off the old carriage road near the parking lot.

Birding the Eastern Slopes

A well-known trail begins at the meditation center on Route 63 (3.0 miles north of Bull Hill Road and just north of a small graveyard), crosses high tension lines and the railroad, and ascends steeply past waterfalls and conglomerate cliffs to a woods road that joins the RFT higher up the mountain. Patches of calcareous bedrock here have one of the region's best collection of spring wildflowers and old growth trees. On the power line cut Prairie Warbler, Field Sparrow, and Indigo Bunting breed. Blue-headed Vireo, Hermit Thrush, Magnolia, Black-throated Blue, Black-throated Green, and Blackburnian Warblers breed elsewhere along this trail.

Birding the Southern End of Mount Toby and the Delta

The Robert Frost Trail leaves for a five-mile ascent to the summit from a small parking area on the north side of Bull Hill Road at another Leverett/Sunderland town line (0.9 mile east of the Bull Hill/Route 116 junction). This route passes through hemlock groves, an extensive thicket of mountain laurel, birch and witch hazel, two ridgetop plateaus of oak-hickory, and a majestic park-like stand of old hemlock, sugar maple, and black birch below the ruins of an old cabin.

Bull Hill Road, especially the open area in Sunderland, has excellent year-round birding. In spring look for soaring Cooper's Hawk, Red-tailed Hawk, and Common Raven, which nest nearby. (Please do not disturb the raven nest on the cliffs.) Eastern Bluebirds nest along the road. Tree, Bank and Barn Swallow zip over the fields. Nesting Vesper Sparrows and American Kestrels perch on the wires along the road; Savannah Sparrows often sit on the fences. Listen for Blue-winged Warbler and Indigo Bunting in spring and summer. Over fifty species of butterflies have been found here.

In winter, check the feeder at #100. The birder who lives here ensures that any visiting Common or Hoary Redpolls, Pine Siskins, or unusual sparrows find enough to eat. Flocks of several hundred Snow Buntings have occurred in the fields across the road. Scan the usual Horned Lark flocks for Lapland Longspur. These fields have also harbored Northern Harrier, Rough-legged Hawk, and Northern Shrike.

Pete Westover

Hubbard Hill Road

Like Bull Hill Road one mile to the north, Hubbard Hill Road starts at the base of a delta of glacial Lake Hitchcock (Route 116), and climbs steeply up the side of the old delta to the flat top (Route 63). The Hubbard Hill Road area has a mix of scrubby, invasive species.

There is a Hubbard Hill sign at the Route 116 junction (1 mile south of Bull Hill Road, 5.1 miles north of the Route 116/Route 9 junction in Hadley). At the Route 63 end of Hubbard Hill Road in Leverett (0.8 mile south of Bull Hill, 1.9 miles north of North Amherst center), the street sign is for Long Plain Road, a paved road that immediately turns north. To get on Hubbard Hill from Route 63, drive straight ahead onto the dirt road, which becomes Hubbard Hill Road at another Leverett/Sunderland town line.

Two cautions: 1) Hubbard Hill is a dirt road not maintained in winter. Do not drive it in winter or early spring. 2) This area is an active gravel pit. Respect No Trespassing signs and stay on the public road.

Hubbard Hill is always interesting. American Woodcock display at dusk from mid-March to mid-May. In late spring and summer Brown Thrasher, Prairie Warbler, and Indigo Bunting nest in years when there are shrubs, while Great Blue Herons commute overhead between nests in Leverett and fish hatcheries along the lower edge of the delta. The most exciting fall spectacle was the night migrating Monarch Butterflies roosted in a tree at the east end of the road. In winter one can often see a Northern Shrike and sometimes, in late afternoon, hundreds of American Robins heading for a winter roost near Bull Hill Road.   *Mary Alice Wilson*

C13. Sunderland and Deerfield

Mount Sugarloaf, Deerfield

From the junction of Routes 47 and 116 at the traffic light in the center of Sunderland, take Route 116 west across the Connecticut River into Deerfield. After 0.8 mile turn right on Sugarloaf Street. The gated entrance to Mount Sugarloaf State Reservation is immediately on your right. When the gate is closed, park outside the gate and walk up the road or adjacent trails.

The summit road leads steeply to a picnic area and observation tower with wonderful views of the Berkshires and the Connecticut Valley. Oaks prevail along the ridge, while mixed hardwoods cover the slopes. There are shrubby black cherry and open lawn at the summit park and steep traprock cliffs on the mountain's east face. Pileated Woodpecker,

Hermit Thrush, Worm-eating Warbler, Scarlet Tanager, Dark-eyed Junco, and Rose-breasted Grosbeak breed and can be encountered along the road. The observation tower, excellent for spring hawk-watching, allows good looks at hawks following the river valley. Common Ravens breed on the cliff (visible from River Road).

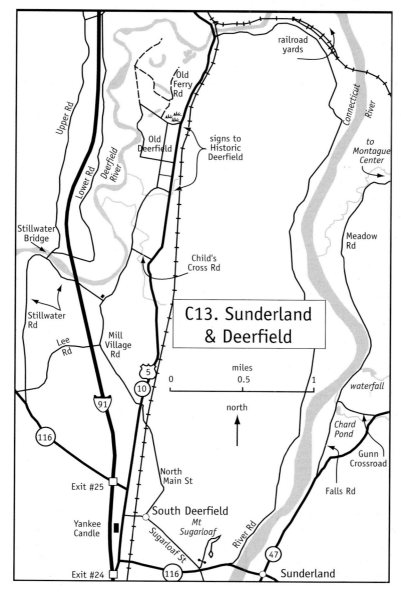

SNOW GOOSE

South Deerfield to Old Deerfield

Return to Route 116 and continue right (west) 1.0 mile to the junction with Routes 5 and 10. Just before the junction, there is an inconspicuous road to the right leading to Tri-town Beach (see map C14. Whately) which is worth checking for migrating waterfowl. In recent years large flocks of Canada Geese have been accompanied by the occasional Snow Goose or Brant. Return to the junction and turn right (north) on Route 5 and 10 and continue 2 miles. Turn left on Mill Village Road through agricultural land, which often has flocks of blackbirds in the spring and Horned Larks in fall and winter. Snow Bunting and Lapland Longspur are possible in winter. At 0.9 mile Wild Turkeys frequently feed in a field opposite Lee Road. As the road enters a dell, check the hemlock stand for nuthatches and Golden-crowned Kinglet. Common Redpoll is possible in invasion years.

Turn left near a brick pump house on the left (1.5 miles from Routes 5 and 10) onto Stillwater Road. A calf-feeding area here sometimes has flocks of blackbirds and, if there is sufficient water during migrations, Solitary, Spotted, Semipalmated, Least and Pectoral Sandpipers. Continue on Stillwater Road 0.9 mile to the Stillwater Bridge. There is parking just before the bridge; be sure to hide valuables and lock your car. In spring this area offers a variety of woodland migrants. Cerulean Warbler has been found here. Much of the canopy is at eye-level from the bridge, making viewing easy.

Return to Mill Village Road. Turn left (north), passing a large dairy barn on the right. Check fields as you drive north for migrating sparrows and warblers and, in winter, for raptors, Northern Flicker, Eastern Bluebird, and American Robin. In winter, check the nursery on your right. In spring and summer check the marsh as you go uphill just before the village of Old Deerfield.

Old Deerfield: Marsh and Fields

At 1.7 miles from Stillwater Road, you enter the village of Old Deerfield at the south end of The Street, also known as Old Main Street. It has no street signs and runs through beautiful Old Deerfield.

Drive the length of The Street to the T. Turn right (east) to the marsh on your left (north).

Alternatively, from Sunderland Center, take Route 116 to the junction with Routes 5 and 10 (1.7 miles). Turn right (north) on 5 and 10 and continue 6.2 miles to the second (northern) entrance to Old Deerfield. There is a sign for Historic Deerfield, but no street sign. Turn left (west). The marsh is immediately on the right (north).

Pull completely off the road. This cattail-sedge marsh is a haven for American Bittern, Virginia Rail, Willow Flycatcher, Warbling Vireo, and Swamp Sparrow in spring and summer, and for many migrants in spring and fall.

From the marsh (see map) head west, bear right (north) and then, at a fork in the road, bear right again. Check the playing fields in spring, fall, and winter. When you reach the end of the paved road, be sure the farm road is passable. If not, park and walk. Continue to the tobacco barns where you can pull well off the road. Throughout this area please respect farmers' fields and **do not block access for tractors and trucks.**

In early spring, if there is sufficient water, these fields provide stopover and feeding areas for migrant waterfowl and shorebirds. Large blackbird flocks often use this area and have included Yellow-headed with the more expected Red-winged and Rusty Blackbirds and Brown-headed Cowbird. In fall after harvest, the area provides habitat for American Golden-Plover, American Pipit, and sometimes Black-bellied Plover, and Upland and Buff-breasted Sandpipers.

South of the tobacco barns on the west side of the road is a large slough; in fall its borders host Savannah, Song, Lincoln's, Swamp, White-throated, White-crowned, and occasionally Vesper Sparrows. The slough may hold Great Blue and Green Herons, Wood Duck, Green-winged Teal, and sometimes Pied-billed Grebe. If the water is low, exposed edges may entice shorebirds. In the fall if the water is extremely low, an overgrown depression may be the only vestige of the slough.

Return to the fork in the road and turn right (west). Continue (0.2 mile) to two sloughs, one on either side of the road. These sloughs often have large numbers of up to five species of swallows in early spring and late summer. Green Herons and Black-crowned Night-Herons sometimes feed in late summer.

Migrant raptors, including Merlin and Peregrine Falcons, may pass through this area. In late fall the fields may have flocks of Horned Larks and Snow Buntings, with lesser numbers of Lapland Longspurs, feeding on freshly spread manure.

Falls Road, Sunderland

From the junction of Routes 116 and 47 (1.8 miles east of Routes 5 and 10) in the center of Sunderland, head north on Route 47 for 1.4 miles. Bear left on Falls Road. Check the Falls Road fields for wintering Eastern Bluebirds. In winter, spring, and fall, Dark-eyed Juncos and other sparrows often flush from the roadside.

At 0.9 mile from the start of Falls Road, pull completely off the road before or beyond Chard Pond. The pond and the area bordering a dirt road along the pond's eastern edge are posted "no trespassing," but Falls Road and Gunn Crossing are public roads and can be used to observe breeders, including Chestnut-sided Warbler, American Redstart, Louisiana Waterthrush, Scarlet Tanager, Rose-breasted Grosbeak, and a variety of spring migrants.

Walk north along Falls Road for a half mile to pretty Whitmore's Falls on the right and a vista of the Connecticut River on the left. Yellow-throated Vireo is often found in breeding season near the falls. The river offers gulls and ducks in winter and spring, and, if one is lucky, a perched Bald Eagle.

The area between Chard Pond and Whitmore's Falls has a bountiful display of early spring wildflowers such as bloodroot, trillium, Dutchman's breeches, and columbine. In winter, the area hosts Red-bellied and Pileated Woodpeckers (both nest), Winter Wren, Golden-crowned Kinglet, and many sparrows.

From Chard Pond, you can continue north; Falls Road becomes Meadow Road in Montague and continues through more fields toward Montague Center. Or you can return along Falls Road to Route 47 and Sunderland center.   *Al Richards*

C14. Whately

For a good birding tour of Whately, start in the center of Sunderland (intersection of Routes 116 and 47). Take Route 116 west. As soon as you cross over the Connecticut River, turn left (south) on River Road.

For the first section of the tour, take River Road south 2.2 miles to the second right onto Straits Road; go 0.4 mile and right again on Long Plain Road for 0.5 mile. River and Long Plain Roads have some of the biggest skies in the Valley, with open fields and skeins of Canada Goose and occasionally Snow Goose overhead in spring and fall, Horned Lark, Snow Bunting, and sometimes Lapland Longspur in the winter. Vesper and Savannah Sparrows nest; Killdeer and Eastern Bluebird are common; and American and Fowler's toads can be heard.

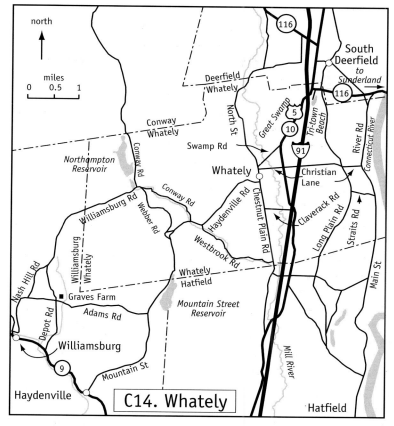

north

miles
0 0.5 1

116

Deerfield
Whately

South
Deerfield
to
Sunderland

116

Conway
Whately

North St

Great Swamp

5

Tri-town
Beach

River Rd

Connecticut River

Northampton
Reservoir

Swamp Rd

10

91

Conway Rd

Whately

Christian
Lane

Williamsburg Rd

Webber Rd

Conway Rd

Haydenville Rd

Chestnut Plain Rd

Claverack Rd

Long Plain Rd

Straits Rd

Nash Hill Rd

Williamsburg
Whately

Westbrook Rd

Main St

Whately
Hatfield

Graves Farm

Depot Rd

Adams Rd

Mountain Street
Reservoir

Williamsburg

9

Mountain St

Mill River

Haydenville

C14. Whately

Hatfield

Take a left from Long Plain Road onto Christian Lane, continue 1.6 miles over Route 91, across Routes 5 and 10 and up a steep hill to a right on North Street. North Street has grassland, marsh, and edge habitat, fading into Whately Great Swamp to the east, with black gum and swamp white oak. To the right (east) of North Street, the Great Swamp (hard to penetrate) is one of the biggest unbroken wooded wetlands in the Valley. The area, some of which has recently come to the Massachusetts Division of Fisheries and Wildlife, has not yet been ornithologically well studied but should be ideal for Red-shouldered Hawk, Barred Owl, Warbling Vireo, Northern Waterthrush, and Swamp Sparrow.

A stop anywhere along North Street produces plenty of warblers in migration. The fields are good for an occasional Wilson's Snipe, American Woodcock, swallows, Bobolink, and Eastern Meadowlark. American Kestrels and a few Virginia Rails occur. Continue birding along the road to the Deerfield town line.

Double back on North Street to the town center (2.4 miles). Turn right at the Whately Inn onto Haydenville Road and continue 1.5 miles to a left on Westbrook Road which follows a beautiful rocky trout stream through a hemlock ravine. Look for Belted Kingfisher, Winter Wren, and Louisiana Waterthrush. Where the road runs through open country, Red-Bellied Woodpecker and Cedar Waxwing are likely.

Backtrack to Haydenville Road and continue on to Webber Road 0.8 mile on the right and the Northampton Reservoir (an additional 1.6 miles). Webber Road traverses coniferous and hardwood forest and successional openings. Look for Least Flycatcher, Red-breasted Nuthatch, Black-throated Blue and Pine Warblers, and Ovenbird nesting in deep woods. Openings produce Brown Thrasher, Blue-winged and Chestnut-sided Warblers, and Eastern Towhee. The dike of the Northampton Reservoir, visible from the northern part of Conway Road, has concentrations of Tree, Cliff, and Barn Swallows in migration. Also during migration, the small pond below the dam often has Ringed-necked Duck, Bufflehead, and Hooded and Common Mergansers. *Pete Westover*

C15. Hatfield

See map C15a. Hatfield & Hadley (south)

In Hatfield's floodplain fields and oxbows, April is best for waterfowl, May for other spring migrants, and August through October for fall migrants, starting with shorebirds. Winter is good for Horned Lark, Snow Bunting and, in the right years, Rough-legged Hawk, Northern Shrike, and redpolls. Hatfield is a good place for Eastern Screech-Owl in any open woodland near water.

Hatfield is best approached from Route 5 and I-91 just north of Northampton (Exit 21 from I-91). Elm Street runs east from Route 5. It becomes Maple Street 1.5 miles east of I-91 just after the Mill River and in another 0.4 mile, at a left-hand turn, it becomes Main Street. Several roads lead right from Elm and Maple toward the floodplain, extensive flat farmland similar to the East Meadows in Northampton. Main Street, which becomes River Road at the Whately town line, runs 3.3 miles north of town through riparian woodland, swamp, marsh, and farmland.

Just 0.2 mile east of the I-91 northbound exit onto Elm Street is Elm Court, a right turn off Elm Street, the first access to the floodplain fields bordered on the south by the Connecticut River and dissected by a meandering Mill River. Elm Court runs back toward I-91 past a small cemetery on the left 0.2 mile from Elm Street. To the left, Little Neponsett Road (dirt road) runs along the far (west) side of the cemetery and down onto the lower floodplain known as Little Neponsett. In April this is often blocked by floodwaters. A walk to the edge of the water can give views of Wood Ducks, Hooded Mergansers, and other waterfowl.

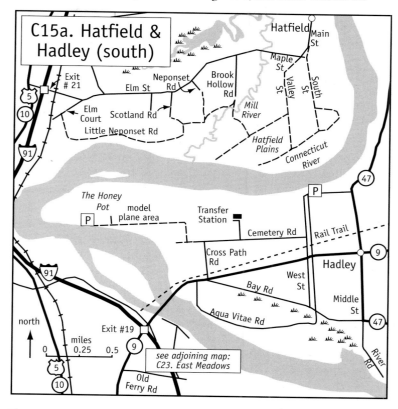

From May on, the road is drivable when dry. It comes back to Elm Street at three places: Scotland Road (a loop of 1.4 miles), Neponsett Road (1.9 miles), and Brook Hollow Road (2.0 miles). The connection between Little Neponsett and Brook Hollow Roads is **quite rough,** especially when wet. There is access to the Connecticut and Mill Rivers at several places along the road.

The woods and fields of Little Neponsett can be productive during migration and winter. A wooded bank along the north side of the fields is a good place to find Eastern Screech-Owl and is nearly always fruitful on moonlit winter nights, even in a wind. The swampy area along the bottom of the bank is a special place for winter birds, including scarce over-winterers such as American Robin and Red-winged Blackbird, because springs there maintain patches of open water.

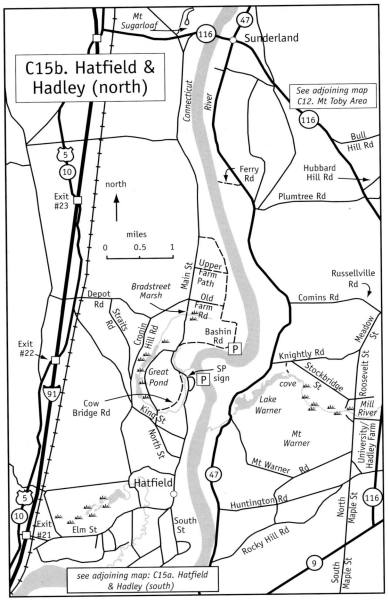

A second large area of fields and riparian woodland is reached by crossing the Mill River over the Underwater Bridge on the dirt continuation of Brook Hollow Road. The bridge is sometimes a poor route during high water; then South or Valley Streets can be used to come onto this area from the east end of Maple Street. This area is best for flocks of winter visitors such as Snow Buntings. A trip to the end of the dirt road to where the Mill River empties into the Connecticut can be productive in migration. The area at the mouth of Mill River is called The Nook and is best reached by turning right off Maple Street onto Valley Street, then turning right after 0.5 mile and continuing another 0.9 mile through the large field. There are normally Great Horned Owl and Red-bellied Woodpecker here. The Mill River holds Wood Duck all year. Checking weedy and brushy areas is always a good idea anywhere in these meadows.

See map C15b. Hatfield & Hadley (north)

Main Street runs north through a variety of habitats. At 1.0 mile north of the convenience store in Hatfield center it goes though some seasonally flooded deciduous woods between a small stream on the left and the Connecticut River. A dirt road makes a short loop to the right at 1.4 miles; turn at a small sign for Connecticut River Greenway State Park just before the water treatment plant. A boat launch on this road has a good view of the river. Brushy areas here are good for migrant sparrows. Return to Main Street and go north as it runs along a small oxbow, which often has Wood Ducks in April. This oxbow is one of four that fan out here, the outermost being Great Pond. The three inner oxbows, all east of the road, are dry except during flooding.

At 0.5 mile beyond the water treatment plant Bashin Road (dirt, no sign) goes off to the right into, you guessed it, The Bashin. Bashin Road makes a long loop through many fields; three roads return to Main Street: Old Farms (a loop of 1.9 miles), Upper Farms (2.3 miles), and the still unmarked Bashin Road (2.6 miles). If the roads are muddy, explore this area on foot. Bashin Road has very good birding in open fields, brushy edges, and riparian hardwoods. A large pool in the Connecticut is approached via a spur to the right of Bashin Road after 0.6 mile. The shore here has been acquired by The Massachusetts Department of Environmental Management (via Valley Land Fund), and there is a small parking area. The river can be good for ducks, and has held Great Cormorant and Black Scoter. In winter it often has Common Goldeneye and Common Merganser. It is favored by Great Blue Heron, Bald Eagle, and Belted Kingfisher. A walk through the woods gives further views of the river and good woodland birding. Pileated Woodpecker is a regular.

Brushy areas in The Bashin are good during migration. Orange-crowned, Connecticut, and Mourning Warblers, along with a good variety of sparrows, are possible. In May, August, and September shorebirds are often found in the plowed fields and wet areas. American Golden-Plover and Buff-breasted Sandpiper are good bets in September. In the first two weeks of April, flocks of Snow Geese may be forced down into this area by bad weather.

Main Street 0.5 mile north of Bashin Road (2.4 miles north of the convenience store), just before a group of houses, crosses the largest oxbow with tall cottonwoods, ponds, and marsh. The Bashin loop bypasses this area, thus requiring backtracking after rejoining Main Street. This excellent spot, Bradstreet Marsh, can be birded from the road and from the north side of the pond on the right (east) side of the road. Virginia Rail and Sora occur. Fall migrants often show up here past their normal departure dates. It is a good place for Eastern Screech-Owl, Red-bellied Woodpecker, Carolina Wren, and Swamp Sparrow. Ducks frequent the ponds and hawks ply their trade. There were two Great Gray Owls here during their 1980 invasion.

Main Street north from here is worth checking in migration for shorebirds, open-country raptors, and vagrants such as Western Kingbird and, in winter, for Northern Shrike, Lapland Longspur and Snow Bunting. Shorebirds such as yellowlegs, Pectoral Sandpiper, and Wilson's Snipe are often here in spring migration, and Wilson's Phalarope has occurred. Keep your eyes open for Gyrfalcon; one was found in Hatfield in 1982.

David Stemple

C16. Fitzgerald Lake Conservation Area
Northampton

The 500 acres of varied habitats in the city-owned Fitzgerald Lake Conservation Area (FLCA) are managed by the Broad Brook Coalition, dedicated to the preservation of the conservation area and the promotion of affordable housing. The organization was founded in response to an effort to build high-end housing around the conservation area. The birding is best in migration and summer; late winter is particularly slow.

Two entrances are described below. If you have a lot of time, try Boggy Meadow Road, the better choice for woodland birds and summer breeders, and a more direct route to the wildlife blind. For an introduction to FLCA and quick access to the lake, use North Farms Road; it has a paved handicapped accessible walkway, a canoe launch, and an interpretive nature trail. The two trails connect at the dam, about a mile walk.

North Farms Road Entrance

From the intersection of Routes 5 and 10 (King Street) with Damon Road and Bridge Road in Northampton, head west on Bridge Road (no sign). Continue on this road 1.8 miles. Turn right on Mountain Road, which becomes North Farms Road. Proceed 0.6 mile to the bottom of the hill and park in the small parking lot on your right. Take a map from the map board.

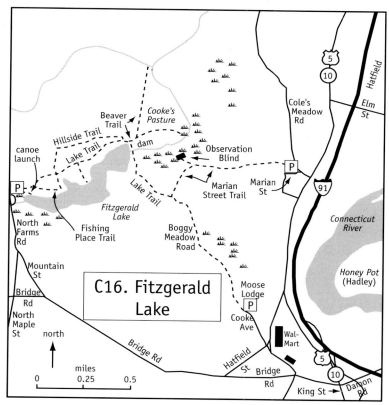

Listen at the parking lot for Pine Warbler and Ovenbird in the large pines and Carolina Wren near the houses. Follow the paved path, good for migrant warblers, Chestnut-sided Warbler (breeding), Louisiana Waterthrush (breeding along the brook near the parking lot and near the end of the walkway), and Golden-crowned Kinglet (winter). Check the pines and hemlocks for Red-breasted Nuthatch (winter), Brown Creeper (year-round), and Yellow-rumped and Pine Warblers.

At the end of the pavement take the short boardwalk to the right and look for Winter Wren (migration), Golden-crowned (winter) and Ruby-crowned (migration) Kinglets, migrant warblers, and Swamp Sparrow. At the end of the boardwalk scan the shallow lake for Pied-billed Grebe (migration), Great Blue and Green Herons, late summer egrets, Wood

BLUE-GRAY GNATCATCHER

Duck, Hooded Merganser (migration), migrating waterfowl, Osprey (migration), shorebirds, and river otter. Listen for Virginia Rail (breeding), Sora (migration), and Marsh Wren (migration) in the cattails.

Return to the beginning of the boardwalk, and turn right onto the other boardwalk/bridge. This is the main Lake Trail, which veers left after about ten yards; stay straight on Fishing Place Trail. After another twenty yards, turn right on a small trail down to the cattails to check for ducks or shorebirds. Backtrack to Fishing Place Trail and take a right to a point and a small cove. Scan for Green Heron, Wood Duck, Northern Goshawk, and Spotted Sandpiper. Backtrack about ten paces and turn right along the cove. Check here for Blue-gray Gnatcatcher (summer) and migrants in the underbrush.

At the end of the cove turn right on the Lake Trail into oak uplands, excellent for woodpeckers, Veery, Hermit and Wood Thrushes. Continue on this trail to the dam where you can see the lake again and scan the sky for possible Osprey (migration), Northern Goshawk (all year), or Red-shouldered Hawk (heard calling in breeding season). Look for Double-crested Cormorant or Wood Duck resting on the rocks. Northern Rough-winged Swallows have bred in the dam culverts.

Backtrack to where Lake and Beaver Trails intersect, take Beaver Trail for about ten yards and turn right toward Cooke's Pasture, with Eastern Bluebird (all year), Blue-winged and Chestnut-sided Warblers, and Baltimore Oriole. If you're quiet you might see a white-tailed deer or black bear feeding on apples in the fall. At dusk listen for American Bittern (migration), American Woodcock, and Whip-poor-will. From the marsh you should hear Alder Flycatcher, Eastern Kingbird, Cedar Waxwing, and Swamp Sparrow. Go down the second narrow tongue of the pasture on your right to a small pine grove, and sneak under the pines to view the marsh. Some possibilities are Great Blue Heron, Green Heron, Wood Duck, Red-shouldered Hawk (breeds), Virginia Rail, and the songsters mentioned above. From the pasture you can return the way you came, or take the Lake Trail straight back. From the dam you can take the first left on the far side of the dam to Boggy Meadow Road, Marian Street Extension, and a blind overlooking the marsh described below.

Boggy Meadow Road Entrance

From the Damon Road/Bridge Road and Routes 5 and 10 intersection, take Bridge Road (no sign) 0.25 mile west to the first light and turn right onto Cooke Avenue. Follow Cooke Avenue 0.4 mile across Hatfield Street to a large parking lot and the Moose Lodge. Park on the right near the map board, and take a map.

From the parking lot follow the line of trees straight to an old woods road where breeding birds include Barred Owl, Yellow-bellied Sapsucker, Eastern Wood-Pewee, Yellow-throated and Red-eyed Vireos, Black-throated Blue and Black-throated Green Warblers, American Redstart, and Scarlet Tanager. Black bears are common along this road.

After about 0.5 mile you'll come to a tiny stream with a shrub swamp on your right, excellent for birds, especially in migration. In summer here you might find Blue-gray Gnatcatcher, Veery, Wood Thrush, Blue-winged and Canada Warblers, American Redstart, Northern Waterthrush, Scarlet Tanager, Rose-breasted Grosbeak, and Purple Finch.

After another 0.3 mile, go past a metal gate and veer left down past swampy woods on your left that sometimes have Winter Wren or Canada Warbler. The thick conifers on your right have Blackburnian Warbler in summer and Golden-crowned Kinglet in winter.

A little farther, at a small open area, take the Marian Street Trail extension on your right, near some boulders and a large oak. Take this trail to the end of the boardwalk, and turn left, veering right under some apple trees and pines. This thick brushy area usually has Ruffed Grouse. After about twenty yards you should see the stairs to the blind. Please be **quiet** so as not to disturb wildlife or other observers. The birds mentioned above for the other side of the marsh and, occasionally, a moose are seen here.

If you go back to the boardwalk and turn left, you'll be on the Marian Street Trail through upland oak woods, with breeding Great Crested Flycatcher and Scarlet Tanager.

Return to the boardwalk, take a right from the blind, retrace your steps to Boggy Meadow Road, and turn right through large pines and hemlocks where Northern Goshawk has bred and where you may see Ruffed Grouse, Blue-headed and Red-eyed Vireos, Brown Creeper, both kinglets (migration), Hermit and Wood Thrushes, Black-throated Blue, Yellow-rumped, Black-throated Green, Blackburnian, and Pine Warblers, and American Redstart. At the end of this road, turn right to the dam (see the North Farms Road section above).

There are many more trails, some on the map, some not. Explore, but be careful not to get lost (easy to do here). *Bob Packard*

C17. Graves Farm Wildlife Sanctuary
Williamsburg

See map C14. Whately

This beautiful 600-acre Massachusetts Audubon Society (MAS) property includes grasslands, old orchard, farm pond, wooded stream, and a variety of forest habitats.

From Route 9 in Williamsburg, turn right (north) on Depot Road near Lashway Logging. At the first intersection turn right (east) on Adams Road. Park in the driveway at the farmhouse immediately on the left. **Do not park anywhere along the road.**

Note: Currently, MAS requires that visitors to the sanctuary be members and that they have attended at least one naturalist-led event at the sanctuary. MAS offers frequent bird walks from spring through fall. The sanctuary is open dawn to dusk.

Wildlife habitat at Graves Farm begins at the barn where as many as 63 pairs of Cliff Swallows have nested. Some years there are none. The re-establishment of the colony was due largely to Mara Silver, who created a mud puddle for nesting material and built clay nest ledges.

Beyond the barn are old hayfield, wet meadow, and apple orchard habitats. Eastern Bluebirds nest in the boxes. The east side of the field is a wet meadow with shrubs along a small channel. Look for Great Crested Flycatcher and Yellow and Chestnut-sided Warblers along the edge, and for American Kestrels patrolling the field. Across the street, Black-billed Cuckoos are seen regularly. Baltimore Orioles nest in large sugar maples near the house. Yellow-bellied Sapsuckers often drum on telephone poles.

To get to the rest of the sanctuary, walk east along Adams Road. The sanctuary is on both sides of the road. Listen for Chestnut-sided Warbler and Swamp Sparrow along Joe Wright Brook. Alder Flycatcher is sometimes found in alder thickets in this abandoned beaver meadow.

Continue along the road to the first small field on the left (north). The three main spokes of access to the inner sanctuary begin here. These old logging roads are not connected. The first road begins at the far right corner of the small field at the north side of Adams Road. The entrance to the trail may be difficult to find, but soon becomes more recognizable in the forest. This trail parallels Joe Wright Brook through hemlock, white pine, and maple forest to a young stand of beech. At this point the trail narrows and winds down a ravine where porcupines are commonly seen in the tops of yellow birches during summer. Eastern Phoebe, Winter Wren, and Louisiana Waterthrush nest here.

The second spoke begins on the south side of Adams Road across from the small field. A giant sugar maple trunk blocks the way to the former parking area. (Police warn folks not to park along the road here, and may issue tickets.) A well-defined logging road leads into the forest at the far end of the abandoned parking area. Blue-headed Vireo and Hermit Thrush are frequently heard among the large white pines. The trail soon crosses Joe Wright Brook where Winter Wrens are regularly heard. Look for Chestnut-sided and Canada Warblers in the thick undergrowth beyond the stream. The trail returns to more mature forest where Eastern Wood-Pewee, Blue-headed and Red-eyed Vireos, Veery, Hermit and Wood Thrushes, Black-throated Blue, Yellow-rumped, Black-throated Green, Blackburnian, and Black-and-white Warblers, Ovenbird, and Scarlet Tanager are common breeders. Magnolia Warbler is an infrequent breeder.

A census plot in this area has revealed fairly stable and abundant numbers of breeding birds since 1993. Ovenbird is by far the most common species, followed by Red-eyed Vireo. Yellow-bellied Sapsucker and Pileated Woodpecker are found here and Barred Owls have nested. Five woodpecker species have nested almost within sight of each other.

Ruffed Grouse, common throughout the sanctuary, can often be seen with broods near the trail. The trail leads to a T at the boundary of the sanctuary, but birding is good for a short distance to the right where you will find an open wet meadow, and for a longer distance to the left through Blue-gray Gnatcatcher habitat.

Back on Adams Road, the third spoke can be reached by continuing east to the entrance to a larger field on the left (north). Just beyond, a smaller field on the right (south) is also worth a check for Indigo Bunting along the edges and vocal Red-shouldered Hawks in the woods at the far end of the field.

The larger field on the left (north) side of Adams Road supports 10 to 20 pairs of breeding Bobolinks. Many more individuals join the ranks in late June and July, as fledglings emerge and adults move in from mowed fields. Indigo Buntings are fairly common along the edges. American Woodcock display here in early spring. This field is a good place to observe raptors. Northern Goshawk, Red-shouldered, Broad-winged, and Red-tailed Hawks fly overhead between the forests on either side of the road. Long-eared Owl has occurred in this area in winter. Great Horned and Barred Owls are resident.

Eastern Bluebirds nesting in the boxes in the field often feed along the roadside. Observations of nesting bluebirds in 1997 revealed that the adults foraged nearly a quarter of a mile away from the nest box, until a small area was mowed near the box. The adults then fed almost exclusively in the mowed area and made more frequent trips to the box to feed the young.

A logging road at the edge of the woods leads into a young aspen, birch, and maple forest where American Redstart is common. This trail eventually intersects Grassy Hill Road at the edge of the property. Deep woods birding is good along this road. To the right, Grassy Hill Road eventually leads through interesting old pasture habitat with Least Flycatcher and Blue-winged Warbler before coming out on Adams Road. Covering this loop requires a few hours.　　　David McLain

C18. Hadley Floodplain
Honey Pot and the Connecticut River, Hadley

See map C15a. Hatfield & Hadley (south)

The Honey Pot has historically been one of the best areas along the Connecticut River for encountering open country birds. In recent years the landscape has changed a bit and may not be quite as good. Instead of corn and asparagus, a large portion of the area has been converted to ornamental shrubbery, which requires more thorough removal of weeds. Even with these changes the Honey Pot is an area not to be bypassed. If you venture into the Honey Pot between April and mid-September, **remember to keep off the farm fields.**

From the intersection of Routes 9 and 47 in Hadley, go west on Route 9 for 0.4 mile and turn right (north) on West Street. (West Street runs on both sides of the Common; both sides are two-way streets.) Turn left (west) on Cemetery Road (0.1 mile from Route 9), which leads straight out into the Honey Pot fields.

Proceed down Cemetery Road and scan both sides of the road, being careful to pull completely off this busy commuter short-cut. In spring and fall you may find American Pipit and Horned Lark. In winter a Snowy Owl has been known to appear. This section of the Honey Pot is not as productive for sparrows as the land west of the earthen dike ahead, although Vesper Sparrows have nested in the ornamental nursery stock.

Cross the earthen dike and go straight ahead; most of the traffic will make a sharp left to Route 9. Once safely beyond the turn, pull off the road. There can be a great number of wintering or migrating sparrows: Field, Savannah, Song, Swamp, White-throated, and White-crowned, especially in the weedy fields. Less likely, but possible, are Clay-colored, Vesper, Lark, and Fox Sparrows. While walking the roads at the edges of the fields you may flush a Short-eared Owl, which has happened on more than one occasion. If it happens to be a finch winter, Common Redpolls may occur by the hundreds.

From late fall through early spring, the Honey Pot can be good for hawks. Scan the trees for Bald Eagle, Red-tailed Hawk (common), and maybe a Rough-legged Hawk (late fall and winter). Tree tops may also have a Northern Shrike. Scan the fields and you may come across a Northern Harrier, Sharp-shinned Hawk, Cooper's Hawk, Merlin, or Peregrine Falcon. In spring, this is a good area to listen for breeding Vesper and Savannah Sparrows.

Continue west and take the first and only right. Follow this road until it bears left and straightens out; park here. In winter, check harvested corn fields for flocks of Horned Larks, and scan for Lapland Longspur (rare) and Snow Bunting (more common). During early spring, Snow Bunting numbers have approached 500. The cornfields can also produce hundreds of Mourning Doves.

A short distance down the road, look for a small airstrip on the right-hand side. The runway is used by a club for remote controlled model aircraft. The road that leads down to the club area has sumac on the left, sometimes producing Eastern Bluebirds. Also check for American Tree, Song, and White-throated Sparrows. If you're feeling adventurous, continue down the road and bird the treeline along the Connecticut River. In winter, you'll probably encounter woodpeckers and maybe a Belted Kingfisher or two. Although this area can be quiet, one observer found a Black-backed Woodpecker a few years back so there's always hope for a surprise.

Back on the main (dirt) road, keep heading west to a wide turnaround. The road continues, but it's private. At the turnaround you'll have a fairly clear view of the river. In winter check for Common Goldeneye and Common Merganser. If the river is low, look for gulls on exposed banks. In spring you may come across Wood, American Black, and Ring-necked Ducks, and Bufflehead.

As you return to the dike, pull over before the intersection and walk Crosspath Road toward Route 9 and the Norwottuck Rail Trail, the paved bike path running from South Amherst across Hadley to Northampton. **Crosspath Road is a commuter short-cut, so be careful.** The Rail Trail is used heavily, especially in the summer and fall, so if you decide to bird anywhere along this route do it in the early morning. The thickets along the path leading either west to the bridge or east to the center of Hadley can be productive throughout the year.

An early morning walk out to the bridge may turn up Great and Snowy Egrets (summer), Hooded and Common Mergansers, or Bald Eagle. If the river is low enough from late July through early September, you may see an occasional shorebird on Elwell Island, just north of the bridge.

Return to your car and go straight over the dike **being careful to avoid oncoming cars turning in front of you.** Continue east on Cemetery Road, and at the stop sign take a left onto West Street. When West Street bends to the right (north along the river), there is a pull-off directly in front of you. The top of the dike has a commanding view of the river. Scan here for waterfowl and raptors. Continue along the road (West Street becomes North Lane) to the next stop sign. Turn right on Middle Street (Route 47) to the center of Hadley (intersection of Routes 9 and 47).

Aqua Vitae Road

This small area of farmland wedged between the Connecticut River, Route 47, and Route 9 is a favorite for local birders. The area is best in spring, fall, and winter. In the summer growing season, crops restrict viewing.

From the intersection of Routes 47 and 9 in Hadley, go south on Route 47 to the stop sign at Bay Road where Route 47 goes left. Turn right (west) on Bay Road 0.35 mile to the small Aqua Vitae Road on the left.

This section of the road is often flooded in March and April; in that case, continue down Bay Road to a set of lights. Turn left onto Route 9 toward Northampton. A short way from that intersection on the left is Aqua Vitae Road, just before the bridge to Northampton.

Over twenty species of waterfowl have been recorded along this part of the river through the years. The most common are Canada Goose, Wood Duck, American Wigeon, American Black Duck, Mallard, Blue-winged Teal, Northern Pintail, Green-winged Teal, Ring-necked Duck, and Hooded and Common Mergansers. Other waterfowl to be on the lookout for include Pied-billed Grebe, rarely other grebes, Gadwall, Northern Shoveler, Canvasback, Greater and Lesser Scaup, scoters (rare), Long-tailed Duck, Bufflehead, and Red-breasted Merganser. Birds to look for around the water's edge or in any small pools in the fields created by floods or spring downpours are herons, most likely Great Blue and Green, both yellowlegs, Solitary Sandpiper, Spotted Sandpiper, and Wilson's Snipe.

In late March and April check the fields for Horned Lark, American Pipit, and Vesper Sparrow (rare). Occasionally you may run into a lingering American Tree Sparrow, Lapland Longspur (rare), or Snow Bunting. Other April migrants to watch for in the open fields or overhead include raptors, Chimney Swift, and swallows.

During the height of spring and fall migration the forests and thickets around the fields can be productive. **Please respect private property** and bird from the road. In these areas look for, in appropriate seasons, all the smaller woodpeckers, flycatchers, vireos, Carolina, House, and Winter (winter and migration) Wrens, migrant kinglets, and warblers, American Tree, Field, Vesper, Savannah, Fox, Song, Lincoln's, Swamp, White-throated, and White-crowned Sparrows, Dark-eyed Junco, and blackbird flocks, including Rusty.

Summer birding on Aqua Vitae Road is on the quiet side. Depending on water level, a fairly large sandbar develops on the river. Access to the sandbar is somewhat difficult, but it can be scoped from the Northampton side. Look for Double-crested Cormorant, Great and Snowy (rare) Egrets, and Great Blue, Little Blue (rare), and Green Herons.

Shorebirding begins around mid-July, and over 18 species of shorebirds have been recorded, including Black-bellied, American Golden- and Semipalmated Plovers, Killdeer, both yellowlegs, Sanderling, and Semipalmated, Least, White-rumped, and Pectoral Sandpipers. Many gulls congregate on the sandbar during the summer, occasionally including Laughing, Black-headed, and Bonaparte's, and Common and Black Terns.

In winter, check the thickets near Route 9 for typical winter birds including American Tree and White-throated Sparrows. Among the winter regulars, birders have found Carolina Wren, Ruby-crowned Kinglet, and Common Yellowthroat. Scan the trees along the fields for Bald Eagle. All three accipiters are possible, and the ever-present Red-tailed Hawk is a good bet. Rough-legged Hawk, Merlin, Peregrine Falcon, and Northern Shrike put in occasional appearances. In the fields, look for Horned Larks and scan the flock for a few Snow Buntings. Walk the weed patches for large numbers of American Tree Sparrows and wintering Savannah Sparrows. During invasion years, I've had over 150 Common Redpolls. If you are very lucky, you may scare up a Short-eared Owl. Birders have also recorded Eastern Screech, Great Horned, and Northern Saw-whet Owls (winter).

The thickets near Bay Road produce about the same variety as those near Route 9. Because this area has some marshy sections, birders have found Winter Wren, Swamp Sparrow, and, on one Christmas Bird Count, a lingering Wilson's Warbler. Some other highlights over the years in the Aqua Vitae area have been Northern Gannet, Glossy Ibis, Greater White-front Goose, Swainson's Hawk, and Sedge Wren.   *Scott D. Surner*

C19. University of Massachusetts Area
Amherst, Hadley

Several productive birding areas are within about a mile of the center of the University of Massachusetts campus in Amherst. In addition to the areas described below, see the University stadium area described in C20, Maple Street Corridor, and visit the varied habitats of Orchard Hill at the northeast corner of the campus (not described, see map).

The pond at the center of the campus has year-round waterfowl. Wood Duck and Northern Pintail sometimes join wintering American Black Ducks, Mallards, and hybrids here. Other waterfowl are sometimes found during migration. The Trumpeter Swans are captives. The red brick W.E.B. Du Bois Library tower, the tallest building on campus, has hosted Peregrine Falcons for several years, and successful nesting is anticipated on this building or in a second nest box on the building just to the north. The peregrines often perch on a pole about 30 feet below the top of the tower on the east side.

University of Massachusetts Cinder Road

From the junction of Routes 9 and 116 in Hadley, take Route 116 north and follow signs to the Mullins Center turning right (east) on Massachusetts Avenue and then left (north) at the light on Commonwealth Avenue. Pass the Mullins Center on the left and continue about

0.2 mile to Parking Lots 25 and 12 on the left. Park in these lots on weekends or in summer **(check signs for current regulations)**; on school year weekdays a sticker is required. Limited parking is available at the Department of Environmental Management Region 4 headquarters around the corner northwest of Lot 25 on Cold Storage Road. There is metered parking just north of the Mullins Center and in the Campus Parking Garage.

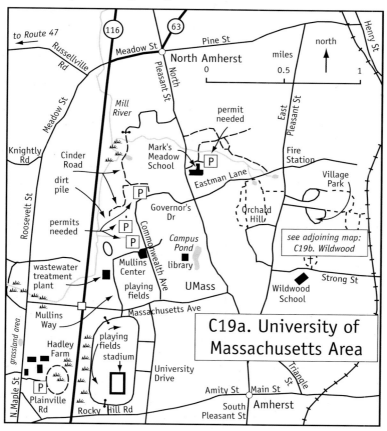

Walk to the back/northwest corner of Lot 12. In front of you is the cinder road proper and to your left a large, ever-changing dirt pile, excellent for sparrows especially in winter. The forest edge and grapevines are best for spring warblers. Along the Cinder Road is an overgrown weedy field; thrushes, warblers and sparrows love the shrubs here, and in winter Pine Siskins are attracted to the weeds. Continue about 100 yards to another path to the left; follow this path to the end past a pond, large marsh, and large field. Ring-necked Pheasant, Red-bellied Woodpecker, and Hermit Thrush may be here in winter. In spring watch for vireos and orioles in the cottonwoods and Virginia Rail and Sora in the marsh. From the marsh you can backtrack or, if time permits, walk the field edges. Horned Larks are common in this area and there are usually Carolina Wrens, Cedar Waxwings, and thrushes.

Return to the main path; a large cinder pile will be on your left and the field previously mentioned on your right. Past the cinder pile a small stream overgrown with autumn olive is on your left, excellent for thrushes. Continue on the path past the soil piles to another road on your left. Take this road up toward the state forestry buildings. The willow trees around a small marshy pond can be loaded with warblers in both migrations. Look in the overgrown nursery and many fruiting plants nearby for thrushes and other skulkers. Bird your way around this area and back to the parking lots.

To bird this area effectively, give yourself at least an hour, or up to three hours for complete coverage. I have had my best birds here in early morning before the University and Route 116 get moving.

To bird the nearby playing fields and Amherst Wastewater Treatment Plant see map C20 Maple Street Corridor (and map C19a. University of Massachusetts Area).   *Dave Ziomek*

Mark's Meadow Area, Amherst

From the Cinder Road, return to Commonwealth Avenue. Turn left and continue 0.6 mile to the traffic light (by then the road is called Governor's Drive). Turn left on North Pleasant Street and in 0.2 mile turn right into the parking lot on the far (north) side of Marks Meadow School/School of Education. At the rear of the first parking lot and before the larger lot, there is a cinder road to the left. Parking is allowed in permit parking area on weekends and in summer (check signs for current regulations). At other times use metered parking on either side of the building.

Alternatively, from the center of Amherst, follow signs to the University via East Pleasant, then left on North Pleasant. Mark's Meadow School is at the north end of campus. See parking instructions above.

Check the bushes near the parking area and the fruit trees around the school for spring and fall warblers. Walk down the cinder road between the two parking lots, just west of the school. House Wrens are frequently active at the beginning of the road. A short distance down the road, look for waterthrushes at a brook in the wooded border. As you continue north toward an intersection, there is a hedgerow on your left and on the other side of it an open meadow to the west. Bobolinks and Eastern Meadowlarks nest in these fields, and Savannah Sparrows are common in spring.

Where the cinder roads intersect, productive birding habitat lies in every direction. As you look at mystifying plant research paraphernalia and piles of landscaping "trash," you may be understandably doubtful. However, this small area has over 120 recorded species and has had more than its share of rarities, especially in fall. Ring-necked Pheasant, Northern Flicker, and Brown Thrasher are regulars here, but it is the prospect of unusual species that keeps local birders returning. On a good migrant day, songbirds are abundant in bushes and surrounding woods, and accipiters may join birders in looking for those songbirds. On several recent occasions Yellow-breasted Chat has emerged from the underbrush, and late in August this is one of the best locations in the area for a Mourning Warbler to "make your day."

A good strategy for birding Mark's Meadow is simply to walk up and down the cinder trails. However, there are two areas that can be particularly lively in fall. First, if you walk the path to the east you soon see a wet, weedy field on your right extending south to a hardwood border. In October this field can be full of sparrows. To check it thoroughly walk in on the edges, where possible, to see what might tee-up on the weeds. Nearby trees and bushes can have warbler activity.

The second hot spot for sparrows is due north of the intersection. Follow the path straight ahead until the hedgerow on your left (west) meets another hedgerow from the east. This hedgerow, nearby trees, and piles of debris can also be blessed with birds on any given day. Lincoln's Sparrow is regular in fall, and LeConte's Sparrow has occurred at least once.

Jan Ortiz

Wildwood Area

See map C19b. Wildwood

The Wildwood complex is one of the most popular birding areas in Amherst for several reasons: the area is accessible and easily explored; there is a variety of habitat; and the area is attractive to migrating birds, with some 125 species regularly recorded, and a rarity list that includes Mississippi Kite, Great Gray Owl, Red-headed Woodpecker, Yellow-bellied Flycatcher, White-eyed Vireo, Purple Martin, Gray-cheeked/Bicknell's Thrush, Golden-winged, Cerulean, Kentucky, and Hooded Warblers, Yellow-breasted Chat, and Summer Tanager. Pileated Woodpecker breeds nearby. In May the Hampshire Bird Club has frequent early-morning warbler walks through the area.

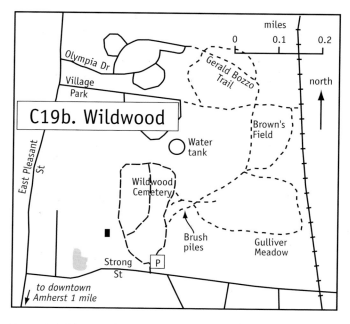

From Mark's Meadow, return to North Pleasant Street and turn left (toward campus) for 0.2 mile. Take a left at the traffic light on Eastman Lane. When Eastman Lane ends at East Pleasant Street, turn right. Continue on East Pleasant Street 0.7 mile, passing the water towers on your right, and turn left on Strong Street. Alternatively, from the center of Amherst, take East Pleasant Street 0.9 mile and turn right on Strong Street. The entrance to Wildwood Cemetery is on the left at the crest of the hill on Strong Street opposite the school (0.2 mile from North Pleasant Street). Do not take the earlier road to the brick house used as the Wildwood Cemetery administration building.

Cars may be left in the parking area on the right just inside the gate. Please do not park or drive on the grass. Please note: The cemetery and the woods downhill to the east are private property. Although birders have been welcome here for many years, **common sense and courtesy should be exercised when birding these grounds.** This is especially true when a funeral is in progress or when people are visiting graves.

Birding the cemetery proper is a simple matter of wandering the grounds at your own pace. Migrant birds are easily seen flitting through the treetops. The hemlocks near the entrance sometimes attract migrating Tennessee and Cape May Warblers, and the larches east of the caretaker's house seem especially attractive to many species of warblers.

From the cemetery parking area, trails lead east and downhill into woods. A short walk from the cemetery proper leads to an opening where brush is dumped. This area can be very good. The southernmost section of the trail where the woods abut the Gulliver Meadow Conservation Area field off Strong Street, especially the southeast corner near the active railroad tracks, can also be rewarding. Listen for both waterthrushes in spring.

Brown's Field, on town conservation land, can be reached by car. Return to East Pleasant Street, turn right/north and continue 0.4 mile. Turn right at Village Park. The trail is at the far end of the parking lot.

Brown's Field is often loaded with migrants in spring. Eastern Kingbird, Eastern Bluebird, Blue-winged and Nashville Warblers, and Field Sparrow breed here. Look for an opening on the north leading to a small field grown up with autumn olive and other shrubs. On a typical spring morning, a Ruby-throated Hummingbird can be observed perched on a dead branch. *James B. Marcum*

C20. Maple Street Corridor
Amherst, Hadley

See map C19a. University of Massachusetts Area

Maple Street, its northward extensions (Roosevelt and Meadow Streets), and adjacent areas in Amherst and Hadley provide year-round open country birds. All the fields bordering these roads, and side roads not covered below, are worth scanning, **if you can find a safe place to pull over.** The birds differ from field to field and year to year with development, changing drainage, and farming practices.

In winter or migration, these fields, especially those spread with manure (a magnet for birds), can have Northern Harrier, Rough-legged Hawk, Merlin, Horned Lark, Lapland Longspur, or Snow Bunting. Cooper's Hawk, Red-tailed Hawk, American Kestrel, and Peregrine Falcon hunt here year-round. Grassland birds breed in pastures and hay fields. Shorebirds occur in both migrations; a field with manure or puddles can attract ten shorebird species at once. American Golden-Plover and Buff-breasted Sandpiper are annual or nearly so early fall migrants.

At least a few Ring-billed, Herring, and Great Black-backed Gulls are present year-round. Iceland, Lesser Black-backed, and Glaucous Gulls occur annually, and Laughing and Black-headed Gulls most years. Patterns of occurrence vary; a species might be found annually for a decade and nearly disappear for another decade. Franklin's, Bonaparte's, Mew, Sabine's, and "Nelson's Gull" (a Glaucous/Herring hybrid) have each been reported at least once. In recent years the Meadow Street fields have replaced the University stadium area as the gull hot spot. Frequent patrolling of all these fields is key to finding rarities. A sudden August or September rain shower is your best chance for another Franklin's or Sabine's Gull, and sifting through the plumages of all the Ring-bills is the route to another Mew Gull.

The roads here are narrow, and even side roads have a lot of traffic. Look for safe pull-off areas, and do not block farm access roads. **Pull completely off the road** without getting your wheels stuck in the mud. Scan from the edges of the fields; there is no need to trespass. A scope is useful.

Russellville Road and Meadow Street, Amherst, Hadley

The account below starts at the north end of the corridor, but all or part of the roads can be conveniently covered in either direction. Begin at the intersection of Maple Street and Route 9, directly across from the two large malls in Hadley. Drive north 3.8 miles on North Maple (which becomes Roosevelt and then Meadow Street). Turn left on Russellville Road, pull completely off the road and scan the first 0.25 mile. You can also walk back to scan from Meadow Street where there are no safe places to pull off the road.

The fields south and west of the junction of Meadow Street and Russellville Road can have thousands of Canada Geese, less frequently Snow Geese, even a Greater White-fronted Goose, a variety of dabbling ducks, and many gulls. A Northern Harrier or Merlin sometimes adds to the mix. There may be Horned Larks and American Pipits and once a Glossy Ibis dropped in. When storms move through, that's the time to keep an eye on these fields. Migrants use them in fall, but late March to late April is when they have produced the most excitement.

The southernmost of these fields can be scanned from Knightly Road, 0.7 mile south of Russellville Road. You will need a scope to sort out individual birds.

The University/Hadley Farm and Vicinity, Hadley

Return along Meadow/Roosevelt/North Maple Street 2.4 miles from Russellville Road to the University/Hadley Farm. Once a working dairy farm, it is now owned by the University of Massachusetts Foundation, Inc., and forms the core of the University's Animal Science/Equestrian Studies Program. The 135-acre farm is known for rarities including many unusual migrants, some uncommon nesting species, and wintering raptors.

Special Note: The University/Hadley Farm grounds are open during posted hours only. See the main gate for current hours and regulations. Generally, if the gate is open, birders can drive into the farm and park in the small lot on the right before the oval track. The staff asks birders not to enter pastures, but instead to bird from fence lines. Birding the farm and adjacent lands from the road can be productive year-round and may be done without permission.

Begin birding this area by scanning the fields on both sides of North Maple Street. **Please use caution; this is a very busy road.** Be patient, as these fields are large, and shorebirds are often resting and difficult to see. Scan treelines for perched raptors. After searching from the road, head into the farm driveway and park. Shorebirds, gulls, sparrows, and other migrants can be in any of the pastures.

In spring, the farm often produces good numbers of migrant herons, geese, ducks, shorebirds, and gulls feeding or resting in muddy, wet, or flooded fields. Visiting in early morning after rain has forced migrants down can be particularly rewarding. After spring rains and runoff, large pools form and remain because of the relatively impermeable clay soils and high water table. Fields closely mowed or grazed provide foraging areas for early Killdeer, yellowlegs, Solitary Sandpiper, Wilson's Snipe, and, once, a Wilson's Phalarope. Some years bare, muddy areas are very productive for shorebirds in fall migration. Walk the large swale running west from the northeast side of the oval track to an old oxbow of the Mill River to check for herons, American Wigeon, American Black Duck, Mallard, Northern Pintail, shorebirds, and gulls.

Savannah Sparrows sing from fence posts throughout the property in breeding season. In fields west of North Maple Street, one of which is owned by Valley Land Fund, Bobolink and Eastern Meadowlark nest in tall grass. American Kestrel, Killdeer, and Spotted Sandpiper regularly breed here; Sedge Wren has bred here at least once. Virginia Rail and Sora nest in the small cattail marsh near the road.

Red-tailed Hawk by day and Great Horned Owl by night sit on the quarter-mile markers of the track. American Kestrels have nested in the Barn Owl box in the middle of the track. A pair of Cooper's Hawks nest near the horse farm. The farm area, with its open fields, perching trees and, what raptors need most, meadow voles, can offer exciting winter birding. In recent winters, the farm has, at times, supported Northern Harrier, Rough-legged Hawk, and Short-eared Owl.

University of Massachusetts Stadium Marsh, Playing Fields and Amherst Wastewater Treatment Plant Area, Amherst, Hadley

The fields and lawns on the flat western edge of the University of Massachusetts are similar in birds and habitat to the Maple Street area. Return to North Maple, turn left (south) and, at the edge of the farm, turn left on Plainville Road which will merge with Rocky Hill Road. Continue for 0.6 mile, turn left (north) into the stadium complex. Park near the circle of stones and chain-link maze and walk left (west) to the marsh.

The marsh between the weeping willows and Route 116 holds breeding Virginia Rail, Sora (sometimes), and Swamp Sparrow. American Bittern is an occasional spring migrant. Careful scanning when hundreds of blackbirds come to roost at sundown in late summer and early fall might turn up a rarity. The trees along the marsh may have a Great Horned Owl visible against the western sky at dusk. Horned Lark, Snow Bunting, and an occasional Lapland Longspur occur in winter.

The lawns around the University football stadium sometimes hold migrant shorebirds, especially if there are puddles, and flocks of gulls. The fenced-off football practice field on the right often has shorebirds when other lawns do not. The fences reduce disturbance, and the practice field is kept watered. In spring and summer swallows hawk insects over the lawns; on a good day all five regularly occurring species can be seen.

Return to your car and drive around the east half of the stadium complex. At the north end of the complex, drive across Massachusetts Avenue to the playing fields and wastewater plant. The playing fields near Mullins Way often have flocks of gulls. The brushy field between the wastewater plant and Massachusetts Avenue often has raptors, including Great Horned Owl at dusk. In winter, check the light towers at the playing fields for roosting raptors. Gulls at the wastewater plant can be viewed from outside the fence. Iceland Gull is as likely to be found at the treatment tanks as on the fields.

South Maple Street

From Route 9, drive south 0.5 mile on South Maple Street between two malls, across the bike path to the first farm (Goulet Trucking/Allard Farm), just before the intersection with Mill Valley Road. Pull to the side of the road, **being sure not to interfere with the busy farm activity.** From spring through fall, check swallow flocks for occasional Bank and Cliff Swallows. Wilson's Snipe occurs in spring and fall, and Short-billed Dowitcher and Blue Grosbeak have turned up in the fall. Cooper's Hawk and Merlin are attracted here, like birders, by seasonal flocks of shorebirds, sparrows, and blackbirds. This area has had winter Dickcissel and Yellow-headed Blackbird.

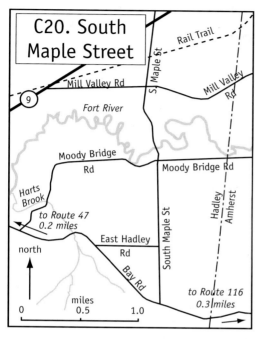

C20. South Maple Street

Rail Trail

S. Maple St

Mill Valley Rd

Mill Valley Rd

9

Fort River

Moody Bridge Rd

Moody Bridge Rd

Harts Brook

to Route 47 0.2 miles

Hadley
Amherst

north

East Hadley Rd

South Maple St

Bay Rd

to Route 116 0.3 miles

miles
0   0.5   1.0

From Allard Farm, it is worthwhile to drive in either direction on Mill Valley Road (0.6 mile south of Route 9). To the east, one may see Eastern Bluebirds year round. Fall shorebirds have included Black-bellied Plover, American Golden-Plover, and Buff-breasted Sandpiper. Lark Sparrow and Nelson's Sharp-tailed Sparrow have been discovered here in fall migration. A Northern Shrike may turn up in the winter. In spring look for Canada Geese, Snow Geese, or even a Greater White-fronted Goose.

Scan the fields to the west, in late fall and winter, for gulls, Horned Lark, and Snow Bunting. Check flocks of Horned Larks for Lapland Longspur. Spring may bring American Pipits to these fields. In summer, check the fields for swallows, Bobolink, and Eastern Meadowlark. In all seasons, check for hawks at the edge of the woods.

Return to the intersection and continue south on South Maple Street. Historically, the birding has been good on South Maple between Mill Valley Road and Bay Road; however, it is difficult to pull completely off the road and except in early morning the traffic is always heavy, making this section very difficult if not dangerous to bird.

Moody Bridge Road (1.4 miles south of Route 9 and 0.9 south of Mill Valley Road) is often productive, especially the portion west of South Maple Street. Any plowed or manured fields on this road in spring or fall (beginning in August) should be checked for shorebirds. In spring check for field birds, including Vesper Sparrow. The scrubby wetland along this road is good for Eastern Screech-Owl year-round;

in winter, the higher and drier areas have hosted Northern Shrike and diurnal raptors. A dip in the road beside Harts Brook near the west end of Moody Bridge Road has been good for winter Wild Turkey and for migrant warblers in spring.

Return to South Maple Street and continue south, turning right on East Hadley Road (2.2 miles south of Route 9). Pull off East Hadley Road as soon as you can safely do so, and scan the fields to the southwest for geese, especially in March, and for gulls and raptors at any time. Check the small pond on the north side of East Hadley Road during migration for herons including Great Blue, Green, and (once) Little Blue Heron. In fall, if rain has brought shorebirds down, you might find Semipalmated, Least, or White-rumped Sandpipers or, if you are very lucky, a Hudsonian Godwit. Grasshopper Sparrows have occurred near the stream in fall. On the south side, across from the houses, there is a wet pasture (0.3 mile west of South Maple Street) that reliably has Wilson's Snipe in late March and early April.

Jan Ortiz, David A. Spector, Scott D. Surner, and Dave Ziomek

C21. Amherst Conservation Areas and Rail Trail
Amherst, Belchertown

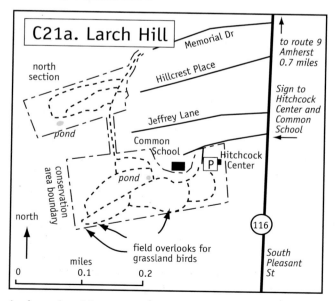

Amherst has 50 town conservation areas with over 1,965 acres and 3 major trails: the 118-mile Metacomet-Monadnock Trail, the Ken Cuddeback Trail, and the 10-town, 40-mile Robert Frost Trail (RFT).

Guides to these areas and trails can be purchased in downtown Amherst bookstores or stationers.

Larch Hill Conservation Area, Amherst

Larch Hill is at 525 South Pleasant Street, 1.1 miles south of Amherst center on the right (west) side of Route 116. There are signs for the Hitchcock Center and the Common School. Larch Hill, a town conservation area, is home to the Hitchcock Center for the Environment, a nature center with interpretive programs. The Larch Hill Accessible Trail affords access for birders with disabilities on a safe, level surface (a boardwalk and an additional crushed-stone path).

Pick up a map from the box at the trailhead near the Hitchcock Center and listen for Carolina Wren. The most productive walks are those over the wheelchair-accessible boardwalk toward the larch stand where Cooper's Hawk and Pine Warbler nest. The thickets along the boardwalk and the swampy area near the first pond can provide fantastic birding, especially in May. Eastern Screech-Owls and Great Horned Owls call at night.

Also visit the agricultural areas and large pond in the northwest section of the conservation area. Use a map to find the right-of-way between Larch Hill South and North and proceed back into the red maple swamp. Scan the fields for resident Red-tailed Hawk and American Kestrel. **Please stay on the fenced right-of-way; the farm fields are not open to the public.** *Dave Ziomek*

Plum Springs

See map C21b. Lawrence Swamp

From Larch Hill (1.1 miles south of the center of Amherst on Route 116), continue south on Route 116 to Shays Street (0.5 mile from the Larch Hill driveway). Turn left on Shays Street and continue to the stop sign (1.0 mile) at the edge of the South Amherst Common. Turn right on Middle Street and continue 1.2 miles. There is a sign to Plum Springs on the left (east) side of the road. Park along the road where you can **pull off completely.** The gravel drive leads to the main pond and foot trail.

The Plum Springs beaver ponds can swarm with swallows and warblers in spring. Warblers noted here and in the gravel pit and fields above it include Blue-winged, Nashville, Chestnut-sided, Black-throated Blue, Prairie, and Palm (migration). Muskrats and beavers are found in the pond. Green Heron, Wood Duck, Belted Kingfisher, Eastern Bluebird, Cedar Waxwing, and Swamp Sparrow nest here.

The main path leads over the pond dike and uphill to an abandoned gravel pit, now partially filled with quaking aspen and black cherry. Breeders in and around this pit include Killdeer, American Woodcock, Willow Flycatcher, Eastern Kingbird, Brown Thrasher, and Field Sparrow.

In the field east of the gravel pit, the Leslie Farm Conservation Area, Bobolink and Eastern Meadowlark nest. Please stay on the paths here and respect homeowners' privacy. *Pete Westover*

Lawrence Swamp

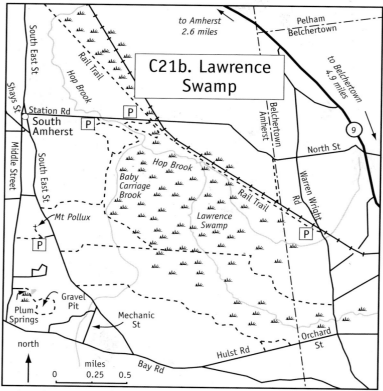

Lawrence Swamp has more than 1,000 acres of hemlock–hardwood forest, swamp, open water, floodplains, and marsh. The swamp is a wonderful place where one can encounter migrating American Bittern, Black-crowned Night-Heron, American Black Duck, Blue-winged and Green-winged Teal, and the full assortment of warblers. Nesting birds include Cooper's Hawk, Virginia Rail, Black-billed and Yellow-billed Cuckoos, Warbling Vireo, Cedar Waxwing, Ovenbird, and Rose-breasted Grosbeak. Spotted, box, and wood turtles have been recorded recently, and in spring the swamp resounds with wood frog and spring peeper calls.

From Plum Springs, return on Middle Street to the South Amherst Common. Turn right (east) and go around the common past the church and library to Station Road on the right. Alternatively, from the intersection of Routes 9 and 116 in Amherst center, take Route 9 east 0.9 mile, turn right (south) on Southeast Street and continue for 2.0 miles bearing left at the South Amherst Common. Turn left on Station Road. Follow Station Road east and downhill for 0.5 mile. Just before the Hop Brook bridge, there is a small pull-off on the right with room for three cars. Park here and walk back a few feet to the western entrance of Lawrence Swamp.

From here one may bird a loop trail following Hop and Baby Carriage Brooks before returning to Station Road or the Robert Frost Trail, which runs south for 3.4 miles from Station Road to Warren Wright Road in Belchertown. Sections of these trails are sometimes flooded by beaver activity. Both routes afford good birding in the spring, summer and fall. A head net, long sleeves, and lightweight gloves help keep mosquitoes at bay. In spring and early summer, the loop trail has Wood Duck nesting along Hop Brook, Swamp Sparrow in open areas, and cuckoos in brushy areas. All three accipiters have been seen in this section. A long hike on the Robert Frost Trail in breeding season will give you Eastern Wood-Pewee, Veery, and Chestnut-sided, Black-throated Blue, Yellow-rumped, Black-and-white, and Canada Warblers.

Another entrance can be reached by driving 0.4 mile farther east to the Norwottuck Rail Trail parking lot. Two trails start on the south side of Station Road a few feet west of the railroad tracks, across the street from the parking lot. Enter here; after about a hundred feet turn right onto a loop trail that eventually exits back onto Station Road, one quarter mile west. This loop, plus the Harvey Allen Trail, have had breeding Green Heron, Barred Owl, Alder Flycatcher, Winter Wren, Veery, and Hermit Thrush.

You can also take the Department of Environmental Management's Norwottuck Rail Trail northwest (toward downtown Amherst). Beaver activity has greatly expanded the wetlands; birders walking along the trail in early May can find themselves surrounded by the nesting activities of Canada Goose, Great Crested Flycatcher, Brown Creeper, Blue-gray Gnatcatcher, Blue-winged Warbler, and Swamp Sparrow.

Winter, with most of the water frozen, is a good time to explore, and with snow on the ground it is a fine time to look for owl pellets below pines and hemlocks. Winter has produced Eastern Screech-Owl, Great Horned, Barred, Long-eared and Northern Saw-whet Owls; at least the first three have bred here. With the help of crows, jays, and chickadees, it is possible to find owls. You don't have to be out at night to locate them.

Harvey D. Allen

GREEN HERON

The Norwottuck Rail Trail, Amherst, Belchertown

If you have access to two cars, drive one to the end of the one-mile Rail Trail in Belchertown. From the Station Road parking lot in South Amherst, go left (east) on Station Road, cross the railroad tracks, and go uphill for 1.1 miles. Turn right on Warren Wright and continue 0.6 mile, cross the tracks again to another Rail Trail parking lot on your right.

From the Station Road Rail Trail parking lot, walk the paved Norwottuck Rail Trail southeast. You will pass a hemlock stand on your right with Golden-crowned Kinglets in the winter and nesting warblers in the summer. After the hemlocks there is a large, shrubby swamp also on the right. The bit of open water in the swamp can have a Great Blue Heron, Green Heron, or Wood Duck. As you continue, white birches on both sides of the road can pack in migrating vireos and warblers during late April and May. The trees are not overwhelming in size, so the observer can get decent looks at most birds. Scarlet Tanager, Swamp Sparrow, and Rose-breasted Grosbeak breed here. In late March and early April, look for Rusty Blackbirds teed up in the dead trees. Before the pump station, there is a deep wooded swamp on the right. From mid- to late April look for Blue-headed Vireo, Blue-gray Gnatcatcher, Palm Warbler, and Northern Waterthrush. Barred Owls can be heard on early summer mornings.

At the pump station leave the trail for a few minutes and turn left (uphill) on the old, unused access road along the Amherst-Belchertown line. Look for Blue-winged Warbler, Eastern Towhee, and, in caterpillar years, Yellow-billed Cuckoo in the first scrub area. In the wet woods farther along the trail Broad-winged Hawk and Barred Owl usually nest.

Return to the Rail Trail and continue south. Near the well buildings, look for nesting Eastern Phoebe, Eastern Bluebird, Eastern Towhee, and maybe a Brown Thrasher. The forest then becomes more swampy with a mix of hemlock, birches, and maples, and more opportunities for Great Crested Flycatcher, House Wren, Hermit and Wood Thrushes, and Ovenbird. The ever-present but elusive Pileated Woodpecker may sound off at any time.

Just after the Rail Trail gate, cross under the power lines to a white pine and pitch pine forest with Golden-crowned Kinglet (November-April), Red-breasted Nuthatch, and Brown Creeper. From late April on, Yellow-rumped and Pine Warblers can be found. The trails that weave to the right under the high tension lines can produce Blue-winged, Yellow, and Chestnut-sided Warblers, Eastern Towhee, Field and White-throated Sparrows, and Indigo Bunting in spring, summer, and fall.

At the parking lot, check for Eastern Bluebird in the fields to the left and check near the tracks and the power line for Eastern Kingbird and Prairie Warbler in spring and summer. Evening walks in spring have produced Eastern Screech-Owl and a number of American Woodcock. The parking lot area has occasionally had a Northern Saw-whet Owl in winter.   *Scott D. Surner*

C22. Holyoke Range and Batchelor Brook
Amherst, Belchertown, Granby, Hadley, and South Hadley
See map C22. Holyoke Range & Batchelor Brook

The Holyoke Range, an east-west series of mountain knobs of sedimentary and volcanic rock, divides Amherst and Hadley from Granby and South Hadley. The range rises abruptly from the valley floor with the north side cool and damp and the south side warm and dry. The elevation changes and varied forest types provide interesting woodland birding. Two places easily reached by car, Skinner Park and the Notch Visitors Center, are described below. The Metacomet-Monadnock (M-M) Trail runs the entire ridge; many other trails crisscross the range. Batchelor Brook flows along the southern edge of the range through Belchertown, Granby, and South Hadley.

Skinner State Park, Hadley, South Hadley
(Also see map C23. East Meadows)

Skinner State Park on the western end of the Holyoke Range has miles of trails and a road to the Summit House, a nineteenth century hotel and restaurant, now a visitors center, atop Mount Holyoke with

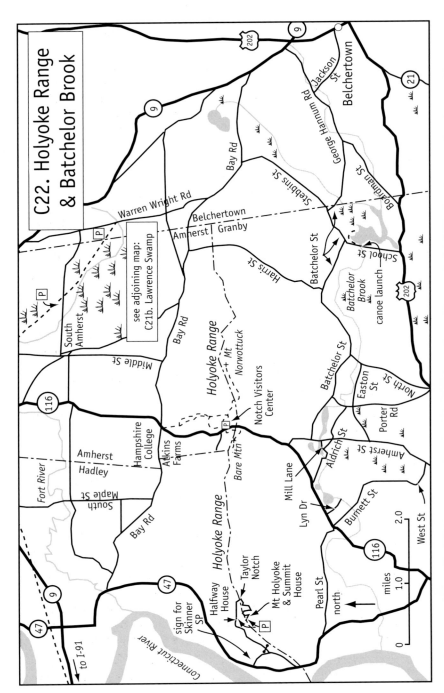

C22. Holyoke Range & Batchelor Brook

202

9

9

Belchertown

21

Jackson St

George Hannum Rd

Boardman St

Stebbins St

Warren Wright Rd

Belchertown
Amherst Granby

P

P

see adjoining map:
C21b. Lawrence Swamp

South Amherst

Middle St

Bay Rd

Harris St

Batchelor St

School St

Batchelor Brook

canoe launch

202

Holyoke Range

Mt Norwottuck

Notch Visitors Center

Batchelor St

Easton St

North St

Porter Rd

116

Hampshire College

Amherst
Hadley

Atkins Farms

Bare Mtn

Aldrich St

Amherst St

Fort River

South Maple St

Bay Rd

Holyoke Range

Mill Lane

Lyn Dr

Burnett St

West St

2.0

9

47

to I-91

Connecticut River

47

sign for Skinner SP

Halfway House

Taylor Notch

Mt Holyoke & Summit House

P

Holyoke Range

116

Pearl St

north

miles

1.0

0

commanding views of the valley. The summit has public restrooms (open when the Summit House is open) and a picnic area.

From the intersection of Route 47 (Middle Street) and Route 9 in Hadley, go 5.0 miles south on Route 47 to the park entrance on the left. Watch for a small sign to the road leading to the entrance. The gated auto road to the Summit House on Mount Holyoke is generally open from April to October. Call 413-586-0350 or the Notch Visitors Center at 413-253-2883 for park hours.

The Summit House provides easily-reached spring and fall hawkwatching. In mid- to late April the Broad-winged Hawk migration peaks, for which the south-facing porch provides the best views. Under favorable weather conditions (party cloudy skies and south or southwest winds), 100 to 300 hawks per hour have been recorded. The best time for hawkwatching is usually from 10 a.m. to 2 p.m. Mixed in with the broad-wings are Ospreys, Sharp-shinned Hawks, American Kestrels, and other raptors.

The fall broad-wing migration peaks mid- to late September. Hawk migration continues into October with good flights of Sharp-shinned Hawks. On days with north or northwest winds, the Sharp-shinned Hawks often ride the updraft off the ridge and pass quite close to the house. The roof observatory (if the house is open) affords good views to the north and is the best location for fall hawkwatching. Arrive early on fall weekends; in the afternoon there can be a wait at the entrance gate because of limited parking at the summit. You can also walk the road or the trail from the Halfway House.

Throughout the year, Common Ravens fly by almost daily. Bald Eagles are often seen near the river. Turkey Vultures roost nearby and are seen regularly from March through October.

In May, watch the shrubby area below the west side of the porch (an old tramway route) for singing Indigo Bunting, nesting Dark-eyed Junco, and, feeding on wild columbine among the rock outcrops, Ruby-throated Hummingbird.

In mid- to late May, Taylor Notch, one mile up the summit road, is an excellent place to look for groups of migrating warblers. There is no parking along the road, so park at the halfway area and walk up the road looking and listening for warblers. Also listen and look for cars. Just north of this notch Winter Wren sings, and at least four Worm-eating Warblers have been found between the summit and Taylor Notch. Two or three Cerulean Warblers have been present in the same area. Yellow-throated Vireo has nested just below the upper parking area.

The deciduous woods in the park have a good variety of nesting songbirds including Black-and-white Warbler, American Redstart, Ovenbird, Scarlet Tanager, and Rose-breasted Grosbeak. The hemlock stands on the west side of Mount Holyoke usually have nesting Blue-headed Vireo, Hermit Thrush, and Black-throated Green Warbler.

See map C23. East Meadows

If you have a few minutes when you return to Route 47, turn left and, just beyond the old brick schoolhouse, pull completely off Route 47 at the entrance to a private farm road. Do not walk beyond the gate, but take the opportunity to view the Bald Eagle nest in the trees at the river's edge. Viewing is best in late winter and early spring before the trees leaf out.

Another good place to visit is across Route 47 from Skinner Park, where DEM has been acquiring land to create the Floodplain Forest Reserve along the old Fort River. The trail from Route 47 is 0.5 mile north of the turn to Mitch's Marina between house numbers 71 and 75. There is parking on the opposite side of Route 47 another 0.3 mile north of the trail. Walk back to the entrance along the woods trails or along Route 47, **being careful to watch for cars.** The path down through the orchard has nesting Blue-winged Warblers and many other warblers during spring migration. Also look for breeding Rose-breasted Grosbeak and Baltimore and Orchard orioles. When you reach the old road turn right. The stagnant river at the old bridge has Wood Duck and Belted Kingfisher and the open field on the right beyond the bridge has displaying American Woodcock in the spring. You may hear an Eastern Screech-Owl on your way back to the car. The Reserve serves as a migrant trap in spring and fall and is a good place to observe migrating Common Nighthawk in late August.

Notch Visitors Center (Holyoke Range State Park), Amherst

See map C22. Holyoke Range & Batchelor Brook

The Notch Visitors Center is at a pass or notch in the middle of the Holyoke Range. The Visitors Center is the trailhead for several miles of trails; hiking these is the best way to see the Range's birdlife. Maps are available at the center.

From Skinner Park, return to Route 47 and turn right (north). Continue 2.9 miles and turn right on Bay Road (sign to Hampshire College). Continue 2.8 miles to Route 116. Turn right (south) on 116 for 1.2 miles. The Visitors Center parking lot is on the left after a long uphill climb. Alternatively, from the intersection of Routes 116 and 9 in Amherst center, take Route 116 south 5.5 miles to the Visitors Center parking lot.

A walk down Laurel Loop to Brookbank Trail in May or June can be productive for breeding birds including Eastern Wood-Pewee, Great Crested Flycatcher, Veery, Hermit and Wood Thrushes, Black-throated Green and Black-and-white Warblers, American Redstart, Ovenbird, Louisiana Waterthrush, Scarlet Tanager, and Rose-breasted Grosbeak. In migration look in flowering oak trees for Tennessee, Northern Parula, Cape May, Bay-breasted, and Blackpoll Warblers.

The trail to Mount Norwottuck branches off the Laurel Loop and soon crosses a powerline where Ruby-throated Hummingbird, Blue-winged, Chestnut-sided, and Prairie Warblers, and Eastern Towhee breed.

Across Route 116 from the Visitors Center, a steep half-mile trail leads to the summit of Bare Mountain. It passes through hemlock woods on the north side of the mountain and crosses to dry oak-hickory forest on the south side where Worm-eating Warbler has been found. Note that Dark-eyed Junco, with a similar song, breeds nearby.

The summit is bare with excellent views in all directions, making it another good location for spring and fall hawkwatching. Scan the skies for Turkey Vulture (March through October), Bald Eagle, Red-tailed Hawk, and Common Raven. In spring watch for locally nesting Cooper's and Red-shouldered Hawks performing courtship flights. Common Ravens nest on the South Hadley side of Bare Mountain.

In winter the woodlands on the range can be quiet, but Golden-crowned Kinglets frequent the many stands of hemlocks. In winter finch years, Pine Siskins occur behind the Visitors Center. Check stands of black birch; look for those with plenty of seeds.

Northern Goshawk, Ruffed Grouse, Wild Turkey, Great Horned and Barred Owls, Pileated Woodpecker, Common Raven, and Brown Creeper occur on the Range year-round. *Bill Lafley*

Batchelor Brook, Belchertown, Granby, South Hadley

Batchelor Brook meanders through some excellent wetland and open field birding, from Belchertown through Granby to the Connecticut River in South Hadley. The trip begins at the junction of Route 9 and George Hannum Road in Belchertown.

From the Notch Visitors Center, turn right (north) on 116. Continue 1.2 miles and turn right (east) on Bay Road. Continue on Bay Road until it ends at Route 9 (6.1 miles). Turn right (east) on Route 9 and continue 0.6 mile to the traffic light. Turn right (south) on George Hannum Road.

Alternatively, from Amherst center, take Route 9 east for 8.7 miles, turn right (south) on George Hannum. From Belchertown, at the junction of Routes 9 and 202, turn left (east toward Amherst) on Route 9. Take the first left (south) on George Hannum.

Just beyond the railroad underpass on George Hannum Road is a large field with a big State Property sign on your right (0.9 mile from Route 9). There is room to pull off on the right. This was once the Belchertown Poor Farm, and, although the buildings have been torn down, the old field trees and fields remain. Rough-legged Hawk occurs here some winters. In both migrations you can expect a variety of open-field birds. Eastern Meadowlark breeds here.

Just beyond the field, Jackson Road is on the left. The farms along this road have a variety of field birds including hawks. Drive up Jackson Road 0.5 mile, turn around just before the railroad tracks, and bird the fields on the way back. In clear weather you have a stunning view of the entire Holyoke Range.

Return to George Hannum Road and turn left. Go straight ahead at the next corner. Continue a short distance to the Belchertown Water Reclamation Facility ponds on the right which were once excellent for migrating ducks and may be so again. If the pools are filled, stop and scan for ducks.

Continue down the road and pull off the road near the fence beyond the stream at the bottom of the hill and walk back to the bridge area. There have been Blue-winged Teal here in migration and, in the marsh beyond, nesting Green Heron, Wood Duck, Virginia Rail, and Sora. Stay by the road; **do not walk into the fenced fields.** Across the road is a marshy area which has had nesting American Kestrel and Savannah Sparrow. Green-winged Teal occurs there in migration.

Just beyond the brook is a large field on your left and a beaver pond beyond it, viewed either by pulling off on the left at the bottom of the field or by bearing left on Boardman Street and pulling off on the left at the top end of the field. You will need a scope for each of these stops. The maple trees lining Boardman Street have had Eastern Screech-Owls.

Return to the Boardman Street corner; turn left onto George Hannum Road, which becomes Batchelor Street at the Granby town line (1.1 miles from the Boardman Street junction). At the T intersection turn left (still on Batchelor Street) toward Forge Pond and continue to bear left to the turn-off on the left (pond) side (you are now on School Street). If you drive a little farther, you can bird the fields on the right at the former Saint Hyacinth's Seminary.

Forge Pond is an excellent place to put in a kayak or to bird on foot (wear boots in the spring). Common Loon, Pied-billed Grebe, both cormorants, Common Merganser, and Osprey have been seen in migration. The trail to the left goes along the edge to a wetland, an oak-pine area with nesting Pine Warbler, and a ledge area with nesting Eastern Wood-Pewee and Hermit Thrush.

From Forge Pond return north on School Street and take the first left onto Batchelor Street which, like the brook, tends to meander. You immediately pass a sign for the Chicopee Sportsmen's Club. At 0.3 mile from the corner, you can pull off the road just beyond a wetland where there have been nesting Northern Waterthrush (on the left) and Canada Warbler (on the right).

When the road splits (2.1 miles from the Sportsmen's Club corner), turn left on North Street. Once over Batchelor Brook, 0.25 mile from the junction, pull over on the right to scan the extensive beaver pond. Just beyond the pond turn right on Easton Street along the south side of Batchelor Brook. At 0.3 mile pull over against the fence across from the sawmill and check out the beaver pond. There is another safe pull-off area farther uphill across from the strawberry fields, where there are nesting bluebirds and an excellent view of the recently enlarged beaver pond. This pond used to be marsh and might become a marsh area again.

At 0.7 mile from the Easton Street corner, turn right on Porter Road bearing right at the junction. After crossing Batchelor Brook, the brook and Granby Conservation Land are on your left. There are safe pull-off areas on the right. This wetland, with nesting Wood Duck, can be birded from the shore or by kayak. Turn left on Batchelor Street, and after 0.1 mile pull off on the right at a gated road, an entrance to the Mount Holyoke Range State Park trails and a good location for Barred Owl. Walk across the road for a view of Aldrich Lake, excellent for ducks in migration.

Continue on Batchelor Street, stopping at the power line (0.5 mile from the corner). The uphill (right) side has nesting Eastern Kingbird, Field Sparrow, and Eastern Towhee. The wetland on the left is worth checking. In another 0.3 mile, Batchelor Street ends at a stop sign where you can pull completely off the road. Directly across is a town-owned pond with a trail (wet and not maintained in some areas) most of the way around. Blue-headed Vireo, Veery, and American Redstart nest here.

Turn left on Amherst Street. This is a busy road; do not stop unless you can pull completely off the road. There is a pull-off area at 0.5 mile. From there you can walk to a spot near the bridge to scan Aldrich Lake in both directions. **Do not stand on the bridge;** there is too much traffic. Immediately beyond the bridge, turn right on Mill Lane. This road will take you along the lake, the dam and mill buildings. There are several places to pull over to check for waterbirds. Aldrich Lake is a wonderful place for birding by kayak above the dam; the water below is too fast-moving.

Mill Lane merges into Aldrich Street before the mill and ends at Route 116. Pull off just before the junction and walk to the corner to scan the large pond on your left (south). Migratory waterfowl here have included Greater Scaup and Hooded Merganser.

Turn left (south) on Route 116 and go 0.4 mile to Lyn Drive, on the left, to the lower end of the same pond. You can park at the head of the dirt road and walk (it may be muddy) across the bridge and on to a second pond with even better summer birding, including nesting Green Heron and feeding Great Blue Heron.

Return to Route 116, turn left (south) and continue past the gas station at Moody Corner (0.3 mile from Lyn Drive) to the low place in the road where 116 crosses Batchelor Brook (0.6 mile from Lyn Drive). There is a pull-off just beyond the bridge on the left (east) side. Blue-winged Warblers nest near the trails beside the brook and parking area. Hooded Mergansers stay into early winter.

Retrace your route on 116 for 0.3 mile to Moody Corner. Take a sharp right on Burnett Street. Pull off just before the stream at 0.3 mile, and walk down to the beaver pond and its Louisiana Waterthrush. Continue on Burnett Street another mile to a wetland viewing area on your left. At 1.7 miles from the beginning of Burnett Street, turn left on West Street. Turn left again and you will shortly come to the junction with Amherst Street. A left on Amherst Street takes you back past Aldrich Lake to Route 116 (2.4 miles). Then a right turn on Route 116 leads to the Notch Visitors Center and Amherst. *Harvey D. Allen*

C23. East Meadows
Northampton

The East Meadows of Northampton is perhaps the best overall birding location in the Connecticut River Valley, a bold statement considering the array of birding locales in the region. Located along the Connecticut River flyway, this extensive farmland is bordered by woods, artificial ponds, and numerous thickets. The East Meadows have a long and storied past, from 1880 when E.O. Damon, cruising the meadows in his horse-drawn buggy, collected a Gyrfalcon in "the great shot of my life," to more recent sightings of Tundra Swan, Eurasian Wigeon, Gyrfalcon, Sandhill Crane, Willet, Burrowing Owl, the Ipswich race of the Savannah Sparrow, Harris's Sparrow, and Blue Grosbeak.

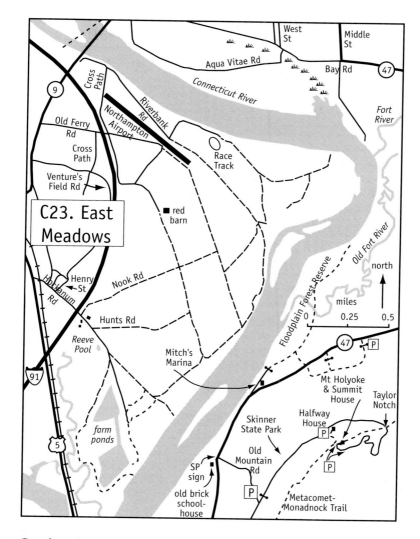

C23. East Meadows

Caution 1: Any time, especially in spring, rain can make these roads slippery, and very soft. So if you venture out there after or during inclement weather, make sure you know where your auto club card is.

Caution 2: The meadows are used by hunters in the fall; use common sense.

There are two main routes into the meadows, Old Ferry Road and Hockanum Road.

Old Ferry Road Access

Old Ferry Road heads southeast from Route 9, 0.4 mile west of the intersection of Route 9 and I-91, just west of the Coolidge Bridge over the Connecticut River, or about a mile east of the intersection of Routes 5 and 9 in the center of Northampton. There is an airport sign at Old Ferry Road. Follow Old Ferry Road under the highway to the next intersection.

Once you go under I-91 you face the Northampton Airport, where you can go left, right, or straight out into the meadows. A right turn leads toward the center of the meadows by the red barn. Straight ahead parallels the airport, past the end of the runway, and out into the meadows. A left turn leads to Riverbank Road, which parallels the Connecticut River. We will take each one in turn.

Right to the Red Barn. Start by taking a right turn; this road briefly parallels I-91 before bearing left and becoming a dirt road. Along this short section are brushy thickets on the right and open fields on the left. Although this area is generally not as productive as other regions of the meadows, it's still worth a quick look. During spring and fall the thickets usually will yield a few warblers and sparrows along with Northern Mockingbird and Northern Cardinal. Check the fields for American Kestrel, blackbirds, and at times numerous sparrows. In winter, when the meadows are snow covered, the only exposed grass is along this street and the other streets directly around the airport runway and taxi areas. At these times, look for Horned Lark, American

AMERICAN GOLDEN-PLOVER

Tree, Savannah, Song and, occasionally, White-crowned Sparrows, Lapland Longspur, and Snow Bunting. Your best bet for the larks, longspurs, and Snow Buntings is around the airport proper.

Continue down the road as it turns sharply to the left, goes from pavement to dirt, and passes a couple of houses. As you break out into more open terrain, the birding abruptly picks up. The fields on both sides of the road have weedy dividers and thickets. This area can be good in early spring for large numbers of blackbirds. The weedy dividers in fall can yield good numbers of Savannah, Song, Swamp, and White-crowned Sparrows and more modest numbers of Chipping and Lincoln's Sparrows. Along with the sparrows are usually a few species of warblers, including Nashville and Palm. In winter these same dividers can host American Tree Sparrows, and, during winter finch irruption years, flocks of Common Redpolls.

Any of the thickets in the meadows can produced uncommon to rare species. Past the last house on the left, continue to an old red barn on the left. This barn is, basically, the center of the meadow and is used from time to time as a landmark on the Western Voice of Audubon to direct birders to sightings.

Depending on road conditions, this is about as far as you should go; from here proceed on foot. Some of the species encountered in the thickets near the red barn are House Wren, Ruby-crowned Kinglet, Blue-gray Gnatcatcher, Gray Catbird, Brown Thrasher, many migrant vireos and warblers, Yellow-breasted Chat (rarely), and American Tree (winter), Chipping, Clay-colored (rare), Vesper, Savannah, Song, Lincoln's, Swamp, White-throated, and White-crowned Sparrows, Rose-breasted Grosbeak, and Indigo Bunting.

From the red barn, farm roads run throughout the fields. Walk or drive the roads and scan. In fall, winter, and early spring check fields for Horned Lark, Lapland Longspur, and Snow Bunting, and check trees, buildings, telephone poles, and farm equipment for hawks. Red-tailed Hawk is by far the most common, but a Rough-legged Hawk or two can show up anytime during the winter. Bald Eagle, Northern Harrier, Sharp-shinned and Cooper's Hawks, American Kestrel, Merlin, and Peregrine Falcon all occur.

Although rare, Snowy Owl has probably been seen here more times than at any other location in Western Massachusetts. Short-eared Owl can be seen at dusk from time to time in late fall, winter, and spring. Northern Shrike occurs in some winters.

Start watching for Tree Swallows in mid- to late March; by mid- to late April, a few Northern Rough-winged, Bank, and Barn Swallows also appear, again not in large numbers. By May you may find a few Cliff Swallows, and if you're really lucky, a Purple Martin. While driving or walking the roads during April and May, you might come across Horned Lark, American Pipit (April, September, and October), Lapland Longspur, and maybe a lingering Snow Bunting.

The best shorebird days are when inclement weather forces birds down. Spring offers a small window of opportunity for shorebirding in the Valley. Good numbers of Killdeer begin to show up by early April. Both yellowlegs, Solitary and Spotted Sandpipers, and Wilson's Snipe show up in the many small pools that develop in spring rains. The occasional Upland Sandpiper is only migrating through. Fall migration is more prolonged and yields better results. Generally, fall shorebird migration picks up in the meadows from about mid–August to the end of September. Make no mistake, we're not talking about a lot of birds probing through the potato and corn fields. Scanning these fields can tax one's patience. American Golden- and Semipalmated Plovers, both yellowlegs, and Solitary, Semipalmated, Least and Pectoral Sandpipers are recorded annually. Baird's and Buff-breasted Sandpipers show up here most years. The fields that seem to be most productive are just beyond the barn up to the next intersection and to the east. Other shorebirds that infrequently put down include Black-bellied Plover, Whimbrel, Ruddy Turnstone, Sanderling, White-rumped Sandpiper, Dunlin, and Short-billed Dowitcher.

If you're in the meadows in April or September, keep an eye to the sky; you might come away with 500 plus Broad-winged Hawks in a morning. Turkey Vulture, Osprey, Northern Harrier, Sharp-shinned, Cooper's Hawks, and Red-tailed Hawk (permanent resident), American Kestrel, Merlin, and Peregrine Falcon are often encountered in migration.

Tree Swallow numbers peak in early to mid–September with estimates of 10,000–15,000. Throw in a couple of thousand Bank Swallows and you've got a nice show. You will also find Barn and maybe a few Cliff Swallows but in much smaller numbers.

Straight Ahead to the Runway. Return to the intersection with Old Ferry Road. This time take the middle road; the airport will be on your left. On the right side of the road is a field and a hedgerow that follows the road to the end of the runway. Bird along the road and look for sparrows, buntings and a few warblers. At the end of the runway continue out into the meadows. This road takes you east of the red barn and offers more of the same field and hedgerow birds. In the last few years just beyond the runway, farmers have piled manure for future use. When the farmers skip a season spreading the manure, a large weedy patch develops, excellent for Indigo Bunting, Dickcissel (rare), and lots of sparrows.

Highlights from this area have included Western Kingbird, Northern Wheatear, Le Conte's and Nelson's Sharp-tailed Sparrows, and Blue Grosbeak. In winter, the exposed areas near the parked airplanes and the runway are the best places for Horned Lark, Lapland Longspur, and Snow Bunting.

Left to Riverbank Road. Return to the intersection of Old Ferry Road and turn on Cross Path Road. The end of the runway will be on your right. Continue a short distance to Riverbank Road. Turn right and park. In late fall, winter, and early spring this spot offers a nice vantage point. Scan the Connecticut River for a Snow Goose or even a Greater White-fronted Goose among the Canadas. Around the marina look for Wood Duck or Northern Pintail among Mallards and American Black Ducks. Look for Common and Hooded Mergansers on open water. In a good freeze, large numbers of gulls, sometimes including an Iceland, Lesser Black-backed, or Glaucous Gull congregate on the ice. Check trees along the river for Sharp-shinned, Cooper's, and Red-tailed Hawks, and, if you're lucky, maybe a Peregrine Falcon strafing the Rock Doves around the Coolidge Bridge. Check the riverbank for Carolina Wren and sparrows.

Continue down Riverbank Road past a small group of houses. A Lark Sparrow spent one winter in the thickets here. A short distance after the last house turn left. Park near the go-cart track, another good vantage point to scan the river. This area can produce a variety of species, including in recent years Clay-colored Sparrow, and Yellow-headed and Brewer's Blackbirds.

Head back to the Riverbank Road, turn left and continue down the road. This road hugs the east side of the meadows. Check the many thickets and sumac hedgerows. A grassy meadow along this road has turned up Short-eared Owl and Grasshopper Sparrow.

Hockanum Road Access

Once you've finished birding around the airport region, you can get to the other section of the meadows by returning on Old Ferry Road under I-91 and taking your first left onto Cross Path Road. (If the road is closed, return to Route 9 and follow the alternate directions below.) The Three County Fair Grounds will be on your right. Turn left at the first stop sign on Venture's Field Road and follow the road as it bends to the right. It parallels I-91. Along this stretch of road you can encounter huge flocks of blackbirds in early spring. Continue down the road and go up and over the earthen dike where it becomes Henry Street. Follow Henry Street to the end. Turn left onto Hockanum Road toward the south end of the East Meadows.

Alternatively, from the intersection of Routes 9 and 5 in the center of Northampton, take Route 5 south 0.4 mile and turn left on Hockanum Road.

Continue on Hockanum Road over the dike to the meadows. Go past a couple of buildings to a row of trees and thickets on each side. This area can produce a variety of species in both migrations. Shortly beyond this area the road branches in three directions. The right-hand fork takes you past the "Reeve Pool" and to the first farm pond. Straight ahead takes you to the second farm pond, and the left fork leads to the center of the meadows and eventually to the red barn (see earlier description).

Reeve Pool and the First Farm Pond. Take the right-hand fork. "Reeve Pool" is a small pool on the right-hand side, named for a Reeve found here several years ago. Check here in April for Wood Duck, Green-winged Teal (occasional), both yellowlegs, and Solitary and Spotted Sandpipers. This a good area for mid- to late April migrants such as Eastern Kingbird, Blue-headed and Warbling Vireos, Ruby-crowned Kinglet, Blue-gray Gnatcatcher, Yellow-rumped and Palm Warblers, and Northern Waterthrush. By early May, you may encounter Least Flycatcher, Yellow-throated and Red-eyed Vireos, Brown Thrasher, many warblers, Eastern Towhee, Savannah Sparrow, Rose-breasted Grosbeak, and Baltimore Oriole. In fall, check the thick underbrush here as well as throughout the meadows for a Connecticut or Mourning Warbler.

Continue down the road to the first farm pond. The first pond is generally less productive than the second, but it's worth a look for migrating Double-crested Cormorant or Osprey in spring. Waterfowl are sometimes plentiful.

Second Farm Pond. Return to the three-way intersection and turn right along the east side of the first farm pond. Park at a large dirt mound. When spring rains flood the area, waterfowl and shorebirds are attracted to the area; walk softly or your opportunity will be lost.

The second farm pond is on your right beyond the woods. Follow the road (a loose term) to the pond. From whenever the pond is free of ice to about mid- to late April is the best time for waterfowl. Wood Duck, American Wigeon, American Black Duck, Northern Pintail, Green-winged Teal, Ring-necked Duck, Hooded and Common Mergansers are commonly found here. Other waterfowl that may be seen include Gadwall, Blue-winged Teal, Northern Shoveler, and Red-breasted Merganser. During May, the woods around the pond can be quite productive for warblers and other migrants. Red-bellied Woodpecker is found here.   *Scott D. Surner*

C24. Arcadia Wildlife Sanctuary
Easthampton, Northampton

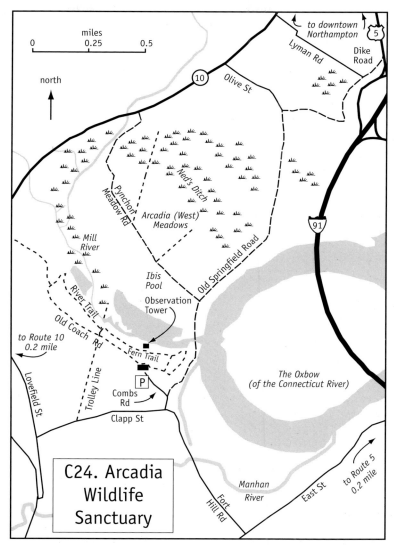

C24. Arcadia Wildlife Sanctuary

Arcadia Wildlife Sanctuary Headquarters Area

Massachusetts Audubon Society's (MAS) Arcadia Wildlife Sanctuary provides diverse bird habitats: lowland oak, maple, pine, and hemlock forest; river; floodplain forest with silver maple, green ash, slippery elm, and cottonwood; open marsh with wild rice, Walter's millet, and rice cutgrass; buttonbush marsh; grass, weedy, and agricultural fields; and an orchard.

From Interstate 91, take Exit 18 in Northampton and turn south (right) on Route 5 for 1.3 miles. Turn right onto East Street and take the first right onto Fort Hill Road (there is an MAS sign). Turn right at the three-way intersection with Clapp Street and Old Springfield Road, and then make a quick left on Combs Road to the parking lot. Alternatively, from Northampton center, take Route 10 south toward Easthampton. Turn left onto Lovefield Street (MAS sign) and take the next left onto Clapp Street. Bear left at the three-way intersection and make a quick left on Combs Road to the parking lot. The sanctuary grounds are open dawn to dusk. Trail maps and brochures are available in the Nature Center and a checklist of birds at Arcadia is available for a small fee.

Near the Nature Center, Eastern Phoebes have nested on the information kiosk, and Great Crested Flycatcher and Eastern Bluebird have nested in boxes in the adjacent field. One box has an infrared camera inside connected to a video monitor in the Nature Center. Cooper's Hawk and Indigo Bunting are frequently found near this field. A productive short loop starting on Tulip Tree Trail is described below.

The lone tulip poplar on Tulip Tree Trail is opposite a wet shrubby area with Chestnut-sided Warbler. Continue straight through the next intersection. Some of the best birding begins on the Horseshoe Trail, between a dense hedgerow and an orchard of crabapples, productive any time. Many spring migrants such as Fox Sparrow, Wilson's Warbler, or more rarely a Yellow-breasted Chat, can be found in the hedgerow. Nesting birds in this area include Brown Thrasher, Blue-winged Warbler, and, occasionally, Indigo Bunting. In fall and winter, the crabapples provide food for an abundance of American Robins, Cedar Waxwings, and, occasionally, Pine Grosbeaks.

The old orchard, with a figure-8 trail winding through the apple trees and dense shrub cover, is good for spring migrant warblers. The Horseshoe Trail then winds back along the top of the high terrace floodplain of the Mill River; the Fern Trail leads into floodplain forest with Pileated Woodpecker, Brown Creeper, Scarlet Tanager, and Baltimore Oriole. Wood Ducks have nested in cavities in the shagbark hickories.

Continue on Fern Trail to the observation tower overlooking a large marsh. In early spring, migrating waterfowl such as Pied-billed Grebe, Gadwall, American Black Duck, Blue-winged Teal, Northern Pintail, Green-winged Teal, Ring-necked Duck, and Hooded Merganser are regular visitors. Later in spring, a large mudflat attracts migrating shorebirds. In breeding season, one can find Great Blue and Green Herons,

Virginia Rail, Sora, Belted Kingfisher, and Warbling Vireo. In August, egrets are commonly found. In September and October, the ripe wild rice attracts waterfowl, Northern Harrier (not feeding on the rice), and large flocks of blackbirds. The marsh is a resting place for hundreds or thousands of Canada Geese, with Snow Geese often among them.

Fern Trail eventually comes out on the Trolley Line. For a longer hike, continue across to the River Trail to Wood Duck Pond. Listen for Red-bellied Woodpecker and Louisiana Waterthrush along the way. Data from a breeding bird census plot, established in 1975 near this trail, indicate a trend from more edge species in the 1970s to more woodland species in the 1990s. Eastern Wood-Pewee, Blue Jay, Black-capped Chickadee, Veery, Wood Thrush, Ovenbird, and Scarlet Tanager are the most common breeders. Less common species include Yellow-throated Vireo, Hermit Thrush, Pine and Black-and-white Warblers, Rose-breasted Grosbeak, and Baltimore Oriole.

Either at the intersection with the Trolley Line or at the end of the River Trail, the Old Coach Trail leads back to the Nature Center. Before reaching the Nature Center, turn right onto the Woodcock Trail to Fire Pond behind the Nature Center. As you wind through the pine forest, watch the ground for Great Horned Owl pellets.

The Arcadia Meadows (formerly the West Meadows) and the Ibis Pool, Northampton

From Arcadia Wildlife Sanctuary, return on Combs Road to the intersection with Old Springfield Road and turn left. Scan the Oxbow for waterfowl. Large flocks of Snow Geese and ducks occasionally congregate near the mouth of the Mill River, especially when surrounding areas are iced over. Cattle Egret, Bald Eagle, Merlin, Caspian Tern, and Fish Crow were seen here at the same time one spring.

After the bridge (which is closed to cars in the winter), a large field on the left has a depression, the Ibis Pool, best reached by turning left onto Pynchon Meadow Road and **carefully** parking at the first turnoff on the left or right, **but not too far in.** More fields are located farther along Old Springfield Road. Several outlets to the Meadows connect to Routes 5 or 10 in Northampton.

The Ibis Pool is named for a Glossy Ibis once seen here, a rare event. Spring is productive for migrating shorebirds and sometimes Black Terns. Semipalmated Plover, Killdeer, both yellowlegs, Solitary, Spotted, Semipalmated, Least and Pectoral Sandpipers, Dunlin, and Wilson's Snipe are seen in spring or fall.

In fall, weeds near the Ibis Pool provide abundant seed and refuge for many species, especially sparrows and finches. The year 1993 was phenomenal: Lark, Grasshopper, Nelson's Sharp-tailed and Harris's Sparrows, Blue Grosbeak, and Dickcissel were found; American Golden-Plover, Dunlin, and American Pipit were recorded in nearby fields. Western Kingbird has occurred in the fall and Rough-legged Hawk in the winter. Quietly watching rain puddles from a discrete distance can be very productive and allows a better view of the birds. MAS is pursuing active management here, with burning, mowing, and tilling to maintain weedy annuals with abundant seeds.

Savannah Sparrow, Bobolink and, occasionally, Eastern Meadowlark breed in the hayfields. Grassland bird numbers doubled from 1996 to 1998 after MAS took control of these fields. Most of the grassland birds are in the large field off Old Springfield Road past the water-ski club. With increasing land acquisition and later mowing schedules, it is hoped that grassland species will benefit.

Past the Ibis Pool on Pynchon Meadow Road, on the other side of the hedgerow (a former trolley line), are more agricultural fields. Watch for Horned Lark in winter. Part of the field on the left has been uncultivated for several years and now has young woody vegetation, ideal for American Woodcock.

The road along the eastern edge of the hedgerow leads north to Ned's Ditch, an old meander of the Connecticut, now a series of ponds and buttonbush marshes with numerous Wood Ducks. Great Blue Herons have a nesting colony here. Red-bellied Woodpecker is common.

David McLain

C25. Mount Tom
Easthampton, Holyoke

Mount Tom is visible from almost anywhere in the central Connecticut River Valley. There are two ways to enter the reservation: on Christopher Clark Road from Route 141 at the Holyoke/Easthampton town line, or on Reservation Road from Route 5 in Holyoke. There is a fee from Memorial Day weekend through Labor Day. In September and October there is a fee only on weekends.

This 1,800-acre area, well known as a premier hawkwatching site, is home to many rare plants, amphibians, and reptiles. Remember, do not pick the flowers. The reservation has huge hemlocks, some over 150 years old, that are falling victim to the invasion of the woolly adelgid insect. The rare northern copperhead and eastern timber rattlesnake are both found here in extremely small numbers and are protected by state law. Be alert when hiking the trails and be sure to look before you sit down.

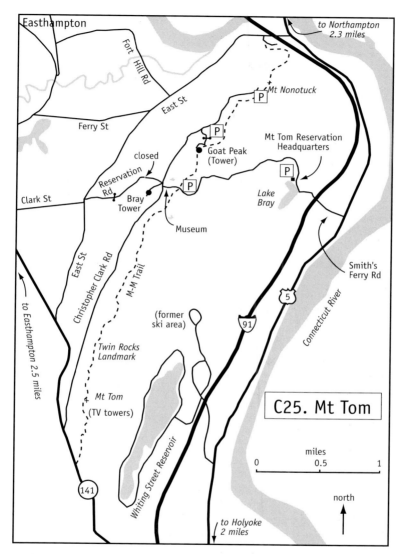

Birding Mount Tom in winter can be done from the two plowed roads or on snowshoes. Mount Tom can be quiet in winter, but a few species can usually be found, including Great Horned and Barred Owls, Pileated Woodpecker, Common Raven, good numbers of Golden-crowned Kinglets, and small numbers of winter finches.

Spring hawk flights start in mid-March with southerly winds. The traditional watching point in spring is Bray Tower, directly accessible by

RUBY-THROATED HUMMINGBIRD

car. On early spring days, fair numbers of Red-tailed and Red-shouldered Hawks have been recorded here with a few Sharp-shinned and Cooper's Hawks, a Northern Goshawk or two, and some Turkey Vultures sprinkled in. In mid-April, several hundred Broad-winged Hawks, several dozen Ospreys, and other raptors are recorded some days. Peak dates are April 17 to 27. In spring, watch for flights of Snow Geese, the first Blue-gray Gnatcatcher of the season in nearby tree tops, or a flock of Double-crested Cormorants flying north.

Beginning about April 20, listen for the sweet song of the Louisiana Waterthrush along the small streams flowing into Bray Lake. By about May 7, the Worm-eating Warbler, Mount Tom's most sought-after warbler, has returned. Several vocal males are usually between the entrance at Route 141/Christopher Clark Road and the Twin Rocks Landmark. Don't get confused by songs of the reservation's breeding Dark-eyed Juncos. Black-throated Blue Warblers nest here in good numbers. A Yellow-throated Vireo usually sings near the entrance of Christopher Clark Road. That road has good numbers of Veery, Swainson's Thrush (migration), Wood Thrush, Scarlet Tanager, Rose-breasted Grosbeak, Indigo Bunting (at the open turnouts), and, high in the canopy, Eastern Wood-Pewee and Great Crested Flycatcher.

About the third week in May, there is a wonderful display of wild columbine at the top of Mount Tom near the television towers, accessible by a hike up the Metacomet-Monadnock Trail. Ruby-throated Hummingbirds feed on the flowers' nectar, and Turkey Vultures and Common Ravens ride the updrafts. After Memorial Day, birding quiets down on the reservation. Summer brings entrance fees, more hikers, picnickers, joggers, and dog walkers. Return in September.

September brings hopes of "that great hawk flight" day, and Goat Peak Tower is the place to be. Park in the large lot off Christopher Clark Road. Put any valuable items in your car out of sight. The long ten-minute walk up the old road to the tower is quite steep. The tower is not for someone afraid of heights. If you choose not to climb the tower, walk past the tower about twenty yards east to Kettlepoint Lookout, with a nice view to the east and northeast at the edge of the cliff. Sometimes if you look down, you may see a flock of migrant warblers. For those who brave the tower, the 360-degree view from Hartford, Connecticut, to Mount Monadnock, New Hampshire, is magnificent on a clear day. Your best chances of catching a fall hawk flight are on days with a northeast or north wind. As many as 10,000 Broad-winged Hawks, 200-plus Sharp-shinned Hawks, 100-plus American Kestrels, 30 Ospreys, and others have been counted here in a single day.

Arrive early (about 9 a.m.); you might be lucky and see a Northern Goshawk circling the tower at eye level as she surveys her dominion. While on the tower keep an eye on the treetops for mixed flocks of warblers and vireos. Occasionally, a Yellow-billed Cuckoo appears. Birds are not the only fall migrants here. Some years big numbers of Monarch Butterflies are counted. On nice sunny days keep an eye on sheltered sunny spots below the tower for Mourning Cloak, Red-spotted Purple, American Lady, and other butterflies.

October brings flights of Red-tailed Hawks, a few Red-shouldered Hawks, an occasional Northern Goshawk, and possibly a Golden Eagle or a flight of Snow Geese. Enjoy your visit, and remember to look not just at the birds but also at the other wonderful creatures of Mount Tom.

As this book is being completed, the Massachusetts Department of Environmental Management, the US Fish and Wildlife Service, The Trustees of Reservations, and the Holyoke Boys and Girls Club have just purchased the former Mount Tom Ski area. Management plans are not complete, but this purchase greatly extends the area of protected land on Mount Tom and opens interesting and varied habitats to birders.

Tom Gagnon

C26. East Mountain Area
Holyoke, West Springfield, and Westfield

See map C26. East Mtn Area

Ashley Reservoir, Holyoke

From I-91 in Holyoke take Exit 15 (Ingleside) and turn west, away from the mall, through the traffic light on Homestead Avenue uphill to a gate, where you can park along the road.

The area just beyond the gate is excellent in winter for Red-breasted Nuthatch, Golden-crowned Kinglet, and, rarely, Boreal Chickadee. Small ponds to the left are good for Wood and Ring-necked Ducks. Swallows and Yellow-rumped, Pine, and Palm Warblers are early spring specialties here. In May the woodland surrounding the ponds is productive for migrant forest landbirds. After a short walk, check the main pond on the right for waterfowl, Osprey, Bald Eagle, and Spotted and other sandpipers. Loons, grebes, and diving ducks are regular here after night rains or storms. The road comes close to an old railroad bed and then turns right at the end of the pond. Across the tracks are trails to the south, where Louisiana Waterthrush nests. Continue along the back of the main pond to a road on the right between two ponds. This road returns through more good habitat to the entrance road, where you turn right and return to your car.

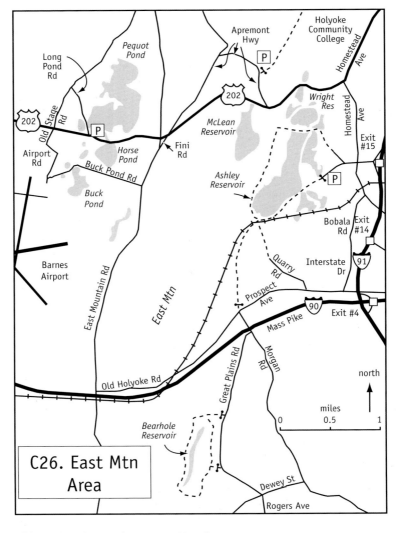

Ashley-Bearhole Watershed, West Springfield

From the Ashley Ponds, return to the light at Homestead Avenue, turn right (south), go 0.3 mile, and turn right on Bobala Road through an industrial park into West Springfield. After about a mile, turn right on Prospect Avenue and follow it until the houses end, the road becomes dirt, and you enter the Ashley-Bearhole Watershed. In spring all through this area there are good chances for unusual warblers. You can drive slowly with windows down or, better, stop and walk periodically. The trail to the right beyond a gate opposite Morgan Road is especially worthwhile. In spring every few days seem to bring a flood of new birds to this area. Dozens of Wood Thrushes and Baltimore Orioles provide background music for other songsters.

Turn left onto Morgan Road opposite the gate, go under the turnpike, and turn right on Great Plains Road. Right after you turn is an excellent location for American Woodcock. Stop anywhere along a 1.3 mile section of road before the rear gate to Bearhole Reservoir (0.2 mile north of the main gate). The complete loop around the reservoir is 2 miles. Check pines for Great Horned Owl, Brown Creeper, Pine Warbler, and, in winter, Red-breasted Nuthatch and Golden-crowned Kinglet. Check the reservoir for Great Blue Heron and Belted Kingfisher. Thrushes and Scarlet Tanagers nest around the reservoir. Eastern Kingbirds are found at the pumping station.

Return to Prospect Avenue and turn left. On this stretch Winter Wren can be found at numerous places, especially where there is winter run-off. Listen for Louisiana Waterthrush near rushing water. Worm-eating Warbler is found after crossing the railroad tracks on the rocky hillside on the right. Continue into Westfield to the road's end, and turn right on East Mountain Road.

East Mountain (North Section), Westfield

Continue on East Mountain Road for 2.5 miles, and bear right on Fini Road (will become Apremont Highway after you cross Route 202). At 0.9 mile beyond Route 202, turn right (still on Apremont Highway), go 0.4 mile, and park at a gate on the left. Follow the trail through a wet area with breeding Northern Waterthrush, then up the ridge where Worm-eating Warblers nest. This trail can be followed for 2 miles to the upper end of Cherry Street near Holyoke Community College.

Hampton Ponds

Return on Apremont Highway, cross Route 202, continue south on Fini/East Mountain Roads 0.6 mile from Route 202, and turn right on Buck Pond Road. Stop when Horse Pond is visible. Scan here for Ring-necked Duck and other waterfowl in spring. Return on East Mountain Road to Route 202. Turn left and take the next right on Long Pond Road and right again along the water into a parking area. Check Pequot Pond for ducks and gulls in season.   *Seth Kellogg and Janice Zepko*

C27. Westfield Area

Barnes Airport

See map C26. East Mtn Area

From Pequot Pond, return to Route 202 and turn right (west). Take the next left on Old Stage Road, which becomes Airport Road. Stop at the Barnes Airport gate and fence to scan the runway fields for American Kestrel, Upland Sandpiper, Horned Lark, and Grasshopper Sparrow. Nearby are Eastern Bluebird, Brown Thrasher, Blue-winged Warbler, Field, Vesper, and Savannah Sparrows, Indigo Bunting, Bobolink, and Eastern Meadowlark.

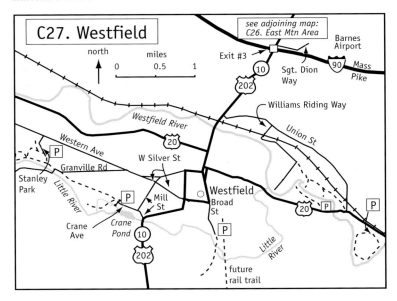

See map C27. Westfield

For another view of the grasslands of Barnes Airport, return to Route 202 and turn left (west), go 1 mile to the junction with Route 10 and turn left on Routes 10 and 202. Continue 2.6 miles south and turn left on Sergeant Dion Way just before you come to the Massachusetts Turnpike. (There is a small fire station on the left at the corner.)

Alternatively, from the Massachusetts Turnpike (I-90), take Exit 3. Turn left (north) and immediately turn right on Sergeant Dion Way.

Continue on Sergeant Dion Way to the gate between the State Police Barracks and the recycling yard. Drive or walk through the gate. Ask permission to go through the recycling yard to the fenceline. At the runway scan the fields from the fence for grassland species. Pine Warblers nest in the woods behind you. Grasshopper Sparrows often perch on the grasses, runway posts, and fence in this area, and nesting Upland Sandpipers are seen here.   *Seth Kellogg*

The Westfield and Little River Floodplains

Crane Pond. Return to Routes 10 and 202, turn left (south) and continue on these routes as they wind through Westfield. Continue through Westfield until you see a bridge ahead of you. Turn right on Mill Street just before the bridge and then left on Crane Avenue. There are two brick factories on the corner; park in the lot behind the second one and walk out on the dike. Check for Northern Rough-winged Swallows. In migration, check the sandbar and marshy area for wading birds and Solitary, Spotted, and Least Sandpipers. Check the pond for Gadwall, American Wigeon, and Hooded and Common Mergansers. Exit left from the parking lot, drive to the end of Crane Avenue (the last section is unpaved), and walk beyond the gate. At the swamp look for herons, ducks, American Woodcock, and warblers. A Prothonotary Warbler has been reported here. In the field listen for Fish Crow, Blue-winged, Yellow and Chestnut-sided Warblers, Field Sparrow, and, in migration, many other species.

Stanley Park and the Frank Stanley Beveridge Sanctuary. To reach Stanley Park from Crane Avenue, turn left on Mill Street, then left at the light on West Silver Street, which runs into Western Avenue. Follow Western Avenue 1.3 miles to the second park entrance on the left.

Go past the playing courts and park at the far end of the parking area. Look for a trail through the tall oaks. Go downhill, turn right, and follow a dirt road along the river. Check for Great Blue Heron, Common Merganser, Spotted Sandpiper, and Belted Kingfisher. Northern Rough-winged Swallows nest nearby (under the bridge on Granville Road reached by turning left at the dirt road). After crossing a small bridge, turn left onto a boardwalk with Swamp Sparrows in cattails and Wood Ducks nesting in sycamores. The boardwalk trail becomes the blue dot trail and parallels the river. In summer look for Cooper's Hawk, Blue-headed Vireo, Winter Wren, and Louisiana Waterthrush. In winter watch for Great Blue Heron, Hooded and Common Mergansers, Belted Kingfisher, Red-breasted Nuthatch, and Golden-crowned Kinglet. Check large pine stands for Great Horned Owl and Brown Creeper. This trail makes a big loop and goes through an open area with edge species. Check gardens and ponds in the developed part of the park for Carolina Wren, and sometimes Gadwall and Northern Pintail among the American Black Ducks and Mallards. The large white pine stand on the northeast side of the park has nesting Fish Crows and Pine Warblers and, in spring and fall, a large roost of Turkey Vultures.   *John Hutchison and Seth Kellogg*

C28. Mount Tekoa
Montgomery, Russell, Westfield

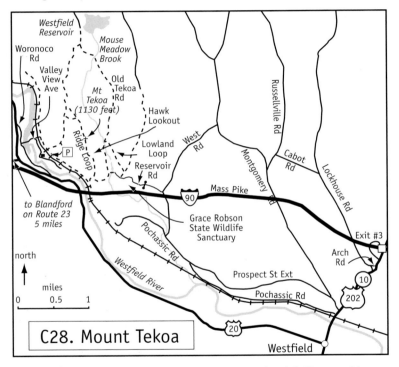

The diverse woodlands surrounding Mount Tekoa's hilltop and imposing rock ledges provide approximately three square miles of productive forest birding. At higher elevations forest fires and minimal topsoil produce habitat of scrub and chestnut oak, pitch pine, lowbush blueberry, and extensive rock outcrops. At lower elevations, vegetation becomes thicker, culminating in beautiful riparian mixed forest around Moose Meadow Brook. The 2.5-mile Lowland Loop takes two to three hours to complete. Other routes through the maze of confusing woods roads and trails can provide a full day of birding.

Grace Robson State Wildlife Sanctuary and the Lowland Loop Trail, Westfield, Montgomery

From Massachusetts Turnpike Exit 3 (Westfield) turn right (south) onto Routes 10 and 202. Turn right immediately at the traffic light onto Arch Road/Lockhouse Road for 1.5 miles, then turn left onto Cabot Road. At the end turn left on Russellville Road and at its end turn right on Montgomery Road. After 1.1 miles, turn left on West Road for 1.3 miles, and take a right on Reservoir Road (just before the turnpike). Park near the Westfield Water Department gate, the entrance to the Grace Robson State Wildlife Sanctuary (no sign) and the Lowland Loop trail.

Enter through the gate and follow Reservoir Road straight ahead for about 0.3 mile and look for woodland thrushes and warblers, including Louisiana Waterthrush. Take your first right onto a well-defined road, watching for nesting Cerulean and Worm-eating Warblers until you come to a trail on your left (150 yards). (You can increase your chances of encountering the warblers by continuing straight ahead on this road past the turnoff to the areas burned by the most recent 1998 fire and then returning to the trail.) Take the trail uphill, bear left at the fork, enjoy a wonderful view of the Tekoa cliffs ahead of you, and follow this woodland path, which will soon begin to go gradually downhill for 0.7 mile through thick underbrush, with Canada and perhaps Hooded Warblers. Near the end of the trail, turn sharply left downhill to the stream at Old Tekoa Road (now closed to traffic).

Turn left, cross the stream and follow the road 1.3 miles back to your car. Watch for Acadian Flycatcher, Winter Wren, and Louisiana Waterthrush along Moose Meadow Brook. At the last crossing a waterfall cascades from the small Tekoa Reservoir. Walk to the top and along the east shore to look for Wood Duck and Belted Kingfisher. Red-breasted Nuthatch and Brown Creeper frequent pine groves around the reservoir. There are more than eight miles of additional trails, including several connecting the Ridge Loop trails and Lowland Loop trails. The white-dot trail, described below, turns south off Reservoir Road just west of the waterfall.

Woronoco and the Ridge Loop Trail, Russell, Montgomery

Drive back to West Road and turn right. Go to the end, turn left on Pochassic Road, follow it for 3 miles, and turn right onto Routes 20 and 202. At the second light turn right on Route 20 and go 4.6 miles to the Russell town line at the Massachusetts Turnpike overpass. At 0.4 mile past the overpass take a right on Woronoco Road. After 0.7 mile

WORM-EATING WARBLER

take a right on Valley View Avenue and cross the one-lane steel bridge over the Westfield River. Follow this road as it bears right past some row houses. Turn left at 0.5 mile into the parking lot just before the paper mill. At the back of the lot, **cross the tracks with caution and park so that you do not block any road or driveway and are not too close to the active railroad tracks.** (Railroad cars are much wider than the rails.)

The Ridge Loop of Mount Tekoa is almost four miles long and can take three to four hours or more to complete. It is **strenuous,** gaining nearly 1000 feet in elevation to the top of Mount Tekoa. The highlight of the first (flat) part of this trip is the surprising ease with which Worm-eating Warblers can be located by their dry buzzy song. Six or more singing males should be encountered in season.

From your parked car, turn right (east) down the cinder road beside the tracks for 0.2 mile and turn left to the dirt road paralleling the railroad tracks. Turn right (southeast) along this dirt road for about 0.5 mile. Listen for Worm-eating Warbler on steep slopes to the left. With luck, you could encounter Common Raven as well as six woodpecker species and four flycatcher species.

When the Massachusetts Turnpike bridge comes clearly into view, you will see a road going down to the railroad tracks. Continue 75 yards past this road to a trailhead on the left that leads to the Mount Tekoa summit. Proceed up the trail about 50 yards from the trailhead to the power line. Turn right on the power line for about 200 yards until it crests at the top of the ridge. Here the partially overgrown trail enters the woods and shortly comes to the white-dot trail maintained by the Appalachian Mountain Club. Go left uphill and follow the trail markers to the top. Past the switchback, after about 200 yards of excellent Blue-gray Gnatcatcher habitat, is the first of two main rock outcrops to climb.

At the top of this outcrop is an open plateau dotted with pitch pines and dense scrub oak, an excellent spot to sit and enjoy a view and listen for Prairie Warbler and Eastern Towhee. Follow white trail markers to the top of a ledge with wonderful views to the south, excellent for migrating hawks in the spring. In another 200 yards is a 360-degree view at the site of the Mount Tekoa fall hawkwatch.

After another 0.3 mile, turn right on a fire road near the main peak. The trail markers disappear as you enter the site of the 1998 Mount Tekoa fire. Walk over the rounded summit, then down a ridge about half a mile, watching for a rock cairn on your left. From the cairn, turn left and continue on the white-dot trail to a washed-out woods road. If you miss the cairn, continue on the fire road, take a sharp left downhill at an obvious old woods road, and continue to its intersection with the white-dot trail. Either way, you will walk through both hardwood forest and burned-over areas with plenty of vireos, wrens, and warblers as you descend to the valley. Continue down the old road past two trails on the right to a right turn at an obvious fork. At a flat dirt road, turn left and continue about 300 yards to your car behind the paper mill.   *Tom Swochak*

C29. Blandford

See map C29. Blandford

From Mount Tekoa in Woronoco, return to Route 20, turn right (west) and almost immediately turn left (also west) on Route 23, which climbs parallel to the turnpike (I-90) toward the center of Blandford.

Alternatively, from Westfield, take Route 20 west 5.5 miles and bear left (west) on Route 23 uphill toward the center of Blandford.

Cobble Mountain, South Otis, and Blair Roads

After 3.6 miles on Route 23, take a left on Cobble Mountain Road. (The road is closed beyond the area you will be visiting.) There will be a beaver swamp on the right and, farther along, an older beaver meadow also on the right. These places can have Hooded Merganser and Alder Flycatcher. Return to Route 23 and turn left. Pass through the center of Blandford and continue to follow Route 23 down a steep hill another 1.6 miles. Turn left on Beech Hill Road.

Continue on Beech Hill Road 2.3 miles to the dirt South Otis Road on the right. In summer and fall you can drive this at least the one mile to the Case Brook bridge, where large beaver swamps stretch right and left. Explore this area for upland species, including Barred Owl and Pileated Woodpecker. Return to Route 23 and turn left. At 0.8 mile turn right on Blair Road.

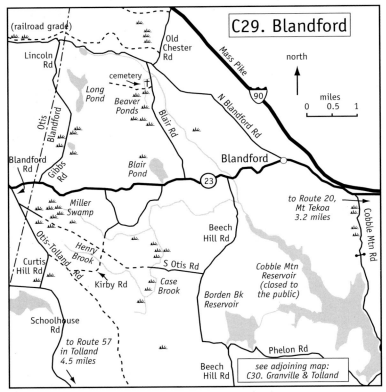

Blair Road eventually goes down a hill; a cattail marsh will be on your left (1.7 miles from Route 23). Check here for American Bittern, Virginia Rail, Alder Flycatcher, and Swamp Sparrow. The road climbs again; as it starts to go down, turn into a small cemetery on the left and park. Walk the trail straight down to a brook and work your way left to a beaver swamp where Great Blue Heron and both waterthrushes nest. Continue by car on Blair Road down to a large wetland with a bridge over the brook. Here Alder Flycatcher is certain and American Bittern is sometimes present.

North Blandford Road and Lincoln/Gibbs Road, Otis, Blandford

The road soon ends at North Blandford Road. Turn left and go 2.4 miles, passing Lincoln Road (very small white signpost) at the Otis town line. As the trees end on the right, the old railroad bed blocks your view. Park and climb to the top to view a large open marsh. Wood Duck and Virginia Rail nest here. Turn around, return 0.4 mile, and turn right on Lincoln Road (which becomes Gibbs Road at the Blandford town line). It climbs to a ranch complex and then through large fields with American Kestrel and Bobolink. After the large farm on the left there are wet overgrown areas with Alder Flycatcher. About 2 miles down, where water comes close to the road on the right, park and climb an embankment on the left to overlook a marsh where Wood Duck and Hooded Merganser nest. Common Moorhen was found here once. After another marsh on the left, the road comes out on Route 23. Turn right, go 0.5 mile, and turn left on Blandford Road, which becomes Otis-Tolland Road at the Blandford town line. Before the town line, at 0.3 mile, the obscure dirt South Otis Road, formerly open to traffic, forks diagonally left. Park on the shoulder just beyond the intersection to explore Miller Swamp (described below). *Seth Kellogg*

Miller Swamp, Blandford

Miller Swamp (see directions above), in the southwest corner of Blandford, is a beautiful 150-acre marsh. South Otis Road, closed to auto traffic, dissects the marsh. The southern end of the swamp is an open wetland with scattered scraggly tamaracks, dead snags, and lush undergrowth of shrubs and grasses. North of South Otis Road the vegetation is thick and visibility is minimal. At 1800 feet elevation, the area surrounding the swamp provides upland mixed forest habitat typical of the foothills of the Berkshires.

As you begin walking down South Otis Road, you may feel that you're trespassing onto the homeowner's property that abuts the road, but this is a public road. As you walk along South Otis Road for the next half mile, you will be absorbed in the songs and calls of a variety of woodland species.

Six-tenths of a mile after leaving your car you arrive at Miller Swamp. For the next quarter mile continue along South Otis Road through this beautiful marsh. Rarely is the interior of a wetland habitat as easily accessible. Expect to hear Nashville and Canada Warblers, Northern Waterthrush, Swamp Sparrow, and a plethora of Common Yellowthroats. Listen for Cedar Waxwing, White-throated Sparrow, Purple Finch, and American Goldfinch on the tops of the dead snags. Turkey Vulture, Red-shouldered, Broad-winged, and Red-tailed Hawks, and all three accipiter species are possible. Five woodpecker species breed in the area and can often be seen feeding on snags throughout the swamp.

At the far side of Miller Swamp, South Otis Road again enters forest. You can retrace your steps to the car or, if you have several hours and a lunch, you can continue on an extended walk over flatter country. Walk along South Otis Road another mile to a well-defined four corners. Turn right here onto Kirby Road. After a quarter mile you cross Henry Brook. Just after crossing the brook, quietly follow a little path to the right about forty yards to the shore of a secluded beaver pond, an excellent location to sit, eat your lunch, and observe whatever nature provides. Great Blue Heron, Wood Duck, Tree Swallow, Cedar Waxwing, and Purple Finch can be expected.

After leaving the beaver pond continue along Kirby Road another 0.7 mile to its end. Turn right onto Otis-Tolland Road and go 0.5 mile until the dirt portion of this road (closed to traffic) turns into a paved public road. The 2.5 miles you have traveled since leaving Miller Swamp holds a high density of many upland species uncommon in lower elevations of Western Massachusetts. A dozen or more of each of the following species should be heard: Yellow-bellied Sapsucker, Eastern Wood-Pewee, Hermit Thrush, Black-throated Blue, Yellow-rumped, and Black-throated Green Warblers, and Scarlet Tanager.

When Otis-Tolland Road turns into a paved town road, turn right and walk about 1.2 miles back to your car. This road is not heavily traveled, and you may add an additional species or two to your trip list.

Tom Swochak

C30. Granville and Tolland

See map C30. Granville & Tolland

Old Westfield and Wildcat Roads, Granville

From I-91 take Exit 3, cross the bridge on Route 5, take the ramp and go around the rotary to Route 57 west. Follow Route 57 for 16.5 miles through Agawam and Southwick (Route 57 turns left then right in Southwick center), through Granville Gorge between Sodom and Drake Mountains, into Granville Village and turn right on Old Westfield Road.

Alternatively, you can reach this section of Route 57 from Otis via Route 8 or from Westfield and Southwick on Routes 10 and 202.

After 0.7 mile on Old Westfield Road check a spruce grove on the right, just before a gated entrance to the Parks Reservoir, for nesting Red-breasted Nuthatch and Golden-crowned Kinglet and migrant Swainson's Thrush and Cape May Warbler. Listen for Yellow-bellied Sapsucker, flycatchers, thrushes, and warblers.

Continue on Old Westfield Road 1.0 mile past the gate and check an overgrown orchard on the right for Blue-winged, Nashville, Chestnut-sided, and Prairie Warblers. Another 0.7 mile brings you to another watershed gate on the right opposite Wildcat Road. Spruces here have nesting Golden-crowned Kinglet. Continuing on the Old Westfield Road another mile affords places to turn off and listen for Blue-gray Gnatcatcher and Canada Warbler. Return to the Wildcat Road junction.

The drive up the dirt Wildcat Road is a treat, with little traffic and just about every upland woodland species on the 1.2 miles to the big water tower and the Little River Gorge. Listen for nesting Acadian Flycatcher on the left, especially near the top as the road levels out.

Phelon and Beech Hill Roads

Stay on Wildcat Road as it curves left and becomes Cobble Mountain Road, skirting the water of Cobble Mountain Reservoir. (The "road closed" signs refer to a different portion of Cobble Mountain Road; your route is not closed.) Blandford Road is on your left 3.5 miles from the beginning of Wildcat Road. Keep right and go down the hill on Phelon Road. At the bottom of the hill stop on the right and listen for Least Flycatcher, Nashville Warbler, and Dark-eyed Junco. Northern Saw-whet Owl has been found here year round. The road then climbs a steep hill to an open area with an apple orchard and old farmhouse (1 mile from the beginning of Phelon Road). This is a good area for American Kestrel, Eastern Bluebird, Nashville and Chestnut-sided Warblers, and Field Sparrow.

When the road turns hard left, Borden Brook Reservoir will be in front of you. You can stop here and scan for waterfowl. Follow the curving road around the reservoir until Beech Hill Road comes in from the left (very inconspicuous vertical sign). Bear right and drive 0.4 mile to the top of the hill to the Ripley Farm and Ski Tour parking lot on the left. Stop here and watch for soaring hawks; then return to Beech Hill Road, continuing to make numerous stops for woodland birds as the road goes through deep forest until it ends at Route 57 in West Granville.

Granville State Forest

From the intersection of Beech Hill Road and Route 57 in West Granville, turn right (west) on Route 57, go 0.8 mile to the next intersection, and turn left (south) on West Hartland Road toward Granville State Forest.

As you enter the forest you descend a steep hill and cross a bridge over the Hubbard River. Park just past the gated entrance to the picnic grounds on the left. Walk down the road through the picnic area and

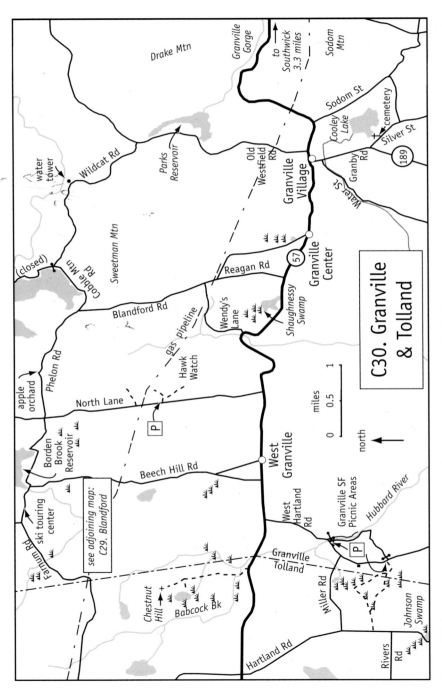

C30. Granville & Tolland

Drake Mtn

Granville Gorge

to Southwick 3.3 miles

Sodom Mtn

Sodom St

cemetery

Cooley Lake

Silver St

189

Granby Rd

Water St

water tower

Wildcat Rd

Parks Reservoir

Old Westfield Rd

Granville Village

Sweetman Mtn

(closed)

Cobble Mtn Rd

Blandford Rd

Reagan Rd

57

Granville Center

gas pipeline

Wendy's Lane

Shaughnessy Swamp

apple orchard

Phelon Rd

Hawk Watch

North Lane

P

miles

0   0.5   1

north

Borden Brook Reservoir

Beech Hill Rd

West Granville

Granville SF Picnic Areas

Hubbard River

Farmum Rd

ski touring center

see adjoining map: C29. Blandford

West Hartland Rd

P

Granville Tolland

Chestnut Hill

Babcock Bk

Miller Rd

Johnson Swamp

Rivers Rd

Hartland Rd

along the river, listening for Acadian Flycatcher and Swainson's Thrush. Return to your car and drive uphill past Miller Road to the headquarters building on the right. There are three spruce groves, one just past the headquarters, another a short distance on the left, and the largest one farther down on the right. To get to the third one, continue on the road and park just past an entrance to a second campground. Take the trail just opposite the entrance and veer off to the left through the spruces. Breeding Red-breasted Nuthatch, Golden-crowned Kinglet, and Magnolia and Blackburnian Warblers are certain and Swainson's Thrush is possible. An old beaver flowage will be on your left; look for Alder Flycatcher and possibly Olive-sided Flycatcher.

Retrace your route on West Hartland Road, then turn left on Miller Road after the headquarters building and before the Hubbard River. You soon enter Tolland; after about a mile, turn left on Hartland Road. The road passes Rivers Road on the right and then becomes **rough but passable except in early spring.** Proceed downhill and pull off at Johnson Swamp, where the beaver dam is beside and above the road. If the water is not too deep, you can walk or drive across. When the main road curves to the right to a camp, walk straight down a dirt track along the swamp. Listen for Red-shouldered Hawk and check the swamp for Hooded Merganser, Eastern Bluebird, Northern Waterthrush, and other swamp species.

Chestnut Hill Area, Tolland

Return on Hartland, Miller, and West Hartland Roads to Route 57. Turn left and go down a steep hill, across a stream and the Tolland town line. As the highway starts to climb (0.8 mile from the turn). There is an inconspicuous dirt road to the right with a metal gate, the entrance to the Fowler Tree Farm (sign says Hull Farmland Management); there is just enough room to park without blocking the gate. This road leads through a series of partially logged hills with several beaver swamps. American Bittern, Hooded Merganser, Least Flycatcher, and Winter Wren are all present in the marshes. There is a bridge over Babcock Brook only 100 yards down. Just after the next major bridge, after a half-mile walk, an obscure trail on the left leads to a large beaver pond where Great Blue Heron, Wood Duck, and Hooded Merganser nest. If you can't find the trail, bushwhacking along the brook will lead you to the pond. Listen for Swainson's and Hermit Thrushes along the way and watch for Evening Grosbeak.

Phelon Forest and Blueberry Hill Hawkwatch, Granville

Head back east on Route 57, and turn left 0.9 mile past West Granville center onto North Lane (4 miles from Granville Village). Go 1.3 miles and look for a good dirt drive on the right, opposite a house. It is ungated and goes slightly uphill about fifty yards to a small parking area. Here the New England Forestry Foundation maintains the 1000-acre Phelon Forest, which is open to passive recreation. On the other side of a small grassy area you will find a trail. Go left to explore part of the forest or right to ascend the hill to the hawkwatch. It is an easy three-minute walk unless you find warblers in the small trees, which you often do, especially in migration.

The view from here is 360 degrees and includes Mounts Greylock, Monadnock, and Wachusett, and downtown Hartford. This site has been used as a hawkwatch since 1970, and recently has been monitored full-time from early September to mid-November. There are two small concrete platforms and a new outhouse. Stay all day in season or linger for a while before continuing on the ridge trail south through more small, second-growth woods where Blue-winged and Nashville Warblers nest. Eastern Bluebird and Savannah Sparrow feed and nest in the wild blueberries here, and American Kestrel hunts in spring and fall. From March to November, Red-shouldered Hawks soar or call nearby and a Barred Owl sometimes calls from the woods in daylight. A good day's watch in season will produce dozens of migrating Osprey, Sharp-shinned Hawk, Red-tailed Hawk, American Kestrel, thousands of Broad-winged Hawks, and good numbers of Turkey Vulture, Bald Eagle, Northern Harrier, and Cooper's and Red-shouldered Hawks. A few Northern Goshawk, Golden Eagles, Merlins, and Peregrine Falcons nearly complete the pantheon. Black Vulture has been sighted, and a Mississippi Kite was once reported.

Wendy's Lane and Shaughnessy Swamp

Return to Route 57 and turn left (east). Go down the steep hill into a hairpin turn and then turn left on Wendy's Lane. Stop after the houses in a turnoff on the left and explore for Acadian Flycatcher. Continue uphill, and at the top listen for Acadian Flycatcher along a brook on the left and then farther along on the right. This road comes out at Blandford Road. Turn right (south) on Blandford Road and then keep straight onto Reagan Road when Blandford Road bears left. Turn right at Route 57 and go a short way to a turnoff on the right beside Shaughnessy Swamp. Check for herons, waterfowl, and Northern Waterthrush.

Water Street, Cooley Meadows, and Cooley Lake

Turn around, head east on Route 57 to Granville Village, and turn right (south) on Granby Road (Route 189). Take your first right on Water

BROAD-WINGED HAWK

Street, go uphill and follow a stream through heavy woods where Louisiana Waterthrush nests. About one mile up on the right Acadian Flycatcher has nested in heavy hemlocks. Return downhill to Granby Road (Route 189) and turn right. Park in a turnoff on the left near the mill with a water wheel to enjoy swallows and Bobolinks in the large meadow. Continue south and take the next left fork on Silver Street. Pull into the cemetery on the left and park in the rear right corner. Walk downhill through tall pines, where Brown Creepers nest, to Cooley Lake, good in spring and fall for Ring-necked Duck, Hooded Merganser, and, sometimes, rarer waterfowl. Return north to Route 57 and turn right to return to Southwick and the Springfield area.   *Seth Kellogg*

C31. Congamond Lakes Area
Southwick

Congamond Lakes

In March to May or October to December a visit here is a must, especially in early morning.

From Granville, take Route 57 east into Southwick. When Route 57 turns left with Routes 10 and 202, go straight ahead on Depot Street.

Alternatively, from I-91 take Exit 3, cross the bridge on Route 5, take the ramp and the rotary to Route 57 west. After you enter Southwick pass Hudson Drive on the right and take the next left on Powder Mill Road. Go to a stop sign and turn right on Depot Street.

From Depot Street, turn south on Sheep Pasture Road. At 0.5 mile bear left on Point Grove Road. Part of the lake shortly appears on your right; turn into the large public boat ramp area.

There are usually only gulls in this area, but American Coot sometimes feeds here. After scanning, turn left out of the lot, go uphill, and take your first left on Berkshire Avenue. At 1.1 miles go straight on Pine Road when Berkshire Avenue curves sharply right, then turn left on Brayton Drive and go to the water's edge. Scan this area, then go up Brayton Drive and turn left to continue on Berkshire Avenue. After 0.4 mile turn left on Echo Road and park at the end where it intersects another short street. The association beach is used only in summer and is a lookout for the largest section of Middle Pond, the most productive for waterfowl.

After checking the pond, return to Berkshire Avenue and turn left. At the stop sign on Congamond Road (Route 168) turn left and go 0.3 mile, crossing into Connecticut, and immediately pull into the turnoff on the right. By special treaty between the two states the entire water body is in the state of Massachusetts, although the east shores of the ponds are in Connecticut. Check South Pond from here for waterfowl. Swallows, sometimes including a few Purple Martins, are often on the wires and trees or feeding over the pond in early morning. Eastern Kingbird and Orchard Oriole sing on either side of the state line. Another lookout is off Second Street (see below).

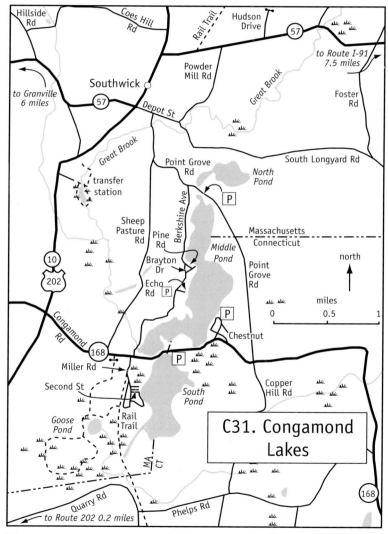

C31. Congamond Lakes

The most common spring and fall migrant waterfowl are Ring-necked Duck, Hooded and Common Mergansers, Ruddy Duck, and American Coot, but most local species of waterfowl have occurred here. The lakes seem to be a magnet for storm-downed or blown birds. Red-throated Loon, Horned and Red-necked Grebes, Canvasback, Redhead, all three scoters, Long-tailed Duck, and Red-breasted Merganser are some of the rarer species found most years. More regular are both scaups, Bufflehead, and Common Goldeneye. Except for American Black Duck and Mallard, dabbling ducks are less regular.

South Congamond Marshes and Goose Pond

Return (go west) on Congamond Road (Route 168). Just past Berkshire Avenue on the right, turn left on Miller Road. The old rail bed, soon to become a rail trail, runs along the road on your right. To view South Pond from another vantage, bear left and then turn left on Second Street. To walk the rail bed to the marshes, park along Miller Road and follow the trail south through the marshes. American Bittern, Virginia Rail, and Sora have nested here, and there is a full complement of breeding wetland songbirds and spring and fall migrants.

Great Brook Marsh Area

Drive west on Congamond Road (Route 168) to the light and shopping center on Routes 10 and 202. Turn right (north) and go 2 miles, turn right into a small industrial park, park at the gate to the transfer station, and walk down the road to view the marshes and beaver ponds. Wood Duck, Hooded Merganser, and migrant dabblers are regular in migration. Swallows often rest on the wires and Orchard Oriole has been present. You can walk upstream on either side of the marsh to another private road crossing and back on the opposite side. Start uphill toward the landfill and turn left on a trail through an overgrown field where Eastern Bluebird, Brown Thrasher, and Blue-winged and Prairie Warblers are regular and Yellow-breasted Chat has occurred.   *Seth Kellogg*

C32. Agawam

See map C32. Agawam

Philo Brook, Hart's and Leonard Ponds, and South Provin Mountain

From the Congamond Lakes, return to Route 57, turn left (east), and continue into Agawam. Turn right (south) on South Westfield Street (Route 187). Alternatively, from I-91 take Exit 3, Routes 5 and 57 west, cross the bridge over the Connecticut River, and exit onto the rotary and Route 57 west. Exit from Route 57 at South Westfield Street (Route 187); turn right at the end of the ramp.

From South Westfield Street turn left at the light (about 0.5 mile) onto Shoemaker Lane and go 1.9 miles to the Crestview Country Club on

EASTERN KINGBIRD

the right. The gate is usually open. Park at the edge of the road to view the meadows on the right, with nesting Savannah Sparrow, Bobolink, and Eastern Meadowlark. The small marsh close to the road often harbors Virginia Rail and Sora.

Retrace your route back on Shoemaker Lane to South Westfield Street and turn left (south) at the light. After 0.5 mile turn left to stay on South Westfield Street. After 0.5 mile park at a metal gate on the left, the access point for a town property that may be developed in the future. Alternatively, park on the grass at the second entrance to the Law Enforcement Academy.

A trail starts through the trees 20 yards south of the gate. Turn right to the top of the hill for an excellent view in all directions. Follow the gas line trail downhill to the left (east), checking the extensive multiflora rose thickets for Blue-winged Warbler and possibly White-eyed Vireo or Yellow-breasted Chat. Many Willow Flycatchers and sometimes an Alder Flycatcher or Nashville Warbler nest on this property. In winter look for raptors, Eastern Bluebird, American Robin, and Cedar Waxwing.

Continue south 0.6 mile on South Westfield Street past Oak Ridge Golf Club, and turn right on Barry Street at the Connecticut state line. Go 1.3 miles to Hart's Pond on your right. Pull onto a dirt road, being careful not to block farm vehicles. Scan for waterfowl and swallows in spring and late summer through fall. Pied-billed Grebe, Northern Shoveler, and Common Moorhen have occurred here. Herons use the west end of the pond. Check the hedgerow along the field for nesting Willow Flycatcher. The trees in this area usually hold an Orchard Oriole pair, and Eastern Meadowlark nests in the hay meadows.

To reach the marshes west of Hart's Pond, go west 0.5 mile, first on Barry Street and then bearing right on Rising Corner Road. At a stop sign turn right on South Longyard Road. Go 0.4 mile and, after a sharp curve, turn into a dirt road on the right between fields. Park at the "no vehicles beyond this point" sign, being careful not to block the farm road. Walk down the road to a marshy pond and check for herons, dabbling ducks, and Virginia Rail. Northern Waterthrush nests in the wooded swamp to the right. At the end of the pond, follow the edge

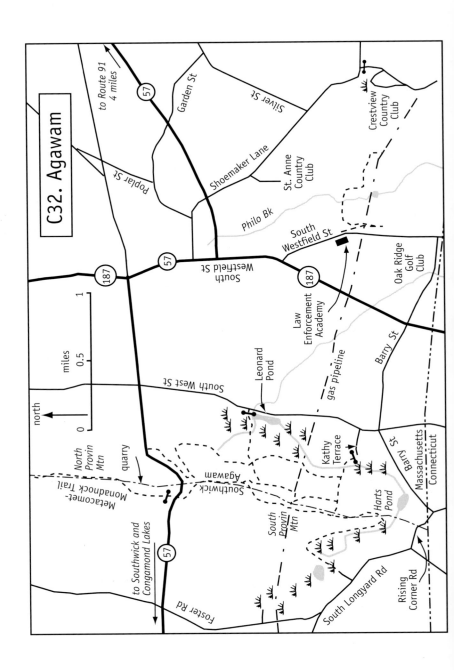

C32. Agawam

of the field to the right and walk a trail through woods along the brook and wetlands. You will eventually see white blazes showing an access point for the Metacomet-Monadnock (M-M) Trail along the Provin Mountain ridge. Either follow the trail up the ridge or return to your car and go back on Rising Corner and Barry Streets. At the stop sign on South West Street, turn left and go 0.1 mile to Kathy Terrace on the left. Go to the end, turn right, and park at a dead end.

Walk past the gate, turning left toward the mountain. This area is a wooded swamp where Pileated Woodpecker, Blue-gray Gnatcatcher, Blue-winged Warbler, and Northern Waterthrush nest. Follow the South Trail straight up the mountain to the M-M Trail or turn right at the foot of the mountain, following another trail to a gas pipeline right-of-way. If you go right, listen for Louisiana Waterthrush at the brook. Turn left (west) uphill on the gas line and look for nesting Indigo Buntings. The main M-M Trail goes right at the top of the first rise, then turns left after a small brook and up to the second rise. Any trails in this area are worth exploring. If you continue south on the ridge trail you come to an evergreen area where Black-throated Green, Blackburnian, and possibly Worm-eating Warbler nest. The latter might be present anywhere along the upper ridge.

Turn left on South West Street and go 0.7 mile to Leonard Pond on your left. Park on the grassy area along the left side of the road, and scan for Green Heron, Wood Duck, and dabblers. Orchard Oriole has nested here.

North Provin Mountain

Continue on South West Street to the intersection with Route 57. Turn left (west) and go uphill 0.8 mile to the crest of the hill and the Southwick town line. Park on the right just beyond the town line in a large dirt entrance to a road blocked with a gate and concrete blocks. If you find yourself at the pull-off by the driving range, park and walk back to the previous pull-off and M-M Trail gate.

Walk north through a gate on the M-M Trail (white-dot trail markings) and into an abandoned stone quarry area where Common Raven and Blue-winged and Worm-eating Warblers have nested. Continue on the blazed trail, which angles up to the top of the ridge and follows it to the TV towers. Along the way are lookouts to the west and more places for Worm-eating Warbler. Beyond the towers, you eventually come to the north end of the ridge and Springfield's holding reservoir with good views for observing migrating hawks. American Kestrels are often present and perhaps nesting.   *Seth Kellogg*

C33. Robinson and Mittineague Parks and East Mountain
Agawam, West Springfield

Robinson State Park, Agawam

At least 166 bird species have been recorded in Robinson State Park, and more than 75 species have nested here. Routinely over 20 species of warblers can be seen along the main road in migration; 12 species regularly nest in the park. The best time to bird here is in May.

From South Provin Mountain, go east on Route 57, take North Westfield Street (Route 187) north 0.8 mile, turn right on North Street and go 0.3 mile. The main entrance is on your left.

Alternatively, from I-91, take Exit 3, Routes 5 and 57 west, cross the bridge over the Connecticut River, and enter the rotary. Take Route 57 west and then turn at the Agawam/Westfield Exit (Main Street). Turn right at the end of the ramp. Go 1.2 miles to a traffic light (there will be a bridge across the Westfield River on your right), and continue straight ahead on Route 147 west. Go 0.6 mile to another traffic light and take the fork to the right on North Street. There is a small sign for Robinson State Park. Go 1.1 miles down North Street to the main entrance on your right.

Park hours are 10 a.m. to dusk in summer and 10 a.m. to 4 p.m. in winter. When the gate is closed, park on Colemore Street opposite the main gate. The main park road is 1.3 miles long and intersects several small trails before it ends at a closed gate just beyond the swimming pond. Check for Red-breasted Nuthatch in pines near the entrance. Louisiana Waterthrush is likely at small streams. Linger around the intersection where a gated road comes in from the left and a power line intersects the road. The brushy understory can have Wilson's and other warblers in migration; Blue-winged Warbler and Indigo Bunting nest here. In spring the swimming pond is usually drained and sandpipers, including Wilson's Snipe, may be in the mud. Check areas with large sycamores and oaks near the river for Cerulean Warbler. Red-bellied Woodpecker nests here.

To get to the James Street section of the park, exit the main gate, turn left onto North Street, and go 0.3 mile. Turn left onto James Street and go 0.7 mile. Park on the left side of the road. Follow the trail from the chain link fence 150 yards to an open field. Look for Eastern Bluebird, Indigo Bunting, and, on the west end of the field in white pines, nesting Cooper's Hawk. The trail traverses the field. Bird the trail along the power lines where you can find Prairie Warbler. Adjacent to the red pine stand an unmarked trail leads to a dam with swallows, including

Cliff Swallow, in spring. The trail continues along the east side of a brook and then doubles back toward the starting point.

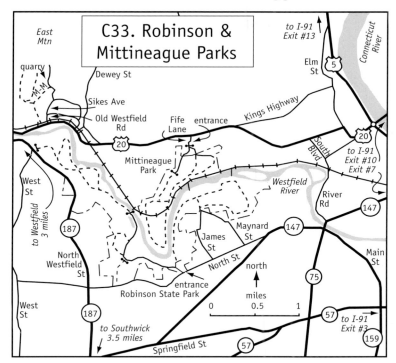

To reach the North Westfield Street section of the park, return to North Street, turn right (west), and proceed to the light on North Westfield Street (which is Route 187 but there is no sign). Turn right and go 1.9 miles to a gate and small parking area on the right, opposite West Street. Just as the road starts downhill look for a trail to the right and follow it along a ridge and then back down to the road at a small brook and pond. Migrant warblers, often near eye level, are likely along this knoll-top trail. Cross the road onto another trail that goes closer to the river through heavy undergrowth. Wilson's and Canada Warblers are reliable here. When the trail loops back to the road, turn right and return along the road to the gate. This tour is excellent for spring and fall migrants, Red-bellied and Pileated Woodpeckers, Brown Creeper, and Pine, Cerulean, and Worm-eating Warblers.   *John Hutchison*

Mittineague Park, West Springfield

Mittineague Park, recently rescued from threatened development, provides a variety of habitat, including riparian areas, grassy meadows, wetlands, and forested hillsides. The Westfield River, with Robinson State Park on the opposite bank, is the southern park boundary. A walk along the roads and trail network through heavily wooded areas should provide fair numbers of thrushes and a good showing in the woodpecker family. Red-tailed Hawks nest in the park. Watch for Osprey over the river, and for occasional Sharp-shinned and Cooper's Hawks. Eastern Screech-Owl and Great Horned Owl are present. When Common Nighthawks migrate in late August, dozens of them can swarm below treetop level over the park's playing fields at dusk, quite a sight for an otherwise rather ordinary spot.

From Robinson State Park, return on North Westfield Street, North Street, and Route 147. Turn left on Route 147 across the Westfield River and immediately turn left on River Road. At the junction (0.8 mile) bear left uphill on South Boulevard. At 0.4 mile, turn left on Route 20. Continue on Route 20 for 1.3 miles to the park entrance on Fife Lane.

Alternatively, from I-91 take Exit 13, Route 5 south. At 0.8 mile take a right fork on Elm Street. After 0.8 mile turn right on Kings Highway. Follow this 1.3 miles until it joins Route 20; the entrance is 0.5 mile on the left at Fife Lane. The gate is closed late at night and opens very early.

Drive into the main park entrance and go straight by the fields, stopping where the road turns sharply to the left. Park by the metal gate to listen. You may hear the "bee buzz" of a Blue-winged Warbler high in the maples bordering the field to the south. A walk down the gated dirt road will get you closer to that field; it is a good area to find Hermit Thrushes as they arrive in spring. This trail eventually leads to a high overlook with views of the Westfield River below and a sense of remoteness difficult to find in such a developed area. Trails to the left go over the top of Buffalo Mountain and down to a small stream with breeding Yellow-throated Vireo, Bank Swallow, and Louisiana Waterthrush. The main paved road dead-ends in a small picnic grove.

To explore the rest of the park return to the turn not taken as you drove in the entrance road, turning left to follow it back past the ball fields. Along the way, with windows down, you will hear an occasional Carolina Wren, Veery, or Wood Thrush. At the end of the road is a parking area and the beginning of a gated woodland trail down to a power line and railroad tracks. Beyond the tracks and downhill to the left is an unmaintained, often obscure trail following the Westfield River as it carves a large bend to the south for approximately a mile. Here is a treasure of warblers in spring. If you are adventurous, this trail can deliver the usual migrants and woodland birds and Great Blue Heron, Wood Duck, Ruffed Grouse, Solitary and Spotted Sandpipers, Belted Kingfisher,

Northern Rough-winged Swallow, Lincoln's Sparrow, and Indigo Bunting. Most warbler species are regular each spring along this trail, and 27 have been recorded in recent years. You never know what to expect when embarking on "the river loop." So take time and enjoy the suspense of what awaits around each bend of the trail along the Westfield River as it journeys through Mittineague Park.

East Mountain (South Section)

To get to the south end of East Mountain, return to the park entrance, turn left (west) on Route 20, and go 1.6 miles to Old Westfield Street. Turn right, go under the railroad and continue uphill on Sikes Avenue 0.2 mile to the sign for the Pioneer Valley Sportsman's Club. This is private property but the club doesn't mind the occasional visit of a quiet birder. **Please be considerate.** Turn left and with your windows open climb the hill slowly listening for Worm-eating Warbler on the left. At 0.2 mile, just before the quarry, you come to the white dots of the Metacomet-Monadnock Trail and a pull-out area on the left. The trail goes through an overgrown gravel pit. A side trail to the right climbs to the top of East Mountain, where a huge water-filled quarry hole attracts Ring-necked Duck and Common Merganser in fall and spring.

Beyond the M-M Trail pull-out, the road goes through the open top of the hill, the easiest place in West Springfield to find Blue-winged and Prairie Warblers and Indigo Bunting. Also possible are Sharp-shinned and Cooper's Hawks, American Kestrel, Common Raven, Eastern Bluebird, and Savannah Sparrow. At dawn try for Great Horned Owl and American Woodcock. *Janice Zepko*

C34. The Connecticut River: Agawam to South Hadley
Agawam, Springfield, Holyoke, and South Hadley

See map C34. Connecticut River (south)

The Longmeadow Sandbar and Bondi's Island, Agawam

To reach these sites along the Connecticut and Westfield Rivers, take Exit 3 (Route 57) off I-91, cross the bridge, enter the rotary, and immediately turn right onto Meadow Street, which becomes River Road (sign "To River Road").

Continue south beside the river on River Road 2.0 miles to a large paved turnoff on the left, and scan the Longmeadow sandbar at a distance. In winter watch for ducks in open water, especially Common Goldeneye and Common Merganser, and scan the ice on the far side for raptors and gulls. Go to the water's edge for a good view of the river.

Return to the rotary, go around the rotary onto Route 5, and go north

0.5 mile. After the sewer beds and incinerator, turn off at the entrance to the Resource Recovery Facility (Bondi's Island), and park in the large lot. In summer and early fall the river may be low; if so, there will be a sandbar with a marshy area just upriver. Egrets, herons, shorebirds, and smaller gulls are regular here. If the Peregrine Falcons are nesting under the bridge, this is the most likely place to catch a glimpse of them as they visit or leave the bridge area. In the coldest weather the river is open here due to heated water from the power plant. Mergansers and gulls lounge on the ice or in the water.

The Exposition Grounds Lagoon, West Springfield

Return to Route 5 and continue north less than half a mile to the Route 147 rotary. Go around the rotary (away from the river) and take Route 147 (Memorial Avenue) west 1.2 miles. There will be a sign at the rotary for the Eastern States Exposition (Big E). Turn left on Circuit Avenue, an entrance to the Big E, and drive 0.2 mile. If there is no event scheduled, you can park in front of the gate (do not block the gate). If an event is going on, there will be a $3 parking fee.

This old tree-lined oxbow of the Westfield River is one of the best places to find Black-crowned Night-Heron and other waders in late summer and early fall. Check the fields on the other side of the lagoon for plovers in the fall. In 2001 and 2002 a pair of Osprey nested on a light pole in the middle of the parking lot, probably the first nesting in our region since the 1930s.

Walk across the parking lot and climb to the top of the dike. You can walk south along the dike to view wetlands, shallows and sandbars.

Chicopee, Holyoke and South Hadley: October to April

Return to the Route 5 rotary and go north 5.7 miles (you will pass the Massachusetts Turnpike interchange, the Holyoke town line, and a hospital on your left). Bear right at a light onto Main Street. The first right is Jones Ferry Road, leading to a paved parking lot and boat ramp with an excellent view of the river. Continue north on Main Street 1.8 miles, turn right on Route 141, go over the bridge into the Willimansett section of Chicopee, park in the lot on the right immediately after crossing the bridge, and walk back onto the bridge to scan the river. To the north are rapids where Common Goldeneyes feed, and Bald Eagles sometimes perch on the east bank bluff. Downstream, ducks and gulls feed at outflows from the canals. Return across the bridge into Holyoke, take the first right on Canal Street, go 0.9 mile to the light on Route 116, and turn right over the bridge into South Hadley Falls.

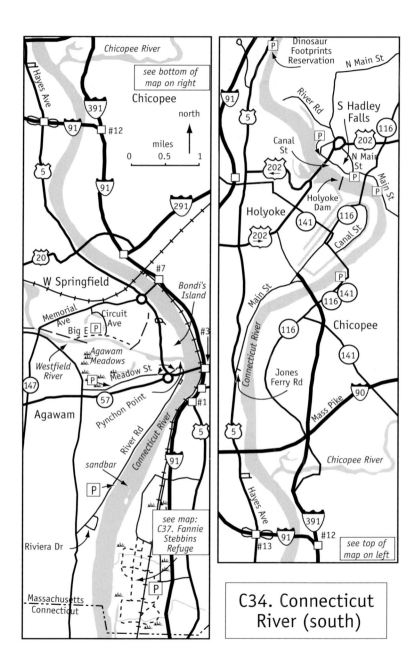

Chicopee

Chicopee River

see bottom of
map on right

north

miles

0   0.5   1

Hayes Ave

391

91

#12

5

291

20

W Springfield

Bondi's
Island

#7

Memorial
Ave

Circuit
Ave

Big E

P

#3

Agawam
Meadows

Westfield
River

P   Meadow St

147

57

Pynchon Point

Agawam

#1

River Rd

Connecticut River

5

91

sandbar

P

see map:
C37. Fannie
Stebbins
Refuge

Riviera Dr

P

Massachusetts
Connecticut

Dinosaur
Footprints
Reservation

P

N Main St

91

River Rd

S Hadley
Falls

5

P

202

116

Canal
St

202

N Main
St

P

Main St

P

Holyoke
Dam

Holyoke

141

116

202

Canal St

141

P

116

116

Chicopee

141

Main St

Jones
Ferry Rd

Connecticut River

Mass Pike

90

5

Chicopee River

Hayes Ave

391

#12

91

#13

see top of
map on left

C34. Connecticut
River (south)

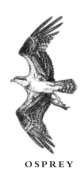

OSPREY

After the bridge turn right at the light on Main Street. At 0.3 mile take a right into a pumping station parking lot after a playground. View the river from this spot or continue another 0.2 mile to a gate with a sign for the Berchulski Fishing Area. Park here and walk down to the river for an excellent view of rapids, outflows, and pools. Iceland and Glaucous Gulls are sometimes here. Common Goldeneye and Common Merganser are regular, sometimes with a Barrow's Goldeneye or other diving species. Return north on Main Street; go straight through the traffic light at the bridge. (Main Street will become Canal Street.) At 0.3 mile pull into a lot on the left, park by a gate to the public fishing area below the Holyoke dam, and walk over the dike to the river, an excellent spot for Iceland and Glaucous Gulls in the rocks at the base of the dam. Continue another 0.4 mile and turn into the Heritage Park lot on the left overlooking the pool above the dam, where an Arctic Tern once spent two weeks in June.

Continue on Canal Street as it curves right, enter the rotary, and take Route 202 west over the bridge. Turn right at the first light, following Route 202 uphill to the light on Route 5, turn right (north), and go 2.7 miles to a paved turnoff on the right with The Trustees of Reservations green sign for the Dinosaur Footprints Reservation, the most reliable spot to find Barrow's Goldeneye with Common Goldeneyes. **Be sure to hide valuables and lock your car.** Walk to the river. **(Be careful; the rail line is active.)** Scan for Bald Eagle and waterfowl.   *Seth Kellogg*

C35. Chicopee and Ludlow

See map C35. Chicopee & Ludlow

Westover Air Reserve Base (Westover ARB), Chicopee

It has sometimes been possible to join pre-arranged, guided tours in June to view nesting Upland Sandpiper, Grasshopper Sparrow, and Bobolink. Contact the base to see if tours are planned. See the rest of this account for a trip along the Chicopee River floodplain and the Westover ARB fences with opportunities to see water, grassland, and marsh birds.

Directions to Westover ARB: From Massachusetts Turnpike Exit 5 (Chicopee), turn left (north) on Route 33. After 0.6 mile turn right on Westover Road (with large signs to the base), and go 1.4 miles to the gate.

Chicopee River Floodplain

From Massachusetts Turnpike Exit 5, turn right (south) on Route 33, and after 0.9 mile turn left at a five-way intersection onto Sheridan Street. Immediately turn right onto Taylor Street. Park at the gate at the end and walk the short way to the bluff overlooking the river. Ducks and gulls feed here throughout the year; herons, egrets, and even Pied-billed Grebe may be present in summer.

Return to the intersection and turn left over the bridge, then left (east) on Route 141 (East Main Street). At 0.7 mile turn left on Bellevue Avenue, which soon ends above a large marshy area on the river. In warm weather Great Blue Heron, egrets, and Osprey sometimes feed here. On two consecutive summers a Least Bittern was flushed here by a canoe. If you wish to launch a canoe, or to explore longer than a few minutes, park on Wildemere Street on the other side of Route 141. In winter Iceland and Glaucous Gulls sometimes lounge with common gulls on the ice here; mergansers and other ducks are often in the river in the distance.

Chicopee Memorial State Park and Westover Grasslands

Return to Route 141, turn left (east), go 1.5 miles, and turn sharply left at the foot of a hill onto Front Street, which immediately curves right over a bridge. Continue 1.9 miles, turn left on Holyoke Street, which becomes Burnett Road, and continue 1 mile to the Chicopee Memorial State Park entrance on your right. Alternatively, to get to the park from the Massachusetts Turnpike Exit 6 turn right (north) on Burnett Road; the entrance is 0.6 mile on the left.

The park is open 10 a.m. to 4 p.m., sometimes with a $5.00 parking fee. Much of the park is pine plantation with Red-breasted Nuthatch and Pine Warbler. Park at the parking lot on the left and walk down the main road past the headquarters, or drive through the gate if there is parking available farther on. A short walk leads to trails to the left to the Westover fence. Scan the runway grasslands for Upland Sandpiper, Field, Savannah, and Grasshopper Sparrows, and Bobolink.

Another way to check for Westover's grassland birds is to return to Burnett Road, which becomes Holyoke Street in Ludlow. At 1.0 mile, turn left at a light onto West Street and after 1.1 miles turn left again on Randall Road. Continue past the county jail and an industrial park. Turn right at the T to the Westover fence. Park and scan for grassland birds.

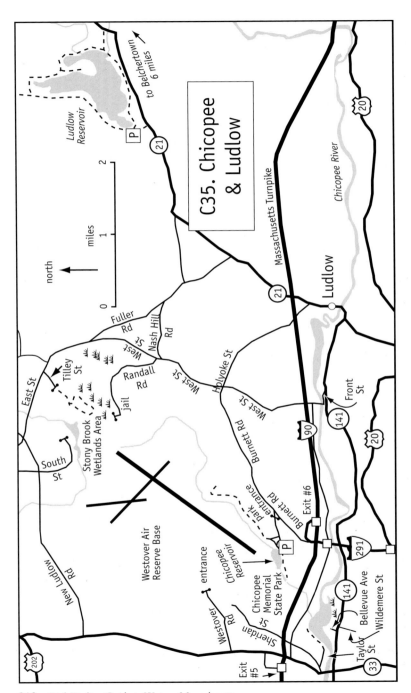

C35. Chicopee
& Ludlow

Westover Marshes, Ludlow

Return to West Street, which becomes East Street, turn left, and continue 1.9 miles to Tilley Street. Turn left and park at the entrance to the
Stony Brook Wetlands Area, a cooperative project of the Town of Ludlow
and the state. Walk along the old road bed through pines and listen for
Red-breasted Nuthatch. After 0.8 mile take the trail to the left into an
overgrown bushy area. White-eyed Vireo has occurred here several times
in May. The trail forks into a loop; take either fork. There are various
places to scan the marsh for bitterns, herons, Wood Duck, teal, rails, flycatchers, and, in cattails, Marsh Wren.

More Westover Grasslands, Chicopee

Return to East Street, turn left, go 1.0 mile, and turn left on New Ludlow
Road. Go another 0.5 mile and turn left on South Street toward the
Westover Golf Course. Stop and check the Westover fields beyond the fence
on the right for Grasshopper Sparrows. Upland Sandpipers are sometimes
seen in the large fields north of the fence, visible from New Ludlow Road.

To return to the Massachusetts Turnpike, continue 2.4 miles on New Ludlow Road and turn left (south) onto Route 33 toward the turnpike entrance (about 2 miles). *Seth Kellogg*

Ludlow Reservoir, Ludlow

The Ludlow Reservoir, part of the Springfield water system, is opening its
trails to the public. Check signs at the parking area for current regulations.
You can walk all or part of the 4.6-mile wide, flat trail around the reservoir. Bring a scope, and expect a pleasant, productive birding experience.

The parking lot is off Route 21, 7.5 miles south of the center of Belchertown and about 4 miles northeast of downtown Ludlow. (From the
Chicopee River Floodplain above, continue east on Route 141 and turn
left on Route 21 through Ludlow.)

The reservoir offers excellent migrant waterfowl from spring thaw (usually March) through May and again from August to freeze-up (usually
mid-December), when you can see Red-throated and Common Loons,
Pied-billed, Horned, and Red-necked Grebes, Double-crested and Great
Cormorants, large numbers of Ring-necked Duck, Common Goldeneye, Common Merganser, Ruddy Duck, and other ducks. Gulls arrive
late in the day, sometimes, in the fall, including Bonaparte's. There is
good, varied passerine habitat along the way.

First check the reservoir from the new boat dock. Then walk north on the
trail, stopping often to check the reservoir. Check red pine plantations for

migrants and resident woodpeckers, nuthatches, and Brown Creeper. Check wetlands for migrating warblers; check open and scrubby areas for resident and migrating sparrows. Migrating Osprey perch in trees on the west side; Common Ravens are often seen. It is about 2 miles to the north end of the reservoir with several wetlands and another half mile to the side trail down the peninsula with good views of the north end of the reservoir. *Harvey D. Allen*

C36. Forest Park
Springfield

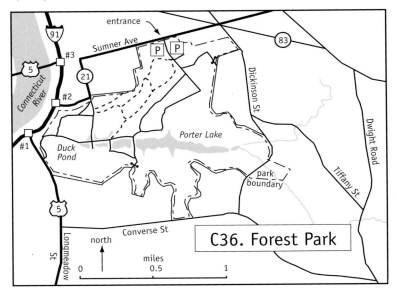

From I-91 take Exit 2 (Route 83 and East Longmeadow). Follow the road as it curves to the left and then turn right at the light on Sumner Avenue. The main park entrance ($2 fee) is 0.6 mile on the right.

You can park in the tennis court lots after the toll booth and walk the trails east or west. The mature trees are prime areas for spring and fall migrants; numbers vary from none to many. One trail to the west goes down a ravine to the duck pond. If you drive on, buildings will be on your left, and a one-way road goes to the right between ball fields and woods. Stop anywhere to explore the tall trees on your right, including many hemlocks infested with woolly adelgid. Turn right at a stop sign, descend to the duck pond, and turn left into the small parking lot. In winter rarer dabblers, from Wood Ducks to Gadwalls, occur with many American Black Ducks and Mallards. Occasionally a Black-headed Gull occurs. From here you can explore trails on the south side of the ponds. Kentucky and Hooded Warblers are occasional in spring, and Winter Wren is regular in cold weather.

Continue on the one-way road to another parking lot near the skate house. Here you can head east into less traveled trails in wilder parts of the park, where anything can show up. If you continue uphill back to the buildings, you find more parking and other trails into less used parts of the park. *Seth Kellogg*

C37. Fannie Stebbins Wildlife Refuge and Longmeadow Conservation Land
Longmeadow

See map C37. Fannie Stebbins Refuge

The floodplain and sandbar here form one of the prime birding areas in Western Massachusetts. Uncommon birds found fairly regularly include Great and Snowy Egrets, Little Blue Heron, Black-crowned Night-Heron, Gadwall, Northern Shoveler, Northern Pintail, Black-bellied, American Golden-, and Semipalmated Plovers, Sanderling, White-rumped, Baird's, and Buff-breasted Sandpipers, Bonaparte's Gull, Common and Black Terns, White-eyed Vireo, Fish Crow, Carolina Wren, and Connecticut, Mourning, and Hooded Warblers.

Coming from the north on I-91, take Massachusetts Exit 1 in Springfield onto Route 5/Columbus Avenue/Longmeadow Street south into Longmeadow. At the fifth light (1.1 miles) turn right onto Emerson Road and pass under I-91 to Pondside Road.

Coming from the south on I-91, take Connecticut Exit 49 in Enfield and turn right at the end of the ramp onto Route 5/Enfield Street, which becomes Longmeadow Street. Continue 2.3 miles on Longmeadow Street, passing the Longmeadow Town Hall and Bay Path College; turn left on Emerson Road and pass under I-91 to Pondside Road.

The Longmeadow Sandbar

From the junction of Emerson and Pondside Roads, continue straight ahead (west) over the railroad tracks and turn left on West Road. Just past a cluster of houses (0.2 mile) there is a parking area on the right, with a short path at the back leading to the river. From here you can view the sandbar.

From mid-July to mid-August the sandbar is a hotspot for migrating raptors, shorebirds, wading birds, gulls, terns, and swallows. The river level varies during this period depending on rain and the need for water at power-generating facilities. During dry periods and weekends the water is lowest and birds most likely. To get closer to the birds, you can brave the first 20 feet of channel (usually only a foot or so deep but the **water levels vary with power dam needs so use caution),** and walk across mud or shallow water to the main sandbar. Rarities reported here include Tricolored Heron, White Ibis, American Avocet, Willet, Red Knot, Western and Stilt Sandpipers, Long-billed Dowitcher, Red Phalarope, Franklin's Gull, Forster's and Sooty Terns, and Northern Wheatear.

West Road

Farther along (0.2 mile), West Road turns to dirt and goes through large town-owned fields used for leaf disposal and leased to vegetable farmers. In spring, low flood pools are favored by ducks and shorebirds, but **beware of muddy roads.** If you can drive to the end of the fields, turn left and return over the railroad tracks on Tina Lane to Pondside Road. Scan the fields for Horned Larks, American Pipits, and Snow Buntings in winter.

Pondside Road

From the Longmeadow Sandbar, return across the railroad tracks to Pondside Road. Before you turn, check the pond at the north end of Pondside along Emerson Road, especially good for wading birds. Then go south on the aptly named Pondside Road which borders shallow ponds its entire length. There are several places to pull over and scan ponds and edges. The ponds between the Bates Trail sign and the Longmeadow Brook culvert are good for Wood Duck, teal, and other dabblers. The marshes just north of Bark Haul Road are places for rails and Swamp Sparrow. Look for swallows over the ponds in early spring and summer. Warbling Vireo is a common nester. The trees to the west of the road and along the edge of the ponds are popular spots for warblers, especially Yellow-rumped and Palm, in migration. This area is one of the most likely places in the region for Least Bittern and Common Moorhen. A Eurasian Wigeon spent a week here one fall.

Old Road Loop and Side Trails

The Old Road Loop is the common walking trip through Fannie Stebbins Refuge and Longmeadow conservation property. The starting point is the intersection of Pondside Road and Bark Haul Road at the refuge sign (1.5 miles from Emerson Road). The sign has a complete map of the trails. The starting point itself is often very productive during warbler migration. As you start on Bark Haul Trail (once part of Bark Haul Road), check the pond immediately on your right and then the one on the left at the railroad tracks for waterbirds. **Walking the**

tracks is illegal and dangerous; trains travel at high speeds here. Cross with care.

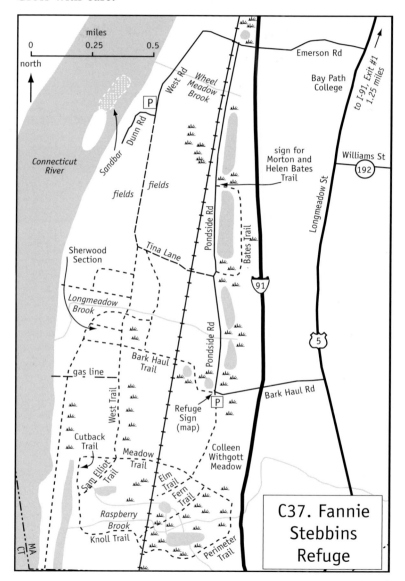

miles
0   0.25   0.5

north

Connecticut River

Sandbar

Dunn Rd

West Rd

P

Wheel Meadow Brook

Emerson Rd

Bay Path College

to I-91, Exit #1
1.25 miles

Williams St
192

sign for Morton and Helen Bates Trail

Longmeadow St

fields

fields

fields

Sherwood Section

Tina Lane

Pondside Rd

Bates Trail

91

Longmeadow Brook

5

gas line

Bark Haul Trail

Pondside Rd

West Trail

Refuge Sign (map)

P

Bark Haul Rd

Cutback Trail

Meadow Trail

Colleen Withgott Meadow

Sam Elliot Trail

Elm Trail

Fern Trail

Raspberry Brook

Knoll Trail

Perimeter Trail

MA CT

C37. Fannie Stebbins Refuge

Past the tracks is an unnamed trail to the right, a side trip that allows you to head north to Longmeadow Brook, and then either turn left to the other trails or cross the bridge straight ahead to the open fields.

NORTHERN PINTAIL

This trail can be productive for flycatchers, thrushes, and warblers in spring migration.

If you continue on Bark Haul Trail, you will come to West Trail (once part of West Road) where you can make other side loops by going straight or turning right (north) and then left after a short way. These trails go west toward the river and make a loop in the Sherwood Section area, with mature silver maples and cottonwoods, and a planting of dense spruce.

If you go left (south) when you reach West Trail, you find an area of large pin oaks and silver maples, good for Red-bellied and Pileated Woodpeckers, vireos, Wood Thrush, and treetop warblers. Farther on you can turn right at a gas line and follow the trail to the Connecticut River. Continuing straight on West Trail you enter two hay meadows, at the end of which is the Meadow Trail.

At the West Trail/Meadow Trail intersection, you can take a side loop straight ahead on the Elliot Trail to a backwater of the river. From there, you can turn right onto the Cutback Trail, bringing you back to the intersection. You can try to go south on Cutback trail and cross Raspberry Brook (sometimes there is no bridge) to reach the Knoll Trail.

Turning left (east) at the junction of Meadow and West Trails, you pass more ponds, which may flood the trail. Woodpeckers, flycatchers, and Eastern Bluebirds are often near the railroad. Farther on is an intersection with the Elm Trail and more worthwhile trail options. If they are not flooded, two of the trails go right (south) across wet areas to the Knoll Trail, which follows along an overgrown gravel pit and Raspberry Brook, ending at the river. Here birds of drier and brushy habitat may be found.

If you turn left (north) at the Meadow Trail/Elm Trail intersection, it is a short distance to your starting point at the refuge sign. American Woodcock display in the Colleen Withgott Meadow on your right. The shrubs in the middle of the meadow are good for Willow Flycatcher and, in fall, Connecticut Warbler.

The most pleasant way to bird the Connecticut River is to put in a canoe and paddle south to the Enfield, Connecticut, boat launch. The river is popular with motor boaters and fishermen, so the best time to bird is at dawn or shortly after. Bald Eagles nest nearby in Suffield, Connecticut, so are usually seen in this area. Herons, egrets, and Osprey can be found in August. A long sandbar straddling the Massachusetts-Connecticut line can have herons, egrets and shorebirds. Carolina Wren song carries far across the water. Belted Kingfishers are common. Farther north you can put in a canoe at the Bondi's Island boat ramp and paddle up the quiet lower Westfield River with more sandbars and fields.   *Bruce Kindseth*

C38. East Longmeadow

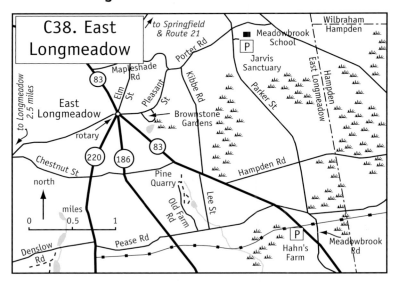

The sanctuaries, farms, and former quarries of East Longmeadow provide diverse year-round birding on the edge of an urban area. Directions to sites in East Longmeadow are from the "rotary" at the center of town, a **very confusing** intersection **to be traversed with caution.**

Pine Quarry Reservation

From the East Longmeadow rotary follow Route 186 (Prospect Street) 1.7 miles south and turn left onto Pease Road. Follow Pease Road 0.4 mile east, turn left, take Old Farm Road 0.7 mile to its end, and park at the cul-de-sac. Walk a short distance along the path, which starts just to the right of the fire hydrant, to an old dirt road, approximately 150 feet east of the cul-de-sac. Turn right (south) following the old dirt road for about 1000 feet as it heads south and then curves eastward downhill to the quarry. There are many trails, all eventually leading to the complex of small quarries and the main quarry. Although the main paths circling the area are safe, **care should be taken** while walking near the steep ravines and quarry hole.

Pine Quarry produced architectural sandstone until the early 1900s; this 16.5-acre property is now a conservation area of the town of East Longmeadow. Although largely forested, habitat diversity at this site makes it a good place for birding year round. In spring migration, canopy-dwelling warbler species are often abundant in hardwood forest surrounding the quarry, while nearby streamside wetlands are good for both waterthrushes. Winter Wrens nest near cool rocky ravines. Broad-winged Hawks occur in woods in summer, and brushy areas near the power line and hedgerows north of the quarry near Chestnut Street provide habitat for Carolina Wren, Blue-winged Warbler, Indigo Bunting, and various sparrows. Patches of pine and hemlock offer suitable year-round refuge for Eastern Screech-Owl and Barred Owl, while forested areas support Red-bellied and Pileated Woodpeckers.

Hahn's Farm and Power Line, Route 83

From Pine Quarry, return to Pease Road and turn left (east). At Route 83/Somers Road, turn right to where the high tension power line crosses the highway. Park on the shoulder near the entranceway to the power line service road; **do not block the gate.**

Alternatively, from the rotary at the center of East Longmeadow, follow Route 83/Somers Road about 2.8 miles southeast to the high tension line. (Parking directions are above.)

Scan the extensive farmed areas adjacent to Route 83, the power lines, and the pylons for Turkey Vulture, Red-tailed Hawk, American Kestrel, and (rare in winter) Rough-legged Hawk. In winter, check the farm fields for Horned Lark, American Pipit, and Snow Bunting; inspect brushy pastures and hedgerows west of the road for Northern Shrike. In spring and summer, particularly if hay has been planted, the fields east of the road are excellent for swallows, Eastern Bluebird, Bobolink, and Eastern Meadowlark.

Walk westward down the power line through varied habitats. White pine stands south of the right-of-way have breeding Pine Warblers in summer, and are frequently good for Red-breasted Nuthatch in winter. Great Horned Owls are regularly found near these pines. Brushy areas along the power line produce cuckoos, Brown Thrasher, and Blue-winged and Prairie Warblers. Low scrub-shrub areas near stream drainages crossing the power line support many breeding bird species. Uncommon spring migrants here have included Yellow-bellied and Alder Flycatchers and Lawrence's Warbler (rare). In early spring, the alder patches are good for American Woodcock. Virginia Rail and Sora have been observed in the marshes, and Solitary and Spotted Sandpipers are often seen near muddy stream edges. Extensive red maple swamps adjacent to the right-of-way are likely spots for Barred Owl. Upland forested areas with tall hardwoods usually produce treetop foragers in migration.

Jarvis Nature Sanctuary

From Hahn's Farm and the high tension lines, continue south 0.3 mile on Route 83 to the end of the field and turn sharply left on Meadow-brook Road (the other side of Hahn's Farm). After 0.4 mile, turn right on Parker Street and follow it 2.4 miles to the entrance to Meadow-brook School on the right.

Alternatively, from the rotary at the center of East Longmeadow, follow Pleasant Street (between the bank and the gas station) east and northeast 1.0 mile to the branching intersection of Mapleshade Road and Porter Road. Bear right (northeast) onto Porter Road and continue nearly a mile to Parker Street. Turn right onto Parker Street and continue about 0.1 mile to the entrance to Meadowbrook School on the left.

Follow the school road to an inconspicuous brownstone sanctuary marker for the Jarvis Nature Sanctuary on the right before the school; park in the school parking lot. Access is easiest on weekends, on school holidays, or after school hours. Do not venture beyond the barbed-wire fence separating sanctuary property from farm fields, which can be adequately surveyed from numerous points along the fence.

Brushy fields at the Sanctuary are often quite productive for sparrows including Fox Sparrow, particularly in fall. In winter scan the farm and athletic fields for Horned Lark and Snow Bunting. Occasional Northern Shrikes have stayed here for weeks, and every year the odd Snow Goose occurs among large flocks of Canada Geese attracted to corn stubble. In early spring, Wilson's Snipe, American Woodcock, and large flocks of Red-winged Blackbirds congregate at the marshy lower ends of farm fields. Eastern Meadowlarks are reliable summer residents, and, if hay is cultivated, Bobolinks may also be present. Red-tailed Hawks are ubiquitous year round, and in summer watch for Red-shouldered Hawk, American Kestrel, Black-billed Cuckoo, Eastern Bluebird, and Prairie Warbler.

Brownstone Quarry

From Jarvis Sanctuary, return to Parker Street and turn right (north). After 0.1 mile turn left on Porter Road toward East Longmeadow.

When Porter Road ends (0.7 mile), bear left on Pleasant Street for 0.6 mile to the inconspicuous brownstone sign for the Brownstone Gardens residential community on the left.

Alternatively, from the rotary at the East Longmeadow town center follow Pleasant Street (between the bank and the gas station) 0.3 mile east to Brownstone Gardens on the right.

Enter the drive and continue to the rear of the property facing the water-filled quarry hole. Do not park in spaces reserved for residents. Although this is private property, there has never been a problem birding here, perhaps because many residents are birders. However, it is probably best that parties not exceed two or three people.

Sandstone from the historic Brownstone Quarry was used for colonnades in the rotunda of the Capitol Building in Washington. The quarry property is now a retirement community. In spring and summer, the large water-filled quarry hole attracts Northern Rough-winged and other swallows including, rarely, Purple Martin. Green Heron is a summer resident, and Great Blue Herons are common in spring and fall. Wetland areas east of the quarry hole often support breeding Virginia Rails and migrant Solitary and Spotted Sandpipers. In spring, tall hardwood trees near the residences and adjacent cemetery are excellent for vireos, warblers, and Baltimore Oriole. Waterfowl such as Gadwall, American Wigeon, Northern Pintail, and Green-winged Teal are occasional in fall. Feeding stations set out by residents are worth checking at any season.   *Tad M. Zebryk*

C39. Wilbraham and Hampden

To reach Wilbraham from the Massachusetts Turnpike, take Exit 7 (Ludlow). Turn right on Route 21 and at 0.4 mile turn right again on Chapin Street. Follow Chapin Street (it goes back under the turnpike) until it ends in 3 miles. Turn right on Cottage Street, go over the bridge and take a sharp right on Route 20 west (Boston Road). Continue 0.2 mile to Main Street. Turn left (south) and follow Main Street 1.1 miles to Delmor Circle on the right.

Cedar Swamp, Wilbraham

Access Point 1: Turn right (west) at the sign "Delmor Circle to Decorie Drive" and then left on Decorie Drive. Drive to the end of the road and park near the Wilbraham Conservation Commission sign. Follow the old road starting behind the sign and enter the swamp. Access Point 2: Follow Decorie Drive 0.3 mile west and turn right onto Leemond Street. Continue on Leemond Street 0.3 mile, turn left on Captain Road, go about 100 feet to a brushy area, and park. An old Cedar

Swamp sign is slightly hidden in the woods. The former trail behind the sign is no longer obvious. Bring the Ludlow USGS topographic map and compass if you plan extensive exploring.

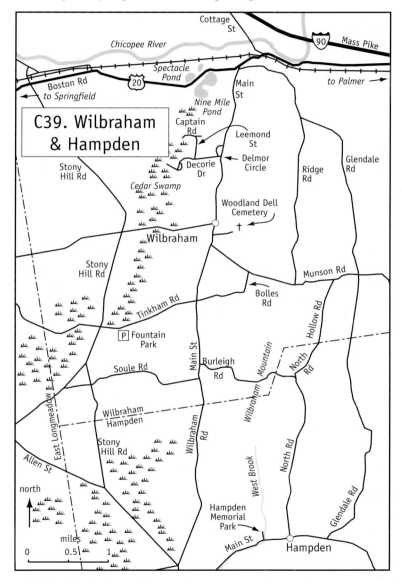

Probably the largest Atlantic white-cedar wetland in the interior of Massachusetts, the Wilbraham Cedar Swamp is worth a visit just to see this unique, rapidly vanishing habitat. Winter is a good time to visit when the barely-maintained muddy trails are frozen and there is a chance to see winter finches. Red-breasted Nuthatches and Golden-crowned Kinglets are usually found. The quiet depths of this densely forested area can produce Eastern Screech-, Barred, and, with luck, Northern Saw-whet Owls. Sharp-shinned Hawk and Northern Goshawk are seen occasionally in winter. This area and its nearby red maple swamp and upland oak forest have Ruffed Grouse and Wild Turkey.

Also worth a visit is the Woodland Dell Cemetery, on Woodland Dell Road south of the center of Wilbraham on Main Street 1.2 miles from Decorie Drive. The cemetery and surrounding woods are good for spring migrants and breeding Yellow-throated and Blue-headed Vireos and Scarlet Tanager.

Laurence R. Fountain Park

From the Woodland Dell Cemetery, return to Main Street and turn left (south). At 0.8 mile, turn right onto Tinkham Road. Follow Tinkham Road 1.0 mile west to the entrance to the old pheasant farm on the left (an old farm house, gazebo, outbuildings, and a Fountain Park sign are landmarks).

Managed by the Wilbraham Nature and Cultural Center as a public nature study and outdoor recreation area, the extensive fields and brush at Laurence R. Fountain Park provide habitat for American Kestrel and other raptors, Snow Bunting, Eastern Meadowlark, and other open-country birds. Fall is an ideal time to search for American Tree, Savannah, Lincoln's, White-crowned, and other sparrows.

Northern Shrike and Dickcissel have been recorded here some winters. In irruption years, Purple Finch, Common Redpoll, and Pine Siskin feed on birch and alder catkins in brushy fields, and crossbills, Pine Grosbeak, and Evening Grosbeak may occur in the Norway spruces lining the service road, particularly if there is a good cone crop. These winter finches and Red-breasted Nuthatch may also occur near the pine stands south of the farm house. Eastern Screech-, Great Horned, and Barred Owls are resident in wooded portions of the property. Check wetlands under the power line for American Woodcock in March, and for American Bittern and rails in summer.

Hampden Memorial Park and Vicinity, Hampden

From Laurence R. Fountain Park, turn right on Tinkham Road and right again on Main Street. Continue south for 3.7 miles (Main Street becomes Wilbraham Road at the Hampden town line). Turn left (east) on Hampden's Main Street and continue 1.2 miles to the entrance to Hampden Memorial Park on the left.

The open brushy areas and forest margins at the park are productive for common spring migrants and summer vireos, warblers, and sparrows, but the main attractions here are the Worm-eating Warblers nesting on the wooded hillside just northeast of the park. From the north end of the park, follow the base of the east-facing hillside northward as it narrows toward the West Brook stream channel; the birds, most easily located by song, are usually found on the lower slopes of this wooded hillside, near West Brook.

North and Hollow Roads, Hampden, Wilbraham

Roadside stops on this route allow sampling of varied habitats otherwise off limits due to posting, including dense mixed hardwood/hemlock forest with logged openings, orchards and fields, open brushy gas and power lines, shrubby wetlands, and streamside wetlands.

From Hampden Veterans Memorial Park, go left (east) 0.2 mile on Main Street to the Town Hall. Turn left on North Road and go 2.1 miles to the junction of Burleigh Road (the paved road heading west) and North Road (the unpaved road heading north, which becomes Hollow Road). Continue north 1.3 miles on Hollow Road to its end at Monson Road. To return to the center of Wilbraham, turn left on Monson Road and head west 1.7 miles.

North Road passes through patches of woods, brushy areas, pasture, and orchards, with open country birds, including Eastern Bluebird. Hollow Road, traversing a densely forested, east-facing hill slope, is much wilder. Common Ravens, more often heard than seen, are permanent residents. Pileated Woodpecker and Ruffed Grouse are commonly seen year-round, along with Wild Turkey and the occasional Sharp-shinned Hawk or other accipiter. Spring warblers can be abundant in the forest canopy. Eastern Wood-Pewee, Great Crested Flycatcher, Yellow-throated and Blue-headed Vireos, Hermit Thrush, Scarlet Tanager, and Rose-breasted Grosbeak are found in spring and summer. In fall and early spring, low roadside swales near the north end of Hollow Road sometimes produce American Woodcock and Wilson's Snipe. *Tad M. Zebryk*

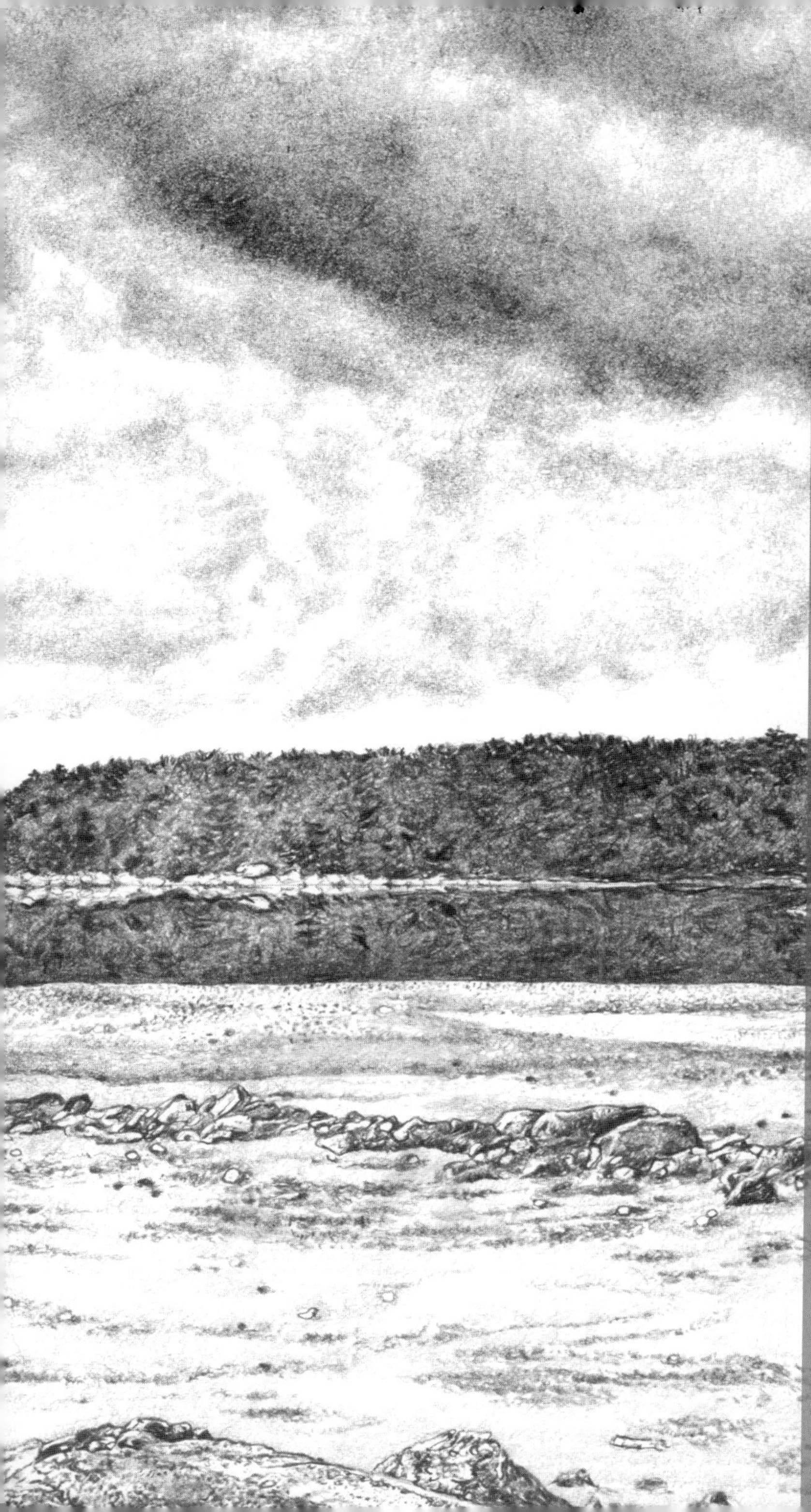

Quabbin Region

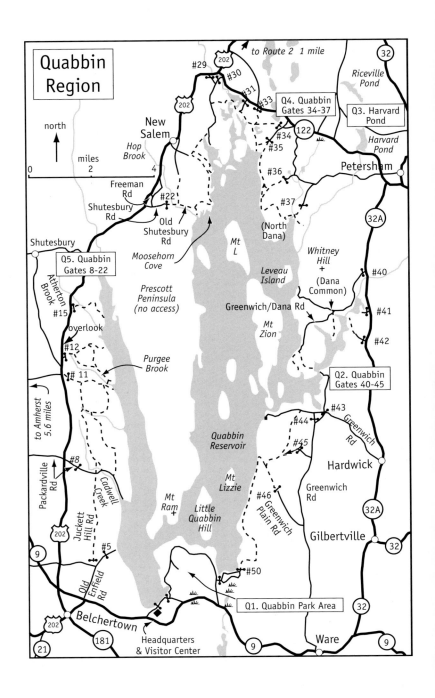

Quabbin Region

north

miles
0   2   4

to Route 2 1 mile

32 Riceville Pond

#29
#30
202
#31
#33

Q4. Quabbin
Gates 34-37

Q3. Harvard
Pond

202

New Salem

Hop Brook

122

#34
#35

Harvard Pond

Petersham

#36

Freeman Rd

#22

#37

32A

Shutesbury Rd

Old Shutesbury Rd

(North Dana)

Shutesbury

Q5. Quabbin
Gates 8-22

Moosehorn Cove

Mt L

Whitney Hill
+
(Dana Common)

#40

Atherton Brook

#15

Leveau Island

Greenwich/Dana Rd

#41

overlook

Prescott Peninsula
(no access)

Mt Zion

#42

#12

Purgee Brook

Q2. Quabbin
Gates 40-45

#11

to Amherst
5.6 miles

Quabbin Reservoir

#43
#44

Greenwich Rd

#45

#8

Packardville Rd

Cadwell Creek

Hardwick

202

Juckett Hill Rd

#5

Mt Ram
+

Mt Lizzie

Little Quabbin Hill

#46

Greenwich Plain Rd

Greenwich Rd

32A

9

Gilbertville

32

Old Enfield Rd

#50

Q1. Quabbin Park Area

32

202

Belchertown

181

Headquarters
& Visitor Center

9

Ware

9

21

Quabbin Region

Introduction

Built as a public drinking water reservoir in the 1930s, the 25,000-acre Quabbin Reservoir is the largest artificial drinking water reservoir in the country. The reservoir and the surrounding 56,000 acres of state-owned watershed lands, the largest contiguous protected open space in southern New England, have been called the "accidental wilderness." Although it might be as close as we get to wilderness in Massachusetts, the watershed has been carefully managed by the Metropolitan District Commission (MDC), both to protect water quality and to preserve and enhance the natural resources of the Commonwealth.

From the vast expanse of open reservoir to the quiet beaver ponds, shady hemlock groves, towering pine forests, stately oak stands, mixed hardwoods, and rocky crags, the Quabbin watershed offers a wonderful mix for birds and birders. Most Quabbin lands are forested, but there are open fields scattered through the watershed.

Because the area is a drinking water supply, there are regulations governing public access to the watershed lands. Swimming, camping, fires, pets, and alcoholic beverages are prohibited; bicycle access is limited to paved roads. Some areas, such as the Prescott Peninsula, are off limits to the public, but there are still more than 30,000 acres of land open by foot. Vehicle access is permitted in the Quabbin Park area although, due to security issues, the Winsor Dam and Goodnough Dike are restricted to pedestrian and bicycle access only. From mid-April to mid-October you can drive down and park for a small fee at the fishing areas (Gates 8, 31, and 43). When parking at any gates, make sure that you do not block the gate or restrict traffic in any way. In recent months there have been several changes in the areas open to the public, and visitors are encouraged to check on access prior to a visit.

The Quabbin Visitor Center at Winsor Dam is a good place to get maps, birding information, and details on policies, management programs, and Quabbin history. As this book goes to press, the Metropolitan District Comission (MDC) is being reorganized. Contact the Visitor Center (413-323-7221) for more information.

The following accounts begin on the south side of the Quabbin in Belchertown and Ware (Quabbin Park Area). The next three accounts

Preceeding Pages: **GOLDEN EAGLE**

take the reader north from Ware to Hardwick (Gates 40–45) and then along the north side of the Quabbin in Petersham and New Salem (Harvard Pond and Gates 34–37). The final account brings the reader south along the west side of the Quabbin from New Salem to Pelham and back to Belchertown (Gates 8–22).

These accounts provide a small sample of the walks possible in this vast area. Every gate and the many connecting roads and paths are worth exploration for breeding warblers and other birds, waterfowl on the reservoir, and hawks overhead. **We recommend that you buy a Quabbin trail map,** available at the Visitor Center at Winsor Dam, and then explore this wonderful area.   *Clif Read*

Q1. Quabbin Park Area
Belchertown, Ware

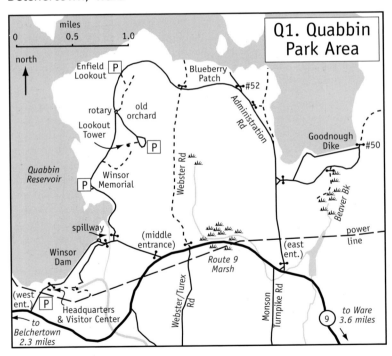

If you have never been to Quabbin before, the Quabbin Park area offers a nice introduction, views of the reservoir, and many bird specialties.

There are three entrance roads to Quabbin Park from Route 9 in Ware and Belchertown. The eastern entrance is 4.3 miles west of the intersection of Routes 9 and 32 South in the center of Ware. The middle entrance (signed as "Winsor Dam/Quabbin Reservation") is 5.5 miles west of Route 32. The western entrance, to headquarters and Winsor Dam only, is 7.2 miles west of Route 32, or 3 miles east of the intersection of Routes 9 and 202 in Belchertown. These gates are generally open 6:30 a.m. to 7:30 p.m. They may be closed for snow and ice. The western gate is always open as far as the headquarters. Expect many other visitors, especially in foliage season.

Route 9 Marsh

A great stop in early morning throughout spring, summer, and fall is the small marsh bisected by Route 9. This marsh, just outside the park, lies between the eastern and middle entrances of Quabbin Park, 5.0 miles west of Route 32 in Ware.

Approaching from the east (Ware), pull into a pull-off on the right just before the marsh. Pull completely off the road. An alternative is to pass the marsh and pull off on the corner of Webster Road, which runs south from Route 9, and walk back along the marsh. Cars often speed along this busy road, so be sure to **pull completely off the road. Do not slow down when on the road, and do not walk in the road.**

Scan the marsh for breeding Great Blue and Green Herons, Wood Duck, Belted Kingfisher, and Swamp Sparrow. Virginia Rails breed, but are difficult to find. Hooded Mergansers, and Solitary and Spotted Sandpipers are noted in migration. River otter and beaver are often seen here. In winter give the frozen, bleak marsh a pass.

Headquarters Area

Entering the western gate, you soon drive under power lines. Bear right, and after 0.25 mile you come to the Regional Headquarters, the Quabbin Visitor Center, and the State Police buildings. Park in the lot on the right just before the buildings. Scope from the overlook in front of the buildings, at the southwest corner of Quabbin, in all seasons for loons, grebes, ducks, and eagles. You can walk onto the Winsor Dam (closed to cars) and scan from there. In fall and winter there are occasionally American Pipits or Snow Buntings on top of the dam or on the rocks along the water. Gulls may seem surprisingly scarce because the staff actively tries to keep gulls off this section of water. The fruit trees near the buildings host Cedar Waxwings, Pine Grosbeaks, or Purple Finches some winters. Northern Mockingbirds, uncommon in the Quabbin, are usually around the buildings. Heated bathrooms, a joy in winter, are located on either side of the overlook and in the Visitor Center, which has exhibits about the Quabbin and maps for sale.

BUFFLEHEAD

A Tour Of Quabbin Park

Middle Entrance to the Rotary. The tour of Quabbin Park starts from the middle entrance on Route 9. The short entrance road has breeding Yellow-throated and Blue-headed Vireos, Blue-gray Gnatcatcher, Chestnut-sided Warbler, Ovenbird, and, near the small stream, Louisiana Waterthrush. Drive in about 0.4 mile and park in the area just before an intersection. (No cars are allowed on the dam.) Walk to the intersection and cross a bridge over the reservoir's spillway. Common Ravens have nested on the east rock wall of the spillway in recent years; they typically fledge around mid-May. Northern Rough-winged Swallows sometimes nest under the bridge or elsewhere in the Winsor Dam area; watch for them especially from the south side of the bridge, where you may look down on Blue-gray Gnatcatcher and other tree-top species. This area usually has migrant warbler activity in spring and fall. Breeding Hermit Thrush, Gray Catbird, and Eastern Towhee can be heard. Bear right at the end of the bridge to walk onto the Winsor Dam and scope the southwest end of the reservoir (see description above under Headquarters Area).

Return to your car and turn right at the intersection, through a gate, onto Administration Road, the main road through the park. You soon pass a scenic little inlet of the reservoir on your left. Pine Warblers breed in the pines across from the inlet and Chestnut-sided Warblers breed on the slope between the inlet and the road. About 0.1 mile past the inlet, park at the Frank E. Winsor Memorial on the left. The deciduous woods along the road from the inlet up to the rotary, about a mile farther along, is superb for spring and fall migrants and breeding specialties. This area is best done on foot (being very alert for traffic) in early morning, but the continuously climbing road may be tough for some. There is also a pull-off on the left just before the rotary.

In spring listen for Eastern Wood-Pewee, Least Flycatcher, Hermit and Wood Thrushes, Yellow-throated and Red-eyed Vireos, Blue-gray Gnatcatcher, Black-throated Blue, Yellow-rumped, Black-throated Green, Blackburnian, and Black-and-white Warblers, American Redstart, Ovenbird, Scarlet Tanager, Eastern Towhee, and Rose-breasted Grosbeak. Worm-eating Warbler is sometimes found, especially near the Winsor Memorial. In recent years, Cerulean Warblers have bred along this stretch of road; watch and listen for them anywhere along this "warbler ridge," but especially at the pull-off lined with rocks about a half mile past the Winsor Memorial. The Ceruleans can be frustratingly tough to see, often remaining down slope high in the canopy, but once you pick out the song, patience is often rewarded with at least a quick view of this beautiful warbler.

The Lookout Tower Area. At the rotary take the road immediately to the right up Quabbin Hill to a large parking area and the Lookout Tower. The bathrooms here are open in summer. The area around the base of the tower hill is good for migrants and breeding Eastern Bluebird, Prairie Warbler, Eastern Towhee, Field Sparrow, and Indigo Bunting. A walk up the small hill and perhaps to the top of the tower, if it is open, offers hawkwatching and dramatic views of the reservoir. The windows at the top of the tower cannot be opened. In late fall and winter, carefully check the parking area for Snow Buntings.

Return to the rotary; look for a gated path with parking immediately on your right. After a short distance on this path; a smaller trail to the right leads to a wonderful old orchard, good for migrant warblers, nesting House Wrens and Eastern Bluebirds, and mixed flocks in winter.

There are birds to be found all along Administration Road from the rotary to Goodnough Dike, so listen, watch, and stop where it looks good. Several traditional stops are described below. Mileage is now given from the rotary.

Enfield Lookout. Continue driving farther down Administration Road from the rotary. At 0.4 mile pull into a parking area on the left, the famous Enfield Lookout where many people come to view Bald Eagles. The lookout is worth a stop any time, but it can get downright crowded in winter eagle-watching season. From this spot, you are looking west and north over the southern terminus of Prescott Peninsula. The prominent hill directly across from you is Mount Ram (see Quabbin Region map.)

Scan the taller pines on Ram and along the whole end of Prescott for Bald Eagles. They have sometimes nested in a large pine along the shore near the terminus of Prescott. If there is an active nest, there are dedicated eagle watchers around who will point it out. If the reservoir is frozen, check the ice for deer carcasses, which attract eagles, crows, ravens, and coyotes. Keep an eye on the sky for eagles and a great variety of raptors. Scope the water, especially the cove to the left of Mount Ram, for loons, grebes, and ducks. Wild Turkeys are sometimes seen along the shore. Migrant landbirds often fly over or put down briefly in the surrounding trees.

Blueberry Patch. One mile from the rotary a large grassy picnic area on the left is known as the "Blueberry Patch." In late spring, summer, and fall, the gate is open, and you can park at the picnic area. In summer there are portable toilets here. In winter, park along the road and hike down. From the picnic parking area, a broad trail leads gently down to the water, a great spot to scan for loons, grebes, waterfowl, and eagles. Migrating warblers and other landbirds are attracted to thickets along the path.

Eastern Bluebirds sometimes nest. In winter, check tops of trees and bushes for Northern Shrike. The meadows here are good for butterflies; in late summer watch for Silver-Bordered Fritillary and Peck's Skipper.

Across Administration Road from the Blueberry Patch road, a broad walking trail, Webster Road, is great in spring and fall for migrant thrushes, warblers, and Black-billed Cuckoo. Watch for the patch of the dangerous-looking shrub Devil's Walking Stick on the right just off the trail. Hermit Thrushes feed on the berries in the fall.

Gate 52. At 1.5 miles from the rotary, pull into a small parking area in front of Gate 52 on your left. Do not block the gate. This short walk (less than a quarter mile) leads to an isolated cove across from Little Quabbin Hill island. (See Quabbin Region map at the beginning of the chapter.) Check here in migration for loons, grebes, waterfowl, and eagles. Ruffed Grouse, Barred Owl, and Pileated Woodpecker occur here.

An Interesting Unnumbered Gate. At 1.7 miles from the rotary, a gated path on the left leads down into pines and a pleasant hike through conifers and mature mixed forest. Bring your scope. When the trail shortly intersects another trail, head left (north). After about a half mile you come to a pleasant overlook of Little Quabbin Hill and the southeastern section of Quabbin. This is another great spot to search for migrant water birds and eagles. Watch for scoters and even Long-tailed Duck here in late fall. This trail hosts breeding Blue-headed Vireo, Hermit Thrush, and Yellow-rumped and Pine Warblers.

Goodnough Dike. At 2.5 miles from the rotary, park at the intersection. The eastern gate exiting onto Route 9 is 0.9 mile straight ahead. Walk left onto the closed road. In less than a half mile you come to a fork, either branch of which takes you onto the 1.8-mile Goodnough Dike loop. The right-hand road descends through birdy mixed forest and eventually passes a large open area of short grass on the steep back of the dike. As you come into the open, a gated path goes right (south) parallel to Beaver Brook Marsh. Follow this path initially, but watch for a smaller path that runs left directly to and then close along the marsh. This path south brings you through good forest and marsh habitat. Watch the marsh for lingering blackbirds or even a snipe in late fall.

As you continue along the loop road and start uphill to the far end of the dike, you may detour to a picnic area among the trees at the base of the dike, worth checking in migration. The road climbs and brings you out onto the dike itself. Scope from the dike for loons, grebes, waterfowl, and Bald Eagles. The loop takes you back across the dike to your car. *Mark C. Lynch*

Q2. Quabbin Gates 40-45
Hardwick to Petersham

Note: Gates are listed in two groups (Gates 43 and 45 along Greenwich Road, and Gates 41 and 40 along Route 32A).

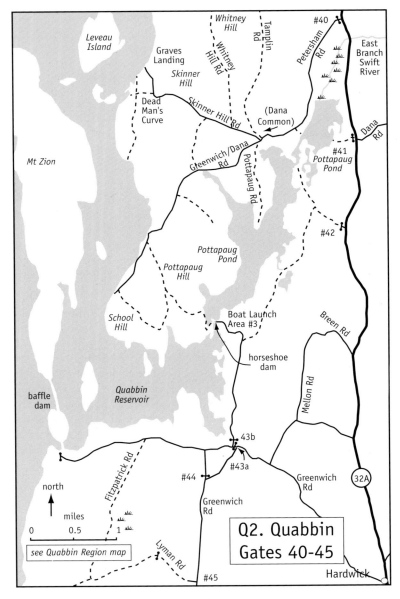

Whitney Hill

Leveau Island

Graves Landing

Skinner Hill

Whitney Hill Rd

Tamplin Rd

#40

Petersham Rd

East Branch Swift River

Dead Man's Curve

Skinner Hill Rd

(Dana Common)

Dana Rd

Mt Zion

Greenwich/Dana Rd

Pottapaug Rd

#41 Pottapaug Pond

#42

Pottapaug Pond

Pottapaug Hill

School Hill

Boat Launch Area #3

Breen Rd

horseshoe dam

baffle dam

Quabbin Reservoir

Mellon Rd

43b

#44

#43a

Greenwich Rd

Greenwich Rd

32A

north

miles

0   0.5   1

Fitzpatrick Rd

see Quabbin Region map

Lyman Rd

#45

Q2. Quabbin Gates 40-45

Hardwick

Along Greenwich Road

Take Route 32 north from Route 9 east of the center of Ware. At 3.3 miles, take Route 32A (restart mileage). At 1.2 miles on Route 32A a wooded marsh on the left can be good for early spring ducks and swallows and for fall shorebirds if water levels are low. At 2.6 miles (in Hardwick center) turn left on Greenwich Road and restart mileage.

Gate 43. A parking area is on the right, 2.6 miles west of Route 32A, as Greenwich Road bends left. Walk through the first gate (43A) and then immediately turn right through the second gate (43B). The road to the right runs about 1.5 miles to a boat launch area and the "horseshoe dam" spillway. This road is open to vehicles with boats and permits in fishing season. When the gate is closed, late fall through early spring, this is an enjoyable hike. The mixed forest has Great Horned Owl and a variety of woodpeckers. The boat mooring area can have migratory waterfowl, including Hooded Merganser. The main road beyond the boat launch becomes dirt and runs between School Hill and Pottapaug Hill. Go right at a T intersection to pass spruces that have had Boreal Chickadee and crossbills. Shortly thereafter, this road joins Greenwich/Dana Road (see Gate 40 below) at the lookout opposite Mount Zion island, a great spot to watch for eagles, about 1.25 miles past the boat launch.

Gate 45. Continue south 1.6 miles from Gate 43 on Greenwich Road. Turn right (east) on Lyman Road (dirt and sometimes impassable in winter and spring). It is approximately 0.75 mile to the gate where you can park. A Quabbin trail map is helpful.

As you walk the first mile beyond the gate the road passes overgrown fields bordered by forest that can be great for migrants in spring and particularly fall. Watch for Olive-sided Flycatcher atop dead snags in late August. After a mile, Fitzpatrick Road on the right goes gently downhill to the northeast for about a half a mile to a nice beaver swamp that sometimes has breeding Hooded Mergansers and other marsh birds. Fitzpatrick Road eventually intersects the paved road from Gate 43A.

Back at the intersection with Fitzpatrick Road, continue walking downhill on Lyman Road (see Quabbin Region map). Past a swampy pond on the left, the road comes to an another intersection in a hemlock stand. The road straight or left (south) leads to Gate 46 on Greenwich Plain Road. The road going sharply to the right and downhill (northwest) along the hemlocks is great for breeding Black-throated Green and Blackburnian Warblers and has been a traditional breeding area for Acadian Flycatcher (not present every year). The road swings sharply left at the shoreline and is close to the shore in places, with good views of Prescott Peninsula, and the Mount Lizzie and Little Quabbin Hill islands. Look for waterfowl, loons and eagles at any time. After several miles this road comes to Gate 50 at Goodnough Dike in Quabbin Park.

Along Route 32A

Gate 41. The gate, with good parking, is opposite Dana Road, 5.4 miles north from the Hardwick Town Hall, or 4.4 miles south from the intersection of Routes 122 and 32A in Petersham.

This 10-minute hike provides a good view of the north end of Pottapaug Pond and its marshes by skirting the edge of the forest to the right after you cross the brook. Look for waterfowl and otters in late fall. By walking to the left at the bottom of the trail after you cross the brook, skirting the small beaver pond and then proceeding to the right, you enter a mixed forest where Ruffed Grouse, American Woodcock, and a variety of warblers breed. Listen for Louisiana Waterthrush along the stream near the gate. Sometimes the waterthrushes are across Route 32A.

Gate 40. The small lot on the west side of Route 32A is easy to miss, 6.7 miles north of the center of Hardwick, or 3.1 miles south of the intersection of Routes 122 and 32A in Petersham. A Quabbin trail map helps if you walk beyond Dana Common.

Gate 40 is the entrance to several popular Quabbin hikes, mostly along paved or hard-packed dirt roads. Try to get here early in summer and fall because these roads are a popular destination. The roads, not plowed in winter, can be difficult walking in snow. Dana, one of four towns destroyed to create the reservoir, is one of the most interesting areas in Quabbin with many cellar holes. *Historic Quabbin Hikes* by J.R. Greene (1994, Highland Press) is a useful guide to the history.

The easy, level hike along Petersham Road from Gate 40 to Dana Common is a bit more than 1.5 miles one way through mixed woods and several fields. This stretch is good in spring, summer, and especially fall. In fall at dawn, numbers of migrants work the sunny forested field edges. Hike down to the north end of Pottapaug Pond, on your left (south) and visible through the trees, to check for waterfowl and otters. Cerulean Warblers have bred several times on the slopes of Whitney Hill to the right (northwest), but require a lot of bushwhacking to find. Just before Dana Common, a short road on your left goes southeast to a narrow part of Pottapaug Pond, a good spot for waterfowl and otters. Northern Saw-whet Owls can be found, especially in winter, along Petersham Road, Dana Common, Greenwich/Dana Road (see below), and Gate 41 (above), but are difficult to find. Listen for mobbing flocks of nuthatches and chickadees to reveal a roosting Saw-whet.

The Dana Common area, with open fields bordered by woods and marsh, is excellent for migrants in spring and especially fall. Watch for Olive-sided Flycatcher in late August and Northern Shrike in late fall and winter. There are sometimes Ruffed Grouse in the bushes in the winter. Several woodpecker species use the dead snags. Black-backed Woodpecker has been found here.

RED-BREASTED NUTHATCH

The directions to several interesting roads beginning at Dana Common are given below clockwise, starting from the south or left if you have just hiked in from Petersham Road.

The level Pottapaug Pond Road goes 0.5 mile south from just past Dana Common and ends in a peninsula in Pottapaug Pond. The mixed forest, some recently logged, has Ruffed Grouse and Pileated Woodpecker and offers views of the lower parts of Pottapaug Pond and Pottapaug Hill and perhaps an eagle. Explore along the water's edge.

Greenwich/Dana Road, not to be confused with the Greenwich Road south of Hardwick center, runs west from Dana Common. Greenwich/Dana Road begins at the far end of Dana Common, and looks like the continuation of Petersham Road. This road, with some small hills, goes through mixed forest, hemlock stands with breeding Black-throated Green and Blackburnian Warblers, and grassy marshes with breeding Virginia Rails. After 1.5 miles, just before the road from the Gate 43 boat launch enters from the left (southeast), there is a terrific view of the Quabbin Reservoir and Mount Zion. This area is great in late fall and winter for waterfowl (Barrow's Goldeneye has occurred) and raptors, particularly Bald Eagle. Golden Eagles have been seen here many times. This a good spot to spend time and see what passes by.

Skinner Hill Road leaves from the far side of Dana Common and goes to the right (northwest). Do not take Tamplin Road, the first road on the right, opposite Greenwich/Dana Road. After about 0.25 mile, Whitney Hill Road enters on the right; the logged area here is good for Wild Turkey and Pileated Woodpecker.

As Skinner Hill Road descends west of Skinner Hill, there is the sharp descending Dead Man's Curve. At this point a trail on the left quickly leads down to an area of evergreens that has had Boreal Chickadee in late fall and winter several times. Here there is an intersection of several trails. The trails that run north-northeast and west end at the water fairly quickly and are not that interesting. The trail left (south) from this intersection goes through forest good for Pileated Woodpecker and many breeding warblers. This side trail ends after about a mile from the evergreen intersection at an overlook of Quabbin and Mount Zion island, a good area for roosting Bald Eagles in early winter.

Skinner Hill Road ends just after Dead Man's Curve at Grave's Landing, a good spot for eagles and ravens, with views of Leveau Island, the North Dana peninsula, and Soapstone Hill. (See Quabbin Region map at the beginning of the chapter.) In severe drought, when extensive mud flats form in late summer, this area is one of the best spots in Western Massachusetts for migrating shorebirds.   *Mark C. Lynch*

Q3. Harvard Pond
Petersham

Harvard Forest, including Harvard Pond (Brooks Pond on some maps), is a research forest of Harvard University. The south end of the pond is adjacent to Route 122 in Petersham, 5.7 miles east of Route 202, or 1.2 miles west of Route 32 in Petersham. There are several convenient places to pull off Route 122; park and scope the pond in spring, summer, and fall.

Migratory waterfowl like Ring-necked Duck, scaup, Bufflehead, Common Goldeneye, and Hooded and Common Mergansers are often present in spring and fall. Wood and American Black Ducks breed. Careful scanning of the numerous bushy islands and floating vegetation mats can reveal migratory shorebirds including Greater Yellowlegs, Solitary and Least Sandpipers, and Wilson's Snipe. Killdeer and Spotted Sandpiper nest. Pied-billed Grebe, and Great Blue and Green Herons are commonly seen. Northern Goshawk, Red-shouldered Hawk, and Broad-winged Hawk breed nearby. Osprey are seen in migration. Barred and Northern Saw-whet Owls occur in the forest. Watch for Olive-sided Flycatcher in late May and late August on exposed tops of conifers. The whole area is good for migrant landbirds and great for odonates and butterflies.

The farthest west parking area, with a Harvard Forest sign and gate, features a trail up the pond's west side, eventually connecting with Tom Swamp Road (see below). You can hike all around the pond on good trails, though you will have to walk along Route 122 to return to your car. Mosquitoes and deer flies are abundant in summer.

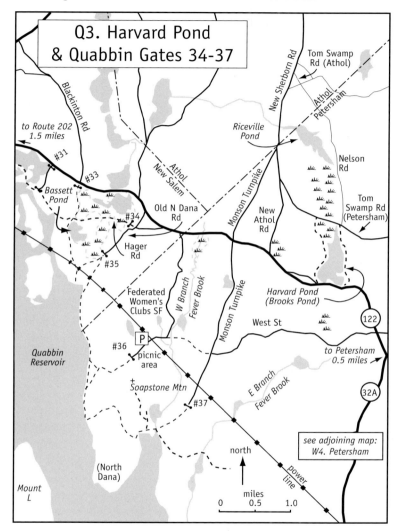

Q3. Harvard Pond & Quabbin Gates 34-37

People with **high carriage vehicles** can drive west 0.9 mile on Route 122 from Harvard Pond and turn right onto New Athol Road. After 1.1 miles, turn right on Tom Swamp Road. This road, initially paved and with houses on it, becomes dirt as it enters Harvard Forest. **This road may not be passable in spring mud.** This road traverses forest with numerous hemlock stands.

Magnolia, Black-throated Blue, Yellow-rumped, Black-throated Green, and Canada Warblers, and Northern Waterthrush breed here. Listen for Pileated Woodpecker, Blue-headed Vireo, Winter Wren, and Hermit Thrush. Eventually the road crosses the north end of Harvard Pond, locally known as Tom Swamp, though the pond may be tough to see through vegetation. The causeway here is *the* place to search in summer for the very rare (in Massachusetts) Bog Elfin butterfly.

Past the causeway, a dirt road on the left runs east and north. This 2.2-mile Nelson Road, which becomes a different Tom Swamp Road in Athol, goes through good habitat, including the Riceville Pond marshes to the left. This road emerges onto New Sherborn Road, the Athol end of New Athol Road.

Another marshy pond is on the left side of South Street, 0.3 mile south from where Routes 32 and 122 separate in Petersham. (See map W4. Petersham.) Pull to the right and behind the town highway garage, where the discreet and quiet birder can scope a wonderful pond with breeding Wood Duck and Virginia Rail and waterfowl like Hooded Merganser in migration.

The Harvard Forest headquarters, on Route 32, 3.3 miles north of where Routes 32 and 122 separate in Petersham, has nature trails and the Fisher Museum with dioramas illustrating the ecological history of the region (open 9 a.m.–5 p.m. most weekdays and 12 a.m.–4 p.m. most weekends May-October; 978-724-3302).   *Mark C. Lynch*

Q4. Quabbin Gates 34–37
Petersham to New Salem

See map Q3. Harvard Pond & Quabbin Gates 34–37

Note: Sites are listed southeast to northwest (Gate 37, Federated Women's Club State Forest, and Gates 34 and 35) along Route 122 between the intersection with Route 32A in Petersham and the intersection with Route 202 in New Salem.

Gate 37

The intersection of Route 122 and West Street is 0.4 mile west of the Routes 32A/122 junction, or 8.3 miles east of the Routes 202/122 junction. Go west 2.6 miles on West Street to Monson Turnpike Road, turn left (south), and go 1 mile to Gate 37. Park beside the gate. The road in from the gate is not plowed in winter. Before Gate 37 you drive under power lines where Prairie Warblers breed.

Walk through the gate; after 0.75 mile there are three options.

The first option is the dirt road to the left, just before the small stone bridge. After another 0.75 mile you pass regenerating red and white pines on the right. Bear left at an intersection and go 0.25 mile farther to the east branch of Fever Brook and a large pond on the right. Look for Wood Duck, American Black Duck, Mallard and, in spring, Ring-necked Duck and Hooded Merganser. Look for snapping, painted, and spotted turtles in June and July when they emerge to look for sand in which to lay eggs.

The second option back at the bottom of the hill is to cross the small bridge and take the first right. This road follows a stream through white pines. After 200 yards you come to a large beaver pond, a good place to view Great Blue Herons, migrant waterfowl and warblers and, in early morning or late afternoon, a busy beaver. As you approach the beaver pond, look for a trail going left to the lookout on Soapstone Mountain. The last 100 yards are fairly steep, but the view is worth the climb. The top is an excellent spot to watch migratory fall hawks drifting south on a lazy fall day.

The third option is to take the old tar road to the left, immediately after the bridge. On hot days northern water snakes bask on rocks in the bridge walls. This road leads to the Quabbin shoreline in the former North Dana. At the water's edge look for Common Loon, Bald Eagle, Common Merganser, and other waterfowl. Golden Eagles are rarely spotted in late fall and early winter from this area. Migrating Osprey can be observed fishing the Quabbin. Watch for mammals in the Gate 37 area, where moose, white-tailed deer, river otter, and black bear all occur.

Dale Monette

Federated Women's Clubs State Forest

Turn south from Route 122, 4.0 miles west of Route 32A, or 4.2 miles east of Route 202. This paved road, not plowed in winter, is in fair condition and ends at parking for a picnic area and Gate 36.

The road winds through mixed forest with hemlock stands and areas of mountain laurel understory. Blue-headed Vireo, Winter Wren, Golden-crowned Kinglet (rare), Hermit Thrush, and Black-throated Blue, Yellow-rumped, Black-throated Green, Blackburnian, Pine and Canada Warblers breed. Louisiana Waterthrush usually breed along the West Branch of the Fever Brook. Listen for nesting Northern Waterthrush along the road. Northern Saw-whet and Barred Owls bred here, but incessant taping from inconsiderate birders has made both species tough to find. **Do not play tapes of these species here in breeding season!**

Park where the stream exits the pond and runs along the road. Hike back to the small pond where Great Blue Herons and Wood Ducks have bred. Small numbers of migrating waterfowl like Ring-necked

COMMON LOON

Duck and Bufflehead occur here. Watch and listen for Red-shouldered and Broad-winged Hawks and Pileated Woodpecker.

The dirt extension of West Street going left (east) from the end of the State Forest paved road (opposite the gate) runs through forest with many breeding species, including Evening Grosbeak, but is **not recommended** for cars with low suspensions.

Gates 34 and 35

Turn south from Route 122 onto Old North Dana Road 4.7 miles east of Route 32A, or 3.1 miles west of Route 202. There is a "Stop" sign on Old North Dana Road and a sign for "C&M Roughcut." Park and walk to Gate 34, taking care not to block the road or the fire station that is shortly before Hager Road. Gate 35 is at the road's end, 1 mile in.

Gate 34 is about a 0.3 mile walk down Hager Road. The road through the gate skirts a swamp that has northern pitcher plants and breeding Northern Waterthrush and Canada Warbler. Watch for migrating Olive-sided Flycatchers atop dead snags. I have turned up fall Connecticut Warblers here several times. The trail then passes through hemlock stands with breeding Black-throated Green and Blackburnian Warblers. After about a mile this road meets the road from Gate 33 (opposite Blackinton Road on Route 122) at Bassett (sometimes called Hacker) Pond.

Gate 35 is great to explore for raptors, especially eagles, in spring and late fall into winter, as you walk the old Athol and Enfield Railroad bed and parts of old Route 21. In summer this gate is often crowded with fishermen but is still interesting. I have found Caspian Terns and Bonaparte's Gulls here in fishing season. Walk through the gate, and immediately swing left. The road quickly turns right, and then proceeds through mixed forest and out under power lines, a good spot for fall migrants. The trail soon comes to the main body of Quabbin and then runs 2.5 level miles alongside the water to a small phragmites area on the North Dana peninsula. Hike as far south as possible. Past the half-way mark, roads from Gate 36 and Gate 37 enter from the left. (Walking straight at Gate 35 leads to another section of the power line and, after an intersection with the road from Gate 33, another place to scan the reservoir.)

Watch for hawks and eagles, including Golden (late fall and winter), particularly around the north end of Mount L island. When the boats have gone in mid-fall, waterfowl, including Red-necked Grebe and scoters are seen. In late fall and winter check trees on the island for Northern Shrike. In fall, migrant passerines sometimes work the shore vegetation. *Mark C. Lynch*

Q5. Quabbin Gates 8–22
New Salem to Belchertown

See Quabbin Region map at the beginning of the chapter

Note: Gates are listed from north to south (22, 15, 12, 8) along Route 202 between Route 122 in New Salem and Route 9 in Belchertown.

Gate 22

From Route 202, turn east onto Freeman Road (sign for South New Salem), 5.4 miles south of Route 122, or 15.4 miles north of Route 9. The road forks 1.0 mile in from Route 202. Stay to the left, and about 100 yards past a barn on the right you come to Gate 22.

Just past the gate, Hop Brook runs along the old Shutesbury Road. In late fall you can see landlocked salmon migrating upstream if you follow the brook up from its mouth at the reservoir. In spring both waterthrushes are seen along this brook.

A half mile in on the right is a large cement slab; continue another 0.5 mile to a fork in the road. If you go right, you will see another fork in the road about 200 yards down. Take the right fork to a bridge removed during the creation of the Quabbin Reservoir in the 1930s. This road originated in Puppyville and headed south to Prescott.

Walk to the edge of the water and look for Common Loon, Common Merganser, Bald Eagle, and assorted waterfowl. In spring and fall Snow and Canada Geese, Ring-necked Duck, and Hooded Merganser are seen. Deer can be seen along the shore when the water is low. When the water is really low, mud flats, excellent for shorebirds, appear.

Return to Old Shutesbury Road and turn right. After another 0.5 mile you are again at water's edge, at the mouth of Moosehorn Cove. Common Loons sometimes echo through the valley, and Bald Eagles soar overhead. You have a good view of Mount L island and surrounding waters. In late summer you can see Great Egrets across the way in phragmites on the north end of Mount L. *Dale Monette*

Gate 15

Park well off the road on the east (reservoir) side of Route 202, 10.2 miles south of Route 122, or 10.5 miles north of Route 9. **Lock up and do not leave valuables in the car.**

This is a traditional spot for breeding Acadian Flycatcher. Hike about 15 minutes down as the old road zigzags through mixed forest with breeding Barred Owl, Yellow-throated, Blue-headed, and Red-eyed Vireos, Winter Wren (occasional), Veery, Hermit Thrush, Black-throated Blue, Yellow-rumped, Black-throated Green, Blackburnian, and Canada Warblers, American Redstart, Louisiana Waterthrush along the stream, and Scarlet Tanager. Look and listen for Acadian Flycatcher in hemlocks especially where Atherton Brook crosses under the old road. **Do not play tapes!** Acadians arrive late, usually by late May or early June. After about another 20 minutes downhill, the trail arrives at the reservoir.

Mark C. Lynch

Pelham Overlook

There is a pull-off on the east side of Route 202 just north of Gate 12 with a great view of Quabbin and the Prescott Peninsula, 12.4 miles south of Route 122 or 8.2 miles north of Route 9. Driving south on Route 202, the pull-off is on your left; **be careful** pulling across oncoming traffic as it is difficult to see cars coming in the opposite direction until you reach the crest of the hill. Be sure to **pull off the road quickly and completely** as traffic really speeds along Route 202.

This is a good spring and fall hawkwatch spot. In winter, scan the Prescott for raptors, including Golden Eagle. Be patient! It may take time before anything flies. During fall hawk migration, kettles of Broad-winged Hawks sometimes soar right overhead. Afternoon light is best. A scope is necessary, as views are often distant. Listen for winter finches flying by in winter, and watch for Pileated Woodpecker and Common Raven. Check the field below the lookout for Indigo Bunting in summer. *Mark C. Lynch and Clif Read*

Gate 12

There is parking for several cars in the gravel lot on the east side of Route 202, just south of the overlook, 8.0 miles north of Route 9 or 12.6 miles south of Route 122.

Before you decide to take this hike, note that there is nearly a 600-foot elevation difference from Gate 12 to the reservoir. The hike back to the gate will be more difficult than the descent.

Past the gate the dirt road drops steadily for 0.5 mile. As the road levels out, it splits at the 0.7 mile mark. The left fork goes 1.2 miles farther to the reservoir through mixed hardwood stands and oak forests, good for Ruffed Grouse, woodpeckers including Pileated, and songbirds.

WESTERN WORCESTER REGION

Introduction

This chapter includes both the western half of Worcester County and the three small towns of Holland, Wales and Monson in Hampden County that jut under southwestern Worcester County.

The avifauna of Worcester County is transitional between western and eastern Massachusetts. Indeed, some breeding species of western Worcester County, like Common Raven, Golden-crowned Kinglet, White-throated Sparrow, and Evening Grosbeak, are more typical of Berkshire and Franklin Counties than of eastern Worcester County. Eastern Screech-Owl, fairly common in eastern Worcester County and even in the city of Worcester, is uncommon and local in the areas discussed in this chapter. Conversely, Northern Saw-whet Owl breeds in several localities in the central and northern sections of western Worcester County, but is extremely local as a breeding bird in eastern Worcester County.

Western Worcester County is typically very hilly with many substantial stands of mixed forest. The Quabbin Reservoir, Massachusetts' largest body of fresh water, forms part of the western border of the county. The Western Worcester area is dotted with numerous small lakes and ponds favored by migratory waterfowl. It also has several of the state's river basins. In the north, Royalston and Gardner are part of the Millers River Basin. The Brookfields, Barre Falls Dam, Rutland State Park, Hardwick, Petersham, and Monson are part of the greater Chicopee River Basin, including the important Ware and Quaboag Rivers. In the southern area, Sturbridge, Wales, and Holland are part of the French and Quinebaug River Basins, both part of the Thames River watershed flowing through Connecticut. Worcester County's largest remaining cattail marsh lies along the Quaboag River in the Brookfields. Extensive farmlands, good for many migrants and breeding species, persist in many areas but are rapidly being developed.

Preceeding Pages: **WILD TURKEY**

A word about weather: In winter, the areas mentioned in this chapter are often colder and icier, and with greater snow depth than central and eastern Worcester County and eastern Massachusetts. The reason for this is simply higher elevation. A cold January rain in the city of Worcester may be an ice event in Barre. Spring comes just a bit more slowly here than in eastern Massachusetts, and snow may remain on the ground weeks after it has melted from eastern Massachusetts or the Connecticut River Valley. With the many hills come numerous valleys and hollows subject to nighttime radiational cooling. Early-morning birders should dress appropriately.

Birding is good any time of the year in western Worcester County. Spring brings many migrant ducks to opening ponds and numerous passerine migrants to woodlots. Spring southern "overshoot" migrants like Hooded and Prothonotary Warblers have been recorded here, but are really not to be expected. Spring hawkwatching can be very good at Barre Falls Dam. Summer is a great time to see and hear a wide variety of breeding warblers, vireos, and thrushes and to search for breeding marsh birds, though mosquitoes and blackflies deter some birders. Fall is perhaps my favorite time to bird these areas, with many migrant passerines moving early in the morning, a great variety of waterfowl, beautiful scenery, and no mosquitoes. Winter can be tough, but the diligent birder can search open sections of rivers for waterfowl. Winter finches and Bohemian Waxwings are sometimes found in Royalston, Petersham, Hardwick, and other sites. Indeed, areas of Royalston and Athol remain the best in the state to find a Bohemian Waxwing or a Pine Grosbeak.

The ten accounts describing this region are arranged roughly north to south. *Mark C. Lynch*

W1. Royalston

Birders come to Royalston in mid-winter to look for winter finches, especially at the classic small New England town common on Route 68 and Athol Road. Park well off the road in front of the town hall or library and walk down the main road. Often Evening Grosbeaks are about, even when they are scarce in the rest of the state. In flight years, Pine Grosbeaks can be found feasting on crabapples behind the houses opposite the library. Sometimes Bohemian Waxwings are here. If no birds are evident, be patient. Often the birds are out of sight and may eventually fly over. Feeders attract Evening Grosbeaks a short distance north of Royalston center, on NE Fitzwilliam Road. Please remember that this is a quiet town whose residents enjoy their privacy. **Do not trespass,** and walk only along the sides of the main roads. Any roads in Royalston may have winter finches "gritting" or in seed-bearing trees.

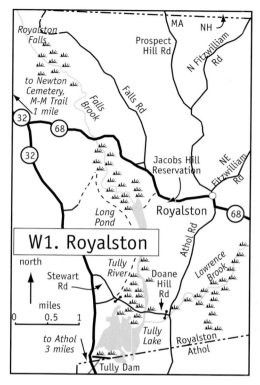

Winter is not the only time to visit Royalston. A spot to explore throughout the year is Jacob's Hill, The Trustees of Reservations (TTOR) area 0.5 mile north and west from Royalston center on the south side of Route 68 (Warwick Road) as you climb a hill. The trail here is good for breeding warblers and has had Northern Shrike along the power lines in winter. Just 0.4 mile beyond this stop on Route 68 is another trailhead for a very short walk to a commanding view of Long Pond and the upper reaches of Tully River. Wild Turkey, Barred and Northern Saw-whet Owls, Pileated Woodpecker, Common Raven, and Winter Wren breed in Royalston.

About 1.4 miles northwest of Royalston Center on Route 68, Falls Road on the right is a dirt road through mixed forest with scattered houses. **Please respect the homeowners' privacy.** Yellow-bellied Sapsucker, Pileated Woodpecker, Eastern Wood-Pewee, Blue-headed Vireo, Hermit Thrush, Yellow-rumped, Black-throated Green, and Blackburnian Warblers, Scarlet Tanager, and, occasionally, Evening Grosbeak breed along this road. The good road ends 2.3 miles from Route 68. The road is maintained irregularly beyond this point and can be rugged; use caution in deciding whether to proceed. However, you can park your car and walk about a mile along the road to Royalston Falls, a beautiful TTOR area where Acadian Flycatcher has bred. The falls can also be reached by returning to Route 68 and continuing northwest to the junction with Route 32. Turn right (north) on Route 32 and go 1.7 miles to the small Newton Cemetery where the Metacomet-Monadnock Trail crosses the road. The trail north to Royalston Falls, which was recently rebuilt, is short but steep.

BARRED OWL

Returning south on Route 32, the Tully Dam Army Corps of Engineers area, along Route 32 and Doane Hill Road, includes Tully Lake and mixed and coniferous forest with marked trails. The dam pull-off just north of the Athol border on Route 32 is good for hawkwatching. Listen for winter finches flying overhead. Common Ravens have bred nearby.

Mark C. Lynch

W2. Crystal Lake and the Mount Wachusett Community College Area
Gardner

Crystal Lake

From Exit 23 off Route 2 in Gardner, go north under the train bridge onto Pearson Boulevard and then 0.2 mile to the traffic light. Go right onto Elm Street and follow Elm 1.0 mile to the rotary. Take the third right off the rotary onto Route 101 south (Central Street). Follow Route 101 for 0.3 mile and then turn right at the common (Park Street). After 0.3 mile on Park Street, turn right at Crystal Lake Drive toward Crystal Lake Cemetery (worth exploring during landbird migration) and Crystal Lake, owned by the city of Gardner.

Gulls roost nightly at Crystal Lake in spring from thaw to late April, and again from September to freeze-up, usually mid-December. After freeze-up, gull numbers diminish but some remain most of the winter. Bonaparte's, Iceland, Lesser Black-backed, and Glaucous Gulls have all occurred. Bonaparte's makes brief appearances, typically for only a few hours in migration (April or November), often in inclement weather.

Although gulls can be present any time, they really begin to congregate from a few hours before dusk until sunset. The afternoon sun is behind you at the cemetery. At sunrise, the gulls disperse, many of them first to the lawns of the community college and golf course (see below). As landfills close, gull numbers are expected to diminish, and gulls may some day be nearly absent from the lake.

Waterfowl are found in both migrations. Look just after spring thaw for Common Loon, Pied-billed Grebe, Ring-necked Duck, Bufflehead, Common Goldeneye, and Hooded and Common Mergansers. Regular early spring dabbling ducks include Wood and American Black Ducks. Gadwall, American Wigeon, and Green-winged Teal have occurred. Many dabbling ducks roost in autumn on Crystal Lake, often arriving after dark.

Rain in late March through early May or late September through November can produce species unusual inland. Horned and Red-necked Grebes, Snow Goose, both scaup, all three scoters, Long-tailed Duck, and Red-breasted Merganser have occasionally been recorded; typically, such species do not linger, and sea ducks usually leave as the weather clears.

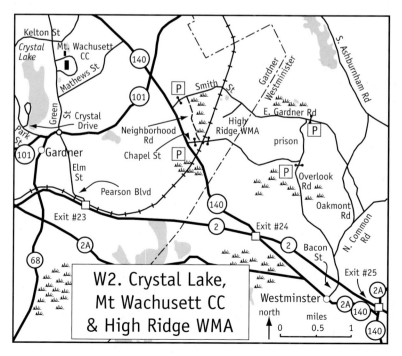

Mount Wachusett Community College (MWCC)

Return to the Route 101 rotary, take the third right onto Green Street. Continue for approximately 0.5 mile to the college on the right (east) and the golf course on the left (west).

A small public bike path parking lot is on the left, just before the first MWCC entrance. In winter, fruit trees attract Eastern Bluebird, American Robin, Cedar Waxwing, and, more unusually, Bohemian Waxwing and Pine Grosbeak. Scan treetops for American Kestrel or Northern Shrike. Eastern Kingbird, House Wren, Blue-winged, Yellow, and Chestnut-sided Warblers breed here. The bike path goes through mixed woods for approximately 0.5 mile with views of Crystal Lake. Both nuthatches, Brown Creeper, Yellow-rumped and Pine Warblers are likely.

Across from the bike path, scan the campus pond for Great Blue Heron, American Black Duck, and Eastern Kingbird. In August and September, mixed flocks of blackbirds roost in the phragmites; Sharp-shinned Hawk, Cooper's Hawk, and Merlin frequent the area to harvest a meal.

In spring and fall, Ring-billed, Herring, Great Black-backed, and sometimes Lesser Black-backed Gulls may search for earthworms on the college lawn and the golf course farther down Green Street. A Snow Goose may join ubiquitous Canadas in autumn. *Tom Pirro*

W3. High Ridge Wildlife Management Area
Gardner, Westminster, and Ashburnham

See map W2. Crystal Lake, Mt Wachusett CC & High Ridge WMA

High Ridge WMA has many side trails and dirt roads worth exploring. Each entrance deserves a field trip of a half-hour to several hours. If two vehicles are available, you can park at one gate and continue to another without backtracking.

Smith Street Entrance

From Crystal Lake and Mount Wachusett Community College, return to the 101 rotary, take 101 north 1.6 miles to the traffic light and junction with Route 140. Turn right (south) on Route 140 and continue 0.5 mile. Turn left on Smith Street.

Alternatively, from Route 2 take Exit 24 (Route 140 Winchendon) and follow Route 140 north 2.3 miles. Turn right on Smith Street.

Follow Smith Street to the dirt and grass parking area at the gate to the WMA. Park so that you **do not block the gate.** Scan here for spring and fall migrants. Past the orange gate look for House Wren in thickets and Scarlet Tanager, Indigo Bunting, and Baltimore Oriole higher up in the vegetation. In late fall and winter the sumacs often harbor Evening Grosbeaks.

Walk down Smith Street, watching for breeding Bobolinks in the first field. After roughly 100 yards look in the woods for Brown Creeper, Chestnut-sided Warbler, and Ovenbird. Take a right onto Neighborhood Road. To the west are mixed woods, excellent for flocks of migrant vireos, kinglets, thrushes, and warblers, particularly on cold mornings just as the early sunlight warms the trees. Tree Swallow and Eastern Bluebird nest in boxes along the road.

Farther down Neighborhood Road is a wetland that beavers sometimes flood. Mid-calf boots may be helpful. To the right is a wooded swamp with snags. To the left is shrubby marsh with breeding Green Heron, Wood Duck, Hooded Merganser, Northern Waterthrush, and Purple Finch. In migration look for Olive-sided Flycatcher, Philadelphia Vireo, both kinglets, Swainson's Thrush, Northern Parula, Cape May Warbler, Lincoln's Sparrow, and Rusty Blackbird. Clay-colored Sparrow has occurred. After a dry summer watch for shorebirds such as Solitary, Spotted, and Least Sandpipers.

Neighborhood Road continues south to the Chapel Street entrance. Follow Neighborhood Road back to Smith Street and turn right (east) under telephone wires. Kentucky Warbler has occurred here. After 100 yards, at the top of an incline, look for an unmarked break in the brush to your right, a dead-end path to a brushy overlook on a marsh with breeding Alder and Willow Flycatchers. Scan for American Bittern, Wood Duck, and Hooded Merganser in spring and summer. Because the marsh attracts numerous swallows and other songbirds, this is a good vantage point to look for Sharp-shinned and Cooper's Hawks, Merlin, and occasionally Northern Harrier, particularly in fall. Scan snags and tree tops during late fall and winter for Northern Shrike. Northern Goshawk is possible throughout High Ridge any time of year. An evening or night visit could produce Great Horned or Barred Owl.

Return to Smith Street and continue down to the marsh; Virginia Rail and Sora probably nest here. High boots help when this section of road is flooded in spring. Continue uphill to an open field on the right that can have Horned Lark, American Pipit, or Snow Bunting in season. The road follows the edge of the field to a railroad where the bridge is out. **This is an active track; be cautious of approaching trains.**

Along the paved road south of the railroad tracks, a field on the left usually has Bobolinks. Ruby-throated Hummingbird is seen along this stretch of road. A small pond to the right may have Great Blue and Green Herons, and Wood Duck. You will soon come to an intersection where you can go right, closer to the pond. Hemlocks beyond the pond are good for migrant warblers such as Tennessee, Cape May, and Bay-breasted, and breeding Yellow-rumped, Black-throated Green, and Pine Warblers. The border of the North Worcester County Correctional Facility is nearby, and is well marked with white signs. **Do not proceed past these signs.** On the way back to Smith Street note a path to the right to a cemetery where Pine Warbler is found. **Do not go beyond the signs at the edge of the prison grounds.** (There is a target range on the prison grounds farther up the hill.)

Along East Gardner Road (the continuation of Smith Street), a stream with Louisiana Waterthrush exits the pond and runs parallel to the road. The road continues past a series of fields, the edges of which may have Blue-gray Gnatcatcher, Blue-winged, Yellow, and Chestnut-sided Warblers, Scarlet Tanager, and Rose-breasted Grosbeak. Tree Swallow, House Wren, and occasionally Eastern Bluebird nest in boxes here. East Gardner Road continues along the stream through wooded habitat to a marsh.

Overlook Road Entrance

Return to Route 140, go left (south) for 3.6 miles (you will go under Route 2) to Westminster. Turn left on Bacon Street (you will again go under Route 2) for 0.7 mile. Bear left at the fork on Overlook Road. There is no road sign, but there is a sign for Urho Sakkinen Square. Follow Overlook 1.5 miles to its end at a gate. Park here even if the gate is open; **be careful not to block the gate or the school bus turn-around.**

Near the gate, look for breeding Yellow-bellied Sapsucker, Winter Wren, and Louisiana Waterthrush. A Kentucky Warbler once summered here.

After the gate, you can go left or straight. The left route goes through spruces. In winter check all spruce stands for Red-breasted Nuthatch, Golden-crowned Kinglet, Pine Grosbeak, and crossbills. In both migrations Tennessee, Cape May, and Bay-breasted Warblers may occur. This road eventually leads to a series of open fields with Savannah Sparrow, Bobolink, and an occasional Eastern Meadowlark. Sumacs often attract wintering Evening Grosbeaks. Occasionally a few of these handsome finches occur during spring and summer. There are currently three abandoned structures about one mile from the Overlook entrance. **Do not venture inside these buildings.** Check shrubbery and thickets around the houses for Gray Catbird, Chipping Sparrow, and possible cuckoos. This wide-open space provides a wonderful southern view for hawkwatching. American Kestrel has nested in the dead trees near the barn. Past the barn are similar habitat and the prison entrance.

Going straight at the Overlook Road gate leads past an open field and through a wooded dry stream bed. Yellow-bellied Sapsucker nests nearby.

RUFFED GROUSE

The road then goes uphill through two fields where Eastern Bluebirds often nest. The berry bushes and crabapple trees near the buildings of the Division of Fisheries and Wildlife's hunter safety headquarters attract American Robin and Cedar Waxwing during late fall and winter. Pine and Evening Grosbeaks are possible in a "finch year." The road continues past the buildings to a wooded section and downhill to the East Gardner Road entrance and the "Lower Marsh" (see below).

East Gardner Road Entrance

Return to the beginning of Overlook Road. Turn left on North Common Road. Continue 0.5 mile and bear left at a fork on Oakmont Road. At the end of Oakmont (0.9 mile), turn left on East Gardner Road. Continue about one mile to its end at an orange gate. Park here (even if the gate is open), being **careful not to block the gate.** This entrance is good if time is limited and marsh habitat is the focus. At the bottom of the hill, continuing to the left leads past a brushy field; just past the field is a dirt path to a marsh with American Bittern, Virginia Rail, Sora, American Woodcock, Alder and Willow Flycatchers, and Swamp Sparrow. Beaver activity has flooded sections of this path. Along East Gardner Road the mixed woodlands to the left may contain Brown Creeper, Winter Wren, Veery, and Hermit Thrush. To the right is a band of secondary growth between the road and the marsh, and after a few hundred yards the road returns to the marsh. East Gardner Road then leads to the section covered above under the Smith Street Entrance.   *Tom Pirro*

W4. Petersham

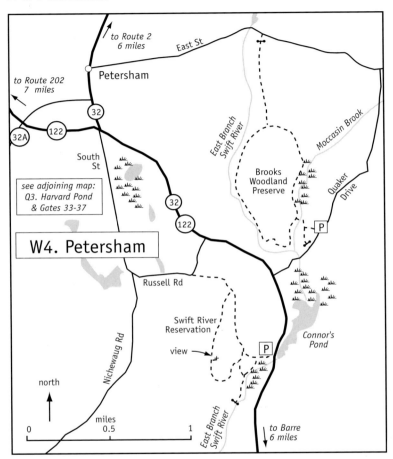

Note: The western part of Petersham is described in two accounts in the Quabbin Region: Q3. Harvard Pond and Q4. Quabbin Gates 34–37.

Brooks Woodland Preserve

From the center of Petersham, take Route 32 for 0.4 mile south to Route 122. Turn left (southeast) toward Barre. After 1.5 miles go left on Quaker Drive (just before a large pond). The road goes over the East Branch of the Swift River (0.2 mile) to the large green The Trustees of Reservations (TTOR) sign for Brooks Woodland Preserve on the left (0.3 mile past the river). Turn up the embankment and park in the grassy opening. An excellent map of the parcel with its miles of trails is available for a small fee from TTOR.

The main parking area on Quaker Drive can be particularly birdy, especially for autumn migrants, including impressive numbers of Pine and Blackpoll Warblers. Evening Grosbeaks have been found singing here in spring and may breed. A short way along the downhill trail is a wet alder thicket, reliable for migrant Fox Sparrows. Soon thereafter a large meadow deserves searching along the edges and treetops during both migrations. In summer watch for butterflies like Common Ringlet and American Copper.

Turn right at the end of the meadow and continue downhill to a bridge over hemlock-lined Moccasin Brook, excellent for breeding Winter Wren and Louisiana Waterthrush and migrant Swainson's and Hermit Thrushes. Shortly after the bridge you will begin a loop that will take you along Moccasin Brook, then along the Swift River and back along Moccasin Brook. Begin by bearing right after the bridge on the trail along the brook. A large, marshy pond, behind the beaver dam to the right, often holds Great Blue Heron and Wood Duck. Alder Flycatcher usually breeds at the far end of the pond, and occasionally a Barred Owl calls at dusk.

The trail continues through hemlock, red pine, and hardwoods. Pileated Woodpecker, Least and Great Crested Flycatchers, Blue-headed and Red-eyed Vireos, Red-breasted Nuthatch, Blue-gray Gnatcatcher, Veery, Hermit and Wood Thrushes, Scarlet Tanager, Swamp Sparrow (at the marshy pond), White-throated Sparrow, and Rose-breasted Grosbeak all breed. Breeding warblers include Blue-winged, Yellow, Chestnut-sided, Black-throated Green, Blackburnian, Pine, American Redstart, Ovenbird, Common Yellowthroat, and Canada (a few). This spot is good in winter for Ruffed Grouse, Red-breasted Nuthatch, Brown Creeper, and Golden-crowned Kinglet.

Continue on this trail, passing a number of inviting trails to the left and the trail to the Indian Grinding Stone on the right, to a T with another wide trail. The trail to the right has views of beaver ponds and a hemlock/red maple swamp before ending at a gate on East Street (0.5 mile). To continue the loop, turn left on the trail along the East Branch of the Swift River (do not cross the river) through beautiful riparian forest of huge hemlock and white pine, another good stretch for singing Winter Wren and Louisiana Waterthrush and a great area to study odonates. The trail turns near the confluence of the East Branch of the Swift River and Moccasin Brook and winds back along Moccasin Brook another 0.25 mile and eventually back to the footbridge.

Chris Buelow and Mark C. Lynch

Swift River Reservation (Route 122 Tract)

From Brooks Woodland Preserve, return to Routes 32/122 and turn left (south). Continue 0.6 mile to the green Swift River Reservation TTOR sign (across from a large pond). Turn in at the sign and park in the lot below. **Caution:** The road down to the parking lot is steep and often not plowed in winter.

From the parking lot cross the gate into open fields of an old farmstead, now just stonewalls and a foundation. These fields are particularly exciting on early spring evenings when American Woodcock display. Autumn is very productive here, especially in thickets dividing the fields from the East Branch of the Swift River. Tangles of alder and grape attract many migrants, especially warblers and vireos, with numbers of Blue-headed and Warbling Vireos, and Tennessee and Wilson's Warblers. In winter, the fields may feature Northern Shrike and Evening Grosbeak. Whistling a Northern Saw-whet Owl call here on winter nights occasionally incites a response.

Follow the trail to the left of the woods road with the alders on your left and the fields on your right. At the end of the fields, continue along the trail, now a woods road, as it parallels the East Branch of the Swift River through dense hemlock and enormous white pine, great for Winter Wren, Hermit Thrush, and Fox Sparrow in spring and fall, and year-round for Red-breasted Nuthatch. After about 0.25 mile, the trail ends at a property-line gate. Return to the field and either return to your car or take a 0.5 mile hike uphill to an incredible view of the Swift River Valley. To reach the view, cross the field and stone wall, turn left, walk uphill and then bear right at the #79 sign. When you see a rocky outcrop on your right, take the trail up to the ridge. *Chris Buelow*

W5. Barre Falls Dam and Rutland State Park
Barre, Hubbardston, Oakham, and Rutland

The great diversity of birds here includes eighteen species of breeding wood-warblers, and the entire area is outstanding for butterflies and odonates. An early start is essential to getting the most out of birding this area.

This large parcel of land is part Rutland State Park, part Army Corps of Engineers flood control project, part Metropolitan District Commission (MDC) Ware River Watershed land, and part Barre Falls Wildlife Management Area. In addition to the area shown on the map in this book, other areas of the Ware River watershed, with trails, lie south of Route 122, and a large, undeveloped wildlife management property is along Route 62. The Barre USGS topographic map covers most of the area, with some areas on the Sterling, Worcester North, and North Brookfield maps. The Army Corps of Engineers distributes a helpful, free map at the Barre Falls Dam.

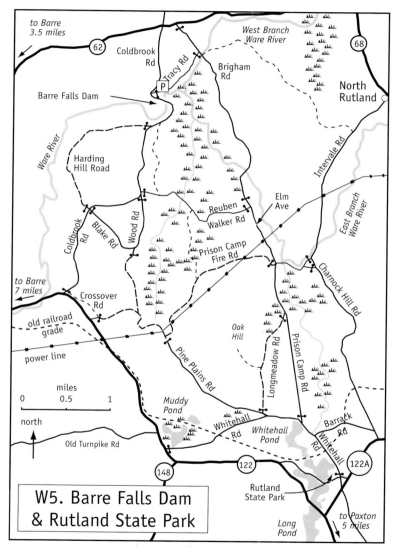

to Barre 3.5 miles

West Branch Ware River

62

68

Coldbrook Rd

Tracy Rd

Brigham Rd

P

North Rutland

Barre Falls Dam

Ware River

Harding Hill Road

Intervale Rd

Elm Ave

Reuben Walker Rd

East Branch Ware River

Coldbrook Rd

Blake Rd

Wood Rd

Prison Camp Fire Rd

to Barre 7 miles

Crossover Rd

old railroad grade

power line

Charnock Hill Rd

Oak Hill

Longmeadow Rd

Prison Camp Rd

miles

0   0.5   1

north

Muddy Pond

Pine Plains Rd

Barrack Rd

Old Turnpike Rd

Whitehall Rd

Whitehall Pond

Whitehall Rd

148

122

122A

W5. Barre Falls Dam & Rutland State Park

Rutland State Park

Long Pond

to Paxton 5 miles

The area is crisscrossed with fair to good dirt roads, all gated. From May through mid-December several major roads are open to cars. The same roads may be closed due to flood control at any time; all are closed in winter. When stopping to bird, **please pull as far off to the**

side as possible! There is always some traffic along these roads, though they often seem deserted. Other gated roads are closed to cars, but may be explored on foot or bike. This is a popular recreation area for swimming (at Rutland State Park beach only), fishing, hunting, biking, and horseback riding. Logging may be underway at any time.

Biting black flies, deer flies, and mosquitoes are abundant in summer. Dog and deer ticks are present. **Do not leave valuables in the car,** and take all the precautions appropriate to deserted wooded roads. Avoid deer-hunting season here.

Below are four car routes that sample some of the best birding spots. Exploration on foot is always exciting. If you are driving, plan on frequent stops, getting out of the car, and poking around where it looks good.

Trip 1: Long Pond to Rutland State Park Beach

Begin at the intersection of Routes 122 and 122A in Rutland. Pull off on Route 122A at the small picnic area at the intersection, or park at the boat launch on Route 122 just northwest of the intersection. The section of Long Pond south of Route 122 is often filled with fishermen in all seasons. The marshy end of Long Pond north of Route 122 is good for Great Blue Heron and Wood Duck. Migrating swallows rest on the phone lines here.

Continue northwest on Route 122 about 0.8 mile to a sharp, paved right turn onto a shortcut connecting Routes 122 and 122A through the southeast corner of Rutland State Park (SP). There is a lot of traffic on this stretch, so pull completely off the road when you stop. Along this shortcut, Long Pond is on both sides of the road. Pull off on the right 0.5 mile from Route 122, a great place to scope marshy and hidden corners of Long Pond. The western, marshy end often has Wood Duck. Hooded Merganser may breed here. Ring-necked Duck occurs in early spring and fall. Least and Great Crested Flycatchers, Yellow-throated Vireo, and Pine Warbler breed in the area. A walk down this road to the causeway over two sections of the pond sometimes yields concentrations of fall migrants (vireos, warblers, orioles). Be careful of traffic.

Continue east a short distance to paved Whitehall Road with a sign for Rutland SP and beach. Turn left. Whitehall Road runs through interesting forest for almost a mile along Long Pond and Whitehall Pond before the swimming area. Birding can be very good early in the morning. Eastern Wood-Pewee, Least Flycatcher, Blue-headed and Red-eyed Vireos, Veery, Hermit Thrush, Scarlet Tanager, and several warblers breed here. Usually at least one Winter Wren can be heard. Barrack Road on the right, 0.6 mile from 122A, winds through more forest to Route 122A. A small wooded marsh on the right just before Whitehall Pond can be good for fall migrants; I have seen Connecticut Warbler here. I usually see only fishermen and bathers on Whitehall Pond.

Back on Whitehall Road, the paved road swings left around Whitehall Pond. Watch for a dirt road with a gate on the right, the starting point for our next tour.

Trip 2: Prison Camp Road to Route 62

This is one of the best bird tours of the area. Start as early as possible and plan on at least 2 to 3 hours. The road is generally good, but some side roads may be suitable only for high clearance vehicles, foot, or bicycle. From Rutland SP and Whitehall Road (see above), start by driving through the gate and down the dirt Prison Camp Road. Measure mileage from the gate. This road is usually gated from mid-December to May. Keep out of here in deer-hunting season unless dressed in regulation hunter's orange.

The first section of this road is mostly flat and straight, through deep deciduous and mixed forest. Stop often and explore, but **pull far to the side of the road and watch for cars.** Common voices in an early morning chorus here include Eastern Wood-Pewee, Blue-headed and Red-eyed Vireos, Veery, Hermit Thrush, Black-and-white Warbler, Ovenbird, and Scarlet Tanager. In conifers listen for Black-throated Green, Blackburnian, and Pine Warblers. In areas with good understory listen for the jumbled notes of the Canada Warbler. Winter Wren can usually be heard on this stretch. Spring and fall bring numerous migrants like Bay-breasted and Blackpoll Warblers, although getting good views in the tall forest can be frustrating.

After 1.3 miles pull over on the left by gated Longmeadow Road; hike or bike this road. Longmeadow Road connects to Whitehall and Pine Plains Roads (see Trip 3) after about 1.5 miles. Halfway down Longmeadow Road is a road that goes uphill to the north through fields and forest to the top of Oak Hill. This area can produce sparrows in fall and early winter, and fruit trees attract waxwings. I have found Common Redpoll here in December. Northern Goshawk has bred nearby.

Return to the intersection of Longmeadow Road and Prison Camp Road. With your car well off the road, explore on foot. Dead trees around the beaver swamp often host nuthatches, Brown Creeper, and noisy crowds of Red-winged Blackbirds and Common Grackles. Watch for Olive-sided Flycatcher late in May and again in late August. Migrant warblers often feed in this area. Across the road and through the brushy tangles lies a marsh of the Ware River. From the road you can sometimes hear Alder Flycatcher.

About 0.2 mile from the intersection, Prison Camp Road is lined with a vast open area of fields with Eastern Bluebirds and Bobolinks. This is a premier butterfly spot.

From here to Prison Camp Fire Road (0.4 mile farther) is a good area to bird fields and forest edge on foot. Many migrant warblers, particularly in fall, can be found at first light along the forest edge. American Kestrels hunt these fields in early fall. Watch bare tree tops for migrating Olive-sided Flycatcher. Northern Flicker, Warbling Vireo, House Wren, Yellow and Chestnut-sided Warblers, and, occasionally, Black-billed Cuckoo breed. Try a walk to the Ware River marsh west of the road, easier in spring but difficult later due to shrub growth; old deer trails can help. Virginia Rail breeds and sometimes American Bittern and Sora are heard. Marsh Wren has occurred. More typical are Willow Flycatcher and Swamp Sparrow. Moose occur here.

At the intersection of Prison Camp Road and Prison Camp Fire Road, pull off on the left and explore the former prison farm, with remnants of a few buildings, notably the small solitary confinement cell block. The prison was established in 1903 as "an industrial camp for prisoners to reclaim and improve wastelands." In 1934, the MDC purchased the land. The area is good for Warbling Vireo, Prairie Warbler, Eastern Towhee, and Brown Thrasher (uncommon in the rest of the area).

BLUE-HEADED VIREO

From late November into December, flocks of Common Redpoll have been found here, and Northern Shrike has been spotted. At all times, listen for Evening Grosbeak.

The Fire Road to the west goes up a small hill, passing a prison root cellar, and soon reaches a gate. The Fire Road to the east crosses the East Branch of the Ware River, a good place for Alder Flycatcher and Swamp Sparrow. Past the river, the Fire Road leaves the park at Charnock Hill Road.

Continue north from the intersection with the Fire Road, keeping mileage from this intersection (Prison Camp Road becomes Elm Avenue). The road first passes fields with Eastern Bluebird and Bobolink. At 0.3 mile pull off on the left (west) side and park near the power lines, good for Eastern Towhee and Field Sparrow. Across Elm Avenue is a footpath that crosses the field and goes under the power lines to a birdy overlook of the Ware River.

At 0.6 mile on Elm Avenue pull over on the right for a path to the conifers, good for Red-breasted Nuthatch, Magnolia Warbler, and White-throated Sparrow. Golden-crowned Kinglets have bred here.

At 0.8 mile, Elm Avenue intersects Reuben Walker Road, which heads west, connecting with Coldbrook Road (Trip 4 below). For now, continue straight through a gate onto Brigham Road through mature deciduous forest. Sometimes birds seem few and far between in the cool woods, but Ovenbird, Scarlet Tanager, and Rose-breasted Grosbeak are common.

One mile from the prison camp a bridge crosses the Ware River, the forest becomes rocky, and the road is less flat. **Drivers of low clearance cars should be careful.** Listen for Winter Wren in this shady stretch.

At 2.1 miles a rough parking area is on the right. Water usually bubbles up from a pipe in an obscured old foundation here, and birds come in early morning to drink. Ruffed Grouse are often in the area.

From here to the next bridge (0.5 mile) are stretches of hemlock with Red-breasted Nuthatch, Black-throated Green and Blackburnian Warblers, and, at boggy spots, Northern Waterthrush. Barred Owl occurs here. The area of the bridge over the West Branch Ware River (2.6 miles from the prison camp) can be alive with spectacular concentrations of Ebony Jewelwing, perhaps the most beautiful damselfly of our state. In late summer cardinal flowers along the river attract Ruby-throated Hummingbirds. Continue straight over the bridge, through more forest, to Route 62 (3 miles from the prison camp). The gate is closed in winter and during flood control periods.

Another option: Just after the last bridge, take a sharp left onto Tracy Road, an attractive way that starts along the bank of the West Branch of the Ware River. It's perfect for a picnic lunch and for Blue-headed Vireo, Winter Wren, and Louisiana Waterthrush. The road turns and rises to an area of red pine. Fall migrants often gather along the road to feed in deciduous saplings. Tracy Road emerges from the forest near Barre Falls Dam (Trip 4 below).

Trip 3: Whitehall Road and Pine Plains Road

This area often has less traffic than Prison Camp Road. This route can be combined with the Long Pond Trip (Trip 1) for a loop tour.

From the intersection of Whitehall Road and Prison Camp Road, bear left (west) around Whitehall Pond past the entrance to the beach on your left. The road becomes dirt and enters forest. Within 0.4 mile is an intersection. Longmeadow Road, on the right, is usually gated at this end (see Trip 2). To the left is the continuation of Whitehall Road.

Straight ahead is Pine Plains Road with Eastern Wood-Pewee, Hermit Thrush, Ovenbird, and Scarlet Tanager. At the road's gated terminus (1.2 miles), listen for Black-throated Blue Warbler, which is local here. This road is good for woodland butterflies like Red-spotted Purple and Northern Pearly-eye. The gate at the road's end connects to a network of popular hiking trails (consult the Army Corps of Engineers' map for details).

Return to the intersection with Longmeadow Road, and drive right (west) down the continuation of Whitehall Road. Near the beginning on the right (north) side is a small marsh, good for migrants, Virginia Rail, and a small patch of northern pitcher plants among the cattails.

Whitehall Road continues 1.2 miles to Route 122. This area is drier than other roads in the tract and has stands of red pine with Pine Warbler and Eastern Towhee. Interesting side trails follow old railroad beds. Just before Route 122, Muddy Pond on your right may have Great Blue Heron, Wood Duck, and, in migration, Ring-necked Duck and Common Merganser.

Trip 4: From Barre Falls Dam Down Coldbrook Road

This route, with more traffic, has lots of birds and several side roads to explore. Allow a minimum of three hours to bird this route thoroughly.

Start at the intersection of Route 62 and Coldbrook Road in Hubbardston, 5 miles east of Barre, 9 miles west of Princeton, and 2.3 miles west of the intersection of Routes 62 and 68. There is a large sign for the dam. Keep mileage from this intersection. **Be sure to pull well off to the side of the road when stopping.**

The entrance road to Barre Falls Dam is paved. Check for breeding Ruby-throated Hummingbirds perched on wires or tips of bare branches. In fall and spring, migrant sparrows find the bushes attractive.

A dirt parking lot on the left, just before the road starts to descend to the dam, is the first stop for Tree Swallow, Eastern Bluebird, Blue-winged Warbler, Prairie Warbler, Chipping Sparrow, and Indigo Bunting. In fall and particularly spring, this is also an excellent hawkwatch location. This high spot is a good place to scope the horizon for locally breeding hawks: Red-shouldered, Broad-winged, and Red-tailed Hawks, and Northern Goshawk. Turkey Vulture and Common Raven are expected. Tracy Road is at the far end of the lot (see Trip 2 above).

At 0.9 mile Coldbrook Road crosses a spillway. Common Ravens have nested under this bridge. These birds are wary and will probably not approach the nest if you hang around. No matter how hard you try, you cannot see the nest far up and under the bridge, but watch for the birds **from your car** in the vicinity.

The road soon crosses Barre Falls Dam. The dammed area sometimes stores water for flood control, but most often is a "dry reservoir." The area near the dam is a popular recreation area, with picnic tables, bathrooms, and parking. Listen for Eastern Phoebe, Wood Thrush, and Pine Warbler. Generally, the road from Route 62 to the recreation area is open year-round. Sometimes in early spring, depending on snowfall and road conditions, Coldbrook Road is open all the way to Route 122, unlike the rest of the roads, which don't open until May. Past a small graveyard, Coldbrook becomes dirt all the way to Route 122. Tall evergreens along the road have Black-throated Blue, Black-throated Green, Blackburnian, and Pine Warblers.

At 2.4 miles Reuben Walker Road enters on your left. This road connects to Elm Avenue (Trip 2 above). Reuben Walker Road is worth a detour. After 0.2 mile, near a small pond on the right, Winter Wren and Yellow-rumped, Black-throated Green, and Pine Warblers breed. The pond is often alive with odonates; look also for greater bladderwort. Reuben Walker Road takes a sharp right turn at a scrubby field and soon crosses Stevens Brook, a good area for migrating Olive-sided Flycatcher and nesting Brown Creeper, and Swamp and White-throated Sparrows.

South and west on Coldbrook Road, just past Reuben Walker Road, is another left onto Wood Road. Wood Road connects with Blake Road and forms a nice 1.5-mile "V," reconnecting with Coldbrook Road. Eastern Wood-Pewee, Hermit Thrush, Yellow-rumped and Black-throated Green Warblers, American Redstart and Ovenbird breed. Red pine stands hold numbers of Red-breasted Nuthatches and Pine Warblers. Evening Grosbeak may breed here.

Where Blake and Coldbrook Roads intersect, pull off on gated Harding Hill Road opposite Blake Road, to explore the hemlocks along Coldbrook Road for breeding Golden-crowned Kinglet and Magnolia Warbler. Evening Grosbeak (may breed) has often been found here, and Boreal Chickadees have occurred in late fall and winter.

Continue down Coldbrook Road. From the intersection with Blake Road it is 1.5 miles to a gate that is closed in winter; Route 122 is 0.3 mile farther. For one more short drive through good habitat, turn left on Crossover Road, a dirt road just before Route 122. This pleasant route (0.5 mile) has had breeding Winter Wren, Golden-crowned Kinglet, and Magnolia, Black-throated Green, Pine, and Canada Warblers. At the bend in the road is a popular gated path to Pine Plains Road. Consult the map for details.   *Mark C. Lynch*

W6. Moose Brook Valley and Winimusset Meadows Wildlife Management Area
Hardwick, New Braintree

Moose Brook Valley, Hardwick

From the center of Barre, take Routes 32 and 122 southeast 1.1 miles until they split. Bear right on Route 32 and continue for 7.1 miles as it twists and turns through South Barre, Barre Plains, and crosses the Hardwick town line. Turn right on Shunpike Road until it ends (0.3 mile). Turn right on Prouty Road for 0.3 mile and turn left onto Brook Road, a dirt road not plowed in winter.

From the intersection of Prouty and Brook Roads, proceed 0.2 mile on Brook Road to a clearing on the left. Park along the right side of the road. On the left behind a hedgerow is a weedy field bordered by an alder marsh on Moose Brook. Belted Kingfisher, Alder and Willow Flycatchers, and Bank Swallows, nest nearby. The weedy field is excellent in autumn for migrating sparrows, with Lincoln's and White-crowned regularly noted.

Return to your car; drive another 0.8 mile to where the road is enveloped in hemlock. Another 0.2 mile on the left is a rough parking area, gateway to a 1,000-acre parcel of unfragmented upland forest partially owned by the East Quabbin Land Trust. Veery and Wood Thrush abound, and occasionally a Hermit Thrush is found. Pileated Woodpecker, Eastern Wood-Pewee, Yellow-throated Vireo, Brown Creeper, Black-throated Blue and Canada Warblers, Scarlet Tanager and Rose-breasted Grosbeak breed. Watch for Cerulean Warbler; a male defended a territory in 2000. The trees here often drip with migrants in spring and fall.

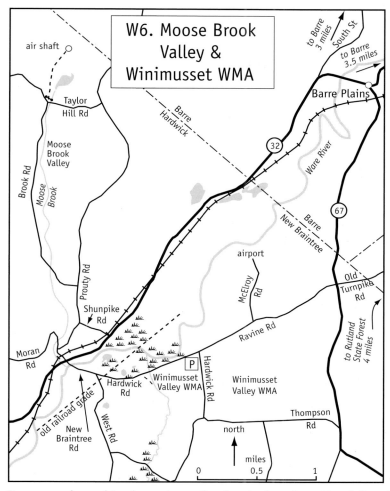

W6. Moose Brook Valley & Winimusset WMA

air shaft

to Barre 3 miles
South St
to Barre 3.5 miles

Barre Plains

Taylor Hill Rd

Barre Hardwick

Moose Brook Valley

Brook Rd

Moose Brook

32

Ware River

Barre New Braintree

67

Prouty Rd

airport

Old Turnpike Rd

McElroy Rd

to Rutland State Forest 4 miles

Shunpike Rd

Ravine Rd

Moran Rd

P

Hardwick Rd

Winimusset Valley WMA

Hardwick Rd

Winimusset Valley WMA

old railroad grade

New Braintree Rd

West Rd

Thompson Rd

north

miles

0   0.5   1

Return to the parking lot and go a few hundred yards on Brook Road to a large, grassy clearing on the left. The borders of this opening often have passerines during migration. This is private property; **please be respectful and stay on the road.**

Finally, continue to the end of the dirt road to Taylor Hill Road (0.7 mile). Directly across from Brook Road is a cable gate with a wide cart road of mown grass beyond it. Park so that you **do not block the gate.** This cart road runs on a level grade about 0.5 mile to a Quabbin Aqueduct airshaft. The tailings from the shaft's construction are now a massive, 100-foot mound with a commanding view of Moose Brook Valley and the immense beaver pond directly below. A well-worn path leads to the top of the mound, an excellent spot to sit with a spotting scope. Ring-necked Duck, Common Goldeneye, Bufflehead, and Hooded and Common Mergansers are plentiful in migration. This is a good hawkwatch spot. In summer Baltimore Orioles attend to their nests at eye level. In winter Eastern Bluebird and the occasional Northern Shrike occur. Ruffed Grouse is common year-round, and American Woodcock is often found feeding along the grassy road from spring through fall. *Chris Buelow*

Winimusset Meadows Wildlife Management Area (WMA), New Braintree

From Moose Brook, return to Route 32 (1.8 miles south of the Barre/Hardwick town line). Turn right (south) on Route 32; continue 0.4 mile. Turn left on New Braintree Road which becomes Hardwick Road and continue an additional 1.2 miles. Park next to the little building at the edge of the field. Note: if you were to continue on this road as it becomes Ravine Road and then (at the junction with Route 67) Old Turnpike Road, you would come to Route 122 in Oakham across from Muddy Pond and Rutland State Park (see W5. Barre Falls Dam and Rutland State Park). If you were to return to Route 32, you would be in Hardwick (see Q2. Quabbin Gates 40–45). The cemetery across the street is a good place to call for Barred Owl and great for Wild Turkey.

In rainy springs the plowed fields pool and almost turn into mud flats, making Winimusset Meadows ideal for migrant shorebirds. In early May the field to your far right usually produces both yellowlegs, Solitary, Spotted, Semipalmated, and Least Sandpipers, and American Pipit. If the season is very wet, larger pools form, and teal (mostly Green-winged) and other migrant dabblers occur. This field is not part of the state WMA, **so stay along the brook or the road.** Along the brook to the left of this field is a good area for Wood Duck, Eastern Bluebird, and sparrows including Savannah and Swamp. Vesper Sparrow is an uncommon spring migrant. About 0.8 mile farther west an old railroad bed crosses the road. Walk in on your right to a fantastic spot for spring warblers. About 0.25 mile down this rail bed an old trestle crosses the Ware River, a pretty spot always good for a duck or two and some big, old snapping turtles.

Back at your car, walk into the field along the path behind the little building in the parking lot. **Boots are advised.** Follow this path along the brook and over a little bridge. Walk into the muddy, tall, tick-infested grass on your right, a great location to listen for Virginia Rail. Walk back to the bridge, brush off the ticks, and head right, down the trail into the fields. There is a little brook that you will have to jump or wade. On spring evenings these fields are great for displaying Wilson's Snipe and American

Woodcock. Walk until you can't go any farther without hip waders and check for American Bittern, Northern Harrier, and Sora. American Kestrel, Bobolink, and Eastern Meadowlark breed here. In 1990 Northern Harrier bred, raising four young. In winter, check the treetops of the entire WMA for Northern Shrike.   *Bill and Nancy Cormier*

W7. The Brookfields and Warren

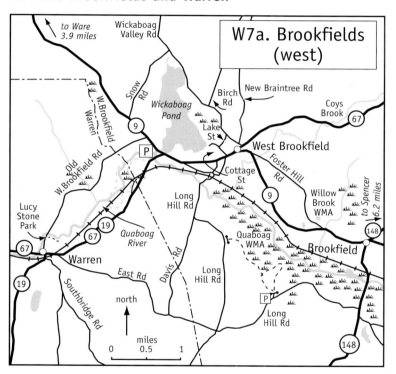

The Brookfields, the four small towns of Brookfield, North Brookfield, East Brookfield, and West Brookfield along Route 9, have several large lakes and a stretch of the Quaboag River with extensive marshes. The Brookfields feature suburban and rural habitat that is being developed. The remaining abundance of farmlands, hedgerows, and woodlots makes exploration of back roads worthwhile, especially in migration. Winter can bring slim pickings, but snow-covered fields can hold lingering sparrows and raptors, while the remaining open water often boasts migrant waterfowl late into the season. Most of this area is in the Sturbridge Christmas Count. The Warren USGS topographic map and a copy of the Street Atlas of Metro Worcester/Central Massachusetts are both useful.

BOBOLINK

The Quaboag Wildlife Management Area (WMA) and the Quaboag River, Brookfield, West Brookfield

There is always something to look at along the Quaboag River throughout the year. One of the best ways to tour the Quaboag marshes is by canoe, but most birders do not have time or equipment to do this, so this section presents a car tour with stops for hiking. Some of the choicest habitat along the Quaboag is the state WMA. Birders should avoid this area in hunting seasons.

Head south on Route 148 from the intersection of Routes 9 and 148 (Upper River Street) in Brookfield. Within 0.6 mile there is a railroad bridge and then a bridge over the Quaboag River. Pull over on the right (west) side before the river, scan up and down the river for dabblers and mergansers, and look for Belted Kingfisher and Swamp Sparrow. During early spring flood waters watch for American Bittern, once a regular breeder, now typically a migrant. Scan forest edges for raptors. The water near the bridge may stay open when other water freezes and is thus good for lingering waterfowl.

Continue south on Route 148, crossing the river. Take the first right after the bridge (about 1 mile south of Route 9) onto Long Hill Road.

Long Hill Road is always worth a drive. Stop wherever it looks good, but **pull over!** This road is busier than it looks. After 1.4 miles on Long Hill Road pull into a small dirt and grass WMA parking area on the right (north). The nice trails here give access to forested sections of the Quaboag WMA. In late spring and summer, predatory insects and ticks can be fierce. On a positive insect note, this is a great place for odonates and butterflies. Bring a compass and topographic map or a good sense of direction. Do not go near these trails in deer hunting season unless you are covered with hunter's orange.

Breeding species along these trails include Ruffed Grouse, Barred Owl, Eastern Wood-Pewee, Blue-headed Vireo, Winter Wren, Veery, Hermit and Wood Thrushes, Scarlet Tanager, Rose-breasted Grosbeak, and warblers such as Blue-winged, Yellow-rumped, Black-throated Green, Blackburnian, Pine, and Ovenbird. Watch and listen for Pileated Woodpecker. During Christmas Counts I have found Northern Saw-whet Owls in the area; they may breed here.

Soon after the gate, the trail enters mixed forest. After about 100 yards, one trail continues straight and to the right, while another trail heads left. The left trail is the better choice. This trail descends, crosses a stream, and winds its way northwest through forested habitats, never quite reaching an overlook of the river. Sections of the trail may be overgrown with grass. This trail has charm and a variety of breeding birds. As the wide trail twists and turns, stay on the well-worn and obvious section. At one point, the trail bends 45 degrees to the right near an overgrown field with old apple trees. After more than a mile, the trail reaches a stream bottom in a hemlock stand and then gently ascends for another mile through deciduous forest. Eventually the trail comes to a gate at another section of Long Hill Road (see below). Leaving a second car here allows a birdy one-way hike.

Back at the WMA parking area continue west down Long Hill Road. A mile from the parking area, Long Hill Road turns right at an intersection. Keeping mileage from this point, continue down this part of Long Hill Road, with several excellent feeders that often host Red-bellied Woodpecker and American Tree Sparrow in winter. Red-headed Woodpecker has occasionally been found. Check the fields for Eastern Bluebird. At 1.5 miles from the corner is the gate at the other end of the trail described above.

Continuing on Long Hill Road 2.0 miles from the corner, bear right where Davis Road comes in from the left. At 2.5 miles from the Long Hill Road corner, the road again crosses the Quaboag River, a good vantage point from which to scope the river after parking before or after the bridge. This isolated, marshy stretch of the Quaboag often has ducks like Ring-necked Duck, and Hooded and Common Merganser, and sometimes Belted Kingfisher well into winter. The ducks are often tucked behind cattails, so be patient. Check the river from both sides of the bridge. Long Hill Road crosses the railroad and reaches a T; either direction shortly leads to Route 9 in or near the center of West Brookfield.

For another productive overlook above the Quaboag River, drive west on Route 9 from the center of West Brookfield about a mile to the intersection with Routes 19 and 67. Take Routes 19 and 67 south 0.1 mile to a small road on the right leading to a rest area along the Quaboag River where Wickaboag Pond flows in. The water is often partially open in midwinter and thus attracts wintering waterfowl.   *Mark C. Lynch*

Lucy Stone Park, Warren

Continue south on Routes 19 and 67. At the center of Warren, where Route 19 goes left (south), turn right (north) on Old West Brookfield Road. After 0.3 mile there is a small gravel parking lot on the left, just before the bridge. The Town of Warren's Lucy Stone Park is across the street.

Lucy Stone Park has a nice walking trail along the Quaboag River, great for migrating spring warblers and fall ducks. The trail follows the river about 0.25 mile and ends behind a factory at a ballfield, great for fall sparrows. Stay to your left at the ballfield; a marker about 50 feet down the left edge of the field gets you back to the river trail, which can be followed for about 200 yards more until it ends at a dilapidated bridge.

When you leave the park, continue on Old West Brookfield Road past the high school. After a couple of miles, check a beautiful swamp on the left, often loaded with Wood Duck, teal, and other swamp birds in the fall. **Be sure to pull completely off the road.** Old West Brookfield Road is lined with picturesque fields and dead snags, excellent for hawks, woodpeckers, and Eastern Bluebirds. After another half mile you return to Route 9 west of the center of West Brookfield.

                    Bill and Nancy Cormier

Wickaboag Pond, West Brookfield

This pond, the most westerly of the four major Brookfield lakes, is an excellent location from late November till freeze-up for Common Goldeneye, Common Merganser (sometimes hundreds), and other ducks. Bald Eagle and Belted Kingfisher occur in late fall. To view the south end of the lake, from West Brookfield take Route 9 west a short distance beyond the junction of Routes 9 and 67 to Cottage Street on the right (north). Follow Cottage Street to the town beach. For a good view of the north end of the lake, drive back on Cottage Street and go left on Lake Street to the T. Turn left on Wickaboag Valley Road for 1.1 miles to a pull-off on the right.

Foster Hill Road

Go east on Route 9 from the center of West Brookfield, and just beyond the Common take Foster Hill Road left as Route 9 bends to the right. The road soon crosses Coys Brook. **Pull completely off the road** and bird this area, good in spring for American Bittern, American Black Duck and teal, and early spring migrant warblers like Yellow-rumped and Palm. Southeast on Foster Hill Road 1.4 miles beyond the Brookfield town line sign is a state WMA along Willow Brook on the left (entrance near a small pond), that is particularly good in fall when numbers of migrants, like White-crowned Sparrow, move through. Stay away in hunting season.

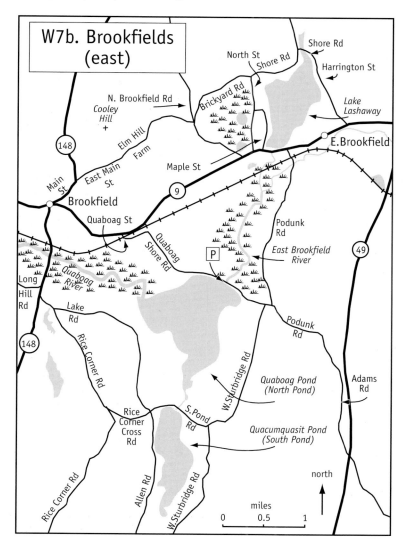

Elm Hill Farm, Brookfield

In 1996 the Massachusetts Audubon Society (MAS) purchased Elm Hill Farm from the Means family, who have farmed this area for over 250 years. The property is a working farm but birders are invited to sample this magnificent parcel by driving north from the center of Brookfield on Route 148 (Main Street). Turn right on East Main Street (0.4 mile). After another 0.6 mile, the road will run through the middle of Elm Hill Farm. MAS signs mark the property; the farm buildings are private, **not** part of the MAS 1000 acres. **Pull completely off the road being careful not to block farm access roads.** Please stay on the farm/woods roads and do not disturb the farming operation. Eastern Bluebird and Cedar Waxwing find the old orchard inviting and are often present in winter. Savannah Sparrow and Bobolink breed. Spring and fall migration brings sparrows to field edges. The view south to the Quaboag Valley from the drumlins on either side of the road are promising hawkwatching sites. When you walk uphill on the north side, please walk along the edge of the corn and hay fields so that you do not destroy any crops. As MAS develops Elm Hill with trails and off-road parking it may become a premier birding spot.

Three Additional Brookfield Lakes, Brookfield, East Brookfield

Lake Quacumquasit, mercifully known to locals as South Pond, is of interest in late fall and early winter. From the center of Brookfield on Route 9, take Route 148 (River Street) south over the railroad and the Quaboag River. At 1.2 miles from Route 9, go left on Lake Road, which winds a bit and joins another road; stay left on Lake Road. This stretch of Lake Road runs through interesting fields and woodlots. After 2.1 miles, the road reaches a T, with Rice Corner Cross Road coming from the right. Go left 0.25 mile to an obvious pull-off and a view of the north end of the lake. Diving ducks are found here, and I have also seen a wintering Northern Pintail and, in 1998, a flock of 12 Tundra Swans. Sections of the south end stay open into December; it is often the last of the four ponds to freeze. The land across the street is a part of the state WMA. Do not visit during hunting season.

Lake Quaboag, locally known as North Pond, is one of the best spots in western Worcester County for migrating waterfowl. Besides Ring-necked Duck, scaup, Common Goldeneye, and mergansers, occasional loons, grebes, scoters, and Long-tailed Ducks drop in. A Great Egret has occurred in late summer. If by mid-July there is low water with exposed mud, shorebirds occur, mostly Greater Yellowlegs and Least Sandpipers, but occasionally something more interesting, like the Long-billed Dowitcher found in 1997. A Sooty Tern and a jaeger (probably Pomarine) appeared after Hurricane David in September 1979. In early 2002, Bald Eagles constructed a nest and are expected to breed. Lake Quaboag is a popular boating and fishing destination, and duck hunters use the far sides of the pond.

From the north end of Quacumquasit, take Lake Road east (it becomes South Pond Road). At 0.4 mile from the pond pull-off, turn left onto West Sturbridge Road, then go 1.7 miles farther to a T. Go left on Quaboag Shore Road. Within 0.5 mile is a small bridge where East Brookfield River flows into Lake Quaboag. This area is often the last to freeze in early winter, so check for ducks. The paved parking lot and boat launch for the pond, in less than 0.5 mile, make the best vantage point on the pond. Be sure not to block the boat launch. Scan with a scope, searching to the back side of the pond. The shore on either side of the parking lot is the place for shorebirds. In spring watch for swallows and Osprey. Working along this shore to where the East Brookfield River enters the pond may reveal waterfowl, Pied-billed Grebe, herons and Wilson's Snipe in season. Quaboag Shore Road becomes Quaboag Street and emerges onto Route 9, 1.5 miles from the Quaboag Pond parking area.

Lake Lashaway in East Brookfield, the least interesting of the four lakes, is worth a check. An easy vantage point is on Route 9 near the center of East Brookfield. Park appropriately and scan for Hooded and Common Mergansers and occasional Bufflehead. Lake Lashaway can also be scanned from Lashaway Park Beach on Maple Street and from where Five-Mile Brook feeds into the northeast corner of the lake (park near the power lines on Shore Road). See map for details. In early winter the northeast corner of the lake often holds lingering Great Blue Herons and lots of ducks and gulls.

Mark C. Lynch

W8. Sturbridge Area

See map W8. Sturbridge Area

Hobbs Brook

Start at the intersection of Routes 20 and 131, just west of the I-84 Exit. If you come from the west on Route 20, you pass the entrance to Old Sturbridge Village on your right and the Sturbridge Information Center on your left. Get in the right lane to turn right at the first set of lights onto Route 131. Alternatively from the Massachusetts Turnpike (I-90), take Exit 9 (Sturbridge). Then take I-84 south to the first exit (Brimfield and Sturbridge, Exit 3B) onto Route 20 west. Turn left (south) on Route 131.

Go south 0.5 mile on Route 131 to the Sturbridge town common. Turn left at the end of the common on Charlton Street, and continue a few hundred yards until it ends at the Army Corps of Engineers Hobbs Brook. Park along the side of the street at the dead end.

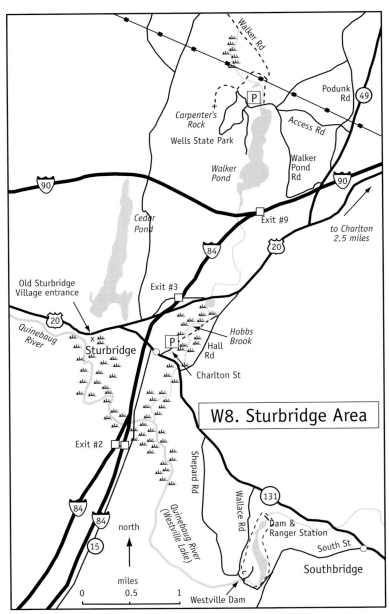

Follow the path to the brook. At the beginning of the path is an overgrown tangle of trees, bushes, and vines, good for migratory sparrows. A cattail marsh farther along the path may have Rusty Blackbirds in migration, and occasionally a Ruby-throated Hummingbird flitting in wildflowers. Check the snags here for woodpeckers. Proceed along the path to the middle section, a good area for Virginia Rail if the water isn't too high. Scan here for Great Blue and Green Herons, Wood and American Black Ducks, Tree and Northern Rough-winged Swallows, and Eastern Bluebird. Farther down the path is a birdy wooded area on the far side of the marsh.

Westville Dam & Recreation Area

From Hobbs Brook, return to Route 131 and go 1.8 miles south. Turn right on Wallace Road and continue 1.0 mile to the sign for the Army Corps of Engineers Westville Dam and Recreation Area on the left (sharp left and steep downhill).

This area can be a fairly large lake during heavy rains, with dramatically different habitat from day to day. When dry, it is a ballfield with marshes, a river, and a small lake. We have often been surprised by the species that turn up here during migration. From the parking lot, follow the road up the river for Belted Kingfisher, Cedar Waxwing, Louisiana Waterthrush, and Indigo Bunting. This walk is about a half a mile, ending at an old dam where Cedar Waxwings feed. If the gate is open you can drive the road to the dam. We have seen nesting Red-tailed Hawk and Red-bellied Woodpecker along the road. After checking this area, walk from the parking lot down the road over the bridge to a small wet area on the right. Both teal and, rarely, Glossy Ibis have been seen here. Hooded Merganser and Killdeer breed nearby. Behind you, depending on water conditions, the ballfield closest to the bend in the river can be very muddy with a wealth of shorebirds.

Starting again from the parking lot, go left up a small trail that becomes a dirt road. This trail leads down to the right along a wildflower meadow and out to the dam and the best view of the lake (a scope helps).

Wells State Park

From Westville Dam, return to Route 131, go back north to the junction with Route 20 and turn right (east) toward Charlton. Continue on Route 20 for 2.4 miles to Route 49. Go left (north) on Route 49 and continue on Route 49 across the Massachusetts Turnpike for 1.0 mile to the Wells State Park access road on your left. Follow the access road 1.4 miles to the main parking lot. There are an intersection and speed bumps on this road, so use caution.

Wells State Park is a fun and easy spot to bird, with plenty of parking, good birds, and bathrooms! Turkey Vulture, Red-shouldered Hawk,

Barred Owl, Yellow-throated Vireo, Red-breasted Nuthatch, Brown Creeper, Winter Wren, and a plethora of warblers breed. Early morning is the best time to bird, before campers and swimmers are up and about. In winter the park is open, but without interpreters or bathrooms.

Park to the right of the ranger station (free trail maps). Across from the ranger station, an old dump with lots of brush is good for sparrows and warblers in spring and fall. If you are very lucky you might see one of the black rat snakes that often hang out fairly high in the nearby trees.

From the parking lot go down the road to the swamp on your left, good for swallows and marsh birds. Don't step on the eastern painted turtles and northern water snakes that sun themselves on the bank. From here either follow the wooded trail on the right side of the road along the brook to the lake or continue up the road and take your next left onto the dirt road. This road parallels the swamp; Yellow-throated Vireo has nested here. Watch for Turkey Vultures and hawks as you follow the power lines to your left. Continue uphill and then down to the swamp where Great Blue Herons nest. Winter Wren is often found here. Return to the top of the hill and follow the trail through the woods to a paved road. Follow the road to your left back to the parking lot. If you have a trail map, it's worth the hike to Carpenters Rock, if only to enjoy the view.   *Bill and Nancy Cormier*

W9. Hopedale Area
Brimfield, Holland, and Sturbridge

Morse Road, Holland

Begin on Route 20 at Holland-East Brimfield Road, 3.4 miles east of Brimfield Town Common and 0.6 mile west of the Brimfield/ Sturbridge town line. **Caution:** There are at least two other Holland Roads that go south from Route 20; pay attention to mileage (and the name Holland-East Brimfield Road) to start on the correct road. From Route 20, go south on Holland-East Brimfield Road past the dam and waterfall 2.0 miles to Morse Road (currently no street sign, but note boat launch sign). Turn right on Morse Road; go 0.7 mile to the end. **Park so you do not block the gate.**

Walk around the gate and down the road to the Quinebaug River, scan, return to just before the gate, and take the foot trail to your left through pines to picturesque riparian habitat, good for a picnic. Continue along the river to birdy overgrown fields. One morning we had eight hawk species in about an hour. This is a good area to listen for Sora. Return to the gate and go down the road to the river. This time continue on the trail, wooded with swampy spots with Blue-headed Vireo, Northern Waterthrush, and Canada Warbler. The trail eventually ends at Five Bridge Road (see below).

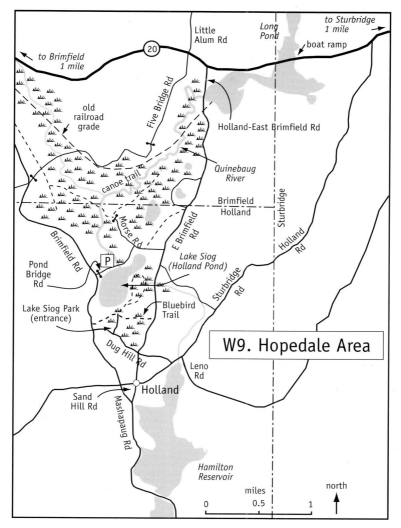

Lake Siog Park

From the Morse Road gate, return to Holland-East Brimfield Road. (Here in Holland, it is called East Brimfield Road.) Turn right (south) and go 1.0 mile. Turn right on Dug Hill Road and go 0.3 mile past a gravel pit on your left, where Bank Swallows and an occasional Belted Kingfisher nest in sand banks, to the Lake Siog Park entrance on your right.

VIRGINIA RAIL

If the park gate is locked, which it often is, park along the road, being **careful not to block the entrance.** The best time to bird here is early spring before the park opens for the season. At the entrance listen for Alder and Least Flycatchers and Magnolia, Yellow-rumped, and Black-and-white Warblers. Walk into the park along the road, listening for Blue-headed, Warbling, and Red-eyed Vireos, Blue-winged and Chestnut-sided Warblers, Ovenbird, and Scarlet Tanager.

After about 100 yards, a path enters the woods on the right. Bushwhack to a small field and go through the field to the muddy edge of a swamp (a scope is helpful here). Great Blue Heron, Wood Duck, Belted Kingfisher, and Swamp Sparrow occur. Virginia Rail, Sora, and Solitary and Spotted Sandpipers are occasional in spring.

Return to the entrance road and head toward the park. Check the gas line right-of-way for House Wren, Eastern Bluebird, and sparrows. Fox Sparrow and Purple Finch occur in early spring. Red-shouldered, Broad-winged, and Red-tailed Hawks and an occasional Northern Goshawk cruise the gas line.

Continue up the road to the pond, checking for shorebirds, ducks, Double-crested Cormorant, and an occasional Osprey. Proceed to the right, stopping at the dead trees and thickets between the path and the parking lot. The trees attract Red-bellied and, less frequently, Pileated Woodpeckers, and both nuthatches. The thickets can have Canada Warbler, White-throated Sparrow, and Northern Cardinal.

Continue through the hemlocks. Great Horned Owls are sometimes seen hunting during early morning. Continue behind the restrooms and follow the trail along the river and swamp, good for early spring Pine and Palm Warblers. Both nuthatches, Brown Creeper, and Golden-crowned Kinglet occur. The trail circles right, ending back in the hemlocks. *Bill and Nancy Cormier and Bill Lafleche*

Hamilton Reservoir Area

From Lake Siog, return to East Brimfield Road, and continue 0.3 mile south to the crossroads in the center of Holland. Turn left (east) onto Sturbridge Road and continue to the Hamilton Reservoir Spillway 0.3 mile on your right.

Park in the dirt lot on Leno Road. The swamp opposite the parking lot can have Great Blue Heron and Belted Kingfisher. The area around the spillway has an occasional Green Heron or Spotted Sandpiper and, in late spring and summer, Tree, Northern Rough-winged, Bank, and Barn Swallows. Scan (a scope helps), especially the cove to your left, for Wood and American Black Ducks.

Return on Sturbridge Road to the center of Holland. Turn left (south) onto Sand Hill Road, which merges with Mashapaug Road. At 0.6 mile from the center of Holland, park next to the Hamilton Reservoir beach. In fall the lake may hold hundreds of mergansers (Hooded and Common) and other migrants, including Common Loon, Bufflehead, Common Goldeneye, and Ruddy Duck. With the lake on your right, walk up the road to observe a protected cove where grebes and Wood Ducks often linger in late fall. Continue on Mashapaug Road 0.6 mile to the causeway, where you can view the same area and look south to the other side of the lake. Most ducks remain north of this causeway.

Quinebaug River Canoe Trail, Holland, Sturbridge

From Hamilton Reservoir, return to the crossroads in Holland. Continue north 0.3 mile on East Brimfield Road. Turn left (west) on Dug Hill Road. Drive the full 0.5 mile of Dug Hill Road past the entrance to Lake Siog. Turn right on Brimfield Road. Continue 0.6 mile and turn right onto Pond Bridge Road for 0.3 mile to the bridge and a small parking lot on your left, the best place to put in. We suggest parking another vehicle at the boat ramp on Long Pond, just north of Route 20, 0.2 mile east of the Brimfield/Sturbridge town line and directly across from Streeter Point. This route, along waterways largely controlled by the Army Corps of Engineers, includes a portage around a small dam at the mouth of the Quinebaug as it enters Long Pond. If you don't park another car at Long Pond, plan on five hours to return.

We prefer canoeing on moonlit summer evenings when cool mist floats along the water transforming the swamp into an alive and magical place. It's an easy two-hour paddle downstream with excellent riparian habitats. Often in the spring wet season the Quinebaug becomes East Brimfield Lake, drastically changing the habitat. Watch the edge for turtles, water snakes, and deer. The remains of fresh water mussels on the banks are a sure sign of river otter. This area is seasonally good for American Bittern, Virginia Rail, Sora, Great Horned and Barred Owls, flycatchers, vireos, and warblers, with an occasional shorebird or raptor.

Five Bridge Road Area, Brimfield

This huge flood control area has many trails through mixed woods and wetlands. Additional spots in the area are discussed above. We recommend purchase of the Southbridge USGS topographic map. The trails discussed here are samples of the many areas accessible from Five Bridge Road. In spring rains this portion of the Quinebaug River becomes East Brimfield Lake. Five Bridge Road is gated at both ends and sometimes closed when flooded. Periodic flooding dramatically affects the flora and fauna in the area from season to season and year to year.

From the parking area on Pond Bridge Road, return to Brimfield Road. Turn right (north) on Brimfield Road and continue 1.2 miles, crossing the Holland/Brimfield town line. Turn right (east) on Five Bridge Road. Park just past the gate at a four-way overgrown intersection (formerly Morse Road, prior to the flood control project).

This road to the left (northwest) goes through mostly deciduous woodland to a cornfield in about 100 yards, to be checked for fall sparrows. To the right (heading southeast) from the intersection, the road goes through dense mixed woods with Barred Owls and thrushes. A little farther on this path is a field, good for Wild Turkeys. The road forks near here. The road to the left becomes Morse Road (see above). The right fork goes to a swamp, excellent for waterthrushes. Beaver activity determines how far you can walk without wet feet.

Farther on Five Bridge Road is a bridge spanning a brook at a heavily vegetated area worth a listen for rails and American Bittern. Continue on Five Bridge Road to a walking trail, part of the never-completed Grand Trunk Railroad from Providence to Palmer. This area is great for rails, spring migrants, and Worm-eating Warblers. The rail bed to your right goes along the edge of the swamp, a good spot to try for Virginia Rail and Sora.

To complete the tour loop, continue on Five Bridge Road until it ends at Route 20, just 0.2 mile west of the Holland-East Brimfield Road where you began. *Bill and Nancy Cormier*

W10. Monson

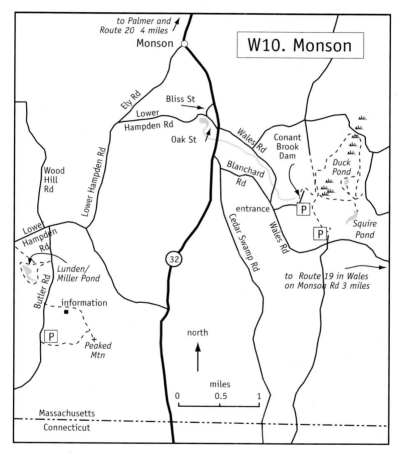

W10. Monson

to Palmer and Route 20 4 miles

Monson

Ely Rd

Bliss St

Lower Hampden Rd

Oak St

Wales Rd

Conant Brook Dam

Duck Pond

Wood Hill Rd

Lower Hampden Rd

Blanchard Rd

entrance

Cedar Swamp Rd

Wales Rd

P

P

Squire Pond

Lower Hampden Rd

32

Lunden/ Miller Pond

Butler Rd

information

P

Peaked Mtn

to Route 19 in Wales on Monson Rd 3 miles

north

miles

0   0.5   1

Massachusetts
Connecticut

Lunden/Miller Pond and Peaked Mountain Reservations

From Route 20 in the center of Palmer, take Route 32 south through the commercial center of Monson. At 0.4 mile south of the gray stone Memorial Hall in downtown Monson, go right onto Bliss Street. Bear right at the Oak Street junction, pass under a railroad bridge, and proceed straight through the next intersection onto Lower Hampden Road. Stay on Lower Hampden Road for 2.9 miles as it twists and turns, then turn left onto Butler Road.

It is 0.4 mile to a small parking area on the right to the trailhead for Lunden/Miller Pond, one part of the TTOR property. The trail circles the pond, alive with odonates, through mixed forest.

Return to Butler Road and continue 1.1 miles to a parking lot on the left and the green sign for Peaked Mountain Reservation. A moderate climb of about a mile on well-marked trails goes to the summit of Peaked Mountain (1227 feet), with a commanding view of central New England from Connecticut to Mount Monadnock in New Hampshire. This spot, a new property of The Trustees of Reservations (TTOR), is promising for spring passerine migration and the fall hawk migration.

These two TTOR areas with tremendous potential have only begun to be explored for birds. Ruffed Grouse, Ruby-throated Hummingbird, Red-bellied Woodpecker, Pileated Woodpecker, Eastern Wood-Pewee, Least and Great Crested Flycatchers, Blue-winged, Nashville, Chestnut-sided, Black-throated Blue and Green, and Blackburnian Warblers, Ovenbird, Louisiana Waterthrush, Scarlet Tanager, Rose-breasted Grosbeak, and Indigo Bunting breed here. *Mark C. Lynch*

Conant Brook Dam

From Peaked Mountain Reservation, return to Route 32 at the junction with Bliss Street. Turn right (south) on Route 32 for 0.3 mile. Turn left on Wales Road; there is a small sign for Conant Brook Dam. Stay on Wales Road 1.4 miles to the dam entrance on your left; follow the road to the parking lot.

This Army Corps of Engineers flood control dam is open during daylight. Check for birds in the trees near the edge of the dam. Several trails lead from the parking lot. See the trail map posted at the entrance; this large area is impossible to cover entirely in a day. Beavers sometimes flood trails. Cross the dam and follow the path to the lower road, near the swamp where you might find a wealth of birds including rails and Belted Kingfisher. Continue to Duck Pond. On your return, continue left down the bike trail to a gate, turn right, and continue down the foot path. Follow this trail to the right to a stand of red pine, good for Barred Owl and Brown Creeper. This trail returns to the bike path. The base of the dam is also productive. *Bill and Nancy Cormier*

Conservation Resources

Bird Clubs in Western Massachusetts

Allen Bird Club *(serving primarily Hampden County)*
www.massbird.org/Allen/
PO Box 1084, Springfield, MA 01101

Athol Bird and Nature Club *(serving primarily the area north of Quabbin)*
www.mrec-athol.org
1978 Chestnut Hill Avenue, Athol, MA 01331-9432

Forbush Bird Club *(serving primarily the Worcester area)*
www.massbird.org/forbush
148 West Main Street, Dudley, MA 01571-3561

Hampshire Bird Club *(serving primarily Franklin and Hampshire Counties)*
www.hampshirebirdclub.org
PO Box 716, Amherst, MA 01004-0716

Hoffmann Bird Club *(serving primarily Berkshire County)*
www.bcn.net/~dcharb/
c/o Berkshire Museum, 39 South Street, Pittsfield, MA 01201

Northampton Bird Watcher's Club *(serving primarily the Northampton area)*
www.massbird.org/Noho
PO Box 76, Northampton, MA 01061

Nature/Environmental Centers in Western Massachusetts

Bartholomew's Cobble Reservation
The Trustees of Reservations
Ashley Falls
Sheffield, MA 01257
413-229-8600
www.berkshireweb.com/trustees/barth.html and www.thetrustees.org

Great Falls Discovery Center
38 Avenue A
Turners Falls, MA 01376
413-863-3221

GREAT BLUE HERON

Hitchcock Center for the Environment
525 South Pleasant Street
Amherst, MA 01002
413-256-6006
www.hitchcockcenter.org

Massachusetts Audubon Society
208 South Great Road, Lincoln, MA 01773
800-283-8266, www.massaudubon.org

Arcadia
127 Combs Road
Easthampton, MA 01027
413-584-3009

Laughing Brook
793 Main Street
Hampden, MA 01036
413-566-8034

Broad Meadow Brook
414 Massasoit Road
Worcester, MA 01604
508-753-6087

Pleasant Valley
472 West Mountain Road
Lenox, MA 01240-2037
413-637-0320

Millers River Environmental Center
100 Main Street
Athol, MA 01331-2222
978-248-9491
www.mrec-athol.org

Norcross Wildlife Sanctuary
30 Peck Road
Monson, MA 01057
413-267-9654
www.norcrossws.org

Northfield Mountain Recreation Center
9 Millers Falls Road (Route 63)
Northfield, MA 01360
413-659-3714
www.nu.com/northfield/

Silvio O. Conte National Fish and Wildlife Refuge
52 Avenue A
Turners Falls, MA 01376
413-863-0209
www.fws.gov/r5soc

Commonwealth of Massachusetts
Executive Office of Environmental Affairs

Forests and Parks *(and State Reservations, and Greenways and Trails)*
Department of Environmental Management (DEM)
  Central: 508-792-7715
  CT Valley: 413-545-5993
  Berkshires: 413-442-8928
for maps and programs: www.state.ma.us/dem/forparks.htm

Metropolitan District Commission (MDC)
Division of Watershed Management
Quabbin Reservoir and watershed, Visitor Center: 413-323-7221
for information: www.state.ma.us/mdc/water.htm

Wildlife Management Areas (WMA)
and Natural Heritage & Endangered Species Program
Massachusetts Division of Fisheries, Wildlife, and Law Enforcement
MassWildlife District Offices:
  Central: 508-835-3607
  CT Valley: 413-323-7632
  Berkshires: 413-447-9789
for maps and information on WMAs:
  www.state.ma.us/dfwele/dfw/dfwrec.htm
for Natural Heritage & Endangered Species Program:
  www.state.ma.us/dfwelel/def/nhesp/nhesp.htm

Land Trusts in Western Massachusetts

The list below includes some of the best known regional and state land trusts serving western Massachusetts. We have not been able to include the many excellent land trusts serving individual towns throughout our region. For an updated list of local and additional regional land trusts and addresses, contact Valley Land Fund (address below) or town Conservation Commissions.

Berkshire County: Regional and Multi-town Land Trusts
Berkshire Natural Resources Council
20 Bank Row, Pittsfield, MA 01201, 413-499-0596, tames@bcn.net

Mahaiwe Harvest Land Trust
679 North Street, Pittsfield, MA 01201, 413-448-2890

Williamstown Rural Lands Foundation
PO Box 221, Williamstown, MA 01267, 413-458-2494
email: ruraland@rnetworx.com

Connecticut River Region: Regional and Multi-town Land Trusts

Franklin Land Trust
PO Box 216, Ashfield, MA 01330, 413-628-4696

Hampden County Land Trust
186 Moulton Hill Road, Monson, MA 01057
413-267-4837

Hilltown Land Trust
PO Box 251, Chesterfield, MA 01012, 413-238-4411

Kestrel Trust
PO Box 1016, Amherst, MA 01004, 413-695-3468

Mount Grace Land Conservation Trust
(also Western Worcester County)
1461 Old Keene Road, Athol, MA 01331, 978-248-2043
email: mglct@shaysnet.com

Valley Land Fund
PO Box 522, Hadley, MA 01035, 413-256-0982

Winding River Land Conservancy
59 Court Street, Westfield, MA 01085, 413-572-6246

Western Worcester County: Regional and Multi-town Land Trusts

East Quabbin Land Trust
PO Box 5, Hardwick, MA 01037, 413-477-8229

Greater Worcester Land Trust
172 Shrewsbury Street, Worcester, MA 01604, 508-795-3838
www.gwlt.org

Mount Grace Land Conservation Trust
(see Connecticut River Region)

North County Land Trust
PO Box 2052, Fitchburg, MA 01420, 978-342-0174
email: jhmorrison@bicnet.net

Opacum Land Trust
Box 233, Sturbridge, MA 01566, 508-347-9144
www.opacumlt.org

State, Multi-state, and National Land Trusts

American Farmland Trust
1200 18th Street NW, Suite 800, Washington DC
202-331-7300, www.farmland.org/northeast/massachusetts.htm

Connecticut River Watershed Council
115 Back Road, Greenfield, MA 01301
413-772-2020, www.ctriver.org

Massachusetts Audubon Society
208 South Great Road, Lincoln, MA 01773
800-283-8266, www.massaudubon.org

New England Forestry Foundation
PO Box 1099, Groton, MA 01450
978-448-8380, www.newenglandforestry.org

The Nature Conservancy, Massachusetts Field Office
205 Portland Street, 4th Floor, Boston, MA 02114
617-227-7017

The Trustees of Reservations
regional office: 5 Strong Avenue, Suite 4, Northampton, MA 01060
413-587-0716, www.thetrustees.org

Trust for Public Land, New England Regional Office
33 Union Street, 4th Floor, Boston, MA 02108
617-367-6200, www.tpl.org/

Important Bird Areas (IBAs)

The international IBA program is a conservation initiative designed to identify and protect areas that provide essential habitat to one or more species of breeding, wintering, and/or migrating birds. Massachusetts Audubon Society is leading a cooperative effort to identify the IBA sites in the state. The final list is not available as we go to print. The following locations are currently being considered as IBA sites. See the index for more information on most of the sites.

Agawam and Konkapot Marshes, Great Barrington, Stockbridge
Arcadia and East Meadows, Easthampton, Northampton
Barton Cove, Gill, Montague
Eugene D. Moran WMA, Windsor
Graves Farm Wildlife Sanctuary, Williamsburg, Whately
High Ridge WMA, Gardner

Hiram H. Fox WMA, Chester, Chesterfield, Huntington,
   Worthington
Longmeadow Flats and Fannie Stebbins Refuge, Longmeadow
Monroe State Forest, Florida, Monroe
Montague Plains, Montague
Mount Greylock State Reservation, Adams, Cheshire, Lanesborough,
   New Ashford, North Adams, Williamstown
Mount Tom Range, Easthampton, Holyoke
Mud Pond and Berkshire Lakes, Pittsfield
Poet's Seat, Greenfield
Quabbin Reservoir Watershed, Belchertown, Hardwick, New Salem,
   Orange, Pelham, Petersham, Shutesbury, Ware, Wendell,
Quaboag Valley, Brookfield, North Brookfield,
   West Brookfield, Warren
Ware River Watershed/Barre Falls Dam/Rutland State Park,
   Barre, Hubbardston, Oakham, Rutland
Westover Air Reserve Base Grasslands, Chicopee

For more information on the IBA program, contact the Massachusetts
Audubon Society (www.massaudubon.org/iba) and the National
Audubon Society (www.audubon.org/iba).

Birds of Western Massachusetts

Introduction

The Bar Charts indicate the relative ease with which a species can be found in Western Massachusetts (in appropriate habitat) rather than its relative abundance. For example, undoubtedly there are more Northern Saw-whet Owls than Bald Eagles in Western Massachusetts, but, as the bar charts reflect, Bald Eagles are much easier to find.

The Footnotes and Species Descriptions below the each Bar Chart are designed to provide the reader with additional information to help find a bird or to learn something about its regional history. Refer to the text and the index for information about specific habitats and locations for each species.

The Bar Charts, Footnotes, and Species Descriptions relied heavily on data from Seth Kellogg. Without his extensive database covering more than 30 years, we could not have prepared this section of the book. The Vagrant Species list, which appears after the bar charts, was prepared by David Spector and Seth Kellogg. A regional editorial committee (Tom Collins, Seth Kellogg, René Laubach, Geoff LeBaron, Mark Lynch, Noreen Mole, Ed Neumuth, Jan Ortiz, David Spector, Scott Surner, and Pete Westover) reviewed and revised all lists, charts, and text. Mary Alice Wilson created the bar charts and served as compiler for the committee. The committee members were selected for both their expertise and their experience in different regions so that the final list would reflect the best possible range of dates and abundance in the area covered by the book. While neither the dates nor abundance will be completely accurate for any given location, our goal was to help the reader learn where and when to expect each species in Western Massachusetts.

BALD EAGLE

Bar Chart Symbols:

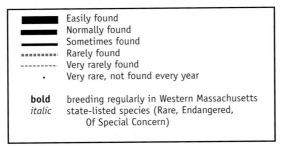

	Easily found
	Normally found
	Sometimes found
	Rarely found
	Very rarely found
	Very rare, not found every year

bold breeding regularly in Western Massachusetts
italic state-listed species (Rare, Endangered, Of Special Concern)

BIRD SPECIES	Footnote	See Below	Months of Occurrence J F M A M J J A S O N D
Red-throated Loon	1		
Common Loon	1, 2	↓	
Pied-billed Grebe	2	↓	
Horned Grebe	1		
Red-necked Grebe	1		
Double-crested Cormorant			
Great Cormorant	1		
American Bittern	2	↓	
Least Bittern			
Great Blue Heron			
Great Egret			
Snowy Egret			
Little Blue Heron			
Cattle Egret	3		
Green Heron			

Common Loon: In migration one or two birds stop on rivers and lakes. There are a few breeding pairs at the Quabbin and in the Worcester area. Some birds stay at the Quabbin and larger Worcester County bodies of water until freeze-out.

Pied-billed Grebe: Migrants dive in shallower water of ponds, marshes, and rivers, where a pair may rarely remain to breed.

American Bittern: This secretive bird stays hidden in marshes among sedges and cattails, and is most easily found when calling in spring.

1. Usually large bodies of water; 2. Rare and local breeder; 3. Primarily farm fields, central Conn. River Valley.

BIRD SPECIES	Footnote	See Below	Months of Occurrence J F M A M J J A S O N D
Black-crowned Night-Heron	4		
Glossy Ibis			
Black Vulture	5	↓	
Turkey Vulture			
Greater White-fronted Goose			
Snow Goose	6	↓	
Canada Goose			
Brant			
Mute Swan	4, 5, 7		
Tundra Swan			
Wood Duck		↓	
Gadwall	8		
American Wigeon			
American Black Duck		↓	
Mallard		↓	
Blue-winged Teal			
Northern Shoveler			
Northern Pintail			
Green-winged Teal	9, 10		
Canvasback			
Redhead			
Ring-necked Duck			
Greater Scaup			

Black Vulture: This species has extended its range north into the lower Housatonic River Valley. Rare elsewhere.

Snow Goose: Large flocks migrate high overhead. They sometimes can be found on fields and rivers when migration is interrupted by inclement weather.

Wood Duck: Breeding birds found throughout the region. In August and September large numbers congregate in marshes.

American Black Duck/Mallard: Often hybridize.

4. Primarily southern Conn. River Valley; 5. Apparently increasing; 6. Brought down by storms; 7. Introduced; 8. More often on Berkshire Lakes; 9. Sporadic rare breeder; 10. Less common in Berkshires.

BIRD SPECIES	Footnote	See Below	Months of Occurrence											
			J	F	M	A	M	J	J	A	S	O	N	D
Lesser Scaup														
Surf Scoter	1, 6													
White-winged Scoter	1, 6													
Black Scoter	1, 6													
Long-tailed Duck	1, 6													
Bufflehead														
Common Goldeneye														
Barrow's Goldeneye	11													
Hooded Merganser	2	↓												
Common Merganser	2	↓												
Red-breasted Merganser														
Ruddy Duck	8													
Osprey	9	↓												
Bald Eagle	1, 2	↓												
Northern Harrier	9	↓												
Sharp-shinned Hawk		↓												
Cooper's Hawk		↓												

Hooded Merganser: Widespread on ponds and rivers in migration. Pairs, or single females, sometimes with young, are uncommon on secluded beaver ponds in breeding season. Uncommon on open rivers in winter.

Common Merganser: Pairs and flocks are found on large lakes and rivers in valleys, with numbers increasing as migration starts. In summer families mostly stay on larger streams in the Berkshire hills.

Osprey: One pair bred successfully in the Springfield area in 2001, probably the first breeding pair in the region since the 1930s.

Bald Eagle: Successfully introduced at the Quabbin in the 1980s. In 2002 at least 9 pairs nested at Quabbin and along the Conn. River. Most easily seen at the nest at Barton Cove, Gill. In the past 2 years, pairs built nests at Lake Quabog, Brookfield, and Colebrook Reservoir, Sandisfield (after a 90+year absence). In winter, 25-40 gather at the Quabbin.

Northern Harrier: Occasionally nests in the northern Berkshires and Winimusset Meadows, New Braintree.

Sharp-shinned Hawk/Cooper's Hawk: In migration best seen from ridges. In winter often found near bird feeders. Difficult to observe in breeding season.

---

1. Usually large bodies of water; 2. Rare and local breeder; 6. Brought down by storms; 8. More often on Berkshire Lakes; 9. Sporadic rare breeder; 11. Primarily Conn. River Valley.

BIRD SPECIES	Footnote	See Below	Months of Occurrence (J F M A M J J A S O N D)
Northern Goshawk			
Red-shouldered Hawk		↓	
Broad-winged Hawk		↓	
Red-tailed Hawk			
Rough-legged Hawk			
Golden Eagle		↓	
American Kestrel	12, 13	↓	
Merlin			
Peregrine Falcon	2	↓	
Ring-necked Pheasant	7, 13, 14		
Ruffed Grouse		↓	
Wild Turkey		↓	
Virginia Rail			
Sora			
Common Moorhen	2	↓	
American Coot			
Sandhill Crane			
Black-bellied Plover			

Red-shouldered Hawk: Most easily found when calling during courtship flights, usually over wooded areas near wetlands.

Broad-winged Hawk: Often detected in breeding season by call. Spectacular flights can occur in fall migration.

Golden Eagle: One or two winter at north Quabbin. Occasionally seen in migration from hawkwatching sites.

American Kestrel: Often seen perched or hovering in fields hunting small mammals and insects.

Peregrine Falcon: Historically bred on cliffs in Western Massachusetts, but disappeared in the 1950s; successfully reintroduced in the 1980s. Currently one pair breeds in downtown Springfield, and another in Erving.

Ruffed Grouse: Listen in spring for the drumming courtship display in areas of woodland. Local populations fluctuate.

Wild Turkey: Extirpated in mid-19th century; successfully reintroduced in mid-20th.

Common Moorhen: In recent years only one pair has been found nesting in the region, typically in the marshes of the Housatonic Valley.

---

2. Rare and local breeder; 7. Introduced; 12. Grasslands; 13. Apparently declining; 14. Most birds released.

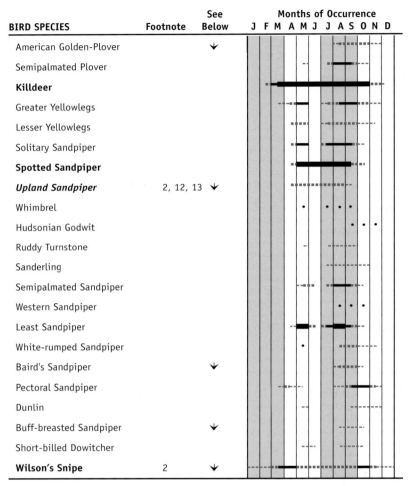

BIRD SPECIES	Footnote	See Below	Months of Occurrence J F M A M J J A S O N D
American Golden-Plover		↓	
Semipalmated Plover			
Killdeer			
Greater Yellowlegs			
Lesser Yellowlegs			
Solitary Sandpiper			
Spotted Sandpiper			
Upland Sandpiper	2, 12, 13	↓	
Whimbrel			
Hudsonian Godwit			
Ruddy Turnstone			
Sanderling			
Semipalmated Sandpiper			
Western Sandpiper			
Least Sandpiper			
White-rumped Sandpiper			
Baird's Sandpiper		↓	
Pectoral Sandpiper			
Dunlin			
Buff-breasted Sandpiper		↓	
Short-billed Dowitcher			
Wilson's Snipe	2	↓	

Shorebirds: Spring migrants are often in fields flooded by rain or high water. In fall, migrants are encountered along river sandbars, on large athletic fields, or on harvested/plowed farm fields. Storms can bring birds down.

American Golden-Plover: In August single birds stop on river sandbars, but in September and October small flocks feed in large plowed fields.

Upland Sandpiper: Pairs and colonies breed only in extensive grassy fields, especially airports.

Baird's Sandpiper/Buff-breasted Sandpiper: Almost all fall migrants are juveniles. In August they are usually found on river edges and sandbars, but in September and October on drier plowed or short-grass fields.

Wilson's Snipe: Migrant groups may be present but are difficult to see in wet fields. A few stay to breed in extensive grassy wetlands, mostly in Berkshire County. (Wilson's Snipe was formerly known as Common Snipe.)

2. Rare and local breeder; 12. Grasslands; 13. Apparently declining.

BIRD SPECIES	Footnote	See Below	Months of Occurrence (J F M A M J J A S O N D)
American Woodcock		↓	
Laughing Gull	11		
Black-headed Gull			
Bonaparte's Gull	1		
Ring-billed Gull			
Herring Gull		↓	
Iceland Gull		↓	
Lesser Black-backed Gull		↓	
Glaucous Gull		↓	
Great Black-backed Gull			
Caspian Tern		↓	
Common Tern		↓	
Black Tern		↓	
Rock Dove	7		
Mourning Dove			
Black-billed Cuckoo	15	↓	
Yellow-billed Cuckoo	15	↓	
Eastern Screech-Owl	16		
Great Horned Owl			
Snowy Owl			
Barred Owl		↓	
Long-eared Owl			

American Woodcock: Difficult to find except in breeding season (late March-May) when displaying males are easily heard and sometimes seen at dusk.

Herring Gull/Glaucous Gull: Hybrids (Nelson's) have been reported in Western Massachusetts.

Iceland Gull/Lesser Black-backed Gull/Glaucous Gull: Single birds feed and rest with other gulls on rivers, in fields, and at landfills.

Terns: Migration can be interrupted by inclement weather forcing terns to put down briefly; they usually leave as soon as the rain stops.

Black-billed Cuckoo/Yellow-billed Cuckoo: Numbers fluctuate with hairy caterpillar outbreaks. Most easily found by call in May and June.

Barred Owl: Most common in wooded area near wetlands, sometimes seen in the day.

1. Usually large bodies of water; 7. Introduced; 11. Primarily Conn. River Valley; 15. Numbers vary from year to year; 16. Primarily valleys and lowlands.

BIRD SPECIES	Footnote	See Below	Months of Occurrence J F M A M J J A S O N D
Short-eared Owl	12		
Northern Saw-whet Owl	15	✔	
Common Nighthawk	13	✔	
Whip-poor-will	13	✔	
Chimney Swift	13		
Ruby-throated Hummingbird		✔	
Belted Kingfisher			
Red-headed Woodpecker			
Red-bellied Woodpecker	5	✔	
Yellow-bellied Sapsucker		✔	
Downy Woodpecker			
Hairy Woodpecker			
Northern Flicker			
Pileated Woodpecker		✔	
Olive-sided Flycatcher		✔	
Eastern Wood-Pewee			
Yellow-bellied Flycatcher	9	✔	

Northern Saw-whet Owl: Occurs in dense stands of conifers or other dense undergrowth. Wintering numbers vary.

Common Nighthawk: In spring small groups swoop back and forth over ponds and pools, especially at dusk and dawn. May still nest on the few remaining gravel rooftops in our cities. Fall migration (late August/early September) can be spectacular.

Whip-poor-will: Most easily heard, and occasionally seen, at the Montague Plains.

Ruby-throated Hummingbird: Single birds search for nectar and insects at forest edges, open woods, and gardens. Readily comes to nectar feeders. Often found in late summer at jewelweed thickets.

Red-bellied Woodpecker: In the 1970s this species extended its breeding range into the southern and lowland areas across our region; it is continuing to expand into the hill country.

Yellow-bellied Sapsucker: This woodpecker's slow syncopated tapping is commonly heard in upland forest areas, primarily west of the Conn. River.

Pileated Woodpecker: Formerly was found only in extensive woodlands. Has become less wary and can be found in more open woods and more populated areas.

Olive-sided Flycatcher: Look for this migrant at the top of trees along edges of woodlands or in swamps. Formerly a very few nested in highland beaver swamps.

Yellow-bellied Flycatcher: Sometimes nests on Mt. Greylock and the Hoosac Range.

5. Apparently increasing; 9. Sporadic rare breeder; 12. Grasslands; 13. Apparently declining; 15. Numbers vary from year to year.

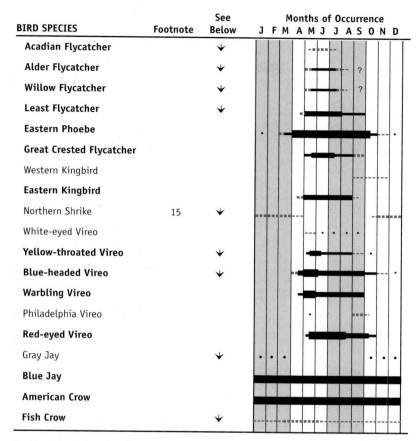

BIRD SPECIES	Footnote	See Below	Months of Occurrence
Acadian Flycatcher		↓	
Alder Flycatcher		↓	
Willow Flycatcher		↓	
Least Flycatcher		↓	
Eastern Phoebe			
Great Crested Flycatcher			
Western Kingbird			
Eastern Kingbird			
Northern Shrike	15	↓	
White-eyed Vireo			
Yellow-throated Vireo		↓	
Blue-headed Vireo		↓	
Warbling Vireo			
Philadelphia Vireo			
Red-eyed Vireo			
Gray Jay		↓	
Blue Jay			
American Crow			
Fish Crow		↓	

Acadian Flycatcher: Very few nest in mixed understory along small streams, usually where hemlocks grow. See index for best locations.

Alder Flycatcher/Willow Flycatcher: The Alder is more common at higher elevations; while the Willow is more common at lower elevations; but there is a broad area of overlap. The bar charts for fall are speculative because visual identification is so difficult.

Least Flycatcher: Breeds in deciduous understory, mostly in highlands.

Northern Shrike: Found in forest openings and edges, most consistently seen at Moran WMA.

Yellow-throated Vireo: Breeds in open deciduous woods, especially with oak predominating.

Blue-headed Vireo: Found in coniferous and mixed forest, mostly in higher country.

Gray Jay: A very rare winter vagrant either found at a feeder in winter or sometimes just by chance while hiking in the forest of the Quabbin and northern highlands.

Fish Crow: Local, permanent resident in the Housatonic and Conn. River Valleys.

15. Numbers vary from year to year.

BIRD SPECIES	Footnote	See Below	Months of Occurrence J F M A M J J A S O N D
Common Raven	5	↓	
Horned Lark	2		
Purple Martin			
Tree Swallow			
Northern Rough-winged Swallow		↓	
Bank Swallow			
Cliff Swallow	2	↓	
Barn Swallow	10		
Black-capped Chickadee			
Boreal Chickadee		↓	
Tufted Titmouse			
Red-breasted Nuthatch	15, 17		
White-breasted Nuthatch			
Brown Creeper		↓	
Carolina Wren	16	↓	
House Wren			
Winter Wren		↓	
Sedge Wren	9	↓	

Common Raven: Has successfully reestablished itself throughout the region.

Northern Rough-winged Swallow: Pairs and small colonies feed over water near steep riverbanks, bridges, and spillways, where they nest.

Cliff Swallow: Colonies nest under eaves of buildings and under bridges. Migrants are sometimes seen with other swallows.

Boreal Chickadee: In winter a few may be present in spruce/fir stands, usually in years when there is an irruption of Black-capped Chickadees.

Brown Creeper: Breeds in deciduous and mixed woods and can be easily located by song in early spring. The rest of the year they often forage with other woodland species.

Carolina Wren: Slowly extending its range northward up the valleys. Populations decline after severe winters.

Winter Wren: Forages on ground around fallen trees and rocks on steep wooded hillsides and cutovers in highlands. Breeds in shady hemlock ravines and woods. More common west of the Conn. River Valley.

Sedge Wren: In May and June males or pairs can appear at any time in wet fields with tall grasses and sedges. Rarely breeds.

2. Rare and local breeder; 5. Apparently increasing; 9. Sporadic rare breeder; 10. Less common in Berkshires; 15. Numbers vary from year to year; 16. Primarily valleys and lowlands; 17. Primarily conifers.

BIRD SPECIES	Footnote	See Below	Months of Occurrence (J F M A M J J A S O N D)
Marsh Wren			
Golden-crowned Kinglet	17	↓	
Ruby-crowned Kinglet			
Blue-gray Gnatcatcher		↓	
Eastern Bluebird		↓	
Veery			
Gray-cheeked Thrush/Bicknell's Thrush		↓	
Swainson's Thrush	2	↓	
Hermit Thrush			
Wood Thrush			
American Robin			
Varied Thrush			
Gray Catbird			
Northern Mockingbird	16		
Brown Thrasher	13, 16, 18		
European Starling	7		
American Pipit			
Bohemian Waxwing	15	↓	
Cedar Waxwing			

Golden-crowned Kinglet: Nests in spruce/fir forests. In winter most often found in mixed flocks with Black-capped Chickadees.

Blue-gray Gnatcatcher: Nesting pairs found in wet lowland deciduous understory, or dry oak woodlands. Locally common at Quabbin.

Eastern Bluebird: Flocks feed on fruits and insects near or on the ground. Starting in early March pairs are found along edges, in orchards, and yards. Populations had declined until the 1980s but are now increasing, with considerable help from well-maintained nest boxes. Flocks are increasingly common in winter around fields that have fruiting shrubs.

Gray-cheeked Thrush/Bicknell's Thrush: Can be distinguished by song. Most historical records are not assignable to species. Bicknell's formerly bred on Mt. Greylock.

Swainson's Thrush: Most easily found as a breeder at Monroe State Forest.

Bohemian Waxwing: In some winters, large flocks can be found feeding on fruit trees and shrubs, but most winters only one or two are found in flocks of Cedar Waxwings.

---

2. Rare and local breeder; 7. Introduced; 13. Apparently declining; 15. Numbers vary from year to year; 16. Primarily valleys and lowlands; 17. Primarily conifers; 18. Shrubby fields, powerlines, and railroad cuts.

BIRD SPECIES	Footnote	See Below	Months of Occurrence J F M A M J J A S O N D
Blue-winged Warbler		↓	
Golden-winged Warbler	9, 13	↓	
Tennessee Warbler			
Orange-crowned Warbler			
Nashville Warbler		↓	
Northern Parula			
Yellow Warbler			
Chestnut-sided Warbler	18		
Magnolia Warbler		↓	
Cape May Warbler	15		
Black-throated Blue Warbler		↓	
Yellow-rumped Warbler			
Black-throated Green Warbler			
Blackburnian Warbler		↓	
Pine Warbler			
Prairie Warbler	18	↓	
Palm Warbler		↓	
Bay-breasted Warbler			

Eastern wood-warblers: In spring and fall flocks move through the region, sometimes in numbers impressive enough to be considered "waves." In fall look for migrant warblers foraging with mixed flocks of chickadees and other resident species.

Blue-winged Warbler/Golden-winged Warbler: The Blue-winged's buzzy song is heard in overgrown fields and thickets with scattered trees. Golden-winged, which once sang in those same fields, has been almost totally replaced by Blue-winged and Blue-winged x Golden-winged hybrids (Brewster's and Lawrence's). Both hybrids occur in the region; Brewster's is more likely.

Nashville Warbler: Nests in overgrown fields and sapling groves of higher country.

Magnolia Warbler: Breeders are present in upland coniferous and mixed woodlands.

Black-throated Blue Warbler: Breeders are found in deciduous and mixed forest understory, especially where mountain laurel is common, mostly in highlands.

Blackburnian Warbler: Nesting birds favor tall conifers. More common west of the Conn. River Valley.

Prairie Warbler: Nests in overgrown fields, gravel pits, powerline and railroad cuts; more common in the Conn. River Valley and to the east.

Palm Warbler: Both subspecies occur. Western is more likely in fall than in spring.

9. Sporadic rare breeder; 13. Apparently declining; 15. Numbers vary from year to year; 18. Shrubby fields, powerlines, and railroad cuts.

BIRD SPECIES	Footnote	See Below	Months of Occurrence J F M A M J J A S O N D
Blackpoll Warbler	2	↓	
Cerulean Warbler	2	↓	
Black-and-white Warbler			
American Redstart			
Prothonotary Warbler			
Worm-eating Warbler	2	↓	
Ovenbird			
Northern Waterthrush		↓	
Louisiana Waterthrush		↓	
Kentucky Warbler			
Connecticut Warbler		↓	
Mourning Warbler		↓	
Common Yellowthroat			
Hooded Warbler			
Wilson's Warbler			
Canada Warbler		↓	
Yellow-breasted Chat			
Scarlet Tanager			

Blackpoll Warbler: Numbers of this treetop species are regular anywhere as migrants. Only a few pairs nest in the highest spruce forests of Greylock and the Hoosac Range.

Cerulean Warbler: Only a few pairs have ventured this far north to nest in small groups in mature oak forests on steep hillsides, primarily in Quabbin and southern Conn. River Valley.

Worm-eating Warbler: This southern warbler sometimes breeds along the steep oak-deciduous hillsides that border the valleys. Most easily found on Mt Tom and Mt Holyoke.

Northern Waterthrush: Breeds near slow-moving or still water in wooded areas.

Louisiana Waterthrush: Usually breeds in woods near moving water, but can also be found near still water.

Connecticut Warbler: Found as fall migrant near wetland edge with dense underbrush, bracken fern and jewelweed.

Mourning Warbler: Breeds in northwestern highland in the kind of thickets found under powerlines or 5-10 years after logging or blow-downs.

Canada Warbler: More common west of the Conn. River Valley. Often breeds in brushy understory and mountain laurel thickets.

---

2. Rare and local breeder.

BIRD SPECIES	Footnote	See Below	Months of Occurrence (J F M A M J J A S O N D)
Eastern Towhee	13		
American Tree Sparrow			
Chipping Sparrow			
Clay-colored Sparrow			
Field Sparrow			
Vesper Sparrow	2	↓	
Lark Sparrow			
Savannah Sparrow	12	↓	
Grasshopper Sparrow	2, 12	↓	
LeConte's Sparrow			
Sharp-tailed Sparrow sp.		↓	
Fox Sparrow			
Song Sparrow			
Lincoln's Sparrow	9	↓	
Swamp Sparrow			
White-throated Sparrow		↓	
White-crowned Sparrow	15		
Dark-eyed Junco		↓	
Lapland Longspur	15	↓	

Vesper Sparrow: This very local nester and rare migrant is found in thickets at the edges of fields where there is bare or plowed ground nearby.

Savannah Sparrow: In the fall flocks congregate in farm fields.

Grasshopper Sparrow: Breeds in a few large grasslands, mostly at airports (Westover, Barnes, Turners Falls, Orange).

Sharp-tailed Sparrow sp.: While Nelson's is more likely, most records precede the split between Nelson's Sharp-tailed and Saltmarsh Sharp-tailed and are, therefore, listed here as "sp."

Lincoln's Sparrow: In spring only a few migrants are found on their way north. Very rarely nests in the edges of beaver swamps in the Hoosac Range. Autumn migrants are more numerous, foraging in weedy fields.

White-throated Sparrow: Breeds in upland forests mostly west of the Conn. River Valley.

Dark-eyed Junco: Breeds in conifers in the highlands; more commonly west of the Conn. River Valley. Western subspecies (usually Oregon) are occasionally reported in winter.

Lapland Longspur: Found in open fields in winter, especially fields with freshly-spread manure, usually in flocks with Horned Larks and Snow Buntings. Most often reported in Hadley/Northampton area.

2. Rare and local breeder; 9. Sporadic rare breeder; 12. Grasslands; 13. Apparently declining; 15. Numbers vary from year to year.

BIRD SPECIES	Footnote	See Below	Months of Occurrence J F M A M J J A S O N D
Snow Bunting	15		
Northern Cardinal	5		
Rose-breasted Grosbeak			
Blue Grosbeak			
Indigo Bunting	18		
Dickcissel			
Bobolink	12	↓	
Red-winged Blackbird			
Eastern Meadowlark	3, 12, 13		
Yellow-headed Blackbird			
Rusty Blackbird	2	↓	
Common Grackle			
Brown-headed Cowbird			
Orchard Oriole		↓	
Baltimore Oriole			
Pine Grosbeak	15	↓	
Purple Finch		↓	
House Finch	7		

Bobolink: Find a lush hayfield and the males will be singing and displaying the instant they arrive from the south. In the fall flocks congregate in farm fields.

Rusty Blackbird: Found in spring in swamps with trees; in fall also found at edges of fields. A few winter in the lowlands.

Orchard Oriole: Western Massachusetts is on the northern edge of this bird's range, but a few pairs breed in the lowlands where there are scattered large trees.

Pine Grosbeak: Loose flocks of this tame finch feed on fruit or buds in trees or shrubs. Some years they are found only in highlands of the north, while in other years they are more widespread. Most years there are none.

Purple Finch: In migration flocks feed on buds in woods and edges. Breeds in upland coniferous and mixed forests. Some winters small wandering groups eat tree seeds in groves and edges, and come to feeders.

2. Rare and local breeder; 3. Primarily farm fields, central Conn. River Valley; 5. Apparently increasing; 7. Introduced; 12. Grasslands; 13. Apparently declining; 15. Numbers vary from year to year; 18. Shrubby fields, powerlines, and railroad cuts.

BIRD SPECIES	Footnote	See Below	Months of Occurrence J F M A M J J A S O N D
Red Crossbill	15	↓	
White-winged Crossbill	9, 15	↓	
Common Redpoll	15	↓	
Hoary Redpoll	15		
Pine Siskin	15	↓	
American Goldfinch			
Evening Grosbeak	2, 15	↓	
House Sparrow	7		

Red Crossbill/White-winged Crossbill: Red Crossbills feed on spruce and pine cones; White-winged feed on spruce and hemlock cones. Both species often call in flight. Occasional migrants of both species pass through, but groups remain for extended periods only in years with good cone crops.

Common Redpoll: Large wandering flocks feed on tree seeds, especially birch catkins, on weeds in fields, and at thistle-seed feeders.

Pine Siskin: Large wandering flocks eat tree seeds in woods, edges; some years only in hills. Eats thistle and sunflower at feeders.

Evening Grosbeak: Uncommon breeder in the hill country.

2. Rare and local breeder; 7. Introduced; 9. Sporadic rare breeder; 15. Numbers vary from year to year.

Vagrant Species

There are at least two confirmed reports for each of the following species in Western Massachusetts in recent decades. These species are likely to occur again and the observer should be alert for these and other species with patterns of vagrancy. Not all reports have been fully documented; anyone finding any unusual bird is encouraged to record and report all the pertinent information.

Leach's Storm-Petrel
Tricolored Heron
Yellow-crowned Night-Heron
Eurasian Wigeon
Common Eider
Gyrfalcon
King Rail
Purple Gallinule
Willet
Red Knot
Stilt Sandpiper
Ruff
Long-billed Dowitcher
Wilson's Phalarope
Red-necked Phalarope
Red Phalarope
Forster's Tern
Barn Owl
Northern Hawk Owl
Great Gray Owl

Chuck-will's-widow
Rufous Hummingbird
Three-toed Woodpecker
Black-backed Woodpecker
Scissor-tailed Flycatcher
Loggerhead Shrike
Northern Wheatear
Yellow-throated Warbler
Summer Tanager
Western Tanager
Green-tailed Towhee
Spotted Towhee
Henslow's Sparrow
Harris's Sparrow
Black-headed Grosbeak
Brewer's Blackbird

There are at least four dozen other species that have been reported in Western Massachusetts, but very rarely.

Escaped or Released Birds

There are also many sightings of escaped or released birds, from Zebra Finch and Eurasian Goldfinch to Egyptian Goose and Greater Flamingo. Some of these species (e.g., Monk Parakeet, Northern Bobwhite, and Trumpeter Swan) are candidates for establishing breeding populations or for occurring as natural vagrants.

Extinct or Extirpated Species:

Eskimo Curlew: presumed to have been a migrant; but now extinct or near extinction.

Greater Prairie Chicken (Heath Hen): formerly a breeder; this subspecies is now extinct.

Northern Bobwhite: extirpated as breeder; recent records are probably of released birds.

Passenger Pigeon: Now extinct; formerly an abundant breeder and migrant.

Barn Owl, Sedge Wren, Bicknell's Thrush, Golden-winged Warbler, and Henslow's Sparrow are all extirpated or nearly so as breeders, but are included in the bar chart or vagrant species list as sporadic breeder, migrant, or vagrant.

Index

*Italicized page numbers
refer to illustrations.*

Eider, King 45
Eliot, Samuel A. 1
Elm Hill Farm 16, 283
Enfield Lookout 240
Eph's Pond 24
Ethics, Code of v
Exposition Grounds
  Lagoon 214

F

Fairfield Pond 47
Falcon, Peregrine 32, 49,
  78, 96, 135, 149, 152,
  157, 177, 178, 179, 202,
  214, 309
Falls Road 136
Fannie Stebbins Wildlife
  Refuge 16, 221, 222
Federated Women's Clubs
  State Forest 249
Felton Lake 66
Fenton Brook 84, 85
Finch
  House 124, 319
  Purple 27, 32, 35, 36,
    41, 58, 65, 103, 104,
    110, 122, 145, 197,
    198, 230, 237, 263,
    290, 319
  winter 4, 32, 40, 58,
    122, 124, 185, 230,
    253, 258, 260
Fisher Museum 248
Fisk Meadow Wildlife
  Management Area 106
Fitzgerald Lake
  Conservation Area 142
Five Colleges, Inc. 17, 101
Five-Mile Brook 285
Flicker, Northern 50, 134,
  155, 194, 272, 312
Floodplain Forest Reserve
  170
Florida 30
Flycatcher
  Acadian 126, 193, 199,
    201, 202, 204, 243,
    252, 253, 259, 313
  Alder 30, 32, 38, 55, 58,
    59, 65, 70, 72, 102,
    103, 106, 109, 145,
    147, 165, 195, 196,
    197, 201, 207, 227,
    263, 265, 267, 272,
    273, 276, 290, 313
  Great Crested 50, 82,
    83, 84, 100, 111, 116,
    117, 119, 124, 146,
    165, 167, 171, 182,
    186, 231, 267, 270,
    294, 313

Least 25, 50, 58, 73, 75,
  81, 82, 83, 84, 89, 91,
  110, 111, 115, 128,
  138, 148, 180, 199,
  201, 239, 267, 270,
  290, 294, 313
Olive-sided 33, 55, 101,
  102, 111, 129, 201,
  243, 244, 246, 250,
  263, 271, 272, 275,
  312
Willow 25, 38, 39, 55,
  59, 72, 86, 91, 103,
  106, 109, 113, 114,
  128, 135, 164, 207,
  224, 263, 265, 272,
  276, 313
Yellow-bellied 36, 66,
  312
Forbes Hill 40
Forbush Bird Club 297
Forest Park 220
Forests and Parks 299
Forge Pond 173
Fountain Pond 77, 78
Fountain, Laurence R.,
  Park 230
Fowler Tree Farm 201
Fox, Hiram H., WMA 108
Franklin Land Trust 300
French River 257
Frost, Robert, Trail 131,
  162, 165

G

Gadwall 25, 45, 46, 55, 86,
  151, 180, 182, 191, 192,
  220, 221, 228, 261, 307
Gallinule, Purple 127, 321
Gannet, Northern 95, 152
Gardner 260, 262
Gill 118
Goldfinch, American 75,
  104, 197, 320
Gnatcatcher, Blue-gray 25,
  60, 61, 75, 84, 85, 113,
  115, 144, *144*, 145, 147,
  165, 166, 177, 180, 186,
  195, 199, 209, 239, 264,
  267, 315
Goat Peak 186
Godwit, Hudsonian 46,
  162, 310
Goldeneye
  Barrow's 216, 245, 308
  Common 61, 68, 86, 91,
    119, 120, 124, 128,
    130, 141, 150, 206,
    213, 214, 216, 219,
    246, 261, 278, 282,
    284, 291, 308
Golden Hill 68
Goodnough Dike 241, 243

Goose
  Canada 128, 151, 158,
    161, 165, 179, 183,
    227, 251, 307
  Greater White-fronted
    45, 86, 152, 158, 161,
    179, 307
  Snow 32, 91, 111, *134,*
    142, 158, 161, 179,
    183, 186, 187, 227,
    251, 261, 262, 307
Goose Pond 206
Goose Ponds 69
Goshawk, Northern 28, 32,
  70, 79, 100, 102, 129,
  144, 146, 148, 152, 155,
  171, 186, 187, 197, 202,
  230, 246, 263, 271, 275,
  290, 309
Goshen 102
Gould/Thiel Roads
  Property 36
Grackle, Common 271,
  319
Granby 167
Granville 198
Granville State Forest 199
Grave's Landing 246
Graves Farm Wildlife
  Sanctuary 146
Great Barrington 77, 79
Great Barrington State
  Forest 78
Great Brook Marsh 206
Great Falls Discovery
  Center 120, 297
Greater Worcester Land
  Trust 300
Grebe
  Horned 46, 119, 128,
    188, 206, 219, 240,
    241, 261, 306
  Pied-billed 45, 86, 102,
    119, 127, 128, 130,
    135, 143, 151, 172,
    182, 188, 207, 217,
    219, 240, 241, 246,
    261, 285, 306
  Red-necked 119, 188,
    206, 219, 240, 241,
    250, 261, 306
Green River Cemetery
  117
Greene, J.R. 244
Greenfield 115
Greenfield Community
  College 116
Greylock Glen 36, 38
Griscom, Ludlow 46
Griswold Wildlife Preserve
  117

Warbling 25, 55, 61, 70,
72, 75, 77, 89, 91, 112,
128, 135, 137, 164,
180, 183, 222, 268,
272, 290, 313
White-eyed 55, 207,
219, 221, 313
Yellow-throated 58, 61,
70, 72, 75, 77, 78, 89,
91, 100, 109, 112, 136,
145, 169, 180, 183,
186, 212, 230, 231,
239, 252, 270, 276,
288, 313
Vulture
Black 77, 85, 88, 89, *90,*
202, 307
Turkey 49, 68, 76, 78,
81, 85, 88, 101, 108,
169, 171, 178, 186,
192, 197, 202, 226,
275, 287, 288, 307

W
Warbler
Bay-breasted 57, 171,
264, 271, 316
Black-and-white 25, 26,
43, 50, 51, 70, 75, 84,
99, 103, 106, 109, 110,
115, 147, 165, 169,
171, 183, 239, 271,
290, 317
Black-throated Blue 27,
32, 38, 39, 41, 43, 51,
58, 65, 66, 70, 75, 78,
81, 83, 85, 99, 101,
103, 104, 109, 110,
112, 114, 124, 126,
131, 138, 145, 146,
147, 163, 165, 186,
198, 239, 248, 249,
252, 253, 274, 275,
276, 294, 316
Black-throated Green
27, 30, 32, 38, 39, 41,
43, 51, 56, 58, 66, 70,
73, 74, 78, 79, 81, 83,
84, 88, 99, 103, 109,
110, 112, 114, 131,
145, 146, 147, 170,
171, 198, 209, 239,
243, 245, 248, 249,
250, 252, 259, 264,
267, 271, 273, 275,
276, 281, 294, 316
Blackburnian *front cover,*
27, 29, 30, 32, 33, 38,
39, 41, 43, 51, 56, 58,
63, 65, 66, 70, 74, 78,
79, 82, 83, 84, 88, 99,
110, 115, 129, 131,
145, 146, 147, 201,
209, 239, 243, 245,
249, 250, 252, 259,
267, 271, 273, 275,
281, 294, 316
Blackpoll 35, 36, 57,
171, 267, 271, 317

Blue-winged 38, 50, 58,
68, 75, 84, 86, 113,
114, 128, 131, 138,
144, 145, 148, 151,
157, 163, 164, 165,
166, 167, 170, 171,
174, 182, 190, 191,
199, 202, 206, 207,
209, 210, 212, 213,
226, 262, 264, 267,
275, 281, 290, 294, 316
Canada 27, 32, 35, 36,
38, 39, 41, 43, 58, 65,
70, 74, 84, 99, 101,
103, 113, 124, 145,
147, 165, 173, 193,
197, 199, 211, 248,
249, 250, 252, 262,
267, 271, 276, 289,
290, 317
Cape May 116, 117,
156, 171, 198, 263,
264, 316
Cerulean *front cover,* 109,
134, 169, 193, 210,
211, 239, 244, 276,
317
Chestnut-sided 30, 43,
50, 55, 70, 75, 82, 84,
99, 106, 109, 110, 115,
136, 138, 143, 144,
146, 147, 163, 165,
167, 171, 182, 191,
199, 239, 262, 263,
264, 267, 272, 290,
294, 316
Connecticut 141, 180,
221, 224, 250, 271,
317
Golden-winged 58, 117,
316
Hooded 221, 258, 317
Kentucky 221, 263, 264,
317
Lawrence's 114, 116,
227, 316
Magnolia 27, 30, 33, 35,
36, 38, 39, 41, 43, 50,
58, 65, 70, 73, 81, 82,
84, 99, 103, 104, 115,
131, 147, 201, 248,
273, 276, 290, 316
Mourning 36, *37,* 38,
41, 43, 58, 65, 66, 102,
108, 117, 141, 149,
155, 180, 221, 317
Nashville 36, 38, 43,
103, 104, 115, 157,
163, 177, 197, 199,
202, 207, 294, 316
Orange-crowned 129,
141, 316
Palm 25, 38, 39, 51, 55,
57, 84, 163, 166, 177,
180, 187, 222, 283,
291, 316

Pine 50, 51, 55, 75, 99,
103, 114, 119, 122,
138, 143, 146, 163,
167, 173, 183, 187,
189, 191, 192, 211,
217, 226, 239, 241,
249, 262, 264, 267,
270, 271, 274, 275,
276, 281, 291, 316
Prairie 50, 73, 75, 122,
131, 132, 163, 167,
171, 195, 199, 206,
210, 213, 226, 227,
240, 248, 272, 275,
316
Prothonotary 191, 258,
317
Tennessee 84, 156, 171,
264, 268, 316
Wilson's 38, 51, 55, 113,
152, 182, 210, 211,
268, 317
Worm-eating 81, 85, 96,
133, 169, 171, 186,
189, 193, 194, *194,*
209, 211, 213, 231,
239, 292, 317
Yellow 43, 50, 55, 70,
84, 106, 112, 146, 167,
191, 262, 264, 267,
272, 316
Yellow-rumped 14, *15,*
25, 32, 35, 36, 41, 43,
58, 65, 82, 84, 110,
115, 143, 146, 147,
165, 167, 180, 187,
198, 222, 239, 241,
248, 249, 252, 259,
262, 264, 275, 281,
283, 290, 316
Ware 236, 242
Ware River 4, 257, 268,
272, 273, 278, 302
Warren 279, 282
Washington 48, 64
Washington Mountain
Meadow 66
Waterthrush
Louisiana 32, 38, 58, 60,
66, 82, 88, 89, 99, 103,
110, 112, 115, 121,
128, 129, 136, 138,
143, 147, 154, 157,
171, 174, 183, 186,
188, 189, 191, 193,
196, 204, 209, 210,
212, 239, 244, 249,
252, 264, 267, 274,
287, 292, 294, 317
Northern 27, 32, 55, 60,
65, 99, 102, 103, 112,
128, 137, 145, 154,
157, 166, 173, 180,
189, 196, 197, 201,
202, 207, 209, 248,
249, 250, 253, 263,
273, 289, 292, 317

Birding Sites

B1. Eph's Pond Area
B2. Clarksburg State Park
B3. Monroe State Forest
B4. Savoy Mountain State Forest
B5. Mount Greylock Area
B6. Moran WMA and Notchview
B7. Gulf Road
B8. The Berkshire Lakes
B9. Berry Hill
B10. Springside Park
B11. Tierny Swamp
B12. Richmond Marsh
B13. Canoe Meadows Wildlife Sanctuary
B14. Pleasant Valley Wildlife Sanctuary
B15. Housatonic Valley WMA
B16. October Mountain State Forest
B17. The Cove Area
B18. Goose Ponds
B19. Tyringham Valley and
     Tyringham Cobble
B20. Ice Glen and Laura's Tower
B21. Alford
B22. Monument Mountain and
     Fountain Pond
B23. Beartown State Forest
B24. Questing Reservation
B25. Three Mile Pond WMA
B26. Jug End Area
B27. Mount Washington Area
B28. Bartholomew's Cobble Reservation
B29. Southern Housatonic River
C1. Heath
C2. High Ledges Wildlife Sanctuary
C3. Hawley Bog and Plainfield
C4. Spruce Corner Roads
C5. Cummington Beaver Pond
C6. Dead Branch Swamp and
    Knightville Dam WMA
C7. Northfield
C8. Greenfield
C9. Turners Falls and Montague Plains
C10. Wendell
C11. Leverett and Atkins Reservoir
C12. Mount Toby Area
C13. Sunderland and Deerfield
C14. Whately

C15. Hatfield
C16. Fitzgerald Lake Conservation Area
C17. Graves Farm Wildlife Sanctuary
C18. Hadley Floodplain
C19. University of Massachusetts Area
C20. Maple Street Corridor
C21. Amherst Conservation Areas and
     Rail Trail
C22. Holyoke Range and
     Batchelor Brook
C23. East Meadows
C24. Arcadia Wildlife Sanctuary
C25. Mount Tom
C26. East Mountain Area
C27. Westfield Area
C28. Mount Tekoa
C29. Blandford
C30. Granville and Tolland
C31. Congamond Lakes Area
C32. Agawam
C33. Robinson and Mittineague Parks
     and East Mountain
C34. The Connecticut River: Agawam
     to South Hadley
C35. Chicopee and Ludlow
C36. Forest Park
C37. Fannie Stebbins Refuge
C38. East Longmeadow
C39. Wilbraham and Hampden
Q1. Quabbin Park Area
Q2. Quabbin Gates 40-45
Q3. Harvard Pond
Q4. Quabbin Gates 34-37
Q5. Quabbin Gates 8-22
W1. Royalston
W2. Crystal Lake and Mount
    Wachusett CC Area
W3. High Ridge WMA
W4. Petersham
W5. Barre Falls Dam and Rutland SP
W6. Moose Brook Valley and
    Winimusset Meadows WMA
W7. The Brookfields and Warren
W8. Sturbridge Area
W9. Hopedale Area
W10. Monson